People and Computers XVIII – Design for Life

Sally Fincher, Panos Markopoulos,
David Moore, and Roy Ruddle (Eds)

People and Computers XVIII – Design for Life

Proceedings of HCI 2004

Sally Fincher, BA, MA, LHG, FSEDA
Computing Laboratory, University of Kent, UK

Panos Markopoulos, MSc, MSc, PhD
Industrial Design, Eindhoven University of Technology, The Netherlands

David Moore, PhD
School of Computing, Leeds Metropolitan University, UK

Roy Ruddle, BSc, PhD, CEng, MBCS
School of Computing, University of Leeds, UK

British Library Cataloguing in Publication Data
A catalogue record for this book is available from the British Library

ISBN 1-85233-900-4 Springer London Berlin Heidelberg
Springer Science+Business Media
springeronline.com

Typeset by *Winder.*
Printed and bound at the Athenaeum Press Ltd., Gateshead, Tyne and Wear
34/3830-543210 Printed on acid-free paper SPIN 11012429

Contents

Preface

The eighteenth annual British HCI Conference chose as its theme Design for Life. 'Life' has many facets, from work (of course, or should we say inevitably!) to travel, fun and other forms of leisure. We selected 23 full papers out of 63 submitted, which covered our interaction with computer systems in a variety of types of life situation — including games, tourism and certain types of work — and also covered a variety of stages in our lives, from the young to the elderly. These papers were complemented by others that described more traditional aspects of research in the field of human-computer interaction.

In putting together the programme we followed a three-stage process. First each paper was reviewed by at least three reviewers. Then a member of the committee conducted a meta-review. Finally, all sets of reviews were considered by the technical chairs who assembled a programme that was submitted to, and approved by, the full committee. This process was greatly assisted by the use of the Precision Conference Solutions web-based submission system. Even more important, of course, were the volunteer reviewers themselves. In recognition, this year we have made an award for the best reviewer as well as one for the best paper.

The conference continues to attract delegates from around the world, and this year the authors of the accepted papers come from Australia, Canada, China, Denmark, France, Malaysia, the Netherlands and Sweden, as well as the UK. Our keynote speakers are also international in outlook, comprising Thomas Erickson (IBM's T. J. Watson Research Center, New York), Wendy Hall (current President of the BCS) and Kees Dorst (Designed Intelligence Research Group, Faculty of Industrial Design Eindhoven University of Technology).

As usual, many people deserve our thanks for helping to put together this conference and these associated proceedings. As well as the reviewers, we would like to express our gratitude to our fellow members on the committee, to Russel Winder for his eagle eye and endless patience, and to the production team at Springer Verlag. All that remains is for us to commend the papers to you and for you to enjoy them.

Sally Fincher, Panos Markopoulos, David Moore, Roy Ruddle

May 2004

The Committee

Conference Chair	Janet Finlay *Leeds Metropolitan University*
Technical Chairs	Sally Fincher *University of Kent*
	Panos Markopoulos *Technical University Eindhoven*
	David Moore *Leeds Metropolitan University*
	Roy Ruddle *University of Leeds*
Industry Day	Dave Roberts *IBM*
Tutorials	Shailey Minocha *Open University*
Workshops	Mary Zajicek *Oxford Brookes University*
Short Papers	Andy Dearden *Sheffield Hallam University*
	Leon Watts *University of Bath*
Interactive Experiences	Barbara McManus *University of Central Lancashire*
Doctoral Consortium	Robert Ward *University of Huddersfield*
	Ann Blandford *UCL*
	Alan Dix *University of Lancaster*
Posters	Nick Bryan-Kinns *Queen Mary, University of London*
Laboratory and	Paul Cairns *UCL*
Organizational Overviews	
Marketing and Publicity	Tom McEwan *Napier University*
	Claire Paddison *IBM*
	Ann Light *Usability News*
Conference Websites	Marc Fabri *Leeds Metropolitan University*
Treasurer & Student Volunteers	Tony Renshaw *Leeds Metropolitan University*
Technical Support	Adrian Williamson *Graham Technologies*
Local Organisation	Meg Soosay *Leeds Metropolitan University*
Social Programme	Liz Allgar *Leeds Metropolitan University*
British HCI Group Liaison Officer	Phil Gray *University of Glasgow*
Previous Conference Chair	Eamonn O'Neill *University of Bath*
Exhibition Management	Peter Gardner *University of Leeds*
Registration &	Jack Hunt *Leeds Metropolitan University*
Exhibition Organisation	

The Reviewers

Hans-Juergen Hoffmann	*Darmstadt University of Technology, Germany*
Liz Allgar	*Leeds Metropolitan University, UK*
Francoise Anceaux	*University Valenciennes / CNRS-LAMIH-PERCOTEC, France*
Rajarathinam Arangarasan	
Sandrine Balbo	*The University of Melbourne, Australia*
Mathilde Bekker	*Technical University Eindhoven, The Netherlands*
Ann Blandford	*University College London, UK*
Richard Boardman	*Imperial College London, UK*
Nathalie Bonnardel	*University of Provence, France*
Marie-Luce Bourguet	*Queen Mary, University of London, UK*
Chris Bowerman	*University of Sunderland, UK*
Nick Bryan-Kinns	*Queen Mary, University of London, UK*
Sandra Cairncross	*Napier University, UK*
Paul Cairns	*University College London, UK*
Gilbert Cockton	*University of Sunderland, UK*
Chetz Colwell	*The Open University, UK*
Karin Coninx	*Limburgs Universitair Centrum, The Netherlands*
Jose Coronado	*Hyperion Solutions Corporation, UK*
Alison Crerar	*Napier University Edinburgh, UK*
Fintan Culwin	*South Bank University, UK*
Liisa Dawson	*The Open University , UK*
Donald Day	*Chapman University, USA*
Andy Dearden	*Sheffield Hallam University, UK*
Anind Dey	*Intel Research, UC Berkeley, USA*
Alan Dix	*University of Lancaster, UK*
Offer Drori	*Hebrew University of Jerusalem, Israel*
Jean-Marc Dubois	*Université Victor Segalen Bordeaux 2, France*
Emmanuel Dubois	*UPS-IRIT-LIIHS, France*
Lynne Dunckley	*Thames Valley University, UK*
Mark Dunlop	*University of Strathclyde, UK*
Alistair Edwards	*University of York, UK*
Florian N. Egger	
Maximilian Eibl	*GESIS*
David England	*Liverpool John Moores University, UK*

Fabio Ferlazzo   *Univertiy Rome "La Sapienza", Italy*

Bob Fields   *Middlesex University, UK*

Sally Fincher   *University of Kent, UK*

Janet Finlay   *Leeds Metropolitan University, UK*

Paola Forcheri   *Istituto Matematica Applicata e Tecnologie Informatiche-Consiglio Nazionale Ricerche, Italy*

Peter Gardner   *University of Leeds, UK*

Gheorghita Ghinea   *Brunel University, UK*

Phil Gray   *University of Glasgow, UK*

Kasper Hornbaek

Steve Howard   *University of Melbourne, Australia*

Ebba Thora Hvannberg   *University of Iceland, Iceland*

Rahat Iqbal   *Coventry University, UK*

Phillip Jeffrey   *University of British Columbia, Canada*

Charalampos Karagiannidis   *Aegean University, Greece*

Susan L. Keenan   *DAVOX Corporation, UK*

Elizabeth Kemp   *Massey University, New Zealand*

Pekka Ketola   *Nokia Mobile Phones, Finland*

Alistair Kilgour   *Heriot-Watt University, UK*

Ann Light   *University of Sussex, UK*

Lachlan MacKinnon   *Heriot-Watt University, UK / University of Porto, Portugal / Buskerud University College*

Thomas Mandl   *Universität Hildesheim, Germany*

Phebe Mann   *The Open University, UK*

Panos Markopoulos   *Technical University Eindhoven, The Netherlands*

Masood Masoodian   *The University of Waikato, New Zealand*

Jon May   *Sheffield University, UK*

Sharon McDonald   *University of Sunderland, UK*

Tom McEwan   *Napier University, UK*

Barbara McManus   *University of Central Lancashire, UK*

Anthony Meehan   *The Open University, UK*

Shailey Minocha   *The Open University, UK*

Sunila Modi   *University of Westminster, UK*

Michelle Mongomery Masters   *Pyrusmalus, UK*

Andrew Monk   *University of York, UK*

David Moore   *Leeds Metropolitan University, UK*

David Morse   *The Open University, UK*

Michael Muller   *IBM Research, UK*

N. Hari Narayanan	*Auburn University, USA*
Ian Newman	*Loughborough University, UK*
Eamonn O'Neill	*University of Bath, UK*
Claire Paddison	*IBM, UK*
Sami Paihonen	*Nokia, Finland*
Philippe Palanque	*LIIHS-IRIT / Université Paul Sabatier Toulouse 3, France*
Rodolfo Pinto da Luz	*Federal University of Santa Catarina, Brasil*
Simon Polovina	*Sheffield Hallam University, UK*
Helen Purchase	*Glasgow University, UK*
Roope Raisamo	*University of Tampere, Finland*
Rakhi Rajani	*HP Labs, UK*
Irla Bocianoski Rebelo	*Federal University of Santa Catarina, Brasil*
Karen Renaud	*GUCSD*
Tony Renshaw	*Leeds Metropolitan University, UK*
Dimitrios Rigas	*University of Bradford, UK*
Dave Roberts	*IBM, UK*
Roy Ruddle	*Leeds University, UK*
M C Schraefel	*University of Southampton, UK*
Helen Sharp	*The Open University / City University, UK*
Andy Sloane	*University of Wolverhampton, UK*
Meg Soosay	*Leeds Metropolitan University, UK*
Jan Stage	*Aalborg University, Denmark*
Phil Turner	*Napier University, UK*
Katerina Tzanidou	*The Open University, UK*
Pedro Valero	*INTRAS Institute of Traffic and Road Safety*
Alfred Vella	
Carol Vella	
Colin C. Ventners	*University of Manchester , UK*
Robert Ward	*University of Huddersfield, UK*
Leon Watts	*University of Bath, UK*
Janice Whatley	*University of Salford, UK*
Peter Wild	*University of Bath, UK*
Adrian Williamson	*Graham Technology, UK*
William Wong	*Middlesex University, UK*
Mary Zajicek	*Oxford Brookes University, UK*

Collaboration at Work and Play

Understanding Interaction in Ubiquitous Guerrilla Performances in Playful Arenas

Jennifer G Sheridan, Alan Dix, Simon Lock & Alice Bayliss[†]

Computing Department, Lancaster University, Bailrigg, Lancaster LA1 4YR, UK

[†] *School of Performance and Cultural Industries, Leeds University, Leeds WF4 4LG, UK*

The inherent freedom of *playful arenas* combined with intimate ubiquitous technologies has led to a new breed of guerrilla performance. We draw on theory from computing, performance and club culture to illustrate the Performance Triad model, a method for the analysis, deconstruction and understanding of tripartite interaction in playful arenas. We then apply the Performance Triad model to *Schizophrenic Cyborg* a part reversal of wearable computing technology where the user is outfitted with an electronic communication display and yet this display is visible to others not the cyborgs themselves. This ubiquitous performance investigates the shifting boundaries between performer, participant and observer and of technology-enhanced guerrilla performance.

Keywords: wearable computing, computing intimacies, ubiquitous computing, performance art, playful arenas, tripartite interaction, performance triad model.

1 Introduction

The empowerment and facility of new ubiquitous sensor technologies combined with the inherent freedom of *playful arenas*, such as nightclubs, has led to a new breed of performance. These new performances meld atoms and bits, performer and audience, fantasy and fact to create an intimate connection between our physical and virtual world and to affectively augment our notion of expectation.

We perceive the underground club space as a playful arena where all who contribute to its status as a communal event embrace participation, performance and play. The clubbing environment invites individuals and groups to gather together, to suspend time and to engage in a social activity, which allows them to play with and destabilize notions of identity and reality. New possibilities are envisaged through collaborative creativity.

Observable participation encouraged by these playful arenas may be planned and intentionally invoked by performance. Alternatively, participation may be unplanned and proactive on the part of the audience. Clubbers (a person present in the club space) themselves add to a sense of the theatrical experience by adopting 'characters' who interact with the crowd over the course of a night. This intentional shape shifting and willingness to 'other' provides us as technologists and performers with a fertile ground for experimentation and innovation.

Low-cost sensing and quick set up allows for more flexible, spontaneous and mobile *guerrilla performances* however, few use high-technology. Guerrilla performance [Hill 2001] is a contemporary hybrid art form which comments on the political and social behaviour of the everyday through performance and is often seen as artistic activism. Performances tend to occur outside the traditional theatre and are not pre-rehearsed like a theatre play but more like experiments, often without a known or explicit outcome.

Steve Mann's *culture jamming* uses of wearable technologies for his politically motivated surveillance performances [see Mann et al. 2003] is one example. However, we are unaware of any work that explores the use of wearable computing for guerrilla performance in playful arenas. In fact, little research exists which explores wearable computing in the arts.

A preliminary study of wearable computing misconceptions [Sheridan et al. 2000] suggests that wearable users and non-users make attempts to communicate with each other without a framework for understanding or interpreting their interactions. For example, when one wearable computer user's frames were white, outside observers assumed that he was visually impaired. We saw this knowledge awareness gap and lack of application breadth as an opportunity to further explore how wearable computing could be used in guerrilla performance to exploit misconceptions about wearable computers:

> "As a schizophrenic cyborg, interacting with other people became
> a strange experience, as often I was instrument in communications,
> without knowing the nature of my input." (post performance interview
> with a cyborg)

Our interest lies in how innovative technologies such as wearable computing stimulates the desire of the clubber and outside observer to create and be performative within playful arenas; how the technology promotes dialogue between itself and the user; how the use of such technology may signal new and innovative performance practices.

An opportunity to explore these connections arose with the announcement of *Art-Cels*, an art and technology performance party and the last event in a three-day celebration with performance artist Stelarc. The event challenged artists and technologists to come together to discuss, display and perform the future of computing and performance art in human-machine communication. Guerrilla performance was encouraged; artists were asked to turn up on the night of the event and perform in any manner they wished. As a result, we formed a collective called .:thePooch:. and performed *Schizophrenic Cyborg* a guerrilla performance that explores the limits of wearable computing in terms of collected identity, technical dependency and technical representation.

In this paper, we discuss use of technology in performance and then present our Performance Triad (PT) model. We then describe our guerrilla performance and conclude with a discussion of our observations and problems associated with evaluating performance art using HCI methodology.

2 Innovative Technologies in Playful Arenas

Use of modern technologies in planned performance is not new. Laurie Anderson, Kraftwerk, and Stelarc, have all paved the way for recent innovations in the cross fertilization between performance and technology using body-worn sensors (see http://www.stelarc.va.com.au/) mobile and wearable computing [Mann & Niedzviecki 2002; Wren et al. 1997], directional audio [Pompei 1999] and interactive projections [Lock et al. 2003]. As we become more familiar with these technologies, and as these technologies become both more affording and more affordable, their use is becoming more diverse and widespread.

The growth in this field has gone hand in hand with the increasing number of performances that seek to investigate and redefine notions of performance and performativity as essential human activity that can occur beyond the tightly bound world of the theatre building. Collaborations between scientists and artists, such as *Uncle Roy Is All Around You* [Flintham et al. 2003], *Art-Cels* (see http://www.art-cels.com/), and *The Brain Stripped Bare* (see http://www.rebeccaallen.com/), take full advantage of technology in performance to extend the physical with the digital.

With the addition of innovative technologies in performance, we see a dramatic shift from traditional, fixed theatre towards a more dynamic form of guerrilla performance, which encompasses audience participation and the integration of the real world and the everyday. Probably one of the best examples of this is pioneering cyborg Steve Mann's sousveillence [see Mann et al. 2003] a form of situationist street theatre.

In this paper, we seek to investigate the use of technology in playful arena performances that have emerged from the vibrant, and often underground, dance music scene of the late 1980s. We perceive clubs as playful arenas, what Fiona Buckland [2002] calls 'playgrounds of culture'; liminal spaces where identities are fluid, boundaries blurred and new meanings made possible. Is it possible to suggest that DJs, dancers, performers and participants are engaged in a creative collaboration, feeding off each other to create a new whole? How can our performative technological interventions promote that state? Jacques Attali [1985] envisaged a world in which technology would become a creative instrument, a tool for performance. We seek to explore that, not by observing what is already there but by pushing the limits of what we know is possible and what we believe might be possible.

In order to assist us with this task of investigation and understanding, we use a new model of technology-based performance. This model allows us to dissect the structure of a performance, in order to examine the various facets involved. By isolating these elements in this manner, we can discuss each in depth, without the issues and complexities associated with the performance as a whole unnecessarily obscuring our investigation.

3 Performance Triad Model

Working with digital technology in performance opens up new opportunities to investigate modes of interaction that exaggerate or break from those experienced in day-to-day life. Performance imposes its own aesthetic and practical constraints, but these are different from those most often associated with computing research. In computing, the demand for face validity, an implied potential utility, restricts the freedom with which we can explore particularly the new forms of interaction afforded by technology. For many the only alternative seems to be purely technology driven exemplars, with a thin veneer of utility! What our digital performance art experiments do is explore the issues around this — the technical requirements and infrastructure, the novel modes of interaction and their new cognitive demands, and the effects of these on social relationships. The Performance Triad (PT) model is the culmination of our initial research of human-computer interaction (HCI) in digital performance.

The PT model raises the technical and practical issues associated with the development and analysis of technology-based performance (Figure 1). In the PT, the observer, participant and performer are equal collaborators in a performance, which lies at the heart of the triad. A performance is, by definition, that which is present between performer, participant and observer. The performance as a whole exists in a particular context and the context occurs within and creates an environment. The model also includes three separate technology layers by which humans interface with the performance, each of which may be of different complexity, sophistication and extent.

This model has a wide variety of uses in the development of complex technology-based performances. As a representation of the performance itself, the model can help promote understanding of that particular performance and all its associated elements. This offers us the ability to investigate the *tripartite interactions* (interaction between performers, participants and observers), and how context and environment affect such activities. In addition to this, it is possible to consider the role technology might undertake in mediating such interactions. The model affords a structuring of experience which is highly valuable in the planning and development of future performances by building on knowledge and experience gained from previous work. Finally, the model provides a common language for the discussion of technology-based performance which supports discourse between performers, curators, technologists, researchers, theorists and so on.

Figure 1: Performance Triad model for the development and analysis of technology-based performance.

In this paper however, we utilize the PT model to deconstruct performances in playful arenas in order to gain a deep insight into their complex structures, anatomies and behaviours. This allows us to separate the various human, technological, contextual and environmental elements of a performance and to execute an in depth investigation of each.

3.1 Technology

Technology is a fundamental yet flexible bounding element of the PT model. The role of technology is to mediate the interaction and interfacing between the people involved in a performance and the performance itself. In this role, technology can support the integration of performers, participants and observers into the performance. The type of technology used in such interfacing will depend upon the extent to which the different people are to be incorporated into the performance as well as the mode of interaction required. Performers, participants and observers form the edges of the technology triangle and play an essential role determining our expectation of the performance. The most popular of these connections are discussed in more detail here.

3.1.1 Interaction between Performer and Performance

This is perhaps the most widespread and diverse method of technology-based interaction in performance. The purpose of these technologies is to support the performer in creating the performance, telling their 'story', imparting a message or engineering an experience.

3.1.2 Involving Participants using Interactive Technologies

Using interactive technologies in playful arenas engages participants in the performance in a controlled manner. Participants differ from performers in that they are not usually 'scripted' into the performance. While they may begin as an outside observer, once they physically interact with the technology they become a participant.

3.1.3   Encouraging Observer Engagement with Performances

When interaction is purely observational, performances tend to involve video displays, computer graphics, audio presentation and so on. However, wireless technologies are beginning to stretch the boundary of observational engagement in performance.

4   Performers

Clubs are spaces where watching and being watched are central tenets. They are places where we observe ourselves and lose ourselves in being observed simultaneously. The liveness of performance no longer lies with the official stars of a club night. The DJs, those paid to appear as licensed performers, are more often than not tucked away, obscured from view, minimal figures on a darkened stage. They play recorded music and any attempt at 'live' reproduction is seen as false. In response to this shift, the performative element of a club night often emanates from the crowd. The gaze is turned back on the observer. As Tony Wilson suggested in Sheryl Garratt's [1988] *Adventures in Wonderland*, the emphasis is no longer with four band members on stage in the spotlight but with the crowd itself. He called it a 'democratic art form' where the people are the spectacle, the participants, or spect-actors (to borrow a term from Boal [1979]) — those who act.

It is worth remembering that whilst performative behaviour may well be central to the club experience, rarely do people chose to go to a club in order to engage in rehearsed, planned or prepared performance of a theatrical nature. If a club welcomes performers and if promoters book acts or artists, it is usually with a view to decorating the space and enhancing the visual element of the event. It is not uncommon for clubs to provide stilt walkers, professional dancers, jugglers and so on to add to the sense of spectacle and carnivalesque. However for most it is essential that performative work does not prevent the clubber from his or her main activity — that is, enjoying a night out dancing with friends.

4.1   Participants

It is not unusual for clubbers to adopt 'alter egos' as they prepare for their night out, and in such roles actively participate in both the event as well as any sense of formal performance therein. Dressing up, costuming and masquerade are all common features of a club night and are often taken to extremes by clubbers adopting and staying in role for the duration of the event. As Matthew Collin [1997] says, rave fulfils 'the role of fantasy theatre, a place where people (can) become the magical characters that their everyday lives would not allow'. This state of mind, this willingness and desire to play and perform is a concept which can be utilized when creating site-specific installations and performances. The artist becomes the facilitator; the artwork becomes the vehicle for the clubbers' innate sense of expressivity.

Most notable to participant acceptance of technology-based performance is the participant's particular background and experience with technology. Whether someone is a technophobe or technophile affects his or her expectation of the technology in the performance and how they approach interaction. In the case where the technology is hidden, a participant's mental model is based solely on observable phenomenon.

4.2 Observers

Observers are defined as the people present at a performance who do not engage with interaction or who do not undertake any performative action. In traditional performance environments, the boundary defining an observer is often fixed and rigid. Take for example a member of an audience at a theatrical performance. Participation and performance on the part of audience members is mainly undesired and thus not encouraged. In playful arenas on the other hand, participation and performance are fluid and individuals can rapidly move from 'observer' status to become a participant or even a performer.

4.3 Context

Performance in the post-modern age is no longer restricted to the firmly bounded world of the theatre stage. If we are to understand the world of performance in all its guises and the world as performance, then it is not difficult to perceive clubs as informal stages that give license for people to revel in spectacular society. If, according to Peter Brook [1968], the Deadly Theatre is one which makes people smile out of recognition and familiarity and the Living Theatre is one that moves and becomes a moving force in the world, then a club has the potential to house permeable, flexible, innovative and startling performative events. This is our context as outlined in the Performance Triad. In our model context is understood as the social, cultural and conceptual placement in which the performance finds itself. A performance may take place in a gallery context, a theatrical context, a pedagogical context and so on. Each of these contexts is associated with its own unique features, dynamics, implicit and explicit rules as well as accepted behavioural norms and conventions.

4.4 Environment

Environment is the physical space and location in which a performance finds itself. Each environment is associated with its own unique set of properties and constraints. The environment of a performance is often linked to the context of that performance, in that particular contexts are often associated with particular environments. For example, a play is usually performed in a theatrical context in a theatre. However, this is not always the case in that our hypothetical play could actually be performed outside in a park.

Probably the most unpredictable factor that can negatively affect a technology-based performance is the environment. The technical components for a performance may run well in a lab, studio or theatre but because of the unpredictable nature of playful arenas, testing a performance in the real world is essential to ensure that the environment is not adversely affecting the technology, performers or observers.

Many technologies are not good at coping with unpredictable events where the dynamism of a playful environment can affect the technology and thus the performance. Technically speaking, fixed locations are much easier to deal with since the technology can be produced to fit predictable events occurring in the environment, such as in 'zones of interaction' or hot spots so that events are predictable and fixed. However, in flexible environments events are often more spontaneous and unpredictable, often creating a tension between performer and participant/observer. A good example of this tension is in *Schizophrenic Cyborg*.

5   Schizophrenic Cyborg

Since we were interested in developing a guerrilla performance that capitalized on an audience's misconceptions about wearable technology, we determined that we needed to design a piece which encouraged participation through a solicitation of appeal, whether physical, emotional or psychological and that we should focus on how to solicit participation between observers and observed. We came up with the idea of a wearable computer user as a 'cyborg': cyborg not really a 'self' at all but rather part of a larger collective; and, cyborg as technically dependent on a parasitic 'other'. Wireless technology could provide a ubiquitous, hidden link between cyborg and 'parasitic other', where the parasite controlled the cyborg and conversely the parasite was dependent on the cyborg for stimulation. A wearable display would reveal this tension in technical dependency between cyborg and parasite and encourage interaction between the cyborg and observers.

5.1   Procedure

Our scenario presented an interesting problem; since we were not conducting an empirical study, we were unsure as to how to collect and evaluate our data. Conventional empirical research seemed inappropriate for this type of study. As a result, we decided that we would observe interaction between participants, performers and observers and record our data on paper and with a video camera. We anticipated that this performance would lead to issues about how to evaluate performance-based HCI.

5.2   Participants: Deconstructing Tripartite Interaction

Our performance, *Schizophrenic Cyborg*, required three types of people: a participant (parasite); a performer (cyborg); and, at least one observer (audience). For our performer, we needed someone who was willing to participate in a live, unplanned performance in a public space. Also, we hope to involve someone who was knowledgeable about the wearable computer without knowing its technical specifications and who did not consider him or herself to be an artist. We considered that this type of person would be less apt to bore an onlooker with technical details about the hardware and to behave naturally during the performance. We compiled a list of people whom we thought would be appropriate and then approached these people. Because of the high cost and fragile nature of the technology we used in the performance, we hand selected our participants from a list of people we generated in our brainstorming session. From those we asked, only one agreed to participate as a cyborg. Our parasitic participant acted as the 'control centre' for the performance had extensive experience setting up and running a wireless local area network (LAN). A member of .:thePooch:. agreed to be this person. Unlike conventional empirical research, we could not control, select or predict our observers. Observers were made up of the random people who turned up at the event.

Figure 2: Cyborg performer and his wearable public display.

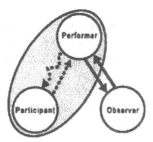

Figure 3: Tripartite interaction in Schizophrenic Cyborg. Solid lines represent physical interaction; broken lines show digital interaction; straight lines show visible awareness; and, jagged lines represent hidden awareness. The oval highlights the physical/digital dependency.

5.3   Method

The cyborg used a wearable computer and positioned the display on a utility vest facing forward so that observers could see the display as they approached him (Figure 2). The cyborg wandered through the environment with the public physical display on his belly. Because of the positioning of the display, only the observers could see the information on the display and not the cyborg himself.

The parasite was in control of the information shown on the display. The parasite hid somewhere in the room so that they were not visible to outside observers and observers were unaware that a parasite was in control of the display (Figure 3). The parasite displayed still images, text or video selected from a collection of saved media or he selected media from the inscribed environment in real time. Although the cyborg was aware of the parasite's existence, they could not directly control or affect the information that the parasite chose to show on the display.

The cyborg and the parasite were encouraged to behave as they normally behaved in social settings. However, the parasite had to maintain enough distance between himself and the cyborg so that observers could not make any connection between the two parties.

During the performance, we did not provide any signage or information about the purpose or function of the wearable computers. However, we did post signs inside the venue that informed attendees that the event was being videotaped.

This work has an intrinsic subjectivity in that one of the crucial aspects is the participants' feelings. John Searle, famous for his Chinese Room Argument, distinguishes two types of subjectivity: epistemic and ontological [Searle 1997]. A statement such as "I think the Empire State building is 1273 feet tall" is epistemicly subjective — it is a matter of belief. In analysis, science prefers epistemic objectivity — the measured height of the building. However where personal preference, aesthetics, pain or other feelings are the domain of discourse, as in this work, then we have ontological subjectivity — where the subjectivity is the very essence of the thing being studied. In such cases it is essential to gather subjective data although we of course need to exercise caution when interpreting it.

5.4   Measures

To record our data, we used qualitative procedures, including observations and interviews. We recorded observations during the event with a video camera and on paper. At the end of the event, an investigator conducted a short interview with the performer, participant and about five observers via face-to-face conversation and through email. Using multiple forms of observation and data collection allowed for detailed evaluation and analysis of user behaviour and interaction.

5.5   Technical Specifications

The parasite was linked to the cyborg over a wireless LAN network. The cyborg node required a display and a RealVNC server running on a wearable computer. VNC (Virtual Network Computing) software makes it possible to view and fully-interact with one computer from any other computer or mobile device anywhere on the Internet. The parasite node required a laptop and VNC client running on the computer. The changing lighting conditions of the environment required that we obtain a Xybernaut high-resolution, flat-panel display.

5.6   Observations

Over 200 technologists and artists from around the UK attended the event and since it was licensed, all attendees were over the age of 18. Attendees came from a wide variety of professional backgrounds (computer scientists, sociologists, artists, philosophers, engineers) and had diverse social and ethnic backgrounds.

5.6.1   Cyborg Experience

When telling investigators about his experience, the cyborg highlighted his conflicting and inconsistent emotional state: one minute he felt excited and aware and another he felt frustrated and out of control.

He expressed his experience in terms of how comfortable and natural interaction felt with observers. When the parasite posted text messages, he said that the conversation felt natural and very comfortable; having the display as a teleprompter for conversation meant that conversation lasted longer since observers were constantly prompted with new discussion points. Even when observers discovered that a parasite was controlling the conversation, observers were content to continue conversation. It was often the case that the parasite couldn't keep up the natural conversational exchange between observers and the cyborg, which was not surprising since they was no audio connection between the two. This resulted in the participant posting questions that didn't follow natural conversational progression. However, rather than this hindering conversational exchange, the cyborg said that he found this highly entertaining for both themselves and observers:

> "From (observers) perspective, they saw a strange looking person who wanted a hug. From my perspective, I was only aware that 'I', or the cyborg within, wanted a hug, after it was received, and needed to adjust my reaction accordingly." (post performance interview with a cyborg)

When observers were relying on the display to direct conversation, the cyborg felt a high level of frustration in that he couldn't control the discussion. As conversation progressed, he felt a 'role reversal' and that he had became the 'object' of conversation and the participants had become the 'subject'; the cyborg felt like he wasn't a part of the shared experience.

During the interview, the cyborg often referred to the parasite as the cyborg rather than himself. He saw his role as a 'conduit for communication' rather than as a performer.

5.6.2   Parasite Experience

The remote display allowed the parasite to behave in ways in which he felt he would be unable or afraid to outside of the performance. Initially, parasite said that he wanted to act like cyborg's subconscious; where text on the display reflected what the cyborg was possibly thinking. The parasite said he switched images and text quite rapidly in an attempt to try and keep observers and the cyborg interacting. But in many cases, the parasite found it too difficult to keep up with conversation, so he resorted to writing suggestive comments in an attempt to regain observers' attention.

The parasite acted fairly subversively. Since he was removed from the immediate situation, he knew that the cyborg was the only person that could hold him accountable for unwanted or negative responses from observers. Because of this, the parasite said that he was interested in seeing what he could get away with saying.

As well, he said he was tempted to provoke more private conversation as interaction continued. One way of doing this was to send more and more personal information about the cyborg or suggestive comments about the observer.

5.6.3   Observer Experience

All of the observers, including several technical experts, said that on their initial encounter with the cyborg, they believed that the conversation was only between the cyborg and themselves. They assumed that the wearable hardware was either controlling something technical in the room or was some kind of communication device.

Initially, observers refused to believe that the cyborg didn't have any control over the public display. They asked the cyborg to take his hands out of his pockets or prove in some way that he had nothing to do with the media being shown. How quickly observers accepted that someone else was in control of the display usually depended on their technical background: expert computer users believed that the cyborg had no control more quickly than beginner users.

The type of text message displayed provoked different types of emotional responses from observers. Observers said that they found the experience very 'creepy' particularly when the text on the display reflected something unique and personal about the observer. As well, simple questions provoked them to approach the cyborg and begin conversation.

How observers responded depended on their familiarity with the technology, their technical background, and their awareness of the existence of a hidden parasite. Many artists wanted to know more about the symbolic significance of the performance whereas technologists were more interesting in knowing about the technical aspects.

5.6.4   Affect of Varying the Type of Media on the Cyborg Display

The wearable display prompted various types of interactions based on the type of media shown. Text messages acted like a teleprompter for observers. For example, if the display suggested, "ask me what I am doing tomorrow" or "ask me why I am doing this" the observer obliged. On several occasions we observed interaction moving from cyborg as subject to cyborg as object. This occurred because of the appealing nature of the display; initially, the display *tempted* observers to interact with cyborgs through personalized text messages (I like your hat. Nice pair of red boots). After approaching the cyborg, observers would wait for the display to pose another question or statement and increasingly paid less attention to the cyborg himself.

A different type of interaction occurred when the parasitic participant streamed video of the inscribed environment in real time. We noticed that when some observers realized that the video was a live stream, they wanted to become part of the display and would search for cameras around the room and then dance or gesture in front of them.

Showing still images on the display had less of an effect on performer-observer interaction. Some observers commented on the image, but the image didn't seem to direct conversation in any particular way.

6   Discussion

The asymmetric, tripartite interaction between the cyborg, parasite and observer breaks and challenges 'normal' interaction and for the cyborg causes a dislocation between 'I' and 'me'. This dislocation is evident in the quotes we have seen cyborg's post event interview. In one he says "as a schizophrenic cyborg" at once identifying himself and yet also distancing the "internal self or 'I' from the external self as acted on and observed by others, the 'me'". This equivocal relationship continues "I was instrument" — the active 'I' becomes subject and passive. In the second quote he says "From (observers) perspective ... from my perspective ...". He feels that only by perceiving others reactions could he know what the 'I' wanted.

6.1   Levels of Awareness

An underlying issue in tripartite interaction and with the wearable technology itself is identifying levels of awareness. When is it important for an observer to be aware of who is in control of the technology or of the hidden participants? How does this change interaction? At what point is it important that observers understand interaction? What is their mental model of this interaction and how do they come to this conclusion? At what point to observers see the screen as having interactive qualities? As we soon discovered, our performance prompted more questions than answers!

The reader of an earlier version of this paper asked how this performance differed from having a 'kick me' sign posted on someone's back.   While *Schizophrenic Cyborg* was indeed created to generate, in some cases, comical and potentially embarrassing situations, observers were tempted into interacting with a hidden participant while being engaged in conversation with a present other. Observers have to come into interaction with the display. Once this happens, levels of responsibility change: Who is in control? Who can be trusted?

These confusions do not happen with the 'kick me sign'; a static sign or message may invite interaction, but is not, except in a very long-term sense, part of interaction. As noted above, static images on the display similarly were objects of discussion but not utterances in the dialogue. Previous knowledge and cultural expectations are important here too; even the streaming video elicited a response from the observer more like that we would expect if the display were mounted on a wall. The observers understood 'television' and this was then perceived as a television that happened to be mounted in someone — Teletubbies indeed! However, when text is displayed that acts in 'conversation', the observers are being called to interact with an agency that is 'behind' the display when what is 'behind' the display is the performer himself. With no previous experience to help the observers were faced with two human agencies occupying the same physical space were often unable to separate the two. *Wearing* the display is not the important issue here; interacting with the display when the wearer is not in control of the display is the issue.

Revealing this spectactorship through hidden technology often brings in to question our notion of accountability and awareness. In some cases, an awareness of the hidden aspect of the technology causes performers to act more subversively. If hidden participants know that they cannot be held immediately accountable for their actions, they often 'misbehave'. This in turn encourages performers to misbehave. The misrepresentation of control causes both participants and performers to act subversively from within the performance parameters, to see what kind of reactions they could get from observers. Clearly elements of both dark and invisible play are at work here, reinforcing our understanding of the performative act as one that is slippery, malleable and ultimately dialogic in nature. For us as researchers it raises particularly interesting questions about control, authority and authoring of the performance text.

6.2   Evaluation Issues

We have clearly gained valuable insight through the *Schizophrenic Cyborg* performance. However this is hard to quantify. Was it a success? Evaluation demands valuation and how do we measure the value of such guerrilla performances? In a playful arena people had fun, but clearly a beach-ball may have had equal affect — what is the 'control' or baseline? Another measure is the artistic merit and here there is an external measure. The performance has been invited to further arts events; amongst other competing performances this has been chosen — an objective measure of subjective satisfaction by the arts community. As is evident these issues of value in an intensely subjective arena are intensely problematic.

7 Future Considerations

We are in the process of improving the performative aspect of *Schizophrenic Cyborg* as well as its costume and technical components. We expect to perform at various arts and technology performance events and conferences over the next year, which will help us to evaluate and to improve upon our PT model.

In future performances, we would improve on our technical components, particularly data capturing techniques. We would like to log all of the messages sent to the cyborg display and match these to observer reactions.

Since the display screen was a bit difficult for observers to read, we would like to experiment with brighter displays. Integrating the display into the cyborg's clothing would also increase the comfort level for the cyborg.

Finally, we would like to improve the sound quality, integrate speakers into the cyborg's outfit so that we can generate audio files, and perhaps outfit the cyborg with a higher quality microphone.

8 Conclusions

Dance music and the subcultural styles that attend it have always provided rich sites for innovative practice. DJs, musicians, artists and producers constantly seek new styles, new forms, and new methodologies to attract and maintain audiences each weekend. Dance music is constantly reinventing itself, surfing the waves of cultural and social change as it does so. A DJ and his decks is a fitting example of how man and machine work together to create something fresh and vibrant, rooted in the here and now, in order to promote and stimulate a collective response in the form of social dancing. This living and fluctuating context provides us as researchers, performers and artists with immensely exciting possibilities. Performance and play can be read as basic human functions. They fulfil a need in us for self-expression. They allow us to challenge, confirm and confront our own identities in dialogue with other people. We perceive clubs as spaces which, potentially, have similar properties, similar functions. By marrying technology, performance and club culture we are not only able to draw on a diverse range of theory and understanding from each field but are also able to learn from each others' disciplines and working practices about what it is to be human. In a world which is seemingly driven and dominated by machines, where the individual can feel powerlessness in the face of complex technologies of varying kinds, our intention is to reconsider the performative conversation that might take place between man and machine and see how that might impact on our understanding of ourselves, each other and of the world around us.

Acknowledgements

We would like to thank Lora Carroll, Peter Phillips, Ken Cosh, Stewart Kember, Hester Reeve and Xybernaut.

References

Attali, J. [1985], *Noise: The Political Economy of Music*, University of Minnesota Press.

Boal, A. [1979], *Theatre of the Oppressed*, Pluto Press.

Brook, P. [1968], *The Empty Space*, Penguin.

Buckland, F. [2002], *Impossible Dance: Club Culture and Queer World Making*, Wesleyan University Press.

Collin, M. [1997], *Altered State — The Story of Ecstasy Culture and Acid House*, Serpent's Tail.

Flintham, M., Benford, S., Anastasi, R., Hemmings, T., Crabtree, A. & Greenhalgh, C. [2003], Where On-Line Meets On-The-Streets: Experiences With Mobile Mixed Reality Games, *in* G. Cockton & P. Korhonen (eds.), *Proceedings of 2003 Conference on Human Factors in Computing Systems (CHI'03)*, *CHI Letters* **5**(1), ACM Press, pp.569–76.

Garratt, S. [1988], *Adventures in Wonderland: A Decade of Club Culture*, Headline.

Hill, L. [2001], *Guerilla Performance & Multimedia*, Continuum International.

Lock, S., Rayson, P. & Allanson, J. [2003], Personality Engineering for Emotional Interactive Avatars, *in* C. Stephanidis & J. Jacko (eds.), *Human–Computer Interaction, Theory and Practice (Part II). Volume 2 of the Proceedings of Human–Computer Interaction International 2003*, Vol. 2, Lawrence Erlbaum Associates, pp.503–7.

Mann, S. & Niedzviecki, H. [2002], *Cyborg: Digital Destiny and Human Possibility in the Age of the Wearable Computer*, Doubleday.

Mann, S., J., N. & Wellman, B. [2003], Sousveillance: Inventing and Using Wearable Computing Devices for Data Collection in Surveillance Environments, *Surveillance and Society* **1**(3), 331–55.

Pompei, F. J. [1999], The Use of Airborne Ultrasonics for Generating Audible Sound Beams, *Journal of the Audio Engineering Society* **47**, 726–31.

Searle, J. [1997], *The Mystery of Consciousness*, Granta.

Sheridan, J. G., Lafond-Favieres, V. & Newstetter, W. C. [2000], Spectators at a Geek Show: An Ethnographic Inquiry into Wearable Computing, *in* T. Starner, C. Thompson, B. MacIntyre & B. Iannucci (eds.), *Proceedings of the 4th International Symposium on Wearable Computers (ISWC 2000)*, IEEE Computer Society Press, pp.195–6.

Wren, C., Sparacino, F., Azarbayejani, A., Darrell, T., Starner, T., Kotani, A., Chao, C. M., Hlavac, M., Russell, K. & Pentland, A. [1997], Perceptive Spaces for Performance and Entertainment: Untethered Interaction using Computer Vision and Audition, *Applied Artificial Intelligence* **11**(4), 267–84.

Towards the Development of CSCW: An Ethnographic Approach

Rahat Iqbal[†] & Anne James[‡]

[†] *Department of Industrial Design, Eindhoven University of Technology, Den Dolech 2, PO Box 513, 5600 MB Eindhoven, The Netherlands*

[‡] *School of Mathematical and Information Sciences, Coventry University, Coventry CV1 5FB, UK*
Email: *a.james@coventry.ac.uk*

Effective and rigorous analysis of cooperative work settings is crucial to the successful development of CSCW systems. This paper investigates the relationship between the social organization of the work settings and the system development. Objectives of this paper are therefore twofold. First, it effectively analyses the social aspects of the work practices using the state-of-the-art techniques of ethnography. Such analysis provides rich and concrete portrayal of the situation thus helps systematic design of CSCW systems. Second it uses the standard Unified Modelling Language (UML) in order to represent and model the findings of the ethnographic analysis. UML-based representation of the findings has proven to be an important aid to the development of CSCW systems.

Keywords: CSCW design, ethnography, UML, user-centred design, education, coordination and communication.

1 Introduction

Ethnographic research has risen to a position of some prominence within CSCW to explore the ways people work. Many researchers and practitioners have found that the ethnographic analyses of work settings can provide useful insights which can be used in the design process of associated systems [Bentley et al. 1992; Hughes et al. 1994; Myers 1999]. Ethnography has successfully been applied to various complex, large scale and domestic workplaces [Crabtree et al. 2003; Clarke et al. 2003;

O'Brien et al. 1999]. The aim is to effectively analyse working practices in order to aid the system development process. Computer systems that are developed without any systematic help from the social sciences (sociology, psychology, linguistics, anthropology, etc.) may not thoroughly address the needs of the users [Goguen & Linde 1993]. Ethnographic research intends to obtain a deep understanding of the people, the organizations, and the broader context of the work, which they undertake.

In this paper, we apply an ethnographic approach to the analysis of cooperative activities. The analysis is based on a real life case study of the cooperative applications in a University environment. An ethnographic study has been carried out in the University in order to understand the needs of the people. This study has been concerned with two administrative systems within the school of Mathematics and Information Sciences (MIS): the Document Management System (DMS); and the Module Assignment System (MAS). The findings of this research enable us to develop appropriate computer support that reflects the needs of people running these crucial operations.

The work we have carried out has gained insights into the working practices involved in the two operations. The development of the system to support the MAS has not been discussed in this paper due to space limit. The methods of data collection used were in-depth interviews, participant observations, documents and informal social contact with the participants over two years. The important information has been extracted and described along the discussion of the DMS. Throughout the research, the focus has been on the analysis of the activities such as monitoring modules, revising modules, and reviewing modules. During this study, different aspects have been highlighted such as, the manuals of instruction and procedures, the job description, the dependencies between the activities, the workflow, the actors involved and their roles.

Some problems related to coordination in the academic environment are also discussed. For example, version control is one of the major issues, which is of intrinsic importance to such an activity.

We do not simply describe the social structure of the academic environment and the cooperation between them but the purpose is to analyse the importance of coordination in the academic environment and to capture the requirements.

The paper presents the findings of the research in a way that can bridge the gap between the two kinds of representation — that is between the expansive textual expositions of the ethnographic research and the abstract, spare graphical depictions which focus on the core concepts of the system design.

The structure of the paper is organized as follows: Section 2 discusses an ethnographic framework and a meta-modelling; Section 3 presents an analysis of the cooperative activities in the University; Section 4 discusses and concludes this paper. This section also outlines some points for future research.

2 Ethnography and Meta-Modelling

In recent years a growing number of CSCW researchers have recognized the value of the ethnographic research for CSCW [Bentley et al. 1992; Hughes et al. 1994, 1997; Myers 1999]. The origins of ethnography lie mainly in anthropology. It became part of the sociological tradition through the research activities of members of the Sociology Department at the University of Chicago in the 1920s and 1930s. It became closely associated with Symbolic Interactionism and latterly with Ethnomethodology [COMIC Project 1993].

Ethnographic research requires an ethnographer to spend a reasonable length of time in the organization, which results in an extensive amount of data being generated. This provides a rich, textual and concrete exposition of the analysis of working practices in the domain of investigation. Many researchers have proposed different approaches for the presentation of research findings in a manner, which can be utilized in the design of the system [Viller & Sommerville 1999; Twidale et al. 1993].

Our approach is based on two existing approaches: (i) the ethnographic framework [Hughes et al. 1997] and (ii) the meta-modelling [Farias et al. 2000b]. The advantage of these approaches is that they can be used to control the extensive amount of information but still provide 'rich' and 'concrete' portrayal of the situation, which can be used to transform the findings to the design of the systems. We use the former approach for 'requirement capture' or 'requirement elicitation'. This is an ethnographic approach, which provides a concrete analysis of the cooperative activities. The later approach based on meta-modelling is used to control the extensive amount of information which transform the findings to the design of the system. The meta-modelling approach is based on UML (Unified Modelling Language).

Using the meta-modelling approach, we have developed the object model for the system in order to understand the main concepts such as activities, interdependencies between the activities, goals, resource and actors involved performing these activities. We have developed the models based on requirements gathering and the experience with the usage of these applications. This high level description (i.e. class diagram) of the system is commonly called conceptual model in the literature [Farias 2002].

An object model aims at capturing the concepts present in the application domain under investigation. An object is a concept or an abstraction with some boundaries and meanings. An object class is a representation of a group of objects with similar structure (i.e. attributes), common behaviour (i.e. operations), common relationship to other objects (i.e. links) and common semantics [Farias et al. 2000b]. The approaches are briefly described below.

2.1 An Ethnographic Framework

The ethnographic framework guides the ethnographers to capture the system requirements through a systemic study of the work place and all the activities of those involved with it [Hughes et al. 1997]. Many ethnographers and practitioners have used this framework to obtain requirement elicitation for the system design, such as 'ethnographic study of the Roughing Mill in a steel plant', which has produced effective results [Clarke et al. 2003]. The framework is shown in Figure 1. It is argued that the role of ethnography is important to the design process.

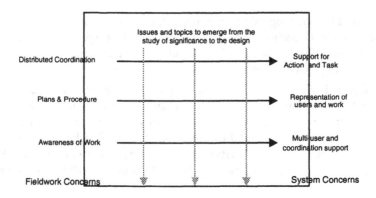

Figure 1: An ethnographic framework [Hughes et al. 1997].

This framework discusses three main dimensions: 'Distributed Coordination'; 'Plans and Procedures' and 'Awareness of Work' based on fields studies and identified how this can be realized in the system design.

Distributed coordination refers to the fact that the tasks performed in complex settings are carried out as part of patterns of activity with the context of a division of labour. Plans and Procedures provide a means by which distributed coordination is organizationally supported. Awareness of work is an expression referring to the way in which the organization of work activities involves making the nature of those activities 'visible' or 'intelligible' to others doing the work [Hughes et al. 1997]. This framework provides a bridge between fieldwork and design decisions.

2.2 Meta-modelling

The Meta-Modelling is used with the ethnographic framework in order to represent the features of work settings captured through ethnographic studies to the design of the system. In the subsequent discussions, meta-modelling will be called a 'meta-model' or 'model' for simplicity.

This model is based on the strengths and commonalities of five different models and theories, viz., Coordination Theory, Activity Theory, Task Manager, Action/Interaction Theory and Object Activity Support Model [Farias et al. 2000b]. Figure 2 depicts the meta-model. This model has used four important concepts, viz. activity, actor, information (i.e. object/resource) and service (i.e. tool) and a set of relationship between them. The concepts of actor, activity, resource (or information) and tool are mapped onto the object classes Actor, Activity, Information, and Tool respectively.

The concept of goal and state is mapped onto a class attribute while the concept of relationship is mapped onto an association class. The multiplicity symbol '*' in the associations between two classes represents zero or more instances of a class in a given association at a time.

An activity is the basic unit of analysis and design. It represents a cooperative procedure. The activities have two properties; a goal and a state. An activity

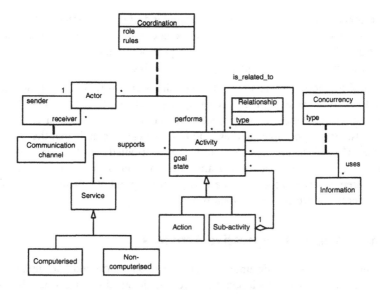

Figure 2: A meta-model [Farias et al. 2000b].

can be decomposed into actions and sub-activities. The activities can be further decomposed while the actions are atomic. The activities can be tied with a relationship. The examples of relationship types include, the disabling of an activity by another, the sequential execution of two activities, and the synchronized execution of two activities [Iqbal et al. 2003].

An actor is an active entity and responsible for performing an activity. The actors may communicate with each other in order to perform the activity properly using different communication channels such as email messages, telephone line, video conferencing, and even a live channel in which the actors are co-located at the same room. Thus, different actors are playing different roles, such as sender and receiver. An actor is not part of an activity but is associated with one or more activities. A role and a set of coordination rules are the attributes of the coordination association class established between the actors and activities. A role describes the part taken by an actor in an association. An actor can be involved in different activities and thus can play different roles in different activities. Coordination rules maintain the relationship between different actors performing the same activity using policies or floor control mechanisms.

The information represents any kind of electronic data such as messages, documents, or database records which is used by an activity. The concept of information is related to resource without any distinction between computerized and non-computerized information. The information can be shared by many actors and multiple activities. The concurrency control mechanisms are provided by the concurrency association class. The class is established between the activity and the shared information.

The concept of the service represents any kind of computerized (i.e. email) or non-computerized service that supports the execution of an activity. This concept is related to a tool, which also extends this concept to non-computerized services, such as the service provided by a secretary [Farias et al. 2000b].

Both of the above models (i.e. ethnographic framework and meta-modelling) are used to analyse and design University systems. The purpose here is not to make a comparison of these models and propose another one, but to use the strength of the both models. Briefly, comparing these models, one can conclude that these models are similar. Most of the concepts present in the 'distributed coordination' and 'plans and procedures' in the ethnographic framework are similar to the meta-model. The major difference between them can be noticed at the point of 'Awareness of Work'. This concept is not present in the meta-model.

3   Analysis of the Cooperative Activities

This section provides a basic understanding of cooperation and coordination. In the literature, CSCW has developed a different understanding of cooperative work and coordination. Some studies emphasize the interdependencies between the actors. Others focus on the interdependencies between the activities [Malone & Crowston 1990]. However, cooperative work is a specific category with certain fundamental characteristic common to all work arrangements [Schmidt & Bannon 1992]. The primary characteristic of all arrangements of work is that the activities of work are distributed and interdependent. The argument is that the activities are not performed in one single place but in a variety of places. For example in an academic environment (i.e. universities or colleges), the activity can be performed in an administrative office, in lecturers room, in resource manager's room etc., and even across international sites such as in partners universities or colleges. The activities of work are spatially and temporally distributed. Each actor or a class of actors is responsible for accomplishing particular activities of work characterized in terms of rules and goals. The activities are also distributed in the same way that responsibilities are distributed. For example two or more lecturers are responsible to write or revise the contents of a module, one may write the objectives of the module while the other writes the contents of the module in order to accomplish their common goal. The activities of work are mutually dependent and the actors like to cooperate with each other in order to achieve their common goal.

The following subsections present a detailed description of the analysis of the cooperative work in the University. These subsections present the material from the field study into a systematic way, which will be used for the development of CSCW system. The discussion is organized in a systematic way. Section 3.1 presents the social description of the DMS. This section is further divided into subsections; Section 3.1.1 discusses a major sub-activity 'revise module'; Section 3.1.2 discusses the second major sub-activity 'review module'; Section 3.1.3 describes the common interdependencies between these activities; Section 3.1.4 describes different roles and responsibilities and finally Section 3.1.5 describes the glossary of terms used for the development of the system.

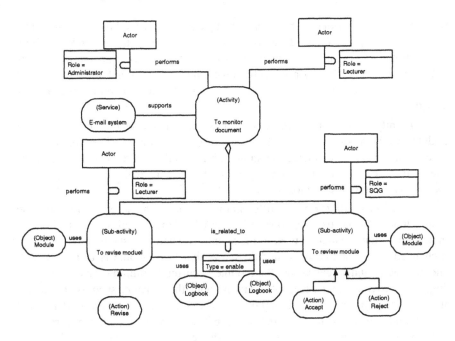

Figure 3: A conceptual model of DMS.

3.1   Document Management System (DMS)

The DMS is used to monitor the modules in the University. The monitoring activity is mainly carried out manually in the academic environment. This application involves two main sub-activities: 'revise the module'; 'review the module'. The conceptual model of DMS is depicted in Figure 3 showing the main activities and sequential dependencies between them. The dependencies make a workflow for the system, which shows how the work is coordinated in the system [Hughes et al. 1997]. This is also related to the concept of plans and procedure as the workflow models shows how the work is done in the organization [COMIC Project 1995].

Distributed coordination is concerned with the different ways in which the coordination of people and task is accomplished as a routine feature of real world, and real time work [Hughes et al. 1997]. The tasks are performed as a pattern of activities. The activities represent a cooperative procedure [Farias et al. 2000b]. The activities are realized as a series of operations within the context of a division of labour [Hughes et al. 1997]. The activities can be further decomposed into sub-activities in order to distribute the work among the actors [Farias et al. 2000b]. For example, in DMS, the main activity is decomposed into two sub-activities; 'revise module' and 'review module'. The activities and the actors are interconnected and they are treated as a part of organization of activities and the actors. The activities are tied with a relationship and this refers to interdependency. The interdependencies between the activities can be analysed in terms of common objects (i.e. module) available to the activities. The common objects such as module constrains how each activity is performed. Thus, the work in the University is concerned with coordinating interdependencies between the activities in order to get the work done. The interdependency between the activities in the University is known in advance that the 'revise activity' will take place first and that it will initiate the 'review activity'.

Currently, Microsoft Word is used to write and revise the contents of the module. All the modules are available in Microsoft Word format. These modules are stored in the machine of the administrator, sitting in the 3rd floor of MIS building. The main objective of this section is to emphasize the 'real world' character of documents (i.e. module and logbook) use within socially organized work activities.

The administrator maintains different folders containing different modules. The administrator also keeps a logbook to keep track of the modules. The logbook is an academic diary, which is used to make entries when the 'status' of the module is changed. The 'status' of a module shows that 'the module is being revised', 'the module is under review' or 'the module is currently running' and so on. The 'logbook' provides contextual information about the module, such as, the status of the module and so on. The administrator has created one main folder called 'Module Information Directory' and four subfolders: 'archive'; 'current'; 'review'; and 'upload' in the machine. The main sub-folders contain some other sub-folders such as 'current folder', which maintains three main list of folder: 'Math', 'Stat', and 'CS (Computer Science)'. The 'Review' folder contains 'Revise' and 'New' folders containing a list of revised and new modules. The 'CS' folder under the 'Revise' folder contains two further sub-folder including 'Pre-SQG' (Subject Quality Group) and 'Post-SQG'. The 'Pre-SQG' contains a list of modules, which have been revised but not yet reviewed by SQG for quality assurance purposes. It contains different versions of the same module, which are received from lecturers time to time. Similarly, the 'Post-SQG' contains those modules, which have been accepted by the SQG. This folder also contains different versions of the same modules.

The hierarchy of the folders containing either sub-folder or a list of modules is shown in Figure 4. The issues related to version control can easily be solved by providing an appropriate computer support with contextual information.

If the changes are required to be made in the module, the concerned member of staff requests the administrator to send the module. The concerned lecturer revises the contents of the module and sends it back to the administrator. The changes made in the module do not take effect immediately. The revised version of the module is used for the next academic year provided that it is approved by SQG (Subject Quality Group). The revised version of the module is kept in the 'revise folder' until the next academic year. According to the University quality process, the new version of the module needs to be approved by SQG if major changes have been made. The major changes involve, changing the contents of the module or write a new module whereas minor changes mean that the name of the book or the lecturer has been changed and so on. The administrator checks the module, which has been changed. The administrator prints the module and sends it to the SQG if the major changes have been made.

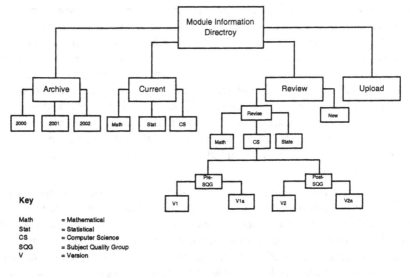

Figure 4: Module Information Directory (MID).

Normally, the module leader is responsible for revising the contents of the module, if it is required, but will also draw on contributions from the other staff involved in the teaching of it. Different communication channels are used to interact with the administrator. The common communication channels include electronic mail and telephone. Sometimes, the lecturers just meet the administrator in the corridor or coffee room and ask to send a particular module through email. Occasionally, this communication channel fails due to some problems such as the administrator might forget due to the pressure of work etc. or problems with the mailing server such as rebooting the servers and so on, which ultimately delayed the whole process.

Another important way in which distributed coordination is achieved is through plans and procedures and their situated interpretation [Hughes et al. 1997]. This refers to formal procedures. For example, in the University, manuals (i.e. instructions) describe the following stepwise procedure: 'how to revise a module'; 'how to review a module', within the context of this application. The two main sub-activities involved in revising and reviewing the module in the University setting are discussed below.

3.1.1 Revise Module

Revising a module is an important activity being carried out in almost all academic institutes. This is similar to editing a document using an editing tool. Currently, in the context of an academic environment, the MS.Word is being used for this purpose, which does not meet the requirements of the University.

More than one lecturer is involved in revising the contents of the module. Mostly, the lecturer who is teaching that module is responsible to make changes in the contents of that module if required. In case of new modules, the administrator assigns the job to one or more than one lecturers to write the contents of the module. The concerned lecturers communicate with each other to discuss the changes they may wish to make. The email systems and telephones are used as the usual communication channels. In addition to it, formal meetings are arranged to discuss the issues related to the revision of the modules. Sometimes, the lecturers also meet in the coffee room or in the corridor by chance. These short and informal meetings help them to discuss some important issues related to the modules they are revising or writing. It shows that the coordination of cooperative work can sometimes be achieved effectively and effortlessly simply by means of everyday modes of interactions.

Both lecturers who are revising the contents of the modules normally have an instance of the module on their machine. They make changes in the contents of the module in their local copies. When, they meet at different occasion, they might like to discuss with each other the changes they have made. They also exchange a copy with each other in order to see the contents written by the other party. Normally, a module leader collects the instance copies of a module and merges them to make a single complete copy maintaining the consistency. The module leader sends this single copy to the administrator who stores it in his/her own machine with an appropriate name such as 225CS-V1 under the sub-folder of CS (Computer Science). Sometimes, it is likely to happen that one of the lectures who has written the contents of the module may ask the administrator for a copy of the module as he/she wants to change a few more things, simply, maybe the name of the book needs to be changed as the previous one is not available in the bookstore and so on. The lecturer gets a copy, revises the contents and sends it to the administrator again. Now, the administrator names this module as 225CS-V1a. After a few days, another lecturer feels that he/she should need to make a few changes in the modules according to his teaching requirements. The lecturer gets the modules, makes changes in the contents of the module and sends to the administrator using email systems. This lecturer names this module as 225CS-latest. The module is stored in the folder of the administrator with the name 225CS-V1b. In this way, different versions of a module are accumulated and this caused many problems in addition to occupying extra space. The entries are made in the 'log book', each time when the lecturer gets a copy of a module from the administrator or sends it back after revising the contents of it. The 'logbook' contains an extensive amount of entries and it has become a complete mess. The advantage of the 'logbook' is that if the administrator is not around, another colleague still keep track of all the records. In this way, it provides a complete set of contextual information to the other actors concerned with that module.

The lecturer sends a different copy to the administrator time to time. Later on, it becomes difficult to decide on the version of the module and find out which one is the latest. In most cases, the lecturer concerned names a module according to his/her wish and the administrator names it based on the available version of the related modules.

3.1.2   Review Module

After the module has been revised or written as a new module, the module must go to a member of Subject Quality Group (SQG) which is one of the mechanisms used within the school to apply quality assurance procedures. The SQG review the modules. As a result of 'review activity' the SQG either accepts the module or reject the module by pointing out the sections, which need further clarification or revision. The following issues are also involved in this process:

- Which one is the latest copy to send to SQG, as there are many versions of the modules are stored. This happens only in the exceptional cases if the administrator does not name the modules according to the available versions.

- There is no record to keep track of the modules sent to SQG. Sometimes SQG do not respond in time about the acceptance or rejection of the module. This delays the process and creates some other problems, which affects the activities involved in Module Assignment System (i.e. spreadsheet), another application used in the University to assign modules to the lecturers. The lecturer or the administrator phones SQG to get to know about the status of the module. The SQG do not keep any appropriate method to record or notify the status of the module to the people concerned.

There should be some mechanism to remind and notify about the status of the module to the concerned people.

3.1.3   Interdependencies between the Activities

" ... within a complex collaborative environment, any individual actor (member of staff) sees 'getting things done' as 'doing-what-I-do' and passing on tasks to other so that they can do what they do." [COMIC Project 1995]

Different interdependencies can be viewed between the activities discussed above. This shows that the modules are the integral features of the orderliness of activities within a complex and dynamic division of labour, which is known in advance in this study. The division of labour shows how the tasks are interdependent, what should I do and what the other people will do, as noted above in the COMIC statement. We are mainly concerned with a kind of interdependencies, which requires sequences in the activities in order to share the common resource (i.e. module), for example, in the case of prerequisite constraints. The output of one activity is required by the next activity. The coordination process for managing interdependency requires ordering the activities, moving information from one activity to the next [Malone & Crowston 1990].

The possible relationships between different classes of objects is seen where the 'revise' activity enables the 'review activity' as shown in Figure 3. There is a sequence in activities and operations. For example, a lecturer performs operations on module first, which enables SQG to review it for quality assurance. Basically, the occurrence of review activity depends on the occurrence of revise activity. The causality relation can be established between two activities such as activity *a* and *b* [Farias 2002]:

- Enabling (*a* enables *b*), in which the occurrence of activity a enables the occurrence of activity *b*, i.e. activity *b* is allowed to occur provided that activity *a* has occurred.

- Disabling (*a* disables *b*), in which the occurrence of activity a disables the occurrence of activity *b*, provided that *b* has not occurred yet nor *b* occurs at the same time as *a*.

The above relationship is similar to a common dependency between a 'producer' activity and a 'consumer' activity, which means that the producer activity must be completed before the consumer activity can begin [Malone & Crowston 1994]. When this dependency exists there should be some notification process to indicate to the consumer activity that it can begin.

3.1.4   Role and Responsibility

The actors are aware of their roles and know their responsibility in the academic environment. The administrator assigns different roles to different actors. The actor has one or more of the following roles:

1. The first role is of a writer who can edit a document (i.e. module). The writer can make necessary changes in the whole document or in the part of the document. In this example, a writer can be a module leader who is allowed to modify or change an existing module or write a new module.

2. The second role is of a viewer who can view the document but cannot modify it. In the example, a viewer can be a lecturer who can view the modules but cannot modify it.

3. The third role is of an administrator who can assign different roles to other actors (i.e. lecturers). The administrator provides different roles to the lecturers. One lecturer can be a viewer at one moment and at the second moment the same can be an editor of a specified module.

4. The fourth role is of a member of a SQG. The member of SQG is allowed to view the module and accept or reject the module. But the SQG is not allowed to make any modifications in the module. The SQG can also identify the section of the document (i.e. module), which needs to be revised for quality assurance purposes.

3.1.5   Glossary of Terms for DMS

Different techniques are used to capture the information present in the application, such as glossary of terms and concept diagrams. A glossary maintains standard terms used a in the system [Farias et al. 2000a]. In software engineering, an engineer uses data dictionary or model dictionary, which is similar to a glossary of terms in UML. An entity in the glossary should contain the name of the term, and its type such as actor, activity, rule or policy. It should also contain a brief description of the term. The glossary is maintained and updated as the development of the system continues. Such a glossary of terms has been developed for the DMS and described in Table 1.

Name	Type	Description
Lecturer	Actor	Person who views and edits the module and log book.
Administrator	Actor	Person who views, adds, deletes, and archives module and views log book.
SQG	Actor	Person who views log book, and module and accepts or rejects module.
Module	Object	The document on which different operations are carried out by different actors.
Log Book	Object	Book on which different operations are carried out by different actors to keep record.
Monitor	Activity	Activity performed by different actors to monitor the module.
Revise	Activity	Activity performed by lecturer to revise the module.
Approval (Review)	Activity	This activity performed by SQG in order to make decision on the acceptance or rejection of modules for quality purposes.

Table 1: Glossary of terms for DMS.

4 Discussion and Conclusions

This paper has investigated the relationship between the social organization of the work settings and the system development of the cooperative activities. We have effectively analysed the social aspects of the work practices using the state-of-the-art techniques of ethnography. Such analysis provides rich and concrete portrayal of the situation thus helps systematic design of CSCW systems. The findings have been employed to complement formal modelling processes. We have used standard Unified Modelling Language (UML) in order to represent and model the findings of the ethnographic analysis. This ensures that features relating to the development of CSCW systems are expressed as richly as possible. For example, UML notations have been used for expressing information about awareness of cooperative work, which ultimately helps software engineers to use them in the development of the systems [Viller & Sommerville 1999]. Another tool, the ethnographers have been using to represent the information, is 'Designers' NotePad (DNP) [Twidale et al. 1993]. DNP is used to organize data produced during an ethnographic study.

Our future work will include a detailed evaluation of the approach discussed in this paper and its comparison with the traditional waterfall model, ISO 13407; human-centred design processes for interactive systems and existing HCI approaches including participative design, and development oriented techniques such as functional, control based and knowledge based approaches.

Due to the sociological perspective, the Participatory Design approaches have been beneficial to CSCW field. A range of systems has been developed using evolutionary approach [Blandford et al. 2002; Singer et al. 1998]. More recently, an ethnomethodological based ethnographic approach has created an association and affinities with the CSCW research focusing on the sociological perception of the system design. The ethnographic approach is the most in-depth method ever emerged, so the results it produces are more effective and concrete which help the design of the system reflecting the context of the work environment.

It is crucial for system design to get requirements right, as errors in requirements lead directly to systems failure. Errors in requirements can remain latent until very late in the design process, the longer that errors remain uncovered, the more they cost to rectify them. So the motivation for applying ethnography to get requirements right is very high [Viller & Sommerville 1999].

The ethnographic approach can also be an important aid to 'Business Process Re-engineering (BPR)' as this method intends to obtain a deep understanding of the people, the organizations, and the broader context of the work in order to provide appropriate computer support to automate and speedup the business processes. Most of the existing techniques applied to BPR have failed due to the lack of concentration on the social aspects. The radical change in the business process based on external observation has failed 70% of the BPR implementations [Herrera et al. 2000]. Therefore, the ethnographic approach should be enforced in this situation.

Acknowledgements

We are very grateful to all staff in the University who has contributed to this study. We would like to thank M. Younas for inspiring and valuable discussions on earlier versions of this paper. Thanks also to J. Terken for backing the conference expenses.

References

Bentley, R., Hughes, J., Randall, D., Rodden, T., Sawyer, P., Shapiro, D. & Sommerville, I. [1992], Ethnographically-informed Systems Design for Air Traffic Control, *in* M. Mantel & R. Baecker (eds.), *Proceedings of 1992 ACM Conference on Computer Supported Cooperative Work (CSCW'92)*, ACM Press, pp.123–9.

Blandford, A. E., Wong, B. L. W., Connell, I. W. & Green, T. R. G. [2002], Multiple Viewpoints on Computer Supported Team Work: A Case Study on Ambulance Dispatch, *in* X. Faulkner, J. Finlay & F. Dètienne (eds.), *People and Computers XVI (Proceedings of HCI'02)*, Springer-Verlag, pp.139–56.

Clarke, K., Hughes, J., Dave, M., Rouncefield, M., Sommerville, I., Gur, C., Hartswood, M., Proctor, R., Slack, R. & Voss, A. [2003], Dependable Red Hot Action, *in* K. Kuutti, E. Karsten, G. Fitzpatrick, P. Dourish & K. Schmidt (eds.), *Proceedings of ECSCW'03, the 8th European Conference on Computer-supported Cooperative Work*, Kluwer, pp.61–80.

COMIC Project [1993], Deliverable 2.1, Technical Report, Lancaster University and Manchester University.

COMIC Project [1995], Deliverable 2.4, Technical Report, Lancaster University and Manchester University.

Crabtree, A., Hemmings, T., Rodden, T. & Mariani, J. [2003], Informing the Development of Calendar System for Domestic Use, *in* K. Kuutti, E. Karsten, G. Fitzpatrick, P. Dourish & K. Schmidt (eds.), *Proceedings of ECSCW'03, the 8th European Conference on Computer-supported Cooperative Work*, Kluwer, pp.119–38.

Farias, C. R. G. [2002], Architectural Design of Groupware System: A Component-Based Approach, PhD thesis, University of Twente.

Farias, C. R. G., Pires, L. F. & van Sinderen, M. [2000a], A Component-based Groupware Development Methodology, *in* K. Shrivastava, L. Bellissard, D. Feliot, M. Herrmann, N. de Palma & S. M. Wheater (eds.), *Proceedings of the 4th International Enterprise Distributed Object Computing Conference*, IEEECSP, pp.204–13.

Farias, C. R. G., Pires, L. F. & van Sinderen, M. [2000b], A Conceptual Model for the Development of CSCW Systems, *in* R. Dieng, A. Giboin, L. Karsenty & G. De Michelis (eds.), *Proceedings of the 5th International Conference on the Design of Cooperative Systems (COOP 2000)*, IOS Press, pp.189–204.

Goguen, J. & Linde, C. [1993], Techniques for Requirements Elicitation, *in* S. Fickas & A. Finkelstein (eds.), *Proceedings of the IEEE International Symposium on Requirements Engineering (RE'93)*, IEEE Computer Society Press, pp.152–64.

Herrera, C., Borges, M. R. S. & Pino, J. A. [2000], CESD: Participatory Selection of Business Process Designs, *in* J. You (ed.), *Proceedings of the 5th Conference on Computer Supported Cooperative Work in Design*, Hong Kong Polytechnic University, pp.269–73.

Hughes, J., King, V., Rodden, T. & Anderson, H. [1994], Moving Out of the Control Room: Ethnography in Systems Design, *in* J. B. Smith, F. D. Smith & T. W. Malone (eds.), *Proceedings of 1994 ACM Conference on Computer Supported Cooperative Work (CSCW'94)*, ACM Press, pp.429–39.

Hughes, J., O'Brien, J., Rodden, T., Rouncefield, M. & Blythin, S. [1997], Designing with Ethnography: A Presentation Framework for Design, *in* I. McClelland, G. Olson, G. C. van der Veer, A. Henderson & S. Coles (eds.), *Proceedings of the Symposium on Designing Interactive Systems: Processes, Practices, Methods and Techniques (DIS'97)*, ACM Press, pp.147–58.

Iqbal, R., James, A. & Gatward, R. [2003], A Practical Solution to the Integration of Collaborative Applications in Academic Environment, *DS Online* **4**(9). Available via http://dsonline.computer.org/collaborative/events/iwces-5/.

Malone, T. W. & Crowston, K. [1990], What is Coordination Theory and How Can it Help Design Cooperative Work Systems, *in* F. Halasz (ed.), *Proceedings of 1990 ACM Conference on Computer Supported Cooperative Work (CSCW'90)*, ACM Press, pp.357–70.

Malone, T. W. & Crowston, K. [1994], The Interdisciplinary Study of Coordination, *ACM Computing Surveys* **26**(1), 87–119.

Myers, M. D. [1999], Investigating Information Systems with Ethnographic Research, *Communications of the Association of Information Systems* **2**(23). Available at http://cais.aisnet.org/.

O'Brien, J., Rodden, T., Rouncefield, M. & Hughes, J. [1999], At Home with the Technology, *ACM Transactions on Computer–Human Interaction* **6**(3), 282–308.

Schmidt, K. & Bannon, L. [1992], Taking CSCW Seriously: Supporting Articulation Work, *Computer Supported Cooperative Work* **1**(1–2), 7–40.

Singer, J., Lethbridge, T. C. & Vinson, N. [1998], Work Practices as an Alternative Method to Assist Tool Design in Software Engineering, *in Proceedings of the 6th International Workshop on Program Comprehension (IWPC 1998)*, IEEE Computer Society Press, pp.173–9. Available at http://citeseer.ist.psu.edu/singer97work.html.

Twidale, M., Rodden, T. & Sommerville, I. [1993], The Designers' Notepad: Supporting and Understanding Cooperative Design, *in* G. de Michelis, C. Simone & K. Schmidt (eds.), *Proceedings of ECSCW'93, the 3rd European Conference on Computer-supported Cooperative Work*, Kluwer, pp.93–108.

Viller, S. & Sommerville, I. [1999], Coherence: An Approach to Representing Ethnographic Analyses in Systems Design, *Human–Computer Interaction* **14**(1 & 2), 9–41. Special Issue on Representations in Interactive Systems Development.

An Evaluation of Workspace Awareness in Collaborative, Gesture-based Diagramming Tools

Christian Heide Damm & Klaus Marius Hansen

Department of Computer Science, University of Aarhus,
Åbogade 34, 8200 Aarhus N, Denmark
Email: {*damm, klaus.m.hansen*}*@daimi.au.dk*

Designing usable real-time, distributed collaboration tools is a complex but important task. *Workspace awareness* **can potentially help in making real-time, distributed collaboration tools more usable through a communication of who is in the shared workspace and what they are doing. We present qualitative evaluations of the workspace awareness features of a gesture-based diagramming tool,** *Distributed Knight,* **that supports real-time, distributed collaboration. These studies suggest that using simple, non-intrusive awareness means results in fewer breakdowns, more symmetric collaboration patterns, better coordination, and higher perceived usability.**

Keywords: real-time distributed collaboration, diagramming tools, gestures, workspace awareness.

1 Introduction

Tools for real-time distributed collaboration are important [CNN 2001], but hard to implement well: Infrastructure, distributed communication, session management, privacy, presence, and awareness are examples of areas that pose design and implementation issues [Beaudouin-Lafon 1999]. When working collaboratively at a distance, the awareness of who is working, where they are working on shared material, and what they are doing becomes particularly important. *Workspace awareness* encompasses means of making this information available in and through the shared workspace that collaborators are working on.

This paper investigates workspace awareness in the context of a distributed version, *Distributed Knight*, of the *Knight* tool for collaborative object-oriented modelling [Damm et al. 2000]. Object-oriented modelling is concerned with creating

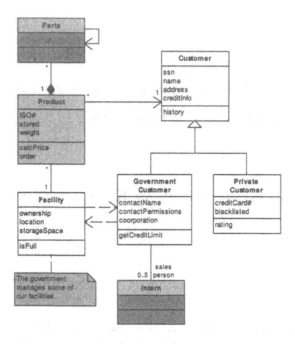

Figure 1: A simple UML diagram.

representations of concepts and phenomena in a problem domain as classes and objects in a solution domain for a software system being developed [Madsen et al. 1993]. The most common way to visualise object-oriented modelling is through the Unified Modelling Language (UML [OMG 2001]) notation. Figure 1 shows an example of a simple model in which, e.g. classes (representing concepts) are visualized as boxes, and associations (representing relationships) are visualized as solid lines between classes.

Whereas the Knight tool was designed to support *co-located* collaborative work (Figure 2), Distributed Knight adds support for *distributed* collaborative work. Tools for distributed work are becoming increasingly important [CNN 2001] as there is an increasing globalisation — also in the domain of software development. Different development groups within an organisation are distributed across geographical locations, and even different organisations may work closely together in joint or out-sourced projects. Consider as an example the following scenario:

> "Alice and Bob are heading a group working in Aarhus, Denmark, on a system for the US Department of Defence. They are collaborating closely with Chris, a domain expert who is located in the US. They often need to discuss specific details of the object-oriented model with Chris while they are in Aarhus. Also, on regular intervals, Alice or Bob or both visit Chris in the US, and during their visits they need to be able to communicate with Aarhus regarding technical details of the project."

Figure 2: Using the Knight Tool on an electronic whiteboard.

To fulfil this scenario a mixture of technology support for co-located and distributed collaboration in software development is needed. We have designed and implemented Distributed Knight to support scenarios such as these.

Although we do not claim that distributed collaboration can replace traditional face-to-face collaboration, we believe that distributed tools may make effective collaboration across geographical locations possible in situations where face-to-face collaboration is not feasible.

This paper is concerned with the usability of Distributed Knight and in particular with the specific use of workspace awareness and how it enhances the usability of the tool. The technical aspects of Distributed Knight have been reported elsewhere [Hansen & Damm 2004].

1.1 Paper Structure

The rest of this paper is structured as follows: Section 2 discusses the design of Distributed Knight for distributed, collaborative modelling with a particular focus on workspace awareness means. Section 3 then presents an evaluation of this design and discusses these results. Next, Section 4 discusses related and future work. Finally, Section 5 concludes.

2 Design of Distributed Knight

The main interaction with the Knight tool is done through *gestural interaction*. In this context, gestures are marks drawn on the workspace and subsequently recognized by a computer tool [Buxton 1986]. In Knight, gestures resemble what a user might have drawn on an ordinary whiteboard during modelling. As an example, Figure 3 shows how a user may create a UML class. This kind of interaction design enhances learnability and also makes it possible for, e.g. domain experts to participate in modelling sessions to a much higher extent than what is possible with traditional UML tools. The Knight tool has been commercialized as *Ideogramic UML* by Ideogramic ApS (http://www.ideogramic.com/products/uml/).

The use of gestural interaction makes Knight usable on a range of input devices ranging from tablet PCs over desktop PCs to electronic whiteboards. The interaction

Figure 3: Left: A box stroke. Right: The class that is the result of a box stroke.

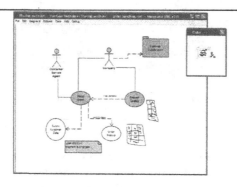

Figure 4: The user interface of the Knight Tool.

style of Knight also makes an effective implementation of real-time distributed collaboration potentially usable on all these devices.

The Knight tool, and subsequently Distributed Knight, has been designed through an iterative, participatory design process. Following observations of object-oriented modelling, we iteratively designed and implemented the Knight tool [Damm et al. 2000]. One of the major outcomes of the observations and participatory design was that there was a need for a tool that supported informal and incomplete models as well as formal. Figure 4 shows the user interface of Knight: It is basically a white surface, much like a whiteboard, on which users draw strokes that are interpreted as gestures.

The informality of the interface and the learnability of Knight were usability characteristics what we decided to pursue in a distributed version of Knight. In particular, we wanted to support ad-hoc collaboration in a fluent way. Take the *Cittera* tool (http://www.canyon-blue.com) as a counter-example. Cittera is a commercial tool that enables real-time distributed modelling in which semantic changes are immediately available to collaborators. To collaborate with others, a user needs to:

1. Coordinate a collaboration session with potential collaborators.

2. Create a model and give it a meaningful name.

3. Make the model a "shared model" so that multiple users may collaborate on it.

Figure 5: AwareMessenger.

---

4. Assign "write" privileges to collaborators.

While reasonable when amortized over the life-time of a long-lived model, this is not very usable for spontaneous collaboration. Based on observations of, interviews with, and logs from instant messaging users, we design the session management component of Distributed Knight to use a context-aware instant messaging client, "Aware Messenger" [Hansen & Damm 2002] (Figure 5).

Using this client, users may see other users' statuses and locations, may initiate and invite to sessions, and may see the active sessions and the participants of these.

2.1   Workspace Awareness

In the evaluations described in this paper, the following workspace awareness facilities in Distributed Knight were relevant:

- *Intermediate updates:* If a user is drawing a gesture, moves an element, or text editing an element, a representation of these actions is shown in the user's collaborators' workspaces while the actions are being carried out. Figure 6 shows an example of this. This functionality basically aims to show what the user is working on.

- *Radar view:* A small radar view shows an overview of the workspace in Knight. In Distributed Knight, the radar also shows the viewports of collaborators (Figure 7). This widget resembles the radar widget of [Gutwin & Greenberg 1999] and aims at showing where the user is working.

- *Cursor representation:* The cursor of a collaborator is shown in a user's workspace if their viewports overlap. If their viewports do not overlap, a line indicating the direction of the collaborator's cursor and the distance to

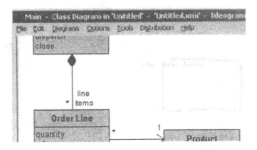

Figure 6: A collaborator is drawing a box gesture.

Figure 7: The radar shows the user's viewport (with handles for zooming) and a collaborator's viewport.

it is shown (Figure 8). This should help in locating where a collaborator is. The cursor line provides information that in some ways overlap with the information of the radar widget (see Section 3).

Other awareness facilities include information on who joins and leaves a session and various awareness information in Aware Messenger.

2.2 *Implementation and Status*

The software architecture of Distributed Knight is based on a peer-to-peer replication of data which eliminates the need for a central server [Oram 2001]. The actual distribution of data is built using a variant of the publish-subscribe paradigm for distributed computing [Eugster et al. 1998]. This allows for a decoupling of clients so that, e.g. Aware Messenger could be implemented without any changes to Distributed Knight.

We have implemented distribution of class diagrams and this part of Distributed Knight is almost complete and has been in use by by members of our research group and people at Ideogramic while being developed. One area in which little work has been done is that of concurrency control, i.e. making sure that actions by one user does not interfere with actions made concurrently by other users. Although this most certainly needs to be implemented, the evaluations showed that the workspace

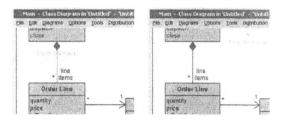

Figure 8: Cursor awareness in Distributed Knight.

awareness features eliminated most concurrency problems (Section 3).

3 Evaluation

To evaluate the design of Distributed Knight, a usability study was made. The study had a particular focus on workspace awareness with the hypothesis that workspace awareness would increase and enhance collaboration. This evaluation is described in detail below.

3.1 Participants

Following a pilot study with two participants, we arranged four sessions with two participants in each session. The participants were volunteers from the Computer Science Department, University of Aarhus and from a private company. None were students and most were experienced with software development. Since the goal was to evaluate Distributed Knight, the participants needed to be familiar with UML-based modelling using and with using stand-alone Knight. Thus, training was part of the study (see Section 3.2).

3.2 Procedure

Each evaluation session consisted of five steps centred around a collaborative modelling task:

1. Participant consent. Introduction to UML and the Knight tool.

2. Presentation of workspace awareness means in Distributed Knight.

3. Introduction to task. Individual reading of requirements.

4. Collaborative modelling task for 2×25 minutes.

5. Post-study questionnaire with a 1-to-5 Likert scale and an open-ended interview.

One experimental condition started with workspace awareness enabled in the modelling task and one started with workspace awareness disabled. After 25 minutes this was reversed. Participant pairs were assigned randomly to each condition. In the experimental condition that started without workspace awareness, Step 2 was performed after the first half of the modelling session (Step 4).

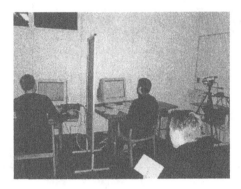

Figure 9: Experimental setup.

In each session, the participants were given a predefined assignment that they needed to work on collaboratively. The assignment was open-ended and complex: The participants had to model an administrative system for the University of Aarhus given a number of requirements that the final system had to fulfil such as handling salary, vacation, employment, students, administrative structure, buildings, and equipment. This assignment was purposely too large to finish in the given time frame meaning that the participants would have the freedom to choose to work in detail in areas or working more broadly on different areas of the model.

Both participants were given a broad description of the domain and requirements for a specific part of the domain. One participant was told to act as a domain expert of the area involving among others personnel and the other participant was asked to act as a domain expert for the area involving among others building administration. All participants reported the task to be realistic in the post-study interview.

The experimental setup is shown in Figure 9. Participants were located in the same room and physical distribution was simulated by placing a board between the workstations of the participants. Thus, no technology was used for audio transmission, and audio was near perfect quality and there was little network latency, eliminating a source of noise in the evaluation. Moreover, the setup enabled us to observe both participants at the same time. When using Distributed Knight in normal work, users are expected to use audio in combination with an instant messaging system or simply by using a phone.

During the evaluation, we observed and videotaped the participants. Observations were made with particular focus on focus shifts and breakdowns [Bødker 1996]. If the participants had trouble using the UML or the Knight tool, we would help them since the focus was on evaluating the usability of the distribution mechanisms in Distributed Knight. The model was saved after 25 and 50 minutes and logs of the users' actions were collected.

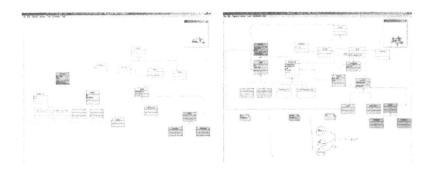

Figure 10: Examples from an evaluation session.

3.3 Discussion

In general, participants found Distributed Knight usable for distributed modelling (4.1 on a Likert scale) and all participants were able to produce quite elaborate models. For the type of scenario in the evaluation, Distributed Knight appears suitable for ad-hoc, real-time, distributed UML modelling.

Figure 10 shows an example of a model produced during the evaluation. The left side shows the model as it looked after the first 25 minutes and the right side shows how the model looked after completion of the evaluation. The figure shows a typical pattern: In the first part of the evaluation, participants would work on the overall structure of the model and in the second part participants would go into detail with the model regardless of experimental condition.

3.3.1 Suitability

Participants found workspace awareness important (3.9) and found the amount of workspace awareness facilities suitable in Distributed Knight (4.0).

The single most important awareness means was awareness through audio, however (5.0). We did not provide video for the evaluation and participants were neutral in whether or not the found video would have been useful (3.1). This evaluation thus adds to the ongoing debate on how important video is for awareness [Isaacs & Tang 1994; Mackay 1999; Veinott et al. 1999]

In this evaluation, the most important workspace awareness features were awareness of movement of elements (4.0) and awareness of collaborators' cursors (3.8). Only the the direction line did not score above neutral in the questionnaire (2.8). This may be due to that the information could be deducted from the radar view and due to the fact that for large parts of the evaluation, participants worked with overlapping viewports. Interestingly, all awareness features except the direction line were either judged very important or important by some participant. Conversely, all awareness features except awareness of movement of elements very either judged very unimportant or unimportant by some participant. This could indicate that all awareness features, except the direction line, were important and that none may be easily removed meaning that the choice of awareness features in Distributed Knight was reasonable and balanced.

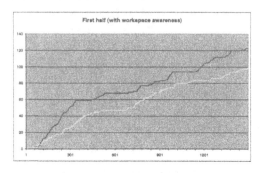

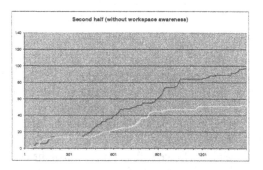

Figure 11: Example of activity levels in an evaluation session. The X axis shows time in seconds. The Y axis shows accumulated number of semantic changes.

It may be surprising that the rather simple awareness features in Distributed Knight provide sufficient support for real-time distributed collaboration. We believe that there are two reasons for this. First, the use of *workspace* awareness seems like a good choice in a diagramming tool such as Distributed Knight, where, by nature, a lot of the work and attention of the collaborators is centred on the shared workspace. Secondly, by using *gestural interaction*, the user can keep focus on the workspace, unlike in many traditional diagramming tools that make heavy use of toolbars, dialogue boxes, etc.

3.3.2 Collaboration Patterns

When working without workspace awareness, participants tended to work more in a turn-taking fashion than in parallel or tightly interleaved. This led to asymmetric collaboration patterns which may be problematic in cases such as the task of the evaluation. Figure 11 shows an example of this. The graphs show the number of semantic changes (creation, update, or deletion of an element) over time.

In the first half, with workspace awareness, the participants are equally active in creating the model, but in the second half, without workspace awareness, one participant does most of the modelling. This pattern was found in three of four evaluations.

3.3.3 Breakdowns and Focus Shifts

In general we experienced very few breakdowns in the workspace awareness condition. In this case most breakdowns were due to technical problems. In fact participants reported that the workspace awareness features of Distributed Knight were non-intrusive (4.1).

Two almost identical incidents in one of the sessions clearly show the importance of workspace awareness: During the first 25 minutes without workspace awareness, the two participants wanted to jointly move two groups of elements. There was some confusion as to which elements should be moved, and who should do it, and in the end, both participants moved a group, but in opposite directions, in effect counteracting each other by accident. During the last 25 minutes with workspace awareness enabled, the two participants wanted to swap two groups of elements, but this time they could see that the collaborator was moving the other group, and were thus able to coordinate their activities.

4 Related and Future Work

Awareness of the work of others is important in collaborative work [Dourish & Bellotti 1992]. In cases such as Distributed Knight in which users can work in a synchronous, decoupled mode on a workspace that is larger than the viewport of a user, workspace awareness becomes particularly important. Gutwin & Greenberg [1999; 2002] have investigated workspace awareness in various settings. We extend this work by looking at workspace awareness in the case of distributed diagramming tools and pointing to how workspace awareness may enhance usability.

There are a number of UML tools for synchronous, collaborative modelling, but none employ workspace awareness features extensively: Workspace awareness in Cittera, e.g. is rather limited; the only indication of where in diagrams collaborators are currently working and what they are currently working on is made through a small lock symbol on UML elements. A textual activity log gives some sense of the history of collaboration and summarises the actions of all collaborators.

Embarcadero Describe (http://www.embarcadero.com/products/describe) also provides real-time collaboration in which changes made are visible to other collaborators after an edited element has been deselected. Embarcadero Describe has even less workspace awareness than Cittera: There is no visual indication of what collaborators are currently working on, and only if a user actually tries to edit an element that is being edited by another user is a dialogue box shown indicating this.

The COAST framework for synchronous groupware [Schuckmann et al. 1996] has a real-time collaborative UML tool, *UMLEditor*, as a demo example with some workspace awareness facilities (http://www.opencoast.org/download/). This demo example was primarily developed as a way of investigating how to develop collaborative applications.

Also, to our knowledge, there have been no studies examining the usability aspects of a tool for distributed, collaborative UML modelling even though the formal and highly structured nature of UML models provide particular challenges. One aspect of this paper is then to report from such a usability study showing that Distributed Knight may be usable for distributed, collaborative modelling. Also, we hypothesize that use of workspace awareness enhances usability in this structured modelling case.

From the evaluation of Distributed Knight, a number of interesting redesign suggestions emerged. Some of these centred around making better use of the radar view: The radar could show actions (such as deletion) on a more abstract level than currently; having a separate radar view for each person would help when working on separate diagrams; and, finally, the radar view could be an anchor for choosing between levels of coupling between collaborators, allowing someone to couple his viewport with a collaborator's viewport.

Another set of redesigns suggested enhancing the semantics of the UML elements. Examples of such enhancements included marking who created an element, emphasizing the most recently used elements, and fading elements that were infrequently used.

An important future direction for Distributed Knight may be to support asynchronous, distributed collaboration. Technically, this involves integrating Distributed Knight with a configuration management system such as CVS (http://www.cvshome.org). A configuration management system allows multiple users to share and version files, a necessary prerequisite for asynchronous collaboration in software development. From a usability perspective, asynchronous collaboration raises a range of issues on how to maintain awareness of others' work across time and place. Ideas from the Notification Collage [Greenberg & Rounding 2001] may help in doing this. Basically, the Notification Collage allows users to upload "media elements" such as sticky notes, video elements, and activity indicators to a server that will redistribute these elements to subscribers. In this way, the Notification Collage becomes a rich resource for awareness and collaboration. Integrating semantic events from Distributed Knight into the Notification Collage itself should be straightforward technically since both a built on a publish/subscribe model of distributed communication. Along these lines, techniques for creating spatial models of interaction and social visualization may also need to be employed to help social interaction [Lee et al. 2001].

A simpler mechanism for sharing semantic events from using Distributed Knight may be to use mechanisms similar to the Tickertape of the Elvin Notification Server [Fitzpatrick et al. 1999]. The Tickertape client provides a single-line, horizontally scrolling text display. Users may publish and subscribe to groups, messages sent to such groups are shown to members in a Tickertape. A Tickertape might combine automatic messages from Distributed Knight clients with messages submitted by users. Having messages visible to group members in this way could give awareness of previous synchronous sessions.

A next major research direction for Distributed Knight could be a stronger focus on pervasive computing issues. Knight can already be used pervasively on a range of input devices, but in order for collaboration to be fluent, supporting for ad-hoc shifts between available devices should be implemented. The range of input devices, on which Distributed Knight is usable, also brings about the interesting issue of mixed single-display and multiple-display groupware [Stewart et al. 1999]: Using Distributed Knight on an electronic whiteboard supports single-display collaboration while collaboration at the distance with another node then can bring about the mix of single- and multiple display groupware. This raises a number of interesting issues to investigate and evaluate such as, e.g. to what degree the physical awareness cues in the single-display location need to be translated into virtual awareness.

5 Conclusion

This paper has presented the Distributed Knight tool for synchronous, distributed collaboration in object-oriented modelling. We have looked in particular at the workspace awareness features of Distributed Knight and discussed a qualitative evaluation of the current design of these features. This evaluation indicates that Distributed Knight is indeed usable for distributed modelling, and that in particular, the workspace awareness features of Distributed Knight may:

- lower the number of breakdowns during collaboration;

- lead to more symmetric collaboration patterns;

- help coordinate work; and

- result in greater perceived usability.

Acknowledgements

Thanks to the people who participated in the Distributed Knight evaluation and to our co-developers of the Knight tool. This work has been partly sponsored by ISIS Katrinebjerg (http://www.isis.alexandra.dk).

References

Bødker, S. [1996], Applying Activity Theory to Video Analysis: How to Make Sense of Video Data in Human–Computer Interaction, *in* B. A. Nardi (ed.), *Context and Consciousness: Activity Theory and Human–Computer Interaction*, MIT Press, pp.147–74.

Beaudouin-Lafon, M. (ed.) [1999], *Computer Supported Cooperative Work*, John Wiley & Sons.

Buxton, W. [1986], There's More to Interaction than Meets the Eye: Some Issues in Manual Input, *in* D. A. Norman & S. W. Draper (eds.), *User Centered System Design: New Perspectives on Human–Computer Interaction*, Lawrence Erlbaum Associates, pp.319–37.

CNN [2001], Telework trend rooted in convenience, http://www.cnn.com/2001/TECH/ptech/11/12/telework.comdex.idg/index.html.

Damm, C., Hansen, K. M. & Thomsen, M. [2000], Tool Support for Object-oriented Cooperative Design: Gesture-based Modeling on an Electronic Whiteboard, *in* T. Turner & G. Szwillus (eds.), *Proceedings of the SIGCHI Conference on Human Factors in Computing Systems (CHI'00)*, *CHI Letters* 2(1), ACM Press, pp.518–25.

Dourish, P. & Bellotti, V. [1992], Awareness and Coordination in Shared Workspaces, in M. Mantel & R. Baecker (eds.), *Proceedings of 1992 ACM Conference on Computer Supported Cooperative Work (CSCW'92)*, ACM Press, pp.107–14.

Eugster, P. T., Guerraoui, R. & Damm, C. H. [1998], On Objects and Events, in J. Vlissides (ed.), *Proceedings of OOPSLA'01, ACM SIGPLAN Notices* **36**(11), ACM Press, pp.254–69.

Fitzpatrick, G., Mansfield, T., Kaplan, S., Arnold, D., Phelps, T. & Segall, B. [1999], Augmenting the Workaday World with Elvin, in S. Bødker, M. Kyng & K. Schmidt (eds.), *Proceedings of ECSCW'99, the 6th European Conference on Computer-supported Cooperative Work*, Kluwer, pp.431–5.

Greenberg, S. & Rounding, M. [2001], The Notification Collage: posting information to public and personal displays, in J. A. Jacko & A. Sears (eds.), *Proceedings of SIGCHI Conference on Human Factors in Computing Systems (CHI'01)*, *CHI Letters* **3**(1), ACM Press, pp.514–21.

Gutwin, C. & Greenberg, S. [1999], The Effects of Workspace Awareness Support on the Usability of Real-Time Distributed Groupware, *ACM Transactions on Computer–Human Interaction* **6**(3), 243–81.

Gutwin, C. & Greenberg, S. [2002], A Descriptive Framework of Workspace Awareness for Real-time Groupware, *Journal of Computer-supported Cooperative Work* **11**(3), 411–46.

Hansen, K. M. & Damm, C. H. [2002], Instant Collaboration: Using Context-Aware Instant Messaging for Session Management in Distributed Collaboration Tools, in O. W. Bertelsen, S. Bødker & K. Kuuti (eds.), *Proceedings of NordiCHI 2002*, ACM Press, pp.279–82.

Hansen, K. M. & Damm, C. H. [2004], Building Flexible, Distributed Collaboration Tools using Type-based Publish/Subscribe — The Distributed Knight Case, in M. H. Hamza (ed.), *Proceedings of the IASTED International Conference on Software Engineering*, ACTA Press, pp.595–600.

Isaacs, E. A. & Tang, J. C. [1994], What Video Can and Can't Do for Collaboration: A Case Study, *Multimedia Systems* **2**, 63–73.

Lee, A., Danis, C., Miller, T. & Jung, Y. [2001], Fostering Social Interaction in Online Spaces, in M. Hirose (ed.), *Human–Computer Interaction — INTERACT '01: Proceedings of the Eighth IFIP Conference on Human–Computer Interaction*, Vol. 1, IOS Press, pp.59–66.

Mackay, W. [1999], Media Spaces: Environments for Informal Multimedia Interaction, in Beaudouin-Lafon [1999], pp.55–82.

Madsen, O., Møller-Pedersen, B. & Nygaard, K. [1993], *Object-oriented Programming in the BETA Programming Language*, Addison Wesley/ACM Press.

OMG [2001], Unified Modeling Language Specification 1.4, Technical Report formal/01-09-67, Object Management Group.

Oram, A. (ed.) [2001], *Peer-to-Peer. Harnessing the Power of Disruptive Technologies*, O'Reilly and Associates.

Schuckmann, C., Kirchner, L., Schümmer, J. & Haake, J. M. [1996], Designing Object-Oriented Synchronous Groupware with COAST, *in* G. Olson, J. Olson & M. S. Ackerman (eds.), *Proceedings of 1996: ACM Conference on Computer Supported Cooperative Work (CSCW'96)*, ACM Press, pp.30–8.

Stewart, J., Bederson, B. B. & Druin, A. [1999], Single display groupware: a model for co-present collaboration, *in* M. G. Williams & M. W. Altom (eds.), *Proceedings of the SIGCHI Conference on Human Factors in Computing Systems: The CHI is the Limit (CHI'99)*, ACM Press, pp.286–93.

Veinott, E., Olson, J., Olson, G. & Fu, X. [1999], Video Helps Remote Work: Speakers Who Need to Negotiate Common Ground Benefit from Seeing Each Other, *in Proceedings of CHI 1999, ACM Conference on Human Factors in Computing Systems*, pp.302–309.

Layers

An Empirical Comparison of Transparency on One and Two Layer Displays

Wael Aboelsaadat & Ravin Balakrishnan

Department of Computer Science, University of Toronto,
10 King's College Road, Toronto, Ontario, Canada M5S 3G4
Email: *{wael,ravin}@dgp.toronto.edu*
URL: *http://www.dgp.toronto.edu*

Two layer displays are constructed by overlaying one transparent flat panel on another, with a discernible physical separation between layers. This layout could increase the available pixels without increasing the width and height of the display. However, it is unclear if the second physical layer provides any advantage over simple alpha-blended transparency on a single layer display. We investigate this issue in two controlled experiments that compare performance between one and two layer displays in users' perception of two potentially interfering virtual layers of information. Results show that for spatially overlapping stimuli, interference from the background stimuli on the perception of foreground stimuli is similar for both displays, while interference from the foreground stimuli on the perception of the background stimuli is higher with two layer displays. For spatially non-overlapping stimuli, perception is degraded on the two layer display if the distracter object is placed on the front layer.

Keywords: two layer displays, interference tasks, transparency.

1 Introduction

Recent technological advances and the demands for more screen real estate, sophisticated methods of interaction, and innovative visualization techniques have engendered a significant interest in non-traditional display designs. Two layer displays (e.g. http://www.deepvideo.com) have been proposed as an efficient alternative, since they can provide additional depth cues for use in 3D applications, and effectively double the available number of pixels with only a small (~1 inch) increase in the thickness of the display. Further, they are largely compatible with existing software and hardware systems, since they can be treated like a two monitor system, driven by a dual-head graphics card.

While these displays appear promising, without appropriate scientific knowledge about the effects of physically layered displays on user performance, interface designers cannot effectively utilize them. For example, one potential application would be to place user interface elements on one layer, and data on another. This notion of multiple layers of information has long been implemented using alpha-blending on a single layer display. Unlike two layer displays, alpha-blending on a single layer display does not increase the actual number of available pixels. In order to justify the cost of a second physical display layer, however, it is critical to understand if and how this setup improves upon alpha-blending on a single layer display apart from the simple increase in pixel count.

In this paper, we present empirical work which compares performance between one and two layer displays when interacting with two virtual layers of potentially interfering information. We explore several questions: Does physical separation change the amount of interference between foreground and background spatial stimuli? With two physical layers, can users better selectively process information on a specific layer and ignore the others? Will this change if the objects are spatially overlapping vs. if they are non-spatially overlapping? What is the effect of varying transparency across the layers? Does colour interact in a different way with interference level?

It is important to note that our experiment only addresses issues surrounding interference in the context of one layer vs. two layer displays. We do not address other possible benefits of two layer displays such as utilizing the physical separation to provide real depth in 3D applications (games, modelling, simulation, . . .). We also do not discuss using the two layer display in creating new information visualization techniques.

2 Background

There are three areas of research that are relevant to our work: attention, interference, and transparency.

2.1 Attention

The ability to direct user attention towards a specific object is a fundamental characteristic of any successful interface design. Several techniques have been proposed for guiding attention: spatial cues, alerts and graphical effects. Zhai et al. [1997] utilized masking to create bleaching, darkening, blurring, or screening effects to de-emphasize background material and thus causing the target to visually pop-up at the user. Harrison et al. [1995a] manipulated transparency to enhance performance in attentional tasks. Most of these techniques are based on colour change. However, perceptual psychologists have shown that depth is potentially more powerful than colour to help find an object [Nakayama & Silverman 1986]. When the number of distracters in a colour-based task goes up, the search time goes up proportionally. On the other hand, when the number of distracters in a depth-based task goes up, the search time stays roughly constant [Triesman & Gelade 1980].

It is unclear from the existing perceptual psychology literature whether users of a two layer display will be able to attend to single layer or not. Some researchers argue that attention cannot be preferentially allocated to specific locations in depth [Iavecchia & Folk 1994; Ghiradelli & Folk 1996; Theeuwes et al. 1998]. Hence, common depth is neither a necessary nor sufficient basis for attentional deployment. Others disagree and suggest that attention can be allocated to a specific location defined by disparity and that, when this is done, there is no interference from distracters in other depth planes [Nakayama & Silverman 1986]. Other studies suggest that the deployment of attention across same-disparity loci is only possible when the elements being attended to are part of a well-formed surface with locally coplanar elements [He & Nakayama 1995]. These studies show that it is difficult to attend to locations that span different surfaces. Further evidence for depth aware attention comes from studies that show that saccades to targets in different depth planes had longer saccadic latencies than saccades to targets in the same depth plane [Atchley et al. 1997]. Several models have also been proposed that attempt to reconcile attentional models in the third dimension. These attribute attentional deployment to the type of stimulus representation used in performing a given task. These reconciliatory models adopt a three level analysis: overall scene depth, layout of objects within the scene, and properties of objects [Andersen et al. 1998].

2.2 Interference

Often described as the index of attention by cognitive psychologists, the Stroop test provides insight into cognitive effects that are experienced as a result of interference [Stroop 1935]. The task takes advantage of our ability to read words more quickly and automatically than we can name colours. If a word is printed or displayed in a colour different from the colour it actually names; for example, if the word 'yellow' is written in blue ink, we will say the word 'yellow' more readily than we can name the colour in which it is displayed, which in this case is 'blue'.

In traditional Stroop tasks, a series of words are presented in randomly chosen colours. Participants must name the ink-colour while ignoring the word. Some of the words are neutral while other words are the names of conflicting colours. Consistent significant performance degradation occurs when conflicting colour words are used and participants attempt to name the colour of the ink. In other studies, a consistent and significant Stroop effect was found even when the word was printed in black ink, presented adjacent to a colour bar [Macleod 1991]. It is virtually impossible to consciously block or prevent the Stroop effect in selective looking tasks, despite numerous experimental permutations (over 700 articles — for reviews see Macleod [1991]). In our present work, we use variants of the Stroop test in evaluating possible differences between two layer displays and alpha-blending on a single layer display.

2.3 Transparency

Objects shown on the first layer of a two layered display are always transparent due to the physical properties of the constituent panels (Figure 1). Transparent interfaces, regardless of the number of physical layers in a display, have been proposed by several researchers to increase screen real estate and to provide interesting visualization and interaction techniques. Bier et al. [1993] proposed a new interface

Figure 1: Two layer display. Front layer is transparent.

paradigm that used transparency to introduce a tight coupling between the tool function and the target object without occluding other interface objects. Harrison et al. [1995b] proposed using transparent user interfaces tools (menus, dialogue boxes, palettes, etc.) and information content windows. Ishii & Kobayashi [1992] used transparency to overlay a drawing surface on a video image of the user's collaborative partner. Lieberman [1994] used multiple translucent layers to overlay zoomed-in and zoomed-out views of a scene. This prior art provides a significant basis for the use of transparent interfaces. However, it is unclear from the literature how a two layer display could change the efficacy of such interfaces compared to using alpha-blended transparency on a single layer display.

3 Goal of the Current Work

Our work is ultimately motivated by the desire to provide guidelines for the development of user interfaces for layered displays. The present work is one step in this direction, and our goal here is to obtain a better understanding of some of the factors that could affect users' ability to discriminate between foreground and background layers of information. We are primarily interested in how alpha-blending on a single layer display fares in comparison to a display with two physical layers. We conducted two experiments: the first investigated the situation where foreground and background stimuli were spatially overlapping, while the second investigated a non-spatially overlapping setup.

4 Experiment 1: Spatially Overlapping Stimuli

Our first experiment compares two layer to alpha-blended one layer displays with regards to users' ability to discriminate between foreground and background stimuli that are spatially overlapping. We use a variant of the Stroop test as our experimental task and vary several parameters, including the colour and content of the foreground and background information, level of transparency of the foreground stimulus, and content congruency between the foreground and background information.

4.1   Apparatus

We used a two layer display developed by Deep Video Imaging[1], which has two panels: the front layer is physically transparent while the back layer is opaque (Figure 1).   The display has a resolution of 1024×768 pixels on each layer, 24-bit colour depth, 170 Cd m^{-2} brightness, viewing angles of 140° horizontal and 110° vertical, and the separation between the two panels is 14.5mm.   The display was driven by a 1GHz Pentium 3 computer running Windows2000. For the single layer display, we decided to use the back layer of the same two layer display to avoid introducing another variable into the experiment.   An ANC-650 (http://www.andreaelectronics.com) close-talk headset microphone with noise reduction facility was used as the input device. The microphone was connected to an Echo Mia high fidelity recording sound card (http://www.echoaudio.com). The experiments were run using Inquisit software (http://www.millisecond.com) and the voice recognition was done using the Microsoft speech recognition engine. Participants sat at a fixed distance of 750mm from the screen.

4.2   Participants

Eighteen volunteers participated in the experiment.   Two participants failed the pre-screening colour blindness test and were disqualified. The remaining sixteen (11 male, 5 female) passed the colour-blindness test, had normal or corrected-to-normal vision, and were naïve as to the purpose of the study. Participants were paid a nominal stipend for their participation, and could voluntarily withdraw without penalty at any time.

4.3   Task and Stimuli

The experiment had two tasks: a foreground focus (FF) task, and a background focus (BF) task. For both tasks, a coloured rectangle appeared in the foreground, and a black word appeared on the background in the same x-y spatial location as the foreground stimulus (Figure 2). This is similar to the set-up used by Harrison et al. [1995a], except that we have two display conditions: in the two layer display condition, the foreground stimulus was displayed on the front display panel, and the background stimulus on the back display panel. For the single layer display condition, both stimuli were alpha-blended and displayed on the back, opaque, display panel of the same two layer display with the front panel left completely transparent.

4.3.1   FF Task

We used the colour-naming component of the Stoop test to measure how the perception of the foreground stimulus is affected by interference from the background stimulus. In this case, participants are asked to ignore the word in the background and name the colour of the rectangle in the foreground. By naming

---

[1] See http://www.deepvideo.com.

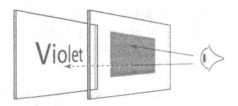

Figure 2: Experiment 1 setup (DUAL layer condition).

the colour and ignoring the word, the user, in effect, is performing a foreground information discrimination task in a spatially overlapping set-up. We will be measuring the time it takes the participant to name the colour, and error rates, on both display types. At high levels of transparency in the foreground stimulus (e.g. 100% — clear), we anticipate that participants will experience high levels of interference from the word when they try to name the colour. As the foreground colour patch becomes more opaque, the interference from the word should decrease.

4.3.2 BF Task

We used the word-naming component of the Stoop test to measure how the perception of the background stimulus is affected by interference from the foreground stimulus. In this case, participants are asked to ignore the colour patch and read the word in the background. The colour patch in the foreground is always clearly visible and perceived. By reading the background word through the colour, the user is, in effect, performing a background information discrimination task in a spatially overlapping set-up. We will be measuring the time it takes the participants to read the word, and error rates, on both display types.

4.4 Procedure

At the start of the experiment, the task was explained to the participants. They were told to fixate on the centre of the display and either name the colour of the rectangle (in the FF task) or read the word (in the BF task). First, participants trained the speech recognition engine on how they pronounce the words and colour names. Next, participants were given a warm-up block of 15 unique trials randomly selected from the possible combinations, just to familiarize them with the task and conditions. Participants received feedback during the practice. If the answer was wrong, a 'WRONG!' message was displayed on screen. No error feedback was given during the experimental blocks. Once a participant provides response, the next trial is immediately displayed. Verbal responses were logged within 1ms of accuracy. The experiment was conducted in one sitting and lasted about 120 minutes per participant. Participants were encouraged, through an on-screen display, to rest in the middle of each block for up to 3 minutes and at the end of each block for up to 15 minutes. At the end of the experiment, participants were debriefed and open-ended comments were recorded.

4.5 Hypotheses

H1: Two layer display will enhance FF performance in a spatially overlapping layout.

H2: Two layer display will enhance BF performance in a spatially overlapping layout.

We anticipate more interference between foreground and background stimulus in the alpha-blended single layer display and therefore reduced performance in both FF and BF conditions.

4.6 Design

There were six experimentally manipulated conditions:

1. Rectangle Colour. Four colours were used: the three primary additive colours — Red, Green, Blue, and the fourth was a secondary additive colour: Yellow.

2. Word. Seven words (Helvetica, 34 point, uppercase) appeared through the colour rectangular patch. We used neutral words: UNCLE, NAIL, and CUTE in addition to the names of the four colours: RED, GREEN, BLUE and YELLOW.

3. Layer. Two set-ups were used. BACK — where the rectangle and word were displayed on a single layer using alpha-blending in the back panel. DUAL — where the rectangle was displayed in the front panel and the word in the back panel.

4. Transparency. Seven transparency levels were used for the colour patch: 5%, 7.5%, 10%, 25%, 50%, 75% and 100% (clear — both the word and colour show). The word naming experiment baseline condition was a word only — presented with no colour rectangle showing. The colour naming experiment baseline condition was a colour only — presented with no word showing.

5. Task. Foreground focus — FF, and background focus — BF.

6. Stroop. Compound independent variable with 3 conditions: NEUTRAL — the word was a neutral word, INCONG — incongruent colour word was present, and CONG — colour word matched the colour of the patch.

A fully randomized, within participant, repeated measures design was used. The two task conditions and the two physical layer conditions were counter balanced between the participants: one group of eight participants did the FF condition first followed by BF condition, while the other group of eight did the BF condition followed by the FF condition. Within the first group, four participants did the BACK layer first and then the DUAL layer, while the other four participants did the DUAL layer first and then the BACK layer. The same treatment was applied to the second group of eight participants. Each participant was presented with three blocks, each consisting of all unique combinations appearing in random order within the block.

The BF task had 406 unique trials calculated as follows:

> 7 words
> × 4 colours
> × 7 transparencies
> × 2 layers
> + 14 baseline cases (2 layers, 7 words)
> = 406 unique trial

The FF task had 400 unique trials calculated as follows:

> 7 words
> × 4 colours
> × 7 transparencies
> × 2 layers
> + 8 baseline cases (2 layers, 4 colours)
> = 400 unique trials

Hence, each participant did 2,418 trials. The total number of trials in the experiment is 38,688.

4.7 Results

4.7.1 FF Task

Data from the warm-up trials was not used in our analysis. Participants' errors in response were very few (~2%) and these error trials were removed before subsequent data analysis. Outliers — calculated as trials with response times more than three std deviations from the mean — accounted for 5.2% of the data, and were removed. A univariate repeated measures ANOVA was carried out on the remaining data. Significant main effects were found for layer ($F(1,47) = 17.16$, $p < 0.0001$), confirming that two physical display layers affect ability to discern foreground stimulus layer differently from alpha-blending on a single display layer. Significant main effects were also found for transparency ($F(6,282) = 22.91$, $p < 0.0001$) and Stroop ($F(1,94) = 379.36$, $p < 0.0001$). This suggests that the Stroop effect was present and that transparency may indeed dilute the interference. Not surprisingly, colour also showed a significant main effect ($F(3,141) = 58.38$, $p < 0.0001$) suggesting that saturation or luminance might dilute the interference.

Post-hoc analyses were carried out to compare means for physical layer. Despite the statistically significant difference, the overall mean for the DUAL condition was only 1.2% faster than the BACK condition. As expected, Stroop had three statistically significant groups: CONG, INCONG, and NEUTRAL. The CONG condition was 5% faster than NEUTRAL, which in turn was 7.4% faster than INCONG. Analysis of variance showed a significant layer × Stroop interaction ($F(5,235) = 77.82$, $p < 0.0001$). However, there was no significant difference between BACK-CONG and DUAL-CONG, BACK-INCONG and DUAL-INCONG, or BACK-NEUTRAL and DUAL-NEUTRAL pairs. Overall, this suggests that in the case where there is spatial overlap between foreground and background stimulus, in a task that requires focusing on the foreground stimulus, there is no difference

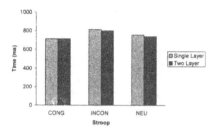

Figure 3: Mean response times for congruent, incongruent, and neutral conditions in FF task for all participants.

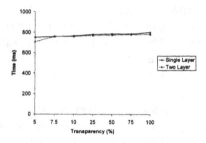

Figure 4: Mean response times for various transparency levels in the FF task for all participants.

of practical significance between single layer and dual layer displays. (Figure 3). Hence, Hypothesis H1 is rejected.

Post-hoc analyses were also carried out to compare means for the transparency levels. The means for transparency levels occurred in three statistically significant groupings: 100%+75%+50%+25%, 10%+7.5%, and 5%. Harrison et al. [1995a] have found similar groupings: 100%+50%+20%, 10% and 5%. Analysis of variance showed a significant layer × transparency interaction ($F(13,611) = 10.18$, $p < 0.0001$). The mean for 5% transparency was 6% faster in the two layer case suggesting that the physical depth decreased interference in this particular transparency level (Figure 4).

4.7.2 BF Task

Data from the warm-up trials was not used in our analysis. Participants' errors in response were very few (~2%) and these error trials were removed from subsequent data analysis. 3.9% of the data were identified as outliers in response time and also removed. A univariate repeated measures ANOVA was carried out on the remaining data. Significant main effects were found for layer ($F(1,47) = 237.21$, $p < 0.0001$),

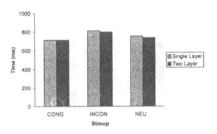

Figure 5: Response times for congruent, incongruent, and neutral conditions in the BF task for all participants.

---

transparency (F(6,282) = 1040, p < 0.0001), colour(F(3,141) = 309.16, p < 0.0001), and word (F(5,282) = 7.71, p < 0.0001). This conforms with Harrison et al.'s [1995a] finding that legibility is affected by not only the level of transparency (visibility) but also the properties of the colour used (saturation and luminance). There was also an unexpected Stroop effect (F(1,94) = 6.47, p < 0.0001).

Post-hoc analyses were carried out to compare means for layer. The mean for the DUAL condition was 8.6% slower than the BACK condition. Analysis of variance also showed a significant layer × Stroop interaction (F(5,235) = 38.81, p < 0.0001). The mean for the INCONG-DUAL trials was 9.6% slower than INCONG-BACK, and NEUTRAL-DUAL trials was 8.8% slower than NEUTRAL-BACK. There was no significant difference between CONG-DUAL and CONG-BACK. This indicates that in the case where there is spatial overlap between foreground and background stimulus, in a task that requires focusing on the background stimulus, two layers will perform ~9.2% worse than a single layer (Figure 5). Hence, Hypothesis H2 is also rejected.

Post-hoc analyses were carried out to compare means for the transparency levels. The means for transparency levels occurred in five statistically significant groupings: 100%+75%+50%, 25%, 10%, 7.5% and 5%. Analysis of variance showed a significant layer × transparency interaction (F(13,611) = 355.63, p < 0.0001). The mean for DUAL-5% trials is 14.1% slower than BACK-5% trials, the mean for DUAL-7.5% trials is 13.1% slower than BACK-7.5% trials, and the mean for DUAL-10% trials is 7.5% slower than BACK-10% trials. This suggests that in the case where there are two spatially overlapping stimulus with the foreground stimulus being transparent by 10% or less, in a task that requires focusing on the background stimulus, two layers will perform on average 11% worse than a single layer (Figure 6).

Post-hoc analyses were also carried out to compare means for colour. The means for colour levels occurred in three statistically significant groupings: Blue, Red, and Green+Yellow. Analysis of variance showed a significant layer × colour interaction (F(7,329) = 57.36, p < 0.0001). The mean for DUAL-Red was 7.9%

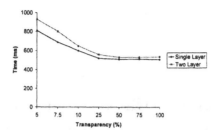

Figure 6: Mean response times for various transparency levels in the BF task for all participants.

slower than BACK-Red and the mean for DUAL-Blue was 11.7% slower than BACK-Blue. Similarly, the mean for DUAL-Yellow was 5.5% slower than BACK-Yellow, and the mean for DUAL-Green was 8.5% slower than BACK-Green. Hence, Yellow was the easiest to see through, followed by Red and Green, and finally Blue.

5   Experiment 2: Spatially Non-Overlapping Stimuli

In this experiment, stimuli are placed in proximity to each other but there is no spatial overlap between them. Our focus here is on the situation where potentially interfering elements are adjacent to the stimulus of interest, rather than overlapping as in the case of our first experiment.

5.1   Apparatus

The apparatus was the same as that in Experiment 1.

5.2   Participants

Twelve (8 male, 4 female) of the sixteen participants who participated in Experiment 1 were randomly selected for this experiment.

5.3   Task and Stimuli

We used the colour-naming component of the Stoop test to measure ability to focus on one portion of the display, while ignoring distracter stimulus on either the same or different layers of the display. In this case, a coloured line, 2 pixels thick, was displayed beneath a black word in the centre of the display (Figure 7). Participants were asked to ignore the word and name the colour of the line. By naming the colour and ignoring the word, the user, in effect, has to ignore the interference stimulus in a non-spatially-overlapping set-up. We will measure the time it takes to name the colour.

5.4   Procedure

A similar procedure to Experiment 1 was followed. The experiment was conducted in one sitting and lasted about 40 minutes per participant.

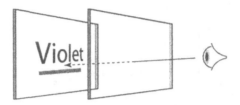

Figure 7: Experiment 2 setup (TextBack_LineBack condition).

5.5 *Hypotheses*

H3: Two layer display will enhance performance in a non-spatially overlapping layout.

5.6 *Design*

There were four experimentally manipulated conditions:

1. Line Colour. Six colours were used; the three primary additive colours: Red, Green and Blue, and three secondary additive colours: Yellow, Magenta and Cyan.

2. Word. Ten words (Helvetica, 34 point, uppercase) appeared above the coloured line. We used four neutral words: UNCLE, NAIL, FOOD and CUTE in addition to the six colour names: RED, GREEN, BLUE, YELLOW, MAGENTA and CYAN.

3. Layer. Three layouts were used: word in the back layer with line in the front layer (TextBack_LineFront), word in the front layer with line in the back layer (TextFront_LineBack), and word in the back layer with line in the back layer (TextBack_LineBack).

4. Stroop. Compound independent variable with 3 conditions: NEUTRAL — the word was a neutral word, INCONG — incongruent colour word was present, and CONG — colour word matched the colour of the line.

Participants were randomly divided into 6 groups of 2 each. Assignment of layer to groups was counterbalanced using a balanced Latin square. Each participant was presented with three blocks, each consisting of all unique combinations appearing in random order within the block. There were 198 unique trials as follows:

10 words
× 6 colours
× 3 layers
+ 18 baseline cases (3 layers, 6 colours)
= 198 unique trials

Hence, each participant did 594 trials. The total number of trials in the experiment is 7,128.

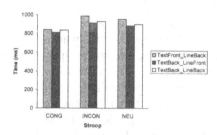

Figure 8: Response times for congruent, incongruent, and neutral conditions for all participants in Experiment 2.

5.7 Results

Data from the warm-up trials was not used in our analysis. Participants' errors in response were very few (~1%) and these error trials were removed from subsequent data analysis. 13.6% of the data were identified as outliers in response time and also removed. A univariate repeated measures ANOVA was carried out on the data. Significant main effects were found for layer ($F(2,70) = 25.46$, $p < 0.0001$) and Stroop ($F(1,70) = 36.85$, $p < 0.0001$). Not surprisingly, there was also a significant main effect for colour ($F(5,175) = 52.37$, $p < 0.0001$), suggesting that saturation or luminance might dilute the interference even in a non-spatially overlapping layout.

Post-hoc analyses were carried out to compare means for layer. The means for layer levels occurred in two statistically significant groupings: TextFront_LineBack and TextBack_LineBack + TextBack_LineFront. The mean for TextFront_LineBack condition was 5.7% worse than the other two conditions. As expected, Stroop had three statistically significant groups: CONG, INCONG, and NEUTRAL. The CONG condition was 8.9% faster than NEUTRAL, which in turn was 4.1% faster than INCONG. Analysis of variance showed a significant layer × Stroop interaction ($F(8,280) = 12.69$, $p < 0.0001$). The mean of TextFront_LineBack − INCONG trials was 7.5% worse than TextBack_LineBack − INCONG and TextBack_LineFront − INCONG. The mean of TextFront_LineBack − NEUTRAL trials was 5.5% worse than TextBack_LineBack − NEUTRAL and TextBack_LineFront − NEUTRAL trials (Figure 8). There was no difference between the other combinations. This suggests that in the case where there are two spatially non-overlapping stimuli, a target and a distracter, two layers will always perform worse by an average of 6.5% if the distracter was placed in the front layer. Hence, Hypothesis H3 is rejected.

Post-hoc analyses were also carried out to compare means for colour. The means for colour levels occurred in four statistically significant groupings: Magenta, Cyan, Green+Blue+Red and Yellow. Analysis of variance showed a significant layer × colour interaction ($F(17,595) = 18.28$, $p < 0.0001$). However, there was no significant difference for the same colour across layers.

6   Discussion and Conclusion

We have presented experimental work that compared one and two layer displays with regards to users' ability to perceive two potentially interfering layers of information. Contrary to our initial hypotheses, the two layer display is not generally better than a single layer display. In a foreground focus task for spatially overlapping stimuli, both one and two layer displays perform similarly except at lower transparency levels where the two layer display performs better. In a background focus task for spatially overlapping objects, performance is dependent on the semantic relationship between the stimuli and also on transparency. In particular, performance of the two layer display degrades when the stimuli compete semantically for user attention. For non-spatially overlapping stimuli, performance is dependent on the assignment of stimuli to the various layers, with the single layer display equalling or outperforming the two layer display in all cases. While it is difficult to pinpoint the precise cause of the relatively poor overall performance of the two layer display in the interference tasks we studied, it is plausible that the physical separation of the two layers causes the human visual system to separate the viewed image into two constituent planes thus incurring additional processing cost. There may also be physical characteristics of the display that could be improved which could lead to performance improvements. However, given that our experiments were conducted using the same display for both the one and two layer conditions, it is unlikely that slight improvements in the (already very good) display quality would change the overall performance ranking. While our results are not terribly encouraging for two layer displays, it is important to note that our work was concerned only with issues surrounding interference between the layers. The other potentially significant benefit of two layer displays is the possibility of enhanced depth cues for 3D applications. Investigating this potential is left for future work.

References

Andersen, G., Braunstein, M. & Saidpour, A. [1998], The Perception of Depth and Slant from Texture in Three-dimensional Scenes, *Perception* **27**, 1087–106.

Atchley, P., Kramer, A., Anderesen, G. & Theeuwes, J. [1997], Spatial Cuing in Stereoscopic Display: Evidence for a "Depth-aware" Attention Focus, *Psychonomic Bulletin and Review* **4**, 525–9.

Bier, E. A., Stone, M. C., Pier, K., Buxton, W. & DeRose, T. D. [1993], Toolglass and Magic Lenses: The See-through Interface, *in* J. Kajiya (ed.), *Proceedings of SIGGRAPH'93 20th Annual Conference on Computer Graphics and Interactive Techniques, Computer Graphics (Annual Conference Series)* **27**, ACM Press, pp.73–80.

Ghiradelli, T. & Folk, C. [1996], Spatial Cuing in a Stereoscopic Display: Evidence for a Depth Blind Attentional Spotlight, *Psychonomic Bulletin and Review* **3**, 81–6.

Harrison, B., Ishii, H., Vicente, K. & Buxton, W. [1995a], Transparent Layered User Interfaces: An Evaluation of a Display Design to Enhance Focused and Divided Attention, *in* I. Katz, R. Mack, L. Marks, M. B. Rosson & J. Nielsen (eds.), *Proceedings of the SIGCHI Conference on Human Factors in Computing Systems (CHI'95)*, ACM Press, pp.317–24.

Harrison, B., Kurtenbach, G. & Vicente, K. [1995b], An Experimental Evaluation of Transparent User Interface Tools and Information Content, *in* G. Robertson (ed.), *Proceedings of the 8th Annual ACM Symposium on User Interface Software and Technology, UIST'95*, ACM Press, pp.81–90.

He, Z. & Nakayama, K. [1995], Visual Attention to Surfaces in Three-dimensional Space, *Proceedings of the National Academy of Science-USA* **92**(24), 11155–9.

Iavecchia, H. & Folk, C. [1994], Shifting Visual Attention in Stereographic Displays: A Time Course Analysis, *Human Factors* **36**(4), 606–18.

Ishii, H. & Kobayashi, M. [1992], ClearBoard: A Seamless Medium for Shared Drawing and Conversation With Eye Contact, *in* P. Bauersfeld, J. Bennett & G. Lynch (eds.), *Proceedings of the SIGCHI Conference on Human Factors in Computing Systems (CHI'92)*, ACM Press, pp.525–32.

Lieberman, H. [1994], Powers of Ten Thousand: Navigating in Large Information Spaces, *in* P. Szekely (ed.), *Proceedings of the 7th Annual ACM Symposium on User Interface Software and Technology, UIST'94*, ACM Press, pp.15–6.

Macleod, C. [1991], Half a Century of Research on the Stroop Effect: An Integrative Review, *Psychological Bulletin* **109**(2), 163–203.

Nakayama, K. & Silverman, G. [1986], Serial and Parallel Processing of Visual Features Conjunctions, *Nature* **320**, 264–5.

Stroop, J. [1935], Studies of Interference in Serial Verbal Reactions, *Journal of Experimental Psychology: General* **18**, 643–62.

Theeuwes, J., Kramer, A., Hahn, S. & Irwin, D. [1998], Our Eyes Do Not Always Go Where We Want Them To Go: Capture Of The Eyes By New Objects, *Psychological Science* **5**, 379–85.

Triesman, A. & Gelade, G. [1980], A Feature-integration Theory of Attention, *Cognitive Psychology* **12**, 97–136.

Zhai, S., Wright, J., Selker, T. & Klein, S. [1997], Graphical Means of Directing Users' Attention in the Visual Interface, *in* S. Howard, J. Hammond & G. K. Lindgaard (eds.), *Human–Computer Interaction — INTERACT '97: Proceedings of the Sixth IFIP Conference on Human–Computer Interaction*, Chapman & Hall, pp.59–66.

User Interface Overloading: A Novel Approach for Handheld Device Text Input

James Allan Hudson, Alan Dix & Alan Parkes

Computing Department, Lancaster University, Bailrigg, Lancaster LA1 4YR, UK

Tel: *+44 1524 592326*

Email: *j.a.hudson@lancs.ac.uk, {app, dixa}@comp.lancs.ac.uk*

Text input with a PDA is not as easy as it should be, especially when compared to a desktop set up with a standard keyboard. The abundance of attempted solutions to the text input problem for mobile devices provides evidence of the difficulties, and suggests the need for more imaginative approaches. We propose a novel gesture driven layer interaction model using animated transparent overlays, which integrates agreeably with common windowing models.

Keywords: text input, PDA, transparent layers, visual overloading.

1 Introduction

The major difficulty with designing graphical interfaces for small touch screen displays is a regular text document has to be divided into very small pages, making comprehension awkward. An additional problem is control elements take up precious display area, making the view of a document ever smaller. One approach is to reduce the size or number of these controls, to free up usable display area, however this affects the usability of an interface. The problem is in maintaining a reasonable sized interface without affecting usability.

This paper considers these problems associated with handheld text input using touch screen graphical interfaces. It proposes the application of superimposed animated graphical layering, which we refer to as *visual overloading*, combined with gestural interaction as illustrated by Belge et al. [1993], Lokuge & Suguru [1995], Meyer [1995] and Silvers [1995] to produce a novel interaction model called User Interface Overloading or UIO [Hudson & Parkes 2003b]. We argue that this approach can help to address the problems of touch screen text input, especially for devices with limited display real estate.

The difficulty in constructing good solutions to interaction for handheld and portable devices with small graphical display has spawned much interest from researchers specializing in multi modal and tangible forms of interaction, however UIO suggests much more can be made of these small graphical displays. This paper examines some of the popular approaches to text input, some of these being currently under development. To set the benefits of the UIO model in suitable perspective, the paper then goes on to identify and discuss the individual features and difficulties of the PDA text input problem as demonstrated by Kamba et al. [1996], Masui [1998], MacKenzie et al. [1999] and MacKenzie & Zhang [1999]. We then introduce our model. Finally, we examine an implementation of a UIO text input application.

2   Handheld Text Input

Many proposed solutions to the handheld text input problem fail to acknowledge the true obstacles of preserving portability and compactness, ease and convenience of interaction and the deft conservation of screen real estate. Before these factors are addressed and in order to illustrate the problem of text input for handheld devices, this section outlines some of the more successful approaches, this section critically examines a number of text input solutions.

Plug-in keyboards or the very appealing laser projected variety, such as iBiz virtual laser keyboard would seem to offer a solution to the problem of easily entering text on small devices. However, this could likened to buying an anchor to make your PDA behave like a desktop. The integration of a full size keyboard into the design compromises the necessary limit on size and ergonomics of use, not to mention the portability of the device, by requiring a flat surface.

A different approach is the chorded keyboard, more usefully implemented for handhelds as a device held in the hand. Here there is a significant learning overhead due to the user having to learn key combinations to select each letter or number, however this approach does outstrip all one handed text input rates at 50wpm. A downside to this approach is with current implementations the need to hold a chorded keyboard in one hand, does affect the ergonomics of interaction. The obvious solution would be to integrate the keyboard into the device itself. Similar to the chorded keyboard is the T9 predictive text found on many mobile phones. Entering a series of keys will generate a list of possible words. This approach does however pose difficulties, if the word is not found in the dictionary or the suggested word is at the bottom of the list of suggestions.

Clip on keyboards may seem to provide a usable text entry facility for small devices, at least on physical grounds. However, they do add bulk, and thus adversely affect the trade-off between size, portability and practicality. An alternative to the clip on is the *overlay keyboard*. Though these do not increase the size of the device, they do have usability implications. The overlay is essentially no different from a soft keyboard (discussed below), and actually is a very expensive sticker that permanently renders the utility of a portion of the display for text input only, restricting the use of an already limited resource.

The soft keyboard is not really too different from the clip-on keyboard, except it is implemented as a graphical panel of buttons rather than a physical sticker. The soft keyboard has the added hindrance of consuming screen display area, as does the overlay approach. However, the soft keyboard does permit the user to free-up display area when required.

The soft keyboard seems to be the most commonly accepted solution [see Kamba et al. 1996; Kölsch & Turk 2002; MacKenzie et al. 1999; MacKenzie & Zhang 1999]. However, it is a solution that is greedy in terms of screen area. Two examples can be used to illustrate the trade off between redundancy, ergonomics of use and visible display. Firstly, a full screen keyboard offers direct manual interaction due to larger keys and a capacity for more keys but at the expense of display real estate. Secondly, the standard split screen keyboard already limited in size, sacrifices redundant controls to permit larger keys and to make more visible display available, yet its small size results in the need to use an additional device, such as a stylus, which results in an approach that is difficult to use dexterously with the fingers.

One approach based on the standard keyboard and akin to one we propose is one that uses a static soft keyboard placed in the background of the display text. A letter is selected by tapping the appropriate region in the background. This solution permits manual input and does preserve some screen real estate. However, the number of available controls and hence redundancy is limited due to the necessary larger size of the controls, required to make the keys legible through the inputted text. This limit on the number of controls necessitates an awkward need to explicitly switch modes for numbers, punctuation and other lesser used keys. Another drawback is the slight overhead in becoming accustomed to the novel layout.

A lot of effort has been expended to improve the soft keyboard approach, however these attempts are still subject to the drawbacks already describe with this approach, moreover they are subject to a learning overhead imposed by remodelling the keyboard layout. On the Unistroke keyboard [Zhai et al. 2000; Mankoff & Abowd 1998] all letters are equidistant, thus eliminating excessive key homing distances. The Metropolis keyboard [Zhai et al. 2000] is another optimised soft keyboard layout, statistically optimised for single finger input, improving efficiency by placing frequently used keys near the centre of the keyboard. Both approaches can be effective, but both impose a learning overhead due to a new keyboard layout. The user must expend considerable effort to become familiar with the keyboard for relatively slim rewards, not to mention the overhead inherent with soft keyboards, such as the consumption of screen real estate.

Handwriting recognition was for some time the focus of PDA text input solutions. However, evaluation revealed that gesture recognition for text input is balky and slower, some 25wpm at best, than that of, say, other less sophisticated approaches, such as the soft keyboard [Dix et al. 1998, p.6]. Problems with handwriting and similar approaches such as 2D gesture interaction, for example Graffiti, is one of learnability, slow interaction and skill acquisition. The obvious problem with handwritten input is the need and time expended to write each letter of a word, whether this is consecutively or all at once, the user must still write the whole thing out, whereas the keyboard solution requires merely the pressing of a button. A problem originally addressed with the invention of the mechanical typewriter. In addition to this difficulty, as with the standard soft keyboard, text input requires the use of a stylus, thus occupying the user's free hand (i.e. the need to hold the PDA) when entering text. The learning curve of this approach is steep due to the need to learn an alphabet of gestures and the saving in real estate is not so apparent, since some approaches require a large input panel.

We now consider alternative, less well known, solutions to the problems of text entry for small devices. One approach to PDA text input is the use of a mitten outlined by Goldstein & Chincholle [1999]. Sensors in the hand units measure the finger movements, while a smart system determine appropriate keystrokes.

This novel approach is an intriguing solution. The main problem is the need to carry around a mitten that is nearly as big as the device itself. Finally, a mitten is not so appealing to the user and the sensors on these devices can be bulky affecting freedom of movement. Dynamic dialogues illustrated by Ward et al. [2000], when applied to limited display size, are a very innovative data entry interface which incorporates language modelling. The animations are driven by continuous two-dimensional gestures, where the user selects strings of letters as they progress across the screen. Letters with a higher probability of being found in a word are positioned close to the centre line. Though the dynamic dialogue approach makes use of 2D gestures, these are supported by affordance mechanisms and they have been kept simple for standard interaction, making them readily learnable. Users achieve input rates of between 20–34 words per minute, which is acceptable when compared with typical one-finger keyboard touch screen typing of 20–30 words per minute [Sears et al. 1993]. However, the input panel for text entry consumes around 65% of the display, leaving as little as 15% remaining for the text field. The approach does not improve on the constraints of limited display area or on text input rates. What it does do is require the user to become familiar with a new technique for no extra benefit.

3   Evaluation of Handheld Text Input

The major problem with many text input solutions is the lack of investigation into the true problem of handheld device text input. The important thing is not the *mechanism* for inputting text in itself but rather the consideration of constraints such as on the available size of a text input panel and free display area.

We next discuss the constraints on the design of text input interfaces for handheld devices, in order to derive several requirements and to set the introduction and discussion of the UIO model in a suitable perspective.

4   Layout Constraints and Ease of Use

The layout of a text input mechanism is subject to some physical constraints which affect usability. In order to free up as much screen display as possible, input dialogues are reduced in size, which reduces the size of individual keys, making them more difficult to select. Increasing the number or redundancy of controls limits the space available. The size of keys is also subject to the population of keys on the keyboard. Lots of keys means less space per key, or a smaller input text panel. Alternatively, to minimise the display area used by the keyboard and maintain a reasonable sized key, designers resort to using menus or modes. Seldom

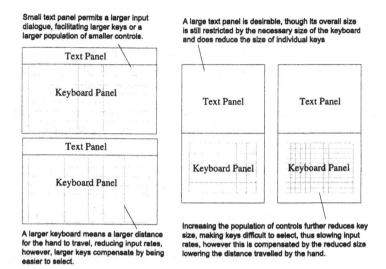

Small text panel permits a larger input dialogue, facilitating larger keys or a larger population of smaller controls.

A large text panel is desirable, though its overall size is still restricted by the necessary size of the keyboard and does reduce the size of individual keys

A larger keyboard means a larger distance for the hand to travel, reducing input rates, however, larger keys compensate by being easier to select.

Increasing the population of controls further reduces key size, making keys difficult to select, thus slowing input rates, however this is compensated by the reduced size lowering the distance travelled by the hand.

Figure 1: The possible combinations of text input panel, the constraints between input rates, size of keys, number or keys with the remaining available display and the size of text input dialogue and display.

used commands inevitably feature in sub-menus, which leads to a slow and awkward interaction approach [Kamba et al. 1996]. These constraints are subject to the constraints defined in Fitts' law, a large dialogue is subject to a time overhead from increased hand travel while smaller keys take up less space and merit a reduced hand travel, yet may incur a time overhead due to a fine motor control requirement in selecting a key. Overly small keys result in either unacceptable increases in error rates or unreasonably slow input rates for text input, due to awkwardness of selecting a key accurately. This suggests a larger keyboard should be favoured.

4.1 Unnecessary Interaction Aids

Pointers, such as a stylus, clip on keyboards and data gloves, impede device usability. To interact with the device the user must either don the interaction accessory or, say, pick up a stylus, which in the case of many portable devices, ties up both hands [Goldstein & Chincholle 1999].

4.2 Learning and Skill Acquisition Overhead

Many small device text input approaches are not easily learned, consider the work by MacKenzie et al. [1999; MacKenzie & Zhang 1999]. The use of 2D alphanumeric gestures is a good example of such an approach. Here the user expends time to learn numerous gestures and the different contexts they can be used in.

5 Design Requirements

Drawing from the evaluation of text input solutions a definition of the design requirements can be constructed, permitting the development of a fresh and fitting solution, rather than, further optimising on approaches that fail to address relevant issues such as screen real estate or convenience of use, for example the over engineered optimisations of the conventional soft keyboards

Consideration of the contributing factors in the design of interaction models for handheld and mobile devices leads to the following design requirements:

- Larger keys for manual interaction should be favoured over interaction aids. For example styluses, obstruct the freedom of a hand, posing a hindrance to handheld interaction.

- We must seek a good balance between redundancy in the number of visible input device features and availability of display area.

- The device must reflect an effective trade-off between display area, size of elements in the input panel, and usability.

- The approach must be easy to learn to use and understand or there must be a justifiable benefit for any learning overhead, as with the chorded approach.

In view of the above requirements, we now discuss our proposed approach to the problem of text input for small devices.

6   User Interface Overloading

Here we introduce a novel system of interaction called user interface overloading, whereby a user can selectively interact with multiplexed or Visually Overloaded layers of transparent controls with the use of 2D gestures.

Transparency is commonly used to optimize screen area, which can often be consumed by menu or status dialogues. The aim is to provide more visual clues [Bier et al. 1994], in the hope the user will be less likely to lose focus of their current activity. Bartlett [1992] and Harrison et al. [1995] consider that the conventional approach of using a layer of transparency to display a menu is done at the cost of obscuring whatever is in the background (Figure 2 right). This is not actually visual overloading, but rather a compromise between two images competing for limited display area. In fact, an underpinning feature of the scheme described by Harrison et al. [1995; Harrison & Vicente 1996] is the investigation of levels of transparency to optimize this compromise.

Visual overloading is different from the use of static layered transparencies. Rendering a transparent animated image or a wiggling panel on a static background, illustrated by Belge et al. [1993], Silvers [1995] and Cox et al. [1998], will visually multiplex or visually overload the overlapping images (see Figure 3). The upshot is a layer of controls appear to float over the interface without interfering with the legibility of the background.

The introduction of gestural input [Meyer 1995] is partly a consequence of implementing visual overloading, since it is necessary to resolve the issue of layer interaction. There is nothing new with gesture activated controls, the concept was first introduced by Kurtenbach & Buxton [1994] with marking menus. However, this approach did only use simple gradient stokes or marks, whereas UIO also makes

Figure 2: The benefits of transparent over conventional solid menus. (Left) the solid menu conceals the background image. (Right) a transparent menu obscures the background image, without completely concealing it.

Figure 3: Three frames from a UIO mobile phone interface with overloaded icons, showing where gestures are executed. The envelope icon is for the messaging function and 'Register' for the call register function. For example a 'C' starting over the envelope will go to a compose dialogue. Please note visual overloading is difficult to present in print.

use of more sophisticated gestures. The underlying principle of marking menus is to facilitate novice users with menus while offering experts a short cut of remembering and drawing the appropriate mark without waiting for the menu to appear. What makes our UIO interaction model novel and where it differs significantly is the use of selective layer interaction. We now discuss some of the features and properties of UIO.

The approach incorporates 2D mouse gestures to activate commands associated with a control (see Figure 3), offering the necessary additional context required beyond that of the restricted point and click approach. This enables the user to benefit from the added properties associated with an overloaded control by enabling the selective activation of a specific function related to a control contained in the layers.

UIO permits the intensive population of a display through the layering of control elements. This we achieve without compromise in size of the inputted text panel or to the size of control elements described by Hudson & Parkes [2003a]. An advantage that effectively gets round the constraints described earlier, (see Figure 1) by permitting background and subsequent layers to occupy the same screen real estate.

Another benefit is the availability of real estate permitting larger controls, which are easier to locate, improving input rates and facilitate manual interaction.

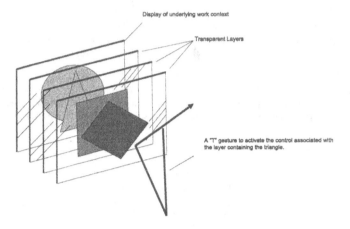

Figure 4: A schematic depiction of an overloaded button or icon. By executing an appropriate gesture, over the collection of layered shapes, such as a 'D' for the diamond or a 'T' for the triangle, etc., a call can be made to the action associated with the desired layer.

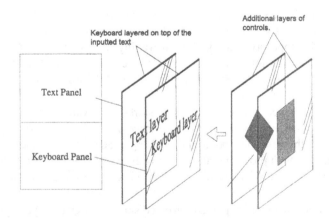

Figure 5: The benefits of layering a keyboard over the text panel, essentially doubling their size and breaking the conventional physical constraints (see Figure 1) associated with user interface design. It is also clear additional layers of controls can be added.

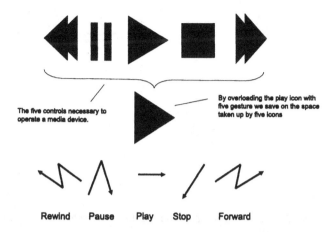

Figure 6: How real estate can be salvaged, by associating gestures with an icon rather than using ever more control elements.

The constraints of this approach are that elements lose coherence gradually or the interface essentially becomes visually noisy as layers are added, however carefully chosen layers permit a good number of controls before this constraint takes effect.

It is clear UIO eliminates the constraints between the size of the display and the input dialogue. In addition the redundancy of controls can be increased in a new way, by overloading the functionality of a control with a selection of gestures (see Figure 6) while avoiding the use of obtrusive context menus.

Expressed in a different way, we can limit population of these controls by overloading their functionality with gesture interaction offering significant savings in screen real estate for handheld devices and other touch screen interfaces.

A problem of gesture interaction is the steep learning curve, because of the need to be familiar with a multitude of gestures and their contexts. An addition to the UIO approach, to support learnability is to introduce a mechanism where an easily remembered '?' gesture will prompt the interface to display the gestures associated with a control or area. In this way the user can become familiar with the system gradually, summoning help in context and when needed. This *blossom help* (described in Figure 7) also functions as a mechanism to support goal navigation and exploration. This help approach is an elaboration on the marking menu reported by Kurtenbach & Buxton [1994]. To improve the usability a function can be activated using the correct gesture or using a text label as a buttons. In addition there is no reason why this help system could not include permitting a straight-line mark from the icon to the label, as with a marking menu, however this will only work with less than eight options and would fail to be useful with layers of controls.

Essentially, a UIO control is a making menu with a transparent graphical image, which means UIO benefits from the properties of marking menus. As with marking menu, UIO requires a procedural memory component, suggesting this style of interaction has a strong cognitive salience.

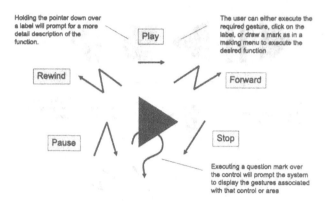

Figure 7: How learnability is supported with the use of help dialogues that 'blossom' when a '?' gesture is executed over a control or area.

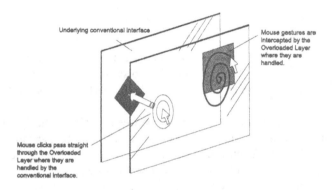

Figure 8: How this approach can be seamlessly incorporated into a conventional point and click interface. Mouse clicks are not intercepted by the Overloaded Layer and pass straight through, where they are handled by the conventional interface, whereas gestures are handled by the Overloaded layer.

A benefit of UIO is that it integrates seamlessly with WIMPS offering extended functionality by intercepting gestures but allowing standard point and click interaction to pass through the layers where they are handled in a conventional way (see Figure 8). An obvious comment is user interface overloading may interfere with drawing packages and text selection. The solution to this is the same used by Sensiva's Symbol Commander, conflicts are avoided with a small time delay to switch modes or simply using the right mouse key to activate gesture input.

There are some downsides to the UIO approach. As with keyboard shortcuts, by letter association, ambiguity can lead to controls possessing the same gesture. This can be overcome with good design either by planning letter associations or incorporating an options dialogue for selecting between commands with the same gesture.

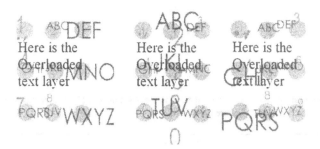

Figure 9: Three frames from a screen shot of the VODKA approach, a mobile keyboard layer over a layer of text. Although, it cannot be seen in print, the layer of letters, when in motion, stand out against the background and appears a lot more coherent.

In practice we found that multiple layers of animated transparent elements were too visually noisy, suggesting only one layer for this type of icon. We did find wiggling or moving non-animated panels [Belge et al. 1993; Lokuge & Suguru 1995] can support in practice up to four layers. We did find that overloaded transparencies work with very low levels of transparencies, lower than the 30% opacity for static images suggested by Harrison & Vicente [1996].

Other restrictions exist that can be avoided with good design are, the choice of colours conflicting with the background, and in the poor choice of animations which may result in difficulties selecting moving elements or distinguishing between layers. However, this is no more an overhead than in designing graphics for a standard interface or website. Another restriction is animated controls can be obscured on a moving background, such as a media clip.

We now examine an implementation of a user interface overloading text input application.

7 Proposed Solution

The user interface overloading technique was implemented in a handheld text input application and evaluated with respect to the specified requirements as follows. Our proposed approach to text entry on small devices the visually overloaded 2D gesture keyboard Application or VODKA utilises the UIO technique. To test the approach a prototype was implemented on an Ipaq 3600 using the Java virtual machine. The graphics were produced using a drawing application. The gesture engine was an optimised version of Javastroke, ported from the open source gesture recognition engine Libstroke.

The implementation of VODKA incorporated a visually overloaded ISO keyboard layout (standard on mobile phones) and a number pad layered over the text. Gestures were incorporated using simple gradient strokes to select a letter and simple meaningful gestures to access other functions, such as numbers and uppercase letters.

Figure 10: In this example a letter is selected by drawing a gradient stroke that begins over the button. The green dots indicate where the gesture must start.

To operate the keyboard (see Figure 10) the user makes very simple gradient gestures, as described by Kurtenbach & Buxton [1994]. To select a letter, a gradient stroke that starts over the selected button is performed. The centre point of a button is indicated with the green dot. The angle of a gesture supplies the context indicating which element is being selected. 'L' would be selected with a right terminating gesture, as above, while 'K' would be selected with a vertical up or downward stroke. To improve usability the 'space' character is easily selected with a 'right-dash' gesture, that can be executed anywhere on the display, similarly a delete command is selected with a global 'left-dash'.

To access lesser used functions other than basic text input, the approach uses more elaborate gestures such as selecting the number '5' with a meaningful and easily associated 'n' gesture.

Other options are, text can be cleared from the screen with a 'C' gesture and a capital can be entered by drawing a 'U' for uppercase after the desired letter. The need to learn these associations does pose a learning overhead, however they are easily learned using the Blossom mechanism (Figure 7). Initially, this use of symbols is no less awkward than selecting a mode or menu option, however as the operation becomes familiar, it ceases to be as obtrusive as the other approaches. Point and click interaction is left alone to demonstrate that the approach could incorporate the T9 approach and could still use standard text interaction, such as with text editing in conventional graphical interfaces.

8 Evaluation

The UIO approach leads to several benefits. The layering of controls increased the size and available population of controls while permitting the largest of text panel. This permits manual interaction obviating the need for a stylus improving the usability of the device. Gestures further reduced the outlay of screen real estate that would be necessary to provide a control for each function. The marking menu style of interaction for regular text input made VODKA simple to use and easily understood. The gradient gestures found in marking menu interaction for simple text input are trivial to parse, with error rates no worse than point and click approaches [Kurtenbach & Buxton 1994]. The use of gestures for more elaborate interaction made it simple to access modes such as capital letters and numbers. The use of Blossom help (Figure 7) offers a good solution to the problem of remembering the associations for more sophisticated gestures, by providing a mechanism that can be configured to passively reinforce these associations. Another example of the usefulness of the blossom approach is in acquiring the skill for the execution of a gesture, by assisting in learning the correct form for that gesture.

Viewed against our set of requirements VODKA does appear a suitable solution:

- There is no reliance on additional interaction aids, since the dialogue elements are large enough to support manual operation.

- The approach reflects an effective combination of redundancy in input device features and availability of display area.

- The approach provides an adequate trade-off between display area, size of elements in the input panel, and usability, with an approach that circumvents these constraints.

- Finally, the approach is easily understood and learned with a simplistic interaction style. Moreover, any learning overhead in learning symbols is arguably justified when weighed against the benefits.

As has been illustrated, our user interface overloading technique resolves the text entry problem and goes a considerable way to satisfying the design requirements.

VODKA is not clearly a gesture input approach, especially for regular input, since gradient gestures are no more difficult to learn and execute than pointing. So, the UIO approach falls under neither point and click or gesture input. Therefore, we decided to not compare it to gesture based input, since VODKA is more like a keyboard than anything else. We decided to test against a qwerty layout, in the hope this would offer a clear indication of the value of our approach when compared with more successful and conventional approaches. We decided not to conduct a longitudinal, (clearly a longer study would be the next step) since we wanted to demonstrate the input rates achievable by a novice. We have avoided predictive text, since it can be introduced to all forms of text input, including our model; our interest is in raw input rates.

To test out approach fifteen subjects were used in a study, all with experience in using the common mobile ISO alphabet keyboard and the qwerty layout, with 30 minutes experience with the VODKA text input approach. We tested the input rates with VODKA and compared them against input rates on the same Ipaq device with a qwerty layout. The average input rate for the qwerty was 27wpm. The average rate for VODKA was 21wpm, with experienced users achieving an acceptable 28wpm.

The results were analysed using an ANOVA of the logarithm of the time spent. Logarithmic analysis was chosen as the data is positive and skewed and most effects were expected to be multiplicative. Because the data was paired differences between the two trial texts were cancelled entirely by the differences between pairs (quotient of raw data).

The VODKA input was slower than soft keyboard by a factor of only 1.11 (from log mean of 0.104). The individual variation was high with one subject nearly twice as slow. Taking into account the variation of the data we can say that at 99% confidence VODKA is on average no slower than 1.21 times the rate of a normal soft keyboard.

Given the novelty of the method for users and the need to further refine the details of the interface this is an encouraging result and makes it a clearly acceptable option where other considerations, such as screen real estate, are critical.

A number of negative comments were reported. The choice of animation for the keyboard did receive some criticism; the frame rate was too quick and the excessive motion made it difficult sometimes to locate the correct control. However, this did appear to improve as the user became familiar with the approach. Therefore, although, the interaction is trivial to understand, there was some difficulty in acquiring the necessary skill, which is possibly due to the unfamiliar design, a bit like using the mouse for the first time.

Finally, the design was to support single handed use, by supporting the device in the palm and entering the gesture with a thumbnail, sadly the physical size of the Ipaq meant that only a few of the users could achieve this, however it is possible a smaller device, such as a mobile phone could support this style of interaction.

9 Conclusion

This paper has illustrated the constraints on and issues relating to, the development of text input for mobile and wearable devices, as illustrated by Dunlop & Crossan [1999] and MacKenzie et al. [1999]. User interface overloading presents a viable approach to screen real estate optimisation and touch screen interaction, offering new twists on the constraints of developing handheld and public access interfaces (see Figures 1 & 5). Solution to these problems and shortcomings of existing schemes were introduced and discussed. A prototype of the solution, making use of user interface overloading, was implemented and evaluated against a set of derived requirements. It was argued that this prototype makes effective use of screen area, yet preserves the portability of the device. The results clearly indicate the approach is comparable with the better input methods available, moreover, the benefits, such as savings in screen area make it a promising candidate, which is full of potential.

This paper has challenged the accepted perspective and assumptions of graphical user interface design to develop this novel user interface overloading model, which integrates agreeably with common windowing systems offering effective, additional tools and functionality rather than the unrealistic proposition of a replacement model or significant remodelling of accepted designs.

10 Further Work

Our current work involves investigating the application of our techniques to support interaction for Databoards, public information kiosks, small devices, such as wearable devices [Masui 1998] and control dashboards for augmented and virtual reality interfaces. We are exploring the effectiveness of UIO itself, and seek to improve touch screen interaction, among other things.

We also intend to explore the use of VODKA in a predictive text application. Consider entering the specific first letter of a word and using a gesture to define the length of a word, then tapping on successive groups of letters, (as with the T9 dictionary), to generate a list of possibilities. Although, with VODKA it remains possible to enter specific letters in order to refine to search.

There are some other aspects of UIO we wish to explore. We noticed that users could perceive controls with indirect gaze making the model useful in peripheral displays, adaptive systems [Hudson & Parkes 2003b; McGuffin & Balakrishnan 2002] and designing interaction for the visually impaired, such as macular degeneration. Adaptive displays could also benefit from the freedom to place new items or reconfigure displays without upsetting the layout of controls.

Another property is, elements sharing the same motion appear grouped together, suggesting this approach could be used to implement widely dispersed menu options on a display without the necessary overhead of bounding them in borders, as is usually required to suggest a group relationship.

Finally, we recognise that our future research will benefit from an investigation into theories of perception. Such work may help us to minimise, and govern the effects of, *visual rivalry*, perhaps by introducing 3D elements and dynamic shading.

References

Bartlett, J. [1992], Transparent Controls for Interactive Graphics, WRL Technical Note TN-30, Digital Equipment Corporation.

Belge, M., Lokuge, I. & Rivers, D. [1993], Back to the Future: A Graphical Layering System Inspired by Transparent Paper, *in* S. Ashlund, K. Mullet, A. Henderson, E. Hollnagel & T. White (eds.), *INTERACT'93 and CHI'93 Conference Companion on Human Factors in Computing Systems*, ACM Press/IOS Press, pp.129–30.

Bier, E. A., Stone, M. C., Fishkin, K., Buxton, W. & Baudel, T. [1994], A Taxonomy of See-through Tools, *in* B. Adelson, S. Dumais & J. Olson (eds.), *Proceedings of the SIGCHI Conference on Human Factors in Computing Systems: Celebrating Interdependence (CHI'94)*, ACM Press, pp.358–64.

Cox, S., Linford, P., Hill, W. & Johnston, R. [1998], Towards Speech Recognizer Assessment Using a Human Reference Standard, *Computer Speech and Language* 12(4), 375–91.

Dix, A., Finlay, J., Abowd, G. & Beale, R. [1998], *Human–Computer Interaction*, second edition, Prentice–Hall Europe.

Dunlop, M. & Crossan, A. [1999], Dictionary Based Text Entry Method for Mobile Phones, *in* S. Brewster & M. Dunlop (eds.), *Proceedings of Second Workshop on Human Computer Interaction with Mobile Devices*, Springer-Verlag.

Goldstein, M. & Chincholle, D. [1999], The Finger-joint Gesture Wearable Keypad, *in* S. Brewster & M. Dunlop (eds.), *Proceedings of Second Workshop on Human Computer Interaction with Mobile Devices*, Springer-Verlag.

Harrison, B. & Vicente, K. [1996], An Experimental Evaluation of Transparent Menu Usage, *in* M. J. Tauber, B. Nardi & G. C. van der Veer (eds.), *Proceedings of the SIGCHI Conference on Human Factors in Computing Systems: Common Ground (CHI'96)*, ACM Press, pp.391–8.

Harrison, B., Ishii, H., Vicente, K. & Buxton, W. [1995], Transparent Layered User Interfaces: An Evaluation of a Display Design to Enhance Focused and Divided Attention, *in* I. Katz, R. Mack, L. Marks, M. B. Rosson & J. Nielsen (eds.), *Proceedings of the SIGCHI Conference on Human Factors in Computing Systems (CHI'95)*, ACM Press, pp.317–24.

Hudson, J. & Parkes, A. [2003a], Novel Interaction Style for Handheld Devices, *in* K. Anind, A. Schmidt & J. F. McCarthy (eds.), *Adjunct Proceedings of UBICOMP'03*, Springer-Verlag, pp.52–5.

Hudson, J. & Parkes, A. [2003b], Visual Overloading, *in* C. Stephanidis & J. Jacko (eds.), *Human–Computer Interaction, Theory and Practice (Part II). Volume 2 of the Proceedings of Human–Computer Interaction International 2003*, Vol. 2, Lawrence Erlbaum Associates, pp.67–8.

Kamba, T., Elson, S., Harpold, T., Stamper, T. & Sukaviriya, P. [1996], Using Small Screen Space More Efficiently, *in* M. J. Tauber, B. Nardi & G. C. van der Veer (eds.), *Proceedings of the SIGCHI Conference on Human Factors in Computing Systems: Common Ground (CHI'96)*, ACM Press, pp.383–90.

Kölsch, M. & Turk, M. [2002], Keyboards without Keyboards: A Survey of Virtual Keyboards, Technical Report 2002-21, Department of Computer Science, University of California, Santa Barbara. http://www.create.ucsb.edu/sims/PDFs/Koelsch_and_Turk_SIMS.pdf.

Kurtenbach, G. & Buxton, W. [1994], User Learning and Performance with Marking Menus, *in* B. Adelson, S. Dumais & J. Olson (eds.), *Proceedings of the SIGCHI Conference on Human Factors in Computing Systems: Celebrating Interdependence (CHI'94)*, ACM Press, pp.258–64.

Lokuge, I. & Suguru, I. [1995], GeoSpace: An Interactive Visualization System for Exploring Complex Information Spaces, *in* I. Katz, R. Mack, L. Marks, M. B. Rosson & J. Nielsen (eds.), *Proceedings of the SIGCHI Conference on Human Factors in Computing Systems (CHI'95)*, ACM Press, pp.409–14.

MacKenzie, I. S. & Zhang, S. X. [1999], The Design and Evaluation of a High-performance Soft Keyboard, *in* M. G. Williams & M. W. Altom (eds.), *Proceedings of the SIGCHI Conference on Human Factors in Computing Systems: The CHI is the Limit (CHI'99)*, ACM Press, pp.25–31.

MacKenzie, I., Zhang, S. & Soukoreff, W. [1999], Text Entry using Soft Keyboards:, *Behaviour & Information Technology* **18**(17), 235–44.

Mankoff, J. & Abowd, G. [1998], Cirrin: A Word-level Unistroke Keyboard for Pen Input, *in* E. Mynatt & R. J. K. Jacob (eds.), *Proceedings of the 11th Annual ACM Symposium on User Interface Software and Technology, UIST'98*, ACM Press, pp.213–4.

Masui, T. [1998], An Efficient Text Input Method for Pen-based Computers, *in* M. E. Atwood, C.-M. Karat, A. Lund, J. Coutaz & J. Karat (eds.), *Proceedings of the SIGCHI Conference on Human Factors in Computing Systems (CHI'98)*, ACM Press, pp.328–35.

McGuffin, M. & Balakrishnan, R. [2002], Acquisition of Expanding Targets, *in* D. Wixon (ed.), *Proceedings of SIGCHI Conference on Human Factors in Computing Systems: Changing our World, Changing Ourselves (CHI'02)*, *CHI Letters* **4**(1), ACM Press, pp.57–64.

Meyer, A. [1995], Pen Computing. A Technology Overview and a Vision, *ACM SIGCHI Bulletin* **27**(3), 46–90.

Sears, A., Revis, D., Swatski, J., Crittenden, R. & Shneiderman, B. [1993], Investigating Touchscreen Typing: The Effect of Keyboard Size on Typing Speed, *Behaviour & Information Technology* **12**(1), 17–22.

Silvers, R. [1995], Livemap — A System for Viewing Multiple Transparent and Time-varying Planes in Three Dimensional Space, *in* J. Miller, I. Katz, R. Mack & L. Marks (eds.), *Conference Companion of the CHI'95 Conference on Human Factors in Computing Systems*, ACM Press, pp.200–1.

Ward, J., Blackwell, A. & MacKay, D. [2000], Dasher — a Data Entry Interface Using Continuous Gestures and Language Models, *in* M. Ackerman & K. Edwards (eds.), *Proceedings of the 13th Annual ACM Symposium on User Interface Software and Technology, UIST'00, CHI Letters* **2**(2), ACM Press, pp.129–37.

Zhai, S., Hunter, M. & Smith, B. A. [2000], The Metropolis Keyboard: An Exploration of Quantitative Techniques for Virtual Keyboard Design, *in* M. Ackerman & K. Edwards (eds.), *Proceedings of the 13th Annual ACM Symposium on User Interface Software and Technology, UIST'00, CHI Letters* **2**(2), ACM Press, pp.119–28.

What is Interaction For?

Designing for Expert Information Finding Strategies

Bob Fields, Suzette Keith & Ann Blandford[†]

Interaction Design Centre, Middlesex University, Bramley Road, London N14 4YZ, UK

Tel: *+44 20 8411 2272*

Email: *{B.Fields, S.Keith}@mdx.ac.uk*

[†] *UCL Interaction Centre, University College London, Remax House, 31–32 Alfred Place, London WC1E 7DP, UK*

Email: *A.Blandford@cs.ucl.ac.uk*

This paper reports on a study of evaluating and generating requirements for the user interface of a digital library. The study involved observation of librarians using the digital library, working on information finding problems on behalf of clients of the library. The study showed that librarians, familiar with the particular digital library system and with information retrieval work in general, possess a repertoire of relatively simple, yet effective, strategies for carrying out searches, and that non-librarians tend not to deploy the same strategies. After describing the study and the most commonly observed strategies, this paper makes some suggestions for how an understanding of how the librarians organize their activities may generate design ideas for user interfaces that aid 'ordinary' users in making use of the strategies that help librarians to be effective users.

Keywords: digital libraries, empirical study, usability, expertise.

1 Introduction

Digital libraries are large repositories of electronic documents, generally gathered together according to defined collection criteria and providing some assurance of quality. Compared to the web, they generally have a clear thematic organization and offer sophisticated document searching and management capabilities. From an HCI perspective, digital libraries are an interesting, and potentially highly fruitful, object of study because they are becoming pervasive (at least within professions such as education and healthcare) and yet they pose substantial usability challenges. They are treated by many as 'walk up and use' systems, and yet learning to use them effectively can take weeks, months or even years. They raise a plethora of use and user experience issues, as well as design issues, many of which have not emerged so starkly in less information-rich applications.

This paper reports on an evaluation and empirical study of the use of a digital library that allowed the researchers to investigate new requirements for the support of searching, browsing and information retrieval tasks. The study began with the unremarkable observation that experienced digital library users are generally more effective at using digital libraries than non experts. The purpose of the study was therefore to investigate in more detail the nature of experienced users' expertise in order to inform the design of user interfaces that will better support non-experts.

The primary goal of this study was to find out what makes experts better at finding information in the library, with a view to re-designing the user interface so as to better aid non-experts. The model of Sutcliffe & Ennis [1998] allows us to make some initial hypotheses about where the nature of expertise might lie. These authors identify four categories of knowledge that are essential for information finding: knowledge about the domain, the available resources the resources and the device or computer system, and also information retrieval skills. In our study, therefore, pertinent research questions relate to the nature of these classes of knowledge possessed and used by experts, and the relative importance of these knowledge domains.

In the following sections we describe the digital library at the centre of our study, the study itself, and some of the resulting observations about the strategies that help librarians to be successful. We are then in a position to make some conjectures about the implications for user interface design. The findings of the observational study will be set in the context of the development of expertise in the use of digital library systems.

2 The Digital Library and its Context

The BT Digital Library has been developed over a number of years by BT to meet the needs of a large and diverse user population within the company. The library gives electronic access to a wide selection of databases of journals, magazines, books, reports, and other digital and online resources. The content of the databases ranges from technical subjects of relevance to engineers and scientists in the company, to business and market oriented material of interest to managers, those charged with following market trends and so forth. A common user interface allows relatively seamless access to these various resources.

The digital library was developed to largely replace an existing paper based library. Existing library staff undertook the task of making the transition from being librarians in a fairly traditional sense, to being digital librarians. Inter alia this meant that the librarians acquired many new skills and became intimately involved in the design, implementation and maintenance of the digital library system itself, in addition to the ongoing requirements of librarianship.

The digital library offers keyword and phrase searching, full-text access to selected journals and a number of browsable links. An 'information spaces' feature provides a monitoring service for new documents on specific themes or categories. The keyword search feature provides a simultaneous search and summary of a number of resources and databases using abstract, index and catalogue data. Two such resources are INSPEC, a scientific and technical resource, and ABI/Inform, which is more business orientated. Each resource can subsequently be searched in more detail, and a number or powerful facilities are provided for specifying searches, viewing search results and how they relate to the underlying indexing mechanisms, and so on.

Following a search, the user is presented with a 'search results' page with a list of documents found. This page gives information about each documents including the title and date of the work, the closeness of match with the search terms, and a few lines of the document's opening text. Links associated with each document found allow the user to click to the document's abstract, full text, and more sophisticated cataloguing and indexing mechanisms.

3 The Trouble with Digital Libraries

While a digital library offers the promise of 'access for all' to a rich variety of information resources, this promise often does not become a reality [Blandford et al. 2001; Stelmaszewska & Blandford 2002] There are several reasons why digital library use has not yet had a deep impact on the information finding practices of potential users, but among the key reasons is the usability of such systems. Users typically find it difficult to arrive at a set of search terms or a query phrase that captures the essence of the information need and produces a sensible set of search results. The problem of information retrieval is sometimes conceived of as one of making a translation between an information need and the language of the search interface. Carrying out such a translation effectively requires knowledge of not only the domain and the syntax for writing queries, but also the indexing and categorization schemes used within the digital library's databases.

Against this kind of background, Dillon [2001] argues that the future of both digital libraries as a technology and HCI as a discipline are bound up together. On the one hand, the promise that digital libraries offer needs a user centred approach in order to become reality. On the other hand, digital libraries provide challenges to HCI that will induce the discipline to develop further.

The goal of the study was to gain a better understanding of the behaviour of expert users (i.e. librarians), or in other words, to determine what our experts are experts in. Is it simply the case that experts have a better knowledge of a difficult-to-use user interface? Or is it that they are better at translating an information need, or what Belkin [1980] calls an "anomalous state of knowledge", into a query that can be entered into a search box to yield an effective set of results from a search engine? The appropriate design response will be different depending on the answers to these questions. Mapping the boundaries of experts' expertise holds the promise of a strategy for designing and formulating requirements for user interfaces that put the experts' knowledge "in the world" in such a way that it can materially affect the practices of non-expert users. The study, therefore sought to explicate a little more clearly what experts do and how they are able to do it.

4 Development of Expertise in Information Seeking

Various studies [for example Blandford et al. 2001; Borgman 1996; Marchionini 1995; Stelmaszewska & Blandford 2002], demonstrate that many typical users of electronic information resources lack both the knowledge and experience to construct organized and disciplined search strategies across individual queries. Inexperienced users often attempt failed queries repeatedly, while partially successful ones are frequently abandoned without development. When such users work across multiple collections of documents, effective combinations of query criteria are often used in one source, but not with others, whereas failed searches are often retried. In contrast, expert librarians rely heavily on systematic approaches to the evolution of their searches and the selection of search criteria. Ellis & Haugan [1997] present a behavioural model of information seeking that lays out a set of user strategies; when compared to this model, experts demonstrate comprehensible strategies, whereas novices can seem perplexingly illogical. In addition, novices seem confused about how to make effective decisions at the tactical level: Sutcliffe & Ennis [1998] outline a set of decision points and effective tactics in their cognitive model, but real users make such decisions poorly. This seems to make the exploitation of such models in interactive system design difficult. Inexperienced users apparently lack some of the decision-making tactics identified by Sutcliffe & Ennis and the coherent strategies suggested by Ellis & Haugan.

Considering the nature of expertise, recent studies have compared some of the search criteria used by expert librarians against those used by less knowledgeable searchers. Two key variables that have been studied are information seeking expertise and subject knowledge.

Some researchers [for example Smith et al. 1989] focus on the importance of domain knowledge as a component of expertise. Vakkari [2001] studied development within one extended searching episode (that took place over several weeks). He reports that earches become more focused as the nature of the information problem becomes better understood. As the search progresses, so the problem definition and query terms become more clearly defined, and users are more easily able to make relevance judgements. In this way, we see a development of searching *with respect to a particular information problem*. Vakkari argues strongly that the effects that are observed are primarily due to development in subject expertise, and not in searching expertise.

Others [for example Dillon & Song 1997; Lucas & Topi 2002] treat expertise as a binary state — either novice or expert. A detailed study of the roles of searching expertise and subject knowledge was conducted by Hsieh-Yee [1993]. One important finding of her study is that experts tend to explore synonyms, to establish what effects these have on search results, whereas novices (even subject experts) do not. However, the effects of differences when they were searching within their area of subject knowledge were relatively small. Outside their area of subject knowledge, differences were much greater: experts were able to use on-line tools such as thesauri to assist in generating alternative search terms, whereas novices relied on their own intuition in selecting terms. In the study reported here, we focus on novice searchers who were knowledgeable within their domain, and on librarians who searched across domains, and acquired limited and focused domain knowledge through the searching activity.

5 The Study

To investigate the expertise displayed by expert digital library users we observed librarians acting as 'intermediaries'. That is, the librarians were acting on behalf of clients of the library who had a real information need and expertise in the problem domain, but lack specific training or skills either in information retrieval in general or in the use of the digital library itself. Librarians, on the other hand, possess a great deal of searching and information finding expertise, as well as proficiency with this particular library system, though they are unlikely to be as familiar with the specific subject area as the client.

In each case, the client had attempted to satisfy their information need using the digital library, but had failed to achieve results they were happy with. Problems were elicited from three users in interviews, and server log data was collected for the clients' own searching attempts. In describing their problems, clients would tend to give a phrase characterizing the problem (e.g. "pleasurable design" or "credit card fraud in Internet commerce") together with synonyms or other key phrases and names of individuals or organizations thought to be relevant (e.g. "card not present transactions").

Two librarians were observed and video recorded working independently on each of the information finding tasks. Each librarian worked on each search problem for around an hour before arriving at a point where an acceptable set of search results had been found, or where more detailed information was needed from the client to improve the search.

The librarians were asked to think aloud while carrying out the search tasks. Actions and verbal commentary on the resulting video recordings were transcribed for later analysis. In analysing the data we were looking for recurrent patterns in the activity of the librarians that seem to characterize aspects of their expertise. As noted above, clients who generated the problems had previously attempted to search themselves, so that log data of their own search attempts was available. This log data reveals something about how they approached the problem before judging their attempts unsuccessful and turning to the librarians for help. The non-expert clients provide a valuable contrast with the librarians, allowing us more clearly to distinguish the expression of expertise from relatively less competent performances.

	Query term	Number of hits
1	fault, diagnosis, ADSL	>7000
2	diagnos*, fault, ADSL	>20000
3	diagnos*, fault, +ADSL	644
4	+fault, +ADSL	6
5	+fault, +de=subscriber	76
6	+de=fault, +de=subscriber	32
7	de=fault, de=subscriber, -optical	>20000

Table 1: Typical series of query reformulations.

5.1 Findings

One striking feature of what the librarians did was the complexity and sophistication of their searching activities. For instance, in all the searches we observed, librarians went through a process of re-formulating a query many times before arriving at a set of search results that they were happy to pass back to the client. Table 1 shows one series of re-formulations undertaken as part of an attempt to find documents relating to "fault diagnosis and ADSL (Asynchronous Digital Subscriber Line)". This series is a subset of the librarian's total search activity while working on this one problem. In the query terms shown, '+' means that the term *must* be included; '*' denotes a 'wild card' (so 'diagnos*' will match with 'diagnosis', 'diagnose', 'diagnosing', etc.); '-' means that the term must *not* appear in the document; and 'de=' means that the term must appear in the list of descriptor terms associated with a document. In this library, the default search is an 'or' search; the effects of this are graphically illustrated in the jump in number of hits from Query 6 to Query 7 (Table 1).

In such a series of queries, and the accompanying verbal protocol, the librarian displays a deep knowledge of the syntax of the query language and the various different resources and databases that the library provides access to. As the sequence progresses, they are also developing a growing awareness of the specific problem domain and how it is represented within the library. In particular, the librarians develop their understanding of which keywords and terms are going to provide the discriminatory power needed.

At numerous stages in the interaction, the librarians display a sensitivity and orientation towards the size of the result set. The size of this set is often used in making the decision as to whether they are happy with the result set. If the set is 'too small' then the search may be too narrow; if it is too large, it is unmanageable and the useful results within it will be hard to find.

A further observation is that librarians in this study appeared to be adept at recognizing deficiencies in the knowledge they possessed (e.g. about the field in which the search is taking place) or the query they had produced. Furthermore, they have ways of working that allow them to recognize and remedy such deficiencies.

However, in addition to such 'low level' knowledge, librarians appear to possess an array of information finding *strategies*, or higher-level ways of organizing their activity. In a sense the root of expertise here seems not to reside in an ability to

Problem:	1	2	3	Mean
Librarian A	20	12	14	17
Librarian B	21	15	18	

Table 2: Numbers of query reformulations per search.

	Query term
1	games
2	+pleasurable, +design, de=interface
3	jordan [the name of a key researcher in the field]

Table 3: Series of queries produced by Client A.

formulate better queries, nor in possessing a deep understanding of the structure and properties of the underlying databases, though these things are important. On the contrary, the librarians' effectiveness seems to rely on being able to strategically organize a series of queries that allow the expert to arrive at an acceptable result by a process of exploration. The librarian does not form any obvious plan in advance — indeed, neither librarian was able to articulate any plan beyond the current step — but has an effective overall strategy for interacting with the available databases that is tightly coupled with, and dependent on, both the information currently displayed and the history of the interaction so far.

A look at the pattern of re-formulations by librarians and clients supports this. Table 2 shows the number of different queries issued by each librarian for each of the problems.

Contrast this with the fact that the non-librarian users produced far fewer queries (mean < 10) for these same problems. Furthermore, a detailed look at the server log data shows that what some client users do is issue a number of separate queries to follow several relatively disconnected hunches or lines of inquiry that they suspect may lead them to useful material. For instance, one client, A, who was interested in the area of emotions and design, issued only three queries, as shown in Table 3.

It is interesting to note not only that A produced only a small number of queries before giving up and turning to the librarians for help, but also that each query is apparently unrelated to the others. This client appeared reluctant or unable to reformulate a query, preferring instead to try a completely different line of attack in the face of unacceptable results.

Another client, M, a frequent user of the library, was both more persistent and more sophisticated in producing a series of queries in order to find material related to specific forms of fraud involving credit cards, as shown in Table 4. Client M, it appears, is much happier to reformulate or re-phrase a query on the basis of the result set returned. However, there still appears to be a tendency to persist with an approach for only a relatively short time before trying a different approach. Coupled to this, M appears to have only a relatively limited set of strategies for modifying

	Query term
1	ecommerce statistics
2	Internet fraud
3	Internet_fraud +de=fraud +de=electronic+commerce
4	Internet_fraud +de=fraud +de=credit+transactions
5	cnp fraud
6	card not present fraud
7	credit card fraud

Table 4: Series of queries produced by Client M.

searches, for example substituting one term for a similar term or synonym (for example, replacing 'cnp' by 'card not present' and then 'credit card').

Librarians, on the other hand, rarely produce an optimal and acceptable set of query terms (and therefore result documents) first time around. As can be seen (e.g. in Table 1), while they might have a number of separate ways of approaching the problem, each approach is likely to be exploratory and will involve carrying out a series of manipulations of a set of search terms. This will progressively modify the search set so as to improve the results obtained, test out hypotheses, or to gain a better understanding of the domain in which the search is taking place.

The skill of librarians, then, seems not (only) to be in accurately translating the needs of the user into an effective set of keywords. Indeed, the figures above suggest that librarians possess ways of going about the tasks of searching, strategies that are different from those used by non-experts.

5.2 Strategies

In interacting with the library, the librarians were able to call upon a number of 'strategies' or 'template' ways of organizing their activity. These strategies allowed the librarians to make use of patterns of action that had proved successful in the past, and which can be flexibly and contingently deployed in future situations. A number of such recurrent patterns of activity were evident in this study in the way that librarians made artful use of the features of the user interface. Three commonly observed strategies are:

- to systematically reformulate queries (rather than just abandon them and try again) in order to improve a search;

- to manipulate a search query in order to increase or decrease the size of the set of search results found; and

- to carry out searches and explore the result sets so as to learn more about the domain of inquiry and the discriminatory power of search terms within it.

Belkin et al. [1995] propose a model of information seeking strategies that operates at a larger scale than ours. Four dimensions (method of interaction, goal of interaction, mode or retrieval and type of resource used) are used to produce a space of sixteen types of strategy. Our strategies then, are much more concerned with the way that searches are carried out, whereas Belkin et al.'s are more concerned with the situation in which searching takes place. Bates [1990] uses the terms 'tactic' and 'stratagem' to refer to something similar to out strategies. Indeed, out strategies could be composed from Bates' tactics.

5.2.1   Reformulate to Improve Search

As has been noted already, non-expert users were frequently observed to issue a series of queries, each reflecting a different approach to finding the required information. If one query fails to return a useful set of results (either because the set contains very few items or, as is more frequently the case, the set contains far too many items) then there is a tendency for the non-librarian to abandon that line of enquiry and attempt another one. As we have seen above, it is relatively rare to see non-librarian users issuing a series of tightly connected queries where each is a reformulation of an earlier one.

Librarians, on the other hand, were observed to issue a series of queries, each building on earlier queries and modified in the light of the results obtained. For instance, one librarian accounted for one particular reformulation in a series of queries, where part of the query is left untouched and part is altered, thus:

> So I am fairly happy about getting towards ADSL words and now I am looking for the diagnosis words. (Librarian B)

Within the strategy of systematically reformulating, librarians displayed a number of tactics that included replacing search terms (e.g. replacing 'ADSL' with 'subscriber' or 'CNP' with 'card not present') and manipulating the query term syntax (e.g. replacing 'fault' by '+fault' and later by '+de=fault').

5.2.2   Expand and Contract

Both librarians and other clients displayed a sensitivity to the size of the set of results returned from a search, but in rather different ways. Put simply, for many of the clients a very large result set was a poor outcome that often engendered a complete change of approach. For the librarians, on the other hand, a large result set was often seen as an opportunity; a set possibly containing useful material that must be 'whittled down' to the useful core:

> This is a complex search, it's not clear from the outset, what is the core and what you are going to use to narrow it down . . . . . . , you've got fraud and you've got credit cards and the Internet. (Librarian B)

Therefore, it was not unusual for librarians to carry out their searching in two relatively distinct phases. The first, exemplified in the fragment of talk below, is concerned with generating a large set of results that will contain the desired material. Sometimes this will involve 'broadening' the search to include more hits, by replacing a specific term or phrase with a more general one:

> I know there are those two terms for ADSL. I'm broadening out ADSL a bit now into subscriber lines. (Librarian B)

The second, embarked upon when the librarian was reasonably certain that the search terms they had found so far resulted in a reasonable selection of useful material, involves narrowing the search once more to eliminate as many as possible of the irrelevant hits:

> It is very difficult to get a tight search that is exactly what you want.
> (Librarian B)

5.2.3   Improve Knowledge of the Domain

A number of episodes were observed in which the librarian carried out searches that did not appear to get them closer to the information-seeking goal. Many such interactions were exploratory sidelines in which the terminology and keywords of the domain were being investigated. In some cases, this reflects the fact that the librarians tend not to be experts in the domain of the search, as reflected in the following account:

> I'm wanting to see what will turn up in general, because I'm looking for
> a bit of help with the terminology. (Librarian A)

In some cases, the problem wasn't simply that the librarian was unable to produce terminology relevant to the search. Rather, the librarian was concerned to find out how the domain was represented in the keywords used by the database:

> I think the problem is we are playing with stuff that is a bit ... they are
> soft terms. (Librarian A)

Librarian B made similar comments on the same search task, remarking that the research area ('pleasurable design') was 'new' and the vocabulary 'soft'. Therefore, it could be some time before agreed key terms emerged and became part of the controlled vocabulary used by the indexers.

Finally on this point, it is worth noting that the librarians' tactics for improving their knowledge of the important keywords in a domain are sophisticated and involve the artful use of the library's facilities. For instance, on more than one occasion, a librarian would conduct a search in one database, INSPEC, which is well known for its robust system of keyword classification, but not with the expectation of finding useful results. On the contrary, they were seeking to improve their knowledge of keywords in the domain, which would then be used to search in another database, ABI, with its less sophisticated classification scheme.

6   User Interface Requirements

6.1   Strategies at the User Interface

An obvious but important conclusion of the above discussion is that one characteristic of non-experts is that they do not possess 'expert' strategies such as those identified above. Among other things, this prevents them from making as effective use of the DL as may be possible. A goal for design, therefore could be to give users of the digital library the information and resources they need in order to be able to carry out some of the strategies that prove so successful what carried out by the librarians.

As an illustration of this, we turn briefly to a simpler case where superficial aspects of a user interface can markedly affect the way users carry out a task. In a study of the use of a simple game, Cockayne et al. [1999] use the concept of strategy that is further developed by Wright et al. [2000]. The point of these papers (especially the former) is to say that we can identify strategies that the design of a user interface makes possible or that the design encourages particular strategies.

Cockayne et al. describe a study of the familiar game, the 8-puzzle, in which a simple strategy exists that will allow players to complete the puzzle quickly and more reliably than most other strategies. However, most players very rarely guess the strategy in the conventional form of the game. If, however, the visual presentation of the game is slightly re-designed, players rapidly acquire and deploy the strategy, allowing them to complete the puzzle more quickly and with fewer moves.

A conclusion that follows from the above-mentioned work is that in order to be able to employ a strategy, or engage in some pattern of behaviour, two conditions must hold. Firstly, the user must be aware of the strategy itself, and secondly, she must be provided, by the user interface, with any information resources that are required for its performance. It is worth noting that apparently trivial changes to a digital library's user interface can produce significant changes in the ways users formulate queries. Belkin et al. [2003] show that the simple addition of a text instruction — "Information problem description (the more you say, the better the results are likely to be)" — adjacent to a digital library search box leads users to enter significantly longer query phrases. This, in turn, leads to significantly better search results than queries produced without the additional instruction.

6.2 Supporting Information Finding Strategies

In the current paper it will only be possible to begin to explore ways that librarians' searching strategies may be supported or 'externalized' in a way that makes them easier for non-librarian users to discover and adopt. Let us illustrate how this might work by taking one of the strategies identified above: that of selectively and deliberately expanding and contracting the set of search results.

A standard search interface, as found on most search engines and digital libraries, permits this kind of strategy, as the user is presented with a 'search box' where arbitrary search terms may be entered. However, such an interfaces does nothing to encourage or suggest strategies for manipulating the search or result set.

Some well-known Internet search engines (such as Google) do appear to have this kind of behaviour in mind and provide some encouragement in the form of a "search within these results" feature. The purpose here is, presumably, to give users a way to progress their search when it initially yields a large set of results. Thus the user is prompted for additional keywords that will narrow down the search space.

Of course this isn't the only way of affecting the size of the results set, and the user interface of a digital library could offer other possibilities, such as the following:

- *Show how discriminating each of the search terms is.* This could be a numeric presentation indicating how many 'hits' each term returns, or could be a graphical representation, such as a Venn-diagram, that shows how the result set relates to the search terms. For instance, Jones [1998] and Jones et al. [1999] describe such a graphical presentation of search queries and results. Recall the librarians' use of the number of 'hits' produced in response to a query; providing additional information in the interfaces may endow non-librarians with some of this sensitivity to search results. It might even help librarians.

- *Provide explicit hints for kinds of reformulation other than simply adding new keywords.* For instance, many search mechanisms distinguish between separate keywords and multi-word phrases, and the user interface could suggest the conversion of one to the other to either expand or contract the result set. Recall the librarians' knowledge of search term syntax that allowed them to change the status of particular search terms within the query. Providing hints may remove the need to be familiar with the syntax, while allowing the non-librarian to see the potential offered by particular kinds of query reformulation.

  Librarians in this study made extensive use of a feature known as the 'keyword browser'. This gave access through a separate page of the user interface to the set of index terms according to which documents in the library are organized. It provided a highly effective means of affecting the selectiveness of searches. However, non-expert users in out study made almost no use of this feature. The reasons for this are likely to include poor visibility on the display, lack of obvious purpose, and poor integration with the more obvious search feature. Clearer presentation and better integration of the keyword browser feature with the core system could empower less sophisticated searchers by giving them easier access to powerful features.

- *Provide context-sensitive help for improving searches.* Part of what librarians are able to do is to make highly tailored responses to search results sets that depend on the size of the results set produced. As noted above, they will explicitly try to expand the set to a large one that includes relevant material, and then will try to reduce that large set to one that has fewer irrelevant hits. Help or hints that offer advice based on the result sets produced could support such a strategy. Search engines such as Google go some way to providing this kind of support when they offer alternative or corrected spellings of search terms.

7   Conclusions and Further Work

We have described a study in which it was observed that 'expert' users of a digital library are, not surprisingly, able to be more successful than 'non-experts' at finding information. In addition to the possession a better and more detailed knowledge of the library, its user interface, and its internal structure, there are other differences between 'expert' librarians and 'non-expert' library clients that allow the former to be very effective at conducting searches and finding information. In particular, it was noted that librarians are able to draw upon an extensive repertoire of strategies for finding information in the library. It has been suggested here that user interfaces should be constructed that will help non-librarians to engage in some of the strategies that allow librarians to be successful.

The study yielded many insights about the nature of our experts' expertise, including the range of strategies to which they appear to have access. This in turn has led to a number or possible design innovations that seek to improve the effectiveness of non-experts. This, of course, leaves open a number of questions that may be explored further. For example, precisely how do librarians make use of the available information in enacting their strategies? Do they direct their attention to the same things as non-librarians? How effective are the design suggestions outlined above?

In addition to showing how an understanding of expert behaviour can guide design, the work carried out here highlights the value of using the difference between user groups with varying forms of expertise as a useful focus in design. A valid goal for design is to accommodate variation and change in expertise by understanding the range of strategies that are employed, and designing so that "expert strategies" are more readily available to non-experts too.

Acknowledgements

We would like to thank the Librarians and Clients who participated in this study as well as members of the Interaction Design Centre at Middlesex University who commented on earlier versions of this work. This work was supported by EPSRC grant GR/N37858/01.

References

Bates, M. J. [1990], Where Should the Person Stop and the Information Search Interface Start?, *Information Processing and Management* **26**(5), 575–91.

Belkin, N. J. [1980], Anomalous States of Knowledge as a Basis for Information Retrieval, *Canadian Journal of Information Science* **5**, 133–4.

Belkin, N. J., Cool, C., Kelly, D., Kim, G., Kim, J.-Y., Lee, H.-J., Muresan, G., Tang, M.-C. & Yuan, X.-J. [2003], Query Length in Interactive Information Retrieval, *in* harles Clarke, G. Cormack, J. Callan, D. Hawking & A. Smeaton (eds.), *Proceedings of the 26th Annual International ACM SIGIR Conference on Research and Development in Information Retrieval (SIGIR'03)*, ACM Press, pp.205–12.

Belkin, N. J., Cool, C., Stein, A. & Thiel, U. [1995], Cases, Scripts and Information-seeking Strategies: On the Design of Interactive Information Retrieval Systems, *Expert Systems with Applications* **9**(3), 379–95.

Blandford, A., Stelmaszewska, H. & Bryan-Kinns, N. [2001], Use of Multiple Digital Libraries: A Case Study, *in* E. A. Fox & C. L. Borgman (eds.), *Proceedings of the 1st ACM/IEEE-CSJoint Conference on Digital Libraries (JCDL'01)*, ACM Press, pp.179–88.

Borgman, C. L. [1996], Why are Online Catalogs Still Hard to Use?, *Journal of the American Society for Information Science* **4**(7), 493–503.

Cockayne, A., Wright, P. & Fields, B. [1999], Supporting Interaction Strategies through the Externalisation of Strategy Concepts, *in* A. Sasse & C. Johnson (eds.), *Human–Computer*

Interaction — INTERACT '99: Proceedings of the Seventh IFIP Conference on Human–Computer Interaction, Vol. 1, IOS Press, pp.582–8.

Dillon, A. [2001], Technologies of Information: HCI and the Digital Library, *in* J. M. Carroll (ed.), *Human–Computer Interaction in the New Millennium*, Addison–Wesley, pp.457–74.

Dillon, A. & Song, M. [1997], An Empirical Comparison of the Usability for Novice and Expert Searchers of a Textual and a Graphic Interface to An Art-resource Database, *Journal of Digital Information* 1(1). http://jodi.ecs.soton.ac.uk/.

Ellis, D. & Haugan, M. [1997], Modelling the Information Seeking Patterns of Engineers and Research Scientists in an Industrial Environment, *Journal of Documentation* 53(4), 384–403.

Hsieh-Yee, I. [1993], Effects of Search Experience and Subject Knowledge on the Search Tactics of Novice and Experienced Searchers, *Journal of the American Society for Information Science* 44(3), 161–74.

Jones, S. [1998], VQuery: A Graphical User Interface for Boolean Query Specification and Dynamic Result Preview, Working Paper 98/3, Department of Computer Science, University of Waikato.

Jones, S., McInnes, S. & Staveley, M. S. [1999], A Graphical User Interface for Boolean Query Specification, *Journal of Digital Information* 2(2-3), 207–23.

Lucas, W. & Topi, H. [2002], Form and Function: The Impact of Query Term and Operator Usage on Web Search Results, *Journal of the American Society for Information Science and Technology* 53(2), 95–108.

Marchionini, G. [1995], *Information Seeking in Electronic Environments*, Cambridge University Press.

Smith, P. J., Shute, S. J., Galdes, D. & Chignell, M. H. [1989], Knowledge-based Search Tactics for an Intelligent Intermediary System, *ACM Transactions on Office Information Systems* 7(3), 246–70.

Stelmaszewska, H. & Blandford, A. [2002], Patterns of Interactions: User Behaviour in Response to Search Results, *in* A. Blandford & G. Buchanan (eds.), *Proceedings of JCDL'02 Workshop on Usability of Digital Libraries — Usability of Digital Libraries, A Workshop at JCDL2002*, Available at http://www.uclic.ucl.ac.uk/annb/DLUsability/JCDL02.html, pp.29–31.

Sutcliffe, A. & Ennis, M. [1998], Towards a Cognitive Theory of Information Retrieval, *Interacting with Computers* 10(3), 321–51.

Vakkari, P. [2001], A Theory of the Task-based Information Retrieval Process: A Summary and Generalisation of a Longitudinal Study, *Journal of Documentation* 57(1), 44–60.

Wright, P. C., Fields, R. E. & Harrison, M. D. [2000], Analysing Human–Computer Interaction as Distributed Cognition: The Resources Model, *Human–Computer Interaction* 15(1), 1–41.

Supporting User Decisions in Travel and Tourism

Andy Dearden & Chiu M Lo

Computing and Communications Research Centre, Sheffield Hallam University, Sheffield S1 1WB, UK

Tel: *+44 114 225 2916*

Fax: *+44 114 225 3161*

Email: *a.m.dearden@shu.ac.uk*

Travel and tourism makes up a large proportion of business to customer (B2C) e-commerce activity, and e-commerce in this sector is growing rapidly. Users can find vast amounts of travel related information and purchase a wide range of travel related goods and services through the Internet. This presents users with a complex decision-making task when planning a trip or a holiday using on-line facilities.

This paper examines a range of accounts of decision making developed both in the context of e-commerce and in travel and tourism. The accounts are compared with data from an investigation using a think-aloud protocol examining a simulated decision task. The results of the investigation suggest that neither the e-commerce models nor the accounts of decision making in travel and tourism, provide completely adequate accounts of user behaviours if used in isolation. Rather elements from both sets of models must be considered relevant. Based on the findings a preliminary framework for the design of new decision-support tools is suggested.

Keywords: e-commerce, decision-support, think-aloud, travel, tourism.

1 Introduction

This paper is concerned with the design of interactive tools for use by end-customers making travel and tourism decisions. Increasing numbers of people are using the Internet to research and purchase travel and tourism services. Travel and tourism make up a significant proportion of business-to-customer e-commerce activity. One major reason for the popularity of the Internet is the opportunity for users to research alternative suppliers, collect detailed information about their travel options and to compare prices across suppliers. However, the high volume of available information and the wide range of possible suppliers present users with a complex decision-making task.

To design a tool to support a pre-existing task, it is of course valuable to develop an account of the task that must be supported. This paper reviews existing accounts of decision-making in e-commerce and in the domain of travel and tourism, (many of which pre-date the development of e-commerce). Using a think-aloud protocol in a simulated tourism decision task, the paper shows that neither existing models of decision-making in e-commerce nor models from the domain of travel and tourism provide completely adequate accounts. Rather, elements from both sets of models should be considered. Based on these findings, the paper proposes a set of requirements for interactive decision support systems for this domain.

2   Accounts of Decision Making in E-commerce

Various accounts of customer purchase decision-making in e-commerce have been proposed. A general model suggested by Turban et al. [1999] consists of five stages: initial need identification; information search; evaluation of alternatives; purchase and delivery; and after purchase evaluation. A very similar account is offered by O'Keefe & McEachern [1998]. The second and third stages (information search and evaluation of alternatives) may be conducted in an iterative cycle, and it is in these two areas where computer support is most likely to be of value.

In the context of business to business e-commerce, Maes et al. [1999] present a six stage model of decision making consisting of: need identification; product brokering; merchant brokering; negotiation; purchase and delivery; and service and evaluation. Merchant brokering recognizes the possibility that users may want to compare between different suppliers for the same goods. In addition to prices, negotiation may include discussions about the details of how a product or service is to be delivered, for example selecting delivery dates and addresses.

Holsapple & Whinston [1996], describe decision-making in terms of three stages of design, intelligence and choice. Miles et al. [1999] build upon Holsapple & Whinston's view, suggesting that decision making in e-commerce can be modelled in terms of three core activities: search for products, management of search criteria, and comparison of found products. Häubl & Trifts [2000] and Jedetski et al. [2002] suggest that on-line shoppers combine an initial screening of alternatives with later detailed comparison of a small number of selected candidates. Combining these views with those of Maes et al. [1999], the two stages of information search and evaluation of alternatives can be viewed in terms of four sub-tasks: search for product-supplier options, management of search criteria, screening of an initial candidate set, and detailed comparison of the selected subset of products-supplier pairings.

A range established interface designs can be used to support these sub-tasks:

- Most e-commerce vendors both in product sales and in travel and tourism provide facilities for searching their own product offerings by establishing queries with respect to a defined set of product attributes. For example, users wanting to purchase computers can specify processor speed, quantity of memory, size of hard drive etc. In the majority of cases only conjunctive queries are supported.

- Many e-commerce vendors provide specific facilities for customers to compare different products within a homogeneous product set. For example, PC World (http://www.pcworld.co.uk/) offer facilities where users can select up to five computers and add them to a comparison table which is organized by the primary attributes that describe these systems. More sophisticated designs are possible, for example the Tete-a-Tete system [Maes et al. 1999] uses 'value bars' to provide visual feedback on the degree to which different products match the preferences declared by a user. This design can be related to the 'Attribute Explorer' described by Spence & Tweedie [1998].

- A number of interaction designs specifically address the question of criteria management. A well known technique in this area is the use of dynamic queries [Williamson & Shneiderman 1992] where results are immediately updated in response to users' adjusting query criteria. In many travel sites, users can adjust date and time of travel to search for earlier trains or flights on a previous day. A novel response is shown by the Leeds based airline Jet 2 where users can obtain a single view that shows how the available fares for a given journey can vary over an entire month (http://jet2.airkiosk.com/cgi-bin/jet2/I6/81015lfa). This design allows a user to see how their preferred travel dates can be traded off against costs.

Naturally, very few suppliers provide the ability to compare products between themselves and alternative merchants, however, similar interaction designs could be incorporated into meta-sites or stand-alone tools, to enable such comparisons.

On the basis of the above discussion, it appears that the general theoretical accounts of decision-making in e-commerce and the interaction designs currently available are reasonably well matched. The next section examines the specific case of decision making in travel and tourism.

3 Accounts of Decision Making in Travel and Tourism

The nature of purchase decisions in travel and tourism has received considerable attention in the field of marketing. Accounts generally cover two broad areas:

1. the various factors that influence the options that a that a customer might select; and

2. the structural make-up of the decision-making process.

Accounts of the factors influencing the selection behaviour of customers highlight a number of distinctive aspects of decisions in tourism:

- Both Wahab et al. [1976] and Moutinho [1987] highlight the degree to which intangible attributes are important in guiding tourism decisions. For example, the quality of the view may have a significant impact on a customer's preferences between different hotels or apartments. Factors such as the customer's self image may play an important part in the decision made. Wahab et al. suggest that "quite often the intangible values far outweigh the tangible ones" [Wahab et al. 1976, p.80].

- Wahab et al. [1976] draw attention to the fact that at the end of the transaction of purchasing and receiving a tourism service, the customer is left with nothing other than the intangible feelings of satisfaction provided by the experience. Given that tourism decisions may involve quite large investments (relative to the income of the traveller) this means that the customer may be very sensitive to the risk of making a poor choice. "The tourist is buying an illusion. He will be embittered by anything or anybody who shatters it." [Wahab et al. 1976, p.74]

- Another important difference is that a tourism experience involves finding a satisfactory combination of many heterogeneous elements, for example: choice of destination, choice of flights, arrangements for travel to and from the airport, choice of activities at the destination [Swarbrooke & Horner 1999]. Fesenmaier & Jeng [2000] show how such sub-decisions form a complex interdependent network that travellers must explore to arrive at suitable plans.

Based on these important differences in the nature of the decision that needs to be made, Wahab et al. and Moutinho provide descriptions of the process of decision making in travel and tourism that include many sub-tasks that are not reflected by the e-commerce accounts considered above.

Wahab et al. [1976] suggest a model of consisting of nine stages, namely:

- Initial stimulus to travel — this is equivalent to the initial need identification noted by Turban et al.'s [1999] e-commerce model.

- Conceptual framework — the decision maker develops various hypotheses about the potential satisfactions that might arise from a trip, for example "Ibiza must be fascinating, and the beaches are lovely ... Let's see Rome, it's Holy Year too." [Turban et al. 1999, p.78]

- Fact gathering — the decision-maker collects information from multiple sources about possible destinations and travel arrangements.

- Definition of assumptions — in this stage the decision-maker develops a range of assumptions about the options available to her and seeks to integrate the information she has obtained in a way that can be used to solve particular planning problems, for example what transport arrangements might be possible, or what hazards might need to be considered.

- Design of alternatives and forecast of consequences — the decision maker iteratively designs a small number of alternative plans and evaluates them in terms of their specific pros and cons.

- Cost-benefit analysis / ranking of alternatives — at this stage only a small number of alternative plans are considered, and their costs and benefits are evaluated.

- Decision — based on the previous actions, the decision-maker commits to one specific choice.

- Outcome evaluation.

Moutinho [1987] presents a similar model including an initial stimulus, the formation of a 'preference structure' that determines the choice criteria (similar to Wahab et al.'s 'conceptual framework'). This stage is followed by a search cycle in which Moutinho suggests that both 'internal' and 'external' search strategies are applied, i.e. the decision-maker uses both their own memory as well as external information sources to inform their decision. Within this search, a process of 'stimulus filtration' occurs in which the decision maker transforms the information that she has obtained, this process includes assessing the reliability of information from different sources. This search is used to construct an 'evoked set' of possible travel options. From this set a 'viable set' is selected for further evaluation. Moutinho claims that a large majority of tourists carefully consider no more than seven alternatives from their 'evoked set'. In evaluating the options within the 'viable set' Moutinho suggests that 'perceived risk' is a major decision criterion. If one particular candidate is selected, a further process of risk reduction is undertaken in which additional information may be gathered to reduce the risk of dissatisfaction with the selected choice.

These more complex accounts of decision-making pre-date the development of e-commerce. For this reason, it is reasonable to question whether the decision-making elements identified for travel and tourism are still observable in the context of e-commerce, or whether accounts developed specifically for e-commerce are more informative. The next section reports on an investigation of this question.

4 An Investigation

Studying consumer decision-making in travel and tourism presents a difficult challenge for HCI. The phenomena of interest may be spread over an extended period in time and space, and involve many cognitive activities that may not result in externally observable behaviours. Given this difficulty, a compromise solution was to apply a think-aloud protocol to a simulated decision-making task. The protocol was similar to co-operative evaluation [Monk et al. 1993], except that users were asked to discuss both their responses to the website and their decision making behaviours. Similar think-aloud protocols have been applied to studying expert decision-making for knowledge based systems development [Hickman et al. 1989].

In this investigation, each subject was given an open task to perform, which was to plan a weekend trip to Paris for themselves and their partner, in a given month (about 2 months from the date of the experimental session). Subjects were asked to find the 'best deal' for their trip (the precise meaning of 'best deal' was not defined). Subjects were provided with two URLs for websites, one of which provided package breaks to the chosen destination (http://www.bargainholidays.co.uk) and one that supported hotel booking in the chosen city (e.g. http://www.france-hotels.net). The task instructions informed the user that if they could not find the accommodation they wanted on the first website, they could visit the second website. The instructions did not forbid the subjects from visiting other websites; nor did the instructions discuss what a 'weekend' might consist of (e.g. Friday to Monday, Friday to Tuesday, Saturday and Sunday only etc.). If the subjects asked about these restrictions, they were informed that they were completely free to interpret the instructions as they wished.

Matchware's ScreenCorder and Camtasia Studio software were used to record interaction behaviour and comments. These tools record on-screen activity and audio input from a microphone. The resulting recordings can then be replayed using a variety of media players. A typical recording session lasted between 30 minutes and 1 hour. Rough working on paper and pencil, or printed output was also retained for later analysis.

The subjects were students and staff at a UK university, including both UK and Malaysian nationals. A convenience sample was used, with the majority of subjects being drawn from within the computing department. All of the subjects were regular computer users and all had experience of researching or purchasing goods and services using the Internet. This subject group was selected to minimize the possibility that basic interaction difficulties would interfere with behaviour in ways that would interfere with subjects ability to progress their decision-making.

The data was analysed by comparing each recording with each of a set of different models that describe users' decision-making behaviour in e-commerce or in travel and tourism. Each model was abstracted to identify a set of key elements, for example stages of the decision-making process or specific activities identified by the model. These elements were then used to create a coding sheet, to identify events within the recordings that corresponded to each given element. Table 1 shows an example coding sheet. The observed events and time of occurrence were noted. Where significant events were observed for which the current model did not provide a suitable account, these events were also noted.

Given the exploratory nature of the study, inter-rater reliability of the coding was not validated. Also, note that the aim of the study was to test the relevance of existing accounts, and therefore any single observation of a behaviour described by an account constitutes evidence that the behaviour described is still relevant in the context of e-commerce.

The main accounts selected for investigation, based on a prior literature review, were the tourism models of Wahab et al. [1976] and Moutinho [1987] and the e-commerce models of Miles et al. [1999] and Maes et al. [1999].

5 Results

Data was collected from nine sessions, four females, four males and one couple. The age range was from 20 to 60. On two occasions technical difficulties resulted in loss of the recording. One subject eventually refused to attempt to find a holiday on the web, explaining that he found the websites visited too difficult to use. The other

Moutinho [1987]	Observed behaviour	[Subject, Time]
Internal information search (use of prior knowledge)	Obtain train information/ticket from Midland Mainline: http://www.midlandmainline.com	[2, 41:25]
	Search for the price and availability of Eurostar to Paris.	[2, 33:00]
External information search (search on web or other means)	Google search for 'Paris airport' to choose the arrival airport from Ryanair.	[2, 18:44]
	Search for accommodation using Google — keyword 'paris, youth hostel'.	[2, 52:44]
	Search for ticket to Paris using Google — keyword 'online flight ticket, Manchester'.	[2, 53:03]
Stimulus filtration (assessment of the reliability of information found)	The price for the train from Sheffield to London was not shown on the Midland Mainline website. The subject needs to make a phone call in order to check out the price. not sure about the price given because the price might not include VAT.	[2, 48:11]
	Does not trust the image of the hostel from the website because it might look different in reality.	[2, 22:18]
Formation of choice criteria	Choice criteria for flight and train is mainly based on the price. For hotel, it is based on the price, the feel of comfortable of the hotel, and the distance to the interesting places. The criteria of hotel are determined based on the images/photos provided.	[2, 27:15]
Exclusion of infeasible options	Gives up the flight after the first search as the flight ticket is more expensive than Eurostar.	[2, 53:45]
	Leaves Easyjet's site: http://www.easyjet.co.uk/en/book/index.asp as it does not offer flight to Paris.	[2, 51:30]
Evaluation of alternatives	Print out the itinerary of train that she wanted to book from London to Paris.	[2, 40:35]
	Evaluate either to go by Eurostar or flight is based on the price criterion.	[2, 53:45]
Exclude alternatives from the choice set	Exclude the alternatives which are over her budget.	[2, throughout the experiment]
Assessment/reduction of perceived risk	The outlook of the hotel, and also the comfortably is based on the image/photo provided by the website.	[2, 30:15]
Selection of final option	Decides to book a train ticket from Midland Mainline which departs from Sheffield to London Waterloo, and then takes a Eurostar from London Waterloo to Paris. Decided to stay in an economy hostel with a private room to share with her partner.	[2, end of observation]
Other events	Abandons bargain holidays because Paris not visible as a destination from Manchester.	[2, 2.30ff]

Table 1: An example coding sheet, based on Moutinho's model

eight sessions all reached the point of considering one or more alternative holiday plans. Events are described using the format S# for subject number, and a four digit time referring to the time shown on the recording.

5.1   Pre-Internet Models of Tourism Decisions

Existing accounts of tourism decision-making provided by Wahab et al. [1976] and Moutinho [1987] both contain many detailed elements that are absent from typical models of e-commerce. The data indicates that these models still contain useful insights for the design of decision-support tools in the context of e-commerce.

Wahab et al. [1976] claim that tourists develop a 'conceptual framework' consisting of hypotheses about alternative satisfactions that guides their decision-making. Subjects made various comments that support this contention, for example one subject explained that it was important to be near to the 'cultural' attractions in Paris [S3, 11.30ff]. Another subject discussed his aim of ensuring he arrived in Paris early enough to enjoy two evenings out, and his desire not to travel too far to the departure airport when planning a weekend trip [S6, File 2, 15.06ff].

Moutinho [1987] distinguishes between 'internal' and 'external' search. All the subjects made some use of their previous knowledge in searching for options (internal search). Many navigated to websites that they already knew. Some made use of their existing knowledge of Paris when selecting hotels [S3, 13.00ff]. External search was also evident with subjects using search engines to look for 'hotels in Paris' or 'Flights to Paris' [S2, File 2, 15:50].

Wahab et al. [1976] suggests that after gathering facts to inform decision making, tourists test the validity of the evidence collected when generating their assumptions. Moutinho [1987] refers to a similar process as 'stimulus filtration'. Some subjects explained that they were extremely suspicious of data provided by web-sites [e.g. S7, 09:30ff; S2, 27:15ff]. Other subjects were concerned whether prices shown included all the elements of the package, including taxes [e.g. S6, File 2, 5.20ff; S2, 22:18ff]. Some subjects were less cautious, but this may reflect the fact that the exercise was simulated and did not involve the subjects in real expenditures.

Wahab et al. [1976] suggest that tourists 'define assumptions' when making their decisions. Two subjects [S1 & S6] discussed the quality and convenience of the Paris Metro and indicated that they would therefore consider hotels over a wider area.

Moutinho [1987] suggests that decision-makers will reject certain alternatives as 'infeasible', and will construct a more limited 'choice set' before actually conducting detailed comparisons. Häubl & Trifts [2000] suggest a similar two-stage process of 'filter' and 'compare'. Many subjects did not construct more than two complete packages. A number of cases were observed where options for one part of the package, e.g. a hotel or flight, were rejected and removed from further consideration before a conducting a more detailed comparison.

Both Wahab et al. and Moutinho include stages where the costs and benefits of different alternatives are evaluated and compared. Similar stages are evident in Miles et al. [1999] and Maes et al. [1999]. All the subjects conducted some comparison.

Finally, Moutinho [1987] suggests that when a small shortlist of alternatives has been constructed, tourists may engage in additional information search to 'reduce the perceived risk' of making a decision that they will regret. One subject explained how photographs of typical rooms, and the area surrounding the hotel helped them 'feel more comfortable' with their decision [S3, 18:00ff].

Thus the data suggests that many elements from the models of Wahab et al. [1976] and Moutinho [1987] remain relevant in the context of tourism decision-making using Internet resources.

5.2 General Models from E-commerce

General e-commerce models such as Miles et al. [1999], Maes et al. [1999] and Silverman et al. [2001] are typically presented at a higher level of abstraction than the models of tourism decision-making discussed above. For example, none of these general models distinguish between 'internal' and 'external' search. Similarly, these models discuss decision criteria, but do not examine its relation to the broader 'conceptual framework' that informs the decision. Silverman et al. [2001] include a discussion of trust, but do not relate it to any process analogous to 'stimulus filtration' as described by Moutinho [1987]. However, these general models do contain some distinct elements that extend beyond the scope of pre-Internet tourism decision models.

Miles et al. [1999] highlight the process of 'criteria management' where a decision-maker adjusts his or her initial criteria in response to data collected. Some examples of this were observed. One subject initially wanted to fly from Manchester airport, but then weakened this constraint by looking for flights from another, slightly less convenient airport [S6, File 2, 14:40]. Another subject made changes to their preferred travel time in an attempt to find cheaper options [S1, 10:40].

Maes et al. [1999] include 'merchant brokering' as a distinct element of e-commerce decision-making. Most of the subjects considered options drawn from a variety of providers.

Such observations suggest that criteria management and merchant brokering should be considered in tools to support tourism decisions. More generally, they suggest that models of decision-making in e-commerce address issues that are additional to those covered by accounts of decision behaviour in travel and tourism.

6 Additional Observations

Some behaviours observed could not be accounted for using either the e-commerce nor the tourism decision-making models. Two main categories of such behaviours were identified.

Firstly, there were a number of situations where the subjects explicitly abandoned their search on a given site expressing specific reasons for doing so:

- Subject 1 abandoned a site having found no results for Paris. The apparent reason for this was that the subject thought of their weekend as a holiday of duration 3 days, rather than using the specific term 'city break' [S1, 06.06ff].

- Subject 3 abandoned a search for flights from their preferred airport because the drop down list of destinations appeared not to include Paris. In fact the drop-down listed a number of major airports in alphabetical order first (from A to Z) before going on to a second list of other airports [S3, 2.16ff].

In both these cases, the subjects appeared to conclude that the site was not able to meet their particular needs. The observations could be related to the concept of 'information scent' [Pirolli 1997].

A second behaviour that was not discussed in any of the models was time spent validating the compatibility of different components of a trip:

- Subject 3 repeatedly switches between an airline site and a rail booking site in order to ensure that the train timings gave sufficient allowances for getting to the airport and checking in [S1, 27.00ff].

- Subject 2 made an error in calculating prices by including travel for two people, but accommodation for only one. [S2, paper calculations]

Fesenmaier & Jeng [2000] explore the interconnected nature of the multiple sub-decisions that are required when planning a trip. These observations support their findings. The idea of presenting tourism products in relation to a 'trip' rather than individual components has been applied in a number of recent systems [for example Rodden et al. 2003; Dunstall et al. 2004].

6.1 Summary

The results suggest that neither pre-Internet models of tourism decision making, nor general accounts of decision-making in e-commerce provide completely adequate accounts of the data observed. Rather, the data can be used to identify a number of elements from the various models that should be considered in designing future tools. Particular elements identified were:

- Recognizing the problem as the organization of a 'trip' [Fesenmaier & Jeng 2000; Rodden et al. 2003; Dunstall et al. 2004].

- Conducting internal and external search [Moutinho 1987].

- Managing criteria for search [Miles et al. 1999].

- Managing mutual constraints between sub-decisions [Fesenmaier & Jeng 2000].

- Forming a choice set [Moutinho 1987].

- Evaluating and comparing alternatives, including price calculation (all) and brokering between multiple merchants [Maes et al. 1999].

- Handling affective and intangible attributes [Wahab et al. 1976].

- Filtering stimuli [Moutinho 1987].

- Reducing perceived risk [Moutinho 1987].

- Developing a conceptual framework [Wahab et al. 1976].

• Defining assumptions [Wahab et al. 1976].

These findings suggest some possible developments for future tools.

7 A Preliminary Framework for New Decision-support Tools

The proposed framework is divided into two sections. The first part addresses basic entities and functions that should be recognized by a tool that aims to support travel and tourism decisions. The second part of the framework highlights some issues that will require creative responses in the design of such tools, and suggests some possible design directions.

7.1 Basic Capabilities

7.1.1 Travel Components and Trip Profiles

Tourism decisions involve both the initial identification of travel services that can be provided, and their integration into completed plans for specific trips. These two categories may be labelled as:

Travel components — individual products or services that will be provided by one supplier. Examples would be a rail ticket, hotel booking or flight. These components may be made up of multiple parts (for example a single flight component might involve travel from a local airport to an international hub, followed by a second flight from the hub to the destination), but are purchased in a single transaction. Such components may involve heterogeneous elements, for example a package trip may include both flights and accommodation purchased in a single transaction.

Trip profiles — a trip profile may include a number of separate travel components, such as flights, accommodation, rail travel (or car parking), car-hire etc. An individual trip profile represents one possible journey or trip that the decision maker might consider.

A decision support tool for travel and tourism must enable users to add, manipulate and remove both travel components and trip profiles.

7.1.2 Supporting Internal and External Search

A suitable tool should allow users to add information and travel components derived from on-line sources; to enter information or travel components arising from off-line sources (e.g. brochures or travel agents' offerings); or to add information derived from their own 'internal' knowledge. Such searches should permit the user to introduce offerings from multiple different merchants.

7.1.3 Managing Search Criteria

In conducting web-based searches, a tool should provide users with opportunities to adjust their criteria in response to results obtained. It may also be useful to support similar criteria management within a decision support tool to filter results sets that have been collected. A further consideration is the ability to manipulate the way that criteria are presented when comparing either sets of related travel components or sets of trip profiles.

7.1.4   Managing Mutual Constraints

As trip profiles are constructed, a computer-based tool could provide support for evaluating the constraints that relate different elements of the trip, for example comparing the details of accommodation to the travel dates and party members.

7.1.5   Support for Formation of Choice Sets

When evaluating and comparing alternative trip profiles, users may want to restrict their attention to a small subset of the possible profiles that they have constructed, or might potentially construct. A tool should provide capabilities to select a subset of profiles for detailed comparison.

7.1.6   Support for Comparison and Price Calculation

Users need to compare both individual travel components, and trip profiles. For most users, price is a relevant criterion in every decision. Users will need to consider the overall costs of different trip profiles. However, tourism products or services may be priced in multiple currencies. Consequently, such price calculation must take into account currency conversion factors.

7.2   Considerations for Interaction Design

The above requirements are directed at particular concrete aspects of the task that must be undertaken. However, there are a number of issues arising from the study that should inform tool design, although they do not necessarily translate into specific functional requirements.

7.2.1   Supporting Consideration of Intangible Attributes

Given the importance of intangible elements in users' decisions, design for new tools should recognize the existence of these considerations. One possible design response would be allowing the user to attach comments or digital images (e.g. of a scenic view, a visitor attraction or a hotel lobby) to travel components or trip profiles.

7.2.2   Recognizing Stimulus Filtration

At the very least, information within such a decision support tool should indicate the original source. Further, some information may relate to confirmed available prices, whereas other information may indicate that a particular price might be available for a travel component but the availability of that price for the chosen dates may not be confirmed. A design should recognize these possibilities, for example, by recording the most recent date and time at which a piece of information was confirmed. Users may also want to add comments of their own regarding the sources of the information that they use.

7.2.3   Supporting Risk Reduction

Before committing to a decision, a user may want to collect additional information and check details of the profile under consideration. It will be important to ensure that the user can obtain a clear overview of the profiles being considered. Creative use of visualizations such as trip time lines may be useful in this respect. The use of 'critics' [Fischer et al. 1991] may also be applicable.

7.2.4　Explicating Conceptual Frameworks or Assumptions

The discussions above have all focused on the case of a single decision-maker. For many trips, multiple users may be involved in the decision. The decision making process could be studied as a type of computer supported co-operative work. In such cases, and even within the single user case, it may be helpful to allow users to make their conceptual frameworks or assumptions explicit within the tool.

8　Conclusions and Further Work

The domain of travel and tourism decision-making presents some distinctive challenges for the design of decision-support tools in e-commerce. This paper reports results of a think-aloud protocol examining a simulated tourism decision situation.

The results show that existing general models of decision-making in e-commerce are insufficiently detailed to account for many of the behaviours observed. More specific accounts of decision making in travel and tourism that pre-date the widespread use of e-commerce provide useful insights into users' possible needs.

Based on the findings from the investigation, a preliminary framework for the design of new decision-support tools was suggested. Future work is planned to design and evaluate new tools using the framework as an initial design guide. Tool design will be targeted at relatively experienced computer users, and will permit such users to collate information from diverse sources and from diverse media (including web-based, paper and 'word of mouth') and to organize the information to support decision-making. The proposed tool should allow the user to configure a trip profile by integrating components from different suppliers, and should support criteria management, support for 'risk reduction' activities, and assist users in considering intangible and affective aspects of the decision.

References

Dunstall, S., Horn, M. E. T., Kirby, P., Krishnamoorthy, M., Owens, B., Sier, D. & Thiebaux, S. [2004], An Automated Itinerary Planning System for Holiday Travel, *Information Technology and Tourism* **6**(3), 195–210.

Fesenmaier, D. R. & Jeng, J.-M. [2000], Assessing Structure in the Pleasure Trip Planning Process, *Tourism Analysis* **5**(1), 13–27.

Fischer, G., Lemke, A. C., Mastaglio, T. & Morch, A. I. [1991], The Role of Critiquing in Cooperative Problem Solving, *ACM Transactions on Office Information Systems* **9**(3), 123–51.

Hickman, F. R., Killin, J. L., Land, L., Mulhall, T., Porter, D. & Taylor, R. M. [1989], *Analysis for Knowledge-based Systems*, Ellis Horwood.

Holsapple, C. W. & Whinston, A. B. [1996], *Decision Support Systems: A Knowledge Based Approach*, International Thomson Press.

Häubl, G. & Trifts, V. [2000], Consumer Decision Making in Online Shopping Environments: The Effects of Interactive Decision Aids, *Marketing Science* **19**(1), 4–21.

Jedetski, J., Adelman, L. & Yeo, C. [2002], How Web Site Decision Technology Affects Consumers, *IEEE Internet Computing* **6**(3), 72–9.

Maes, P., Guttman, R. & Moukas, A. [1999], Agents That Buy and Sell, *Communications of the ACM* **42**(3), 81–91.

Miles, G. E., Howes, A. & Davies, A. [1999], A Framework for Understanding Human Factors in Web Based Electronic Commerce, *International Journal of Human–Computer Studies* **52**(1), 131–63.

Monk, A., Wright, P., Haber, J. & Davenport, L. [1993], *Improving Your Human Computer Interface*, Prentice–Hall.

Moutinho, L. [1987], Consumer Behaviour in Tourism, *European Journal of Marketing* **21**(10), 5–44.

O'Keefe, R. M. & McEachern, T. [1998], Web-based Customer Decision Support Systems, *Communications of the ACM* **41**(3), 71–8.

Pirolli, P. [1997], Computational Models of Information Scent-following in A Very Large Browsable Text Collection, *in* S. Pemberton (ed.), *Proceedings of the SIGCHI Conference on Human Factors in Computing Systems (CHI'97)*, ACM Press, pp.3–10.

Rodden, T., Rogers, Y., Halloran, J. & Taylor, I. [2003], Designing Novel Interactional Workspaces to Support Face to Face Consultations, *in* G. Cockton & P. Korhonen (eds.), *Proceedings of 2003 Conference on Human Factors in Computing Systems (CHI'03)*, *CHI Letters* **5**(1), ACM Press, pp.57–64.

Silverman, B. G., Bachann, M. & Al Akharas, K. [2001], Implication of Buyer Decision Theory for Design of E-commerce Websites, *International Journal of Human–Computer Studies* **55**(5), 815–44.

Spence, R. & Tweedie, L. [1998], The Attribute Explorer: Information Synthesis via Exploration, *Interacting with Computers* **11**(2), 137–46.

Swarbrooke, J. & Horner, S. [1999], *Consumer Behaviour in Tourism*, Butterworth–Heinemann.

Turban, E., Lee, J., King, D. & H.M., C. [1999], *Electronic Commerce: A Managerianl Perspective*, Prentice–Hall.

Wahab, S., Crompton, L. J. & Rothfield, L. [1976], *Tourism Marketing*, Tourism International Press.

Williamson, C. & Shneiderman, B. [1992], The Dynamic HomeFinder: Evaluating Dynamic Queries in a Real-estate Information Exploration System, *in* N. Belkin, P. Ingwersen & A. M. Pejtersen (eds.), *Proceedings of the 15th Annual International ACM SIGIR Conference on Research and Development in Information Retrieval (SIGIR'92)*, ACM Press, pp.338–46.

Constructing a Player-Centred Definition of Fun for Video Games Design

Stephen Boyd Davis & Christina Carini

Lansdown Centre for Electronic Arts, Middlesex University, Cat Hill, Barnet, Hertforshire EN4 8HT, UK

Email: *s.boyd-davis@mdx.ac.uk*

Research was carried out with twenty-seven games players, using a number of techniques. This was academic research, but intended to be useful in the development of existing and new genres of game. Considering the future application of such techniques, perhaps outside academia, their cost-benefit will be important. The authors report both on what they discovered about the two games studied, and also on the strengths and weaknesses of the techniques employed.

Keywords: fun, video games, game play, play testing, engagement, user testing, repertory grid, personal construct.

1 Introduction

Games are fun to play. People who do not play games may not understand why this is. In fact, people who do play games may not understand why either. In this research, we explore the concept of fun in games and attempt to define fun through study of the player's experience. We set out to determine which aspects of games design promote fun and which aspects disrupt it. The long term aim of this research is to produce a set of guidelines for designing fun in games and a set of evaluative techniques which are useful for detecting detailed issues in the design of individual games.

2 Video Games: The Context and the Problem

There is no question that video games are becoming more popular. In 2002, more money was spent on games-related software and hardware than at the cinema and on video rental together [Hermida 2003a]. According to the Entertainment and Leisure Software Publishers Association, there was buoyant growth in the UK computer and video games market last year, with sales of leisure software products reaching £1.26 billion, an increase of 7.1% over the previous year. However, at the same time, much of the industry is in crisis. A combination of escalating costs with an inability to charge more per game is leading to business failures worldwide [Lewis 2003]. One of the allegations often made is that the industry has lost sight of fun in the pursuit of other goals such as photorealism [Hermida 2003b]. At the Game Developers Conference in London in August 2003, Laura Fryer of the Xbox Advanced Technology Group asserted that, 'Games are still too difficult for a mass audience ... People don't focus on game play. Instead they make a beautiful game that is no fun' [Hermida 2003c].

Understanding what enables some games to be fun will provide insight into designing games that are more successful. The possible application of the concept of fun to designing other, more task-oriented software has often been discussed [for example Hassenzahl et al. 1999; Monk et al. 2002]. While we offer no evidence that the positive emotional response that can be found while playing games is the same in other types of computing (as believed for example by Malone [1980; 1982]) defining fun in gaming may offer some solutions for defining fun in computing generally.

3 Aspects of Fun

Fun is an elusive concept. Read & MacFarlane [2000] define it as "expectations, engagement and endurability", while Malone [1980] and Malone [1982] considers it to comprise challenge, fantasy and curiosity. His lack of emphasis on engagement *per se* is surprising: Dix [2003] has suggested that it is difficult to find cases of fun which are not also engaging. Certainly the kind of fun in which a game offers a special intrinsic satisfaction to the player, leading ultimately to the purchase of further games, is more than simply being amused in a detached way, or even than being 'enchanted' by a digital system [McCarthy et al. 2004]. Anecdotal accounts of the pleasures of game play, informal observation and our own experience all suggested that engagement is a vital aspect of fun. Like Draper [1999] and Knight & Jefsioutine [2003], we have borrowed from the concept of flow, described as the optimal experience [Csikszentmihalyi 1992], in which engagement is also considered to be a key characteristic. Although flow theory helped us to construct a preliminary definition of engaged game play and how it relates to fun, it is not player-centred. Pagulayan et al. [2003] make the important point that if games are by definition intended to be fun, then to assess fun is just to assess the overall quality of the game, but they also remark that it may be necessary to consider fun as being different for every user. In this respect it clearly differs from the objective criteria which can be derived from the achievement of extrinsic goals in using productivity software, being concerned instead with the player's perception of a process. We therefore wanted to find a way to assess fun from the player's perspective. In so doing we hoped to discern in games some of the design characteristics which promote or threaten the 'representational context' — the coherence and consistency of a user-experience — which Laurel identified as an important feature of engagement [Laurel 1991, pp.113-6]. This would be a step towards discerning the principal design features of games which either afford fun or militate against it.

4 Factors in Engaged Game play

We started this process by reading twenty games reviews by both professional critics and players. They spanned most genres: action, adventure, fighting, first-person-shooters, platform, puzzle, role playing games, racing, simulation, sports, etc. We looked especially for those that the reviewer related to fun. We combined the comments and complaints to form a rough set of heuristics for designing a game:

- Camera — in a 3D world, the player should be able to look wherever she wants; if she can't, there should be a logical reason why.

- Characters (not enemies) — are likeable; the player can identify with them.

- Consistency — cohesive world and behaviours; nothing seems out of place; things remain where and how the player left them.

- Controls — not too simple, not too complex.

- Dialogue — not too long or overly complex; the player should have the ability to skip past it.

- Enemies — should be intelligent and unpredictable.

- Exploration — the player should feel like she is free to go anywhere she wants; if she can't, there should be a logical explanation why.

- Game play — a variety of ways to play the game; keep game play fresh and interesting.

- Geography — the ability to create a clear mental map of the game world; the layout or geography of the world makes sense.

- Goal — clear idea of what should be done next.

- Graphics — high quality, smooth rendering.

- Help — easily accessible, not interruptive.

- Incentive — a reason for playing; advancing the story, unlocking boards, etc.

- Loading — not too long, kept at a minimum.

- Pace — not too fast, not too slow.

- Saving — the ability to easily save whenever the player wants to.

- Text — not too long or overly complex; the player should have the ability to skip past it.

- Travelling — it should not take too long to get from one place to another in the game world.

Of course, this list was just a starting point. Whether or not these heuristics would be born out by the responses of users was another issue.

5 Methods

Several methods for testing various aspects of game play are used commercially. While some of the methods are applicable to this particular research (such as usability testing, focus groups and consumer feedback) we felt that these methods, which are questionnaire-based [Fulton 2002], would not provide us with a methodology that was truly user-centred. We sought to design a methodology that allowed users to evaluate games based to some extent on their own criteria, which would emerge during the process.

The methods used were interviews, questionnaires, a modified repertory grid technique and participant observation. Interviews and questionnaires are used in commercial play testing, whereas repertory grid technique and participant observation are used little or not at all. We wanted to discover whether they had any special merits in this context.

Because one of our main objectives in this research was to design a methodology that was truly user-centred, the repertory grid technique (RGT) was chosen as the starting point. We wanted a broad but sensitive approach to the many issues that might impact on the user's engagement. As newcomers to the process of HCI evaluation we were nervous of imposing our own agenda and in doing so missing many important clues. RGT was originally created by Kelly as a qualitative method used to determine test subjects' perceptions as a means of learning more about the test subject, rather than about the world they were perceiving [Kelly 1955]. One of the principal benefits claimed for this technique is that the researcher does not impose a predefined set of constructs on the evaluation process, such as must occur when devising a set of questions for a questionnaire or interview [Fransella & Bannister 1977]. Instead, experimental subjects are offered the domain objects or elements (in our case games) and are invited to differentiate them using constructs which they themselves propose. In the traditional use, a construct elicitation session would begin by giving the test subject three similar things to compare. The test subject would be asked how the two of the three things are similar, but different from the third (Kelly believed that we make sense of our world by constantly comparing likenesses and differences). Through this comparison, bipolar constructs emerge. It is through these bipolar constructs that a grid is created. On one side of the grid are positive constructs; on the other, negative constructs. This grid then acts as the test subject's ranking system. We benefited from the work of Wessler & Ortlieb [2002] who used a form of RGT to compare the user appeal of websites, in particular from their modifications designed to make the process more efficient. We were attracted by suggestions that the method was well suited to separating valuable design ideas from those not so valuable [Hassenzahl & Wessler 2000].

Important components related to fun may be difficult for users to verbalize. As an elicitation technique, RGT has another potential advantage. It may enable subjects to make distinctions explicit that were previously only tacit [Speel et al. 1999]. Another obvious solution to the problem of verbal articulation is to use observation. Participant observation allowed us to look for particular behaviours during the play tests. Given the focus of our study, the think aloud protocol, commonly used in usability testing, was avoided, since it requires the test subject to

Negative View	-1	0	1	Positive View
cartoony			x	realistic
blocky			x	smooth
serious		x		exciting
childish			x	fun

Table 1: Fragment of traditional repertory grid, showing constructs and scores.

talk aloud while under observation [Berney 1999]. During the play test, we wanted to recreate an environment closely resembling where the test subject usually plays games. Requiring the test subject to do something that would not normally be done during their usual playtime would skew the results and disrupt the engaged elements of game play.

In summary, the schedule of each trial was:

- Short pre-test questionnaire to establish prior experience and personal details.

- Construct elicitation using modified repertory grid technique.

- One hour play test with live and video-recorded observation.

- Scoring of game played against player's own construct grid.

- Post-play questionnaire.

5.1 Modifying the Repertory Grid Technique

If using RGT to assess the appeal of the graphics in a car racing game, the test subject might be given three screen captures from three other car racing games. The test subject would be asked how the screen captures compare; how two are the same but different from the third. The test subject might say that the first and third screen captures look 'cartoony' while the second looks 'realistic'. The test subject is then asked which of the two bipolar constructs — 'realistic' or 'cartoony' — she perceives to be positive. The test subject indicates that she prefers the 'realistic' one. The two constructs are then considered as opposites and are placed into the appropriate column (positive or negative). The elicitation process continues until the test subject cannot think of any more likenesses or differences. When finished, the subject would be given a fourth screen capture — one from the game that is being evaluated. The subject would then evaluate that screen capture using the grid of constructs, typically numerically with a three-point scale -1 to 1 (see Table 1). The result is a structured description of the test subject's positive and negative views on the graphics with little interference from the researcher's assumptions.

A major drawback of the RGT is that the elicitation may take a long time. This may cause the test subject to become fatigued or bored. With such a long process, the last game played will be the freshest in the memory, which may skew the results. Or, when playing three games of the same genre, the details from the individual games may become blurred. The test subject may not want to go through the evaluation process after playing three games. A subject who comes back another day to evaluate the games may not remember details. A solution to these problems is to use a modified RGT [Wessler & Ortlieb 2002]. We discuss below whether in the process we managed to preserve some of the alleged benefits.

Our first objective was to design a methodology that would require a test subject to play only one game. This would mean that the subject would not have anything to compare for the elicitation process, so we decided to undertake the elicitation through interviewing.

The types of interview questions that were most useful to us in the construct elicitation process were: *grand tour* questions; *mini-tour* questions and example questions [Jorgensen 1989], for instance:

Q: What do you think about the graphics in Grand Theft Auto: Vice City (a video game by Rockstar Games, 2003)? (Grand tour question)

A: They're not that great, but the rest of the game makes up for it.

Q: What do you mean by 'not great'? (Mini-tour question)

A: The graphics are blocky and the textures are not detailed.

Q: Can you give me an example of that from the game? (Example question)

A: The characters look a bit square — especially in the head and shoulders and the textures on the buildings are blurry, but you can't really tell when you're driving around.

Another type of question we found useful was the experience question:

Q: How did you feel about the puzzles in Eternal Darkness (a video game by Silicon Knights, 2002)?

A: A lot of it was repetitive seek-and-find type of puzzles ... But some of it didn't make sense because you'd have to enchant something for key to appear and it would seem very random. It was OK at first, but the randomness became really frustrating and I lost interest about midway through the game.

We aimed to devise questions that would facilitate answers about certain aspects of games design without excessively leading the test subject. We referred to our original list of design concepts taken from the games reviews and began to construct questions that were intended to cause the test subject to discuss the concepts on that list. The questions were general:

- What qualities should the main character have in a game?

- What makes a good story for a game?

- What kind of sound should be used in a game?

- What qualities should the graphics have in a game?

- What characteristics should an enemy or opponent have in a game?

- What should the interface in a game be like? (The interface can be menus, start and save screens, maps, etc.)

Negative View	-2	-1	0	1	2	Positive View
loony lonely child						clever has friends grown up

Table 2: Fragment of the repertory grid used, showing constructs.

- What sort of environment is best for playing games?

- What characteristics should a game controller have?

The last two questions were meant to investigate how much the physical interaction and environment affected the test subject. We considered these questions to be tentative because physical interaction was not the focus of this research. There were two last questions that we included for the sake of experimentation. They were:

- What makes a game good?

- What makes a game fun?

These questions were meant to elicit ideas the test subject had about games design and as a way to evaluate the test subject's expectations. The answers to these questions went into the 'positive view' column on the grid. To fill the 'negative view' column of the grid, we went back through the questions with the test subject, read back the answers given and asked for their opposites (see Table 2).

At first this worked only poorly because the test subject was inclined to give a simple linguistic opposite to what had been said in the first place, instead of thinking about it. A test subject asked, 'What makes a good story for a game?' might say, 'It should be exciting.' When going back through, a simple opposite would be given — 'boring'. While this is a valid answer, we wanted a method that would challenge the test subject to be critical. We changed the method, rewording the question the second time around, so the question would itself be opposed to the original. If the first question was, 'What kind of sound should be used in a game?' the second time around the question would be, 'What kind of sound shouldn't be used in a game?' This produced more thoughtful answers. After all of the questions were answered, we reviewed them with the test subjects. Once the interview was complete, test subjects had made their own grid of positives and negatives of games design elements.

We used a combination of a formal and informal interview style. While the main questions remained the same for every test subject, we questioned further or asked for an example when we wanted a test subject to expand. This was different in every test subject's case. For example, when we asked, 'What qualities should the main character in a game have?' the answer may have been, 'Smart and strong.' However, if the answer was, 'I should like them,' we would probe further with a question like, 'What would the character have to be like for you to like them?'

While the interview was being conducted, we wrote the elicited constructs in the appropriate place in the grid. Each question had its own grid so that the test subject would not become confused when it was time to rate the game.

The modified RGT produces both quantitative and qualitative results, discussed below.

5.2 Participant Observation

During initial trial play tests, we noticed that the test subjects behaved in similar and specific ways while playing the games. We wondered if this sort of physical reaction was linked to engagement and fun, and began to experiment with participant observation [Jorgensen 1989; Oates 2000]. We observed the frequency of particular behaviours that seemed to be related to playing the game, and their duration. Preliminary findings are discussed below.

5.3 Post-play Questionnaire

At the conclusion of each play testing session, the subjects were also asked to complete a conventional questionnaire using a 5-point Likert scale. It included such questions as:

- The pace of the game is appropriate.

- The controls for the game confused me.

- I understood the goal of this game.

- There were parts of the game that didn't make sense.

- I like my character in the game.

- If I were interrupted while playing the game, I would have been annoyed.

5.4 The Test Subjects

Since we believed that engaged game play was not a concept exclusive to any specific type of gaming community, age group or gender, we required test subjects who varied in gaming skill level, age and gender. Another requirement was that test subjects should not previously have played the game we were testing. Advertising on our University's internal email system, we hoped to attract test subjects interested in playing the stated game. We did not have enough resources to be as selective as we should have been — we would have liked to have test subjects who normally play sports games to only test sports games, RPG players to test RPGs, etc. Some test subjects did not like the genre of the game we were testing; some of these ended up not liking the game, while some changed their mind. We would have preferred this aspect of the test subject recruitment to be more controlled.

In all, we ended up with twenty-seven play test subjects who went through the entire test (this is exclusive of some early trial play tests conducted prior to confirming our methodology). They ranged in age from eight to forty, both men and women. The number of men who volunteered greatly outnumbered women, by nearly nine to one. The test subjects were diverse in their preference of game genres and games titles and in their skill levels.

5.5   The Testing Environment

All of the testing took place in a basic usability lab at Middlesex University's Lansdown Centre for Electronic Arts. Using three cameras and a video feed, the usability lab can provide four different views of the play test: the display on the TV monitor, a view focusing on the play test subject's hands, a general view of the subject and a close-up view of the subject's face. Each of these different cameras can be viewed individually or all four at once, split-screen, and can be recorded to tape with sound recorded from a single microphone.

As this usability lab was designed for evaluating functional usability and not for the evaluation of fun or engaged game play, there were some problems from its use, not least that it looked and felt like a lab. This conflicted with our wish to evaluate engaged game play in a way that closely resembled what would occur in a player's normal gaming environment. This requires attention for future work.

Other weaknesses included that the usability lab was not very comfortable: subjects sat in a standard office chair. Also, the lab was not sound-proofed against its surroundings. While noise interruptions could be expected in a player's normal gaming environment, we would have preferred to control this aspect so that each play test would be standardized.

The interviewer was in the same room as the play test subject. While this was sensible for observational purposes, it enticed some test subjects to speak while playing and ask for game hints instead of attempting to work out the game puzzles on their own. Again, this may be expected in a player's normal gaming environment, especially when friends are playing games socially, but we would have liked to keep the test standardized.

5.6   The Play Test

While the test subject filled out the questionnaire and form, we offered to get them a (non-alcoholic) drink. Their having a drink would allow us to observe when the test subject found it suitable, during the game, to put down the controller and take a drink. About half of the test subjects accepted the invitation to a drink. Along the same lines, we left the manual out for the game that was play tested to observe when, and under what circumstances, the test subject would look through it. These actions were used as indicators of partial disengagement.

When the test subject was finished with the pre-gaming questionnaire and release form, we began the interview/elicitation process. As the interview progressed, we wrote down the test subject's answers in the labelled grids, which had been pre-printed.

When the interview/elicitation process was over, it was time for the test subject to play the game. Test subjects were not told how long they would be playing, but rather that they would be completing one level of the game. We wanted to discover how much their awareness of time might be suppressed by the sought-after engagement.

While playing, the test subject was observed. We took note of any behaviour that stood out. We also answered questions when asked.

5.7   The Games

The two games that were play tested were *Legend of Zelda: The Wind Waker* (a video game by Ninetendo, 2003) and *Animal Crossing* (a video game by Nintendo, 2002). We chose these two games because they are very different in game play. The graphics are similar, rather childish and cartoony in both cases. Wind Waker is an adventure/role-playing game with clearly defined goals, tasks and enemies. The game is narrative-driven. The graphics are impressive; everything is rendered very smoothly and there is a great attention to detail. Animal Crossing is more of a simulator. The player takes on the life of a character, engaging in life's menial tasks: buying and paying off a house, fishing, gardening and interacting with other characters. There is no narrative or set path. It is completely up to the player which tasks to participate in. There are no enemies or fighting and, aside from paying off the mortgage, there are no defined goals. Animal Crossing's graphics are more minimal. There is little detail in the textures, and the shapes are rendered with a low polygon count.

We wanted to test games with two very different types of game play to see how test subjects' ratings differed between the two. We also thought that the difference in graphical sophistication would give some insight into how test subjects perceived graphics in relation to game play. Since both games had a childish feel (although neither are strictly aimed at children), a comparison between juvenile and adult games was not evaluated.

6   Quantitative Results

There were twenty-seven play test subjects in all, the average age being twenty. Only three of the twenty-seven subjects were female. On average, the test subjects played games five times a week and had been playing video games for six years. Nineteen subjects normally played on a PC and fifteen on PlayStation 2. Only four were familiar with Nintendo's GameCube on which the play tests were conducted.

Eight of the subjects each played the game Animal Crossing for approximately an hour. During the construct elicitation process, 151 constructs were generated. Against their own constructs each subject rated the game, immediately on completion, on a scale of -2 (worst) through 0 (neutral) to 2 (best). The mean score across constructs was 0.53.

Nineteen subjects each played Wind Waker. During the construct elicitation process, 293 constructs were generated. Against their own constructs each subject rated the game as just described. The mean score across constructs was 0.79.

In the conventional questionnaire, with eight subject scoring nineteen statements on a similar five-point scale, Animal Crossing scored 0.54. Wind Waker with nineteen subjects scored 0.71.

It can be seen when the results from the two forms of evaluation are compared, that the mean scores from the modified RGT are very similar to those from the conventional post-play questionnaire. This raises an issue of cost-effectiveness. For each subject, using both methods together, 10 minutes was spent on a standard pre-questionnaire and introduction; 30 minutes on elicitation of constructs; 60 minutes on game playing; 10 minutes on evaluation against the constructs and 10 minutes on the final questionnaire; total 2 hours. The increased time in using RGT alone over using a conventional questionnaire alone was thus 30 minutes per subject. The results suggest that the less expensive conventional technique is equally effective as an overall measure of quality. However, that is not our main goal, which is rather to provide the designer with a full understanding of those qualities in a game which will cause the user to perceive it as fun. For this purpose the more lengthy and expensive repertory grid elicitation is better suited. The benefits of using RGT lie in the elicitation of detailed issues for further attention, rather than in quantitative overall evaluation of game play.

7 Qualitative Results

The constructs offer interesting oppositions. For example, of the main character it was felt by one subject that *no presence* (a negative) was in opposition to *not too realistic and not too cartoony* (a positive). Another view was that the character should not be *strong in the beginning* but should be *weak in the beginning, getting stronger*.

Of course, by their nature, these constructs are the products of a single individual's responses. This has some value in its own right, reminding us that there is no such thing as 'the user' but a multitude of different individuals; but it may also happen that an individual articulates a view which turns out to be more widespread. Some constructs clustered naturally in apparent consensus. For example, the ideas of coherence and consistency recurred often. For one player, the worst characteristic of an interface was *doesn't make sense* while the best was that *the way it is accessed fits the game play*. *Appropriateness* to the game was a positive construct that appeared several times in relation to graphics, character, sound and music.

Complexity was also valued in many constructs, with positive features listed such as (for the main character) *has a lot of moves and you can build them up*. For the story, similar positives included *not too obvious or too simple, complicated, ambiguity, plot twists, mystery, complex plot, has depth, characters are complex* and so forth. Subjects created the polarities in their constructs shown in Table 3.

In relation to realism some interesting things were said. The opposition of *no presence to not too realistic and not too cartoony* has already been noted. *Graphics show off, gets in way of game* was noted as a negative. For another player also *graphics are the point of the game* was a negative while *graphics do not matter* was positive. On the other hand, there were also several examples of a more conventional attitude to realism, the most frank being: *doesn't look real* (negative) vs. *looks real* (positive). Further use of modified RGT may enable us to get a better grip on what exactly a player means by a term such as *realistic*.

7.1 Insights from Participant Observation

Whereas modified RGT is intended to capture as directly as possible internal states of the player, participant observation was adopted to identify states of the world. The use of such a technique has a different motivation when evaluating *fun* than in looking at some other kinds of systems. Whereas in the task-oriented testing of a functional system the state of the world is in itself significant (for example the user

	Negative (aspects of games design)	Positive (aspects of game design)
Main Character	loony	clever
	does not give player options when talking	someone you can identify with
	does not respond no sense of humour	normal interaction with environment
	no sense of humour	is funny
Story	mystical	true life
	straight-forward narrative	different narrative structure
	morally black and white	ambiguity
	contradictive	consistent
Sound	limited sound effects	range of sounds to complement character
	same commentary over and over	varied
	evil music for no reason	cheery music on a level, evil music for a boss
	music is repetitive	music is complementary
Graphics	doesn't look real	looks real
	graphics are the point of the game	graphics do not matter
	can't see what is important	shows things that are important
	graphics show off, gets in way of game	style appropriate to the game
Enemy	normal person	evil, bad
	has no reason to be the enemy	has a reason for being an enemy
	stereotypical	has some of the same qualities as you undefined in the beginning
	constant reminder of the enemy throughout	builds up
Interface	doesn't have music	has music
	tiny map	map can be zoomed in and out
	too many menus	inventive
	cannot change the settings	changeable settings
Environment	sitting on the floor	chair
	noisy / public	single player / dark room
	interruptions	game must be the centre of the space
	too many people around	quiet
Controller	must take hands off to press something	easy to hold
	must stretch thumbs	buttons are under thumbs
	doesn't use conventions	uses button conventions
	extra buttons	know what controls are before the game begins
Good	not real	real
	simple, repetitive story	pulls you into a good story
	limited exploration	freedom
	set route, linear story	choices in the story
Fun	nothing to do	mission objectives
	you must read manual before you play	instant playability
	can't set your own pace	have time to get to know your character / town
	no interaction with other characters	interaction with other characters

Table 3: Sample of elicited constructs for each question asked.

fails to complete a particular task on the task list) in our case we were using player behaviour as an index of engagement. Although our participant observation has not yet been resolved into a coding scheme, the play test subjects' behaviour during the sessions tended to be revealing.

Before each testing session we asked test subjects if they wanted something to drink. This was to provide an intentional distraction. Since all the drinks were bottled, two hands were needs to unscrew the top — this meant that the test subject would have to put the controller down to take a drink. During the testing sessions, we took note of when the test subject did this. During the use of Wind Waker nearly all the test subjects who had a drink put the controller down during dialogue from the characters or the long introduction to the narrative, both of which are text on screen. Those who did not have a drink often browsed through the manual. In all, 16 of the 27 play test subjects put down the controller at least once during the course of the game, without pausing the game first.

Another widely observed behaviour was the repeated pressing of the A button on the GameCube controller throughout the large amounts of text during dialogue or the long introduction sequence. The A button on the GameCube controller is the main action button. Pressing it while text is on screen in Wind Waker does not in fact allow the player to skip the text or make it go faster. Even though this soon becomes obvious to the player, test subjects continually pressed the A button anyway. Nearly all the subjects who played Wind Waker did this, especially during the opening sequence, which is three minutes and forty seconds long. Some subjects settled for browsing the manual or drinking when they finally gave up hope of the A button working.

Clearly the main problem with the introduction sequence to this game is that players cannot read the screens at their own pace. This in turn causes another problem. In this game there are often useful directions, clues and hints in the text dialogue. With many test subjects becoming bored with large amounts of text, useful information was overlooked because the subject was not paying attention. This resulted in the test subject often becoming stuck or not knowing what to do next. When important directions are mixed in large amounts of text, they tend to be disregarded and the player becomes frustrated too early in the game by a simple task.

8 Discussion of Techniques

In this study it seems that the expensive user-centred evaluation offered by the modified repertory grid technique produces the same overall score for the fun qualities of a game as does the traditional method of a simple questionnaire. However, we are as interested in seeing better games designed as we are in summative evaluation. This is where the benefits of the modified repertory grid technique appear to lie. Whereas a score for a simple questionnaire may yield clues to gross misjudgements in the design which can then be avoided, such a questionnaire is too blunt an instrument to offer specific solutions — in the sense of showing how the fun or engagement factor of the game play can be enhanced.

Rich findings such as those emerging from the modified RGT may be helpful in pointing to characteristics that players want. Using a personal construct elicitation technique, ideas are uttered by players which we suspect would not emerge under another method, because it invites a form of structured introspection which may not otherwise occur. Considered just as an elicitation technique therefore, even this attenuated form of RGT seems to offer some of the benefits of its original, in particular in separating valuable design ideas from those not so valuable and highlighting patterns of user likes and dislikes.

In the full results, one can discern how problematic much evaluative language is. Terms, such as *realism* or *complex*, are seen to b very much contingent on their context. The modified RGT helps to discern what test subjects 'really' mean, by capturing the oppositions they make between these terms and others.

Further benefit from the modified RGT is likely to emerge when its results are more closely tied to other techniques used in conjunction, especially participant observation. Participant observation offers some insight into what the participants are feeling or thinking during game play. This is especially important because some feelings are unconscious or not easily expressed by the participant and would not therefore be expressed even during the RGT elicitation process.

Other work has been done in the area of fun and games design. Other research discusses ways to design games to maximize fun, but we believe none of them defines fun richly though the users' experience in a way which will assist the developer.

9 Further Work

This study has created a full agenda of enquiries which seem worth pursuing. Since our goal with this research is to produce a set of truly user-centred guidelines for designing fun video games, it has been necessary to establish a play testing methodology that focuses on fun. Refining our methodology will help ensure the final guidelines are reliable, but in addition we hope it will produce detailed results valuable to games developers throughout the design process.

Having compared the mean overall scores from modified RGT and conventional questionnaire for two games, we need to repeat the exercise for other games to see if the closeness of the results is repeated.

While the modified RGT offered insights into specific aspects of each game, it would be productive, after the play test is finished and the test subject has completed the repertory grid, to go back through the videoed record of the play test and discuss the specific elements of the games design and game play that were rated both positively and negatively on the play test subject's grid. In the participant observation, many test subjects looked at the manual to pass time during pauses in the game play. Why, specifically, were they looking? While we can infer it was out of boredom, a video review of the play test with the subject would be useful to discover more. Thus the results of one test method become an elicitation tool for another.

With more test subjects, it will also be revealing to map patterns of constructs to player type. Categories of player have been noted to behave differently during the play test: this requires further investigation. Children are the most expressive; they talk aloud when they play and sit up in their chairs during action and fighting sequences. With a larger sample size, an appropriate coding scheme will be devised which might eventually be put to quantitative use.

In addition, the application of such techniques to other gaming platforms including mobiles can be considered. This is not simply a practical difference: *what* is being captured may be as different as *how*. Can engaged game play exist while riding the bus to work or in a busy café? Will multi-player gaming need the same guidelines for engaged game play as single player gaming? Is there a difference in engaged game play if the players are in the same room or across a network?

References

Berney, J. W. [1999], Human Factors and Usability in User Interface Design, http://www.usability.com/umi_amfm.htm. The Usability Group LLC.

Csikszentmihalyi, M. [1992], *Flow — The Psychology of Happiness*, Rider Publishing.

Dix, A. [2003], Being Playful — Learning from Children, *in* S. MacFarlane, T. Nicol, J. Read & L. Snape (eds.), *Small Users — Big Ideas: Proceedings of Interaction Design and Children 2003 (IDC 2003)*, ACM Press, pp.3–9.

Draper, S. W. [1999], Analysing Fun as a Candidate Software Requirement, *Personal Technologies* 3(3), 117–22.

Fransella, F. & Bannister, D. [1977], *A Manual for Repertory Grid Technique*, John Wiley & Sons.

Fulton, B. [2002], 'Beyond Psychological Theory: Getting Data that Improve Games, *in Proceedings of the Game Developer's Conference 2002*, CMP Media. Available at http://download.microsoft.com/download/3/3/c/33c82055-c4bc-4354-bb1b-24358a950937/mgsut_F02.doc.doc.

Hassenzahl, M., Burmester, M. & Sandweg, N. [1999], Perceived Novelty of Functions — A Source of Hedonic Quality, http://www-users.york.ac.uk/~am1/C&F2abs.PDF. Paper presented at the Computers and Fun Meeting of British HCI Group, York University, 1999.

Hassenzahl, M. & Wessler, R. [2000], Capturing Design Space From a User Perspective: The Repertory Grid Technique Revisited, *International Journal of Human–Computer Interaction* 12(3), 441–59.

Hermida, A. [2003a], Britons' Love Affair with Games, BBC News Online, http://news.bbc.co.uk/1/hi/technology/3188873.stm.

Hermida, A. [2003b], Game Graphics Hit Their Limits, BBC News Online, http://news.bbc.co.uk/1/hi/technology/3189537.stm.

Hermida, A. [2003c], Games Suffer from 'Geek Stereotype', BBC News Online, http://news.bbc.co.uk/1/hi/technology/3197911.stm.

Jorgensen, D. L. [1989], *Participant Observation: A Methodology for Human Studies*, Sage Publications.

Kelly, G. A. [1955], *The Psychology of Personal Constructs*, Norton Publishing.

Knight, J. & Jefsioutine, M. [2003], 'The Experience Design Framework: From Pleasure to Engagability, http://www.hiraeth.com/conf/HCI-arts-humanities-2003/papers.html. Position Paper for the workshop 'HCI, the Arts and the Humanities' held at York University.

Laurel, B. [1991], *Computers as Theatre*, Addison–Wesley.

Lewis, L. [2003], Merger Game Played to Rising Degree of Difficulty, Times Online, http://www.timesonline.co.uk/article/0,,5-650669,00.html.

Malone, T. [1982], Heuristics for Designing Enjoyable User Interfaces: Lessons from Computer Games, *in* J. A. Nichols & M. L. Schneider (eds.), *Proceedings of the 1982 Conference on Human Factors in Computing Systems (CHI'82)*, ACM Press, pp.63–8.

Malone, T. W. [1980], What Makes Things Fun to Learn? Heuristics for Designing Instructional Computer Games, *in* P. Lehot, L. Loop & G. W. Gorsline (eds.), *Proceedings of the 3rd ACM SIGSMALL Symposium / 1st SIGPC Symposium on Small Systems*, ACM Press, pp.162–9.

McCarthy, J., Wright, P., Wallace, J. & Dearden, A. [2004], The Experience of Enchantment in Human-Computer Interaction, http://www.shu.ac.uk/schools/cs/cri/adrc/research2/enchantment.pdf.

Monk, A., Hassenzahl, M., Blythe, M. & Reed, D. [2002], Funology: Designing Enjoyment, *ACM SIGCHI Bulletin A Supplement to* interactions p.11.

Oates, J. [2000], fOCUS, CD-ROM, Open University and BBC.

Pagulayan, R. J., Keeker, K., Wixon, D., Romero, R. L. & Fuller, T. [2003], User-centered Design in Games, *in* J. A. Jacko & A. Sears (eds.), *The Human–Computer Interaction Handbook: Fundamentals Evolving Technologies and Emerging Applications*, Lawrence Erlbaum Associates, pp.883–906.

Read, J. C. & MacFarlane, S. J. [2000], Measuring Fun — Usability Testing for Children, *Interfaces* **46**, 6–7. Paper presented at the "Computers and Fun 3" Workshop. See also http://www-users.york.ac.uk/~am1/C&F3abs.PDF.

Speel, P.-H., Shadbolt, N., de Vries, W., van Dam, P. H. & O'Hara, K. [1999], Knowledge Mapping for Industrial Purposes, *in Proceedings of the 12th Workshop on Knowledge Acquisition Modeling and Management*. Available at http://sern.ucalgary.ca/KSI/KAW/KAW99/papers/Speel1/index.html.

Wessler, R. & Ortlieb, M. [2002], A User Centred Approach to Measuring a Web Site's Appeal Using the Repertory Grid Technique, *in* H. Sharp, P. Chalk, J. LePeuple & J. Rosbottom (eds.), *Proceedings of HCI'02: Volume 2*, British Computer Society, pp.70–8. Paper presented at EUPA 2002 the proceedings of which are included in the HCI 2002 conference proceedings.

Cradle to Grave

The Usability of Handwriting Recognition for Writing in the Primary Classroom

Janet C Read, Stuart MacFarlane & Matthew Horton

Child Computer Interaction Group, University of Central Lancashire, Preston PR1 2HE, UK

Tel: *+44 1772 893285*

Fax: *+44 1772 894913*

Email: *jcread@uclan.ac.uk*

URL: *http://www.chici.org*

This paper describes an empirical study with children that compared the three methods of writing — using pencil and paper, using the QWERTY keyboard at a computer, and using a pen and graphics tablet. The children wrote short stories. Where the graphics tablet was used, the text was recognized and presented to the children as ASCII text. Measures of user satisfaction, quantity of writing produced, and quality of writing produced were taken. In addition, the recognition process was evaluated by comparing what the child wrote with the resulting ASCII text. The results show that for the age group considered, writing at the tablet was as efficient as, and produced comparable writing to, the pencil and paper. The keyboard was less efficient. Key usability problems with the handwriting recognition interface are identified and classified, and we propose some solutions in the form of design guidelines for both recognition-based and pen-based computer writing interfaces.

Keywords: handwriting recognition, usability, text entry, writing, pen computers, children, education.

1 Introduction

This paper presents results from a classroom study to compare three methods of writing with children aged 7 and 8. This experiment is part of a larger investigation that was motivated by a desire to establish whether young children could use handwriting recognition technology, and to identify key usability problems. The context of the work reported in this paper is that of free writing (composition) in the classroom with children aged 7–10.

Children spend between 30% and 60% of their school classroom time doing writing activities [McHale & Cermak 1992]. Most of this involves composition work where the child writes down his or her own words in response to some stimulus. Written work is often revised both during and after the initial draft. These revisions include spelling changes, the insertion of missed words, and sometimes, rearrangements of phrases. It is usual for children to limit themselves to revisions that will not 'mess up' their work too much. As the process is difficult, it can sometimes happen that a child begins a correction, only to forget what he was going to write by the time he has finished with the eraser [Swanson & Berninger 1996].

The word processor was designed for revising and manipulating language and so it would appear to have a useful role in written language improvement. Several studies have shown that the use of a word processor can assist in developing written language skills [Sturm 1988; Newell et al. 1992]. A study by Kurth [1987] suggested that, although the use of a computer did not always improve the literal quality of children's writing, the high visibility of text on the screen fostered more conversation about the writing, and the spelling was improved. Papert [1980] suggests that a computer with word processing software affords the child the luxury of being able to revise and rework their ideas, and therefore becomes a powerful intellectual product.

Children in school are encouraged to use word processors to produce electronic text. However, access to the software is traditionally via a QWERTY keyboard, which novices find difficult to master. Hermann [1987] suggested that handling the keyboard interferes with the writing process, and if this is the case, then the use of more natural interfaces, such as speech and handwriting recognition, may be desirable. The affordability of graphics tablets and pens, and the development of the tablet PC, make handwritten input to the computer a feasible alternative to the QWERTY keyboard.

We begin with a brief summary of research into the usability of handwriting recognition for text input, and specifically into its usability with children. We then describe an empirical study that compares writing outputs from the three methods of pencil and paper, handwriting recognition and keyboard. In the following section we look at recognition rates for both copied and composed text and use this information, together with observations from previous work to derive a list of usability problems and solutions for handwriting recognition technology.

2 Background

Handwriting recognition is the automated process of turning handwritten work into a computer readable form. There are two different technologies, one for off-line recognition and one for on-line recognition. In off-line recognition, the writing is initially captured using traditional means (on standard paper) and is then digitized by scanning technology or by photographic capture; this results in a bitmap or vector image of the writing. The work reported in this paper concerns on-line recognition.

Here, the user's writing is digitally captured at the point of creation; this is generally done with a graphics tablet or tablet PC and a special stylus or pen. The user's writing is initially displayed as script and is stored as an 'ink' data type. This data type contains information about position and time, and it is this data that is subsequently 'recognized' by the recognition algorithms. This process results in a stream of ASCII characters that is displayed on the screen and is hereinafter referred to as 'transcribed text'. It is common for this text to include errors, as the recognition algorithms generally have to make sense of incomplete or 'noisy' script. Users are likely to include dashes and flourishes and some of their characters will be badly formed.

Research into the usability of handwriting recognition interfaces for text entry tends to focus on the rates of recognition achieved by the human-computer interface and on the elimination or reduction of recognition errors [Read et al. 2001; Frankish et al. 1995; MacKenzie & Chang 1999]. In a handwriting recognition interface, both the user and the system can initiate errors. There have been some guidelines drawn up for the design of recognition based interfaces; these include minimizing the incidence of errors, maximizing their discovery and making recovery easy [Norman 1981; Lewis & Norman 1986; Mankoff & Abowd 1999]. Improving the recognition algorithms, constraining the system, and constraining the user can all reduce the number of recognition errors that occur [Plamondon & Srihari 2000; Tappert et al. 1990]. Constraining methods include limiting the vocabulary, making the user write in boxes, using a reduced alphabet, or using discrete (non-cursive) writing [Frankish 1999; Goldberg & Goodisman 1991; Mankoff 2000; Noyes 2001].

Text input methods are normally evaluated by focusing on the three usability measures of efficiency, effectiveness and user satisfaction [MacKenzie & Soukoreff 2002b]. Efficiency is typically measured by counting the number of characters entered per second and effectiveness is measured by making comparisons between two strings, these being the presented text (that which was intended to be written) and the transcribed text (that which was produced) [MacKenzie & Soukoreff 2002a]. For handwriting recognition a CER (Character Error Rate) is derived which is the ratio of the number of errors to the number of characters in the presented text. There have been some longitudinal studies on text input that consider the effect of training and learning [MacKenzie & Chang 1999; Card et al. 1978].

Children develop their handwriting skills in a developmental way with factors such as size, quantity, proportion and spacing all improving with age. Handwriting competence is measured by the legibility of the resulting work and the attainment of a reasonable speed. People are often judged by their handwriting, and it is not unusual for a child with poor handwriting to develop a poor self-image [Sassoon 1990].

Handwriting may be 'joined up' (cursive) or it can be 'printed' (discrete). It has traditionally been the case that English schoolchildren learn to write using discrete writing, and then move onto cursive writing at around age eight or nine. There is considerable support in the research community for a change to this pattern, with researchers suggesting that children should use cursive script at a much younger age. Peters' [1985] view is that children should learn cursive writing as early as possible in the school curriculum, because:

- It results in children understanding the concept of a word at an earlier age.

- It results in better letter formation.

- Children don't have to 'adapt' at age eight.

- The movements involved in cursive writing produce better spelling.

This last claim is particularly interesting; Peters claims that *'quality of handwriting is highly correlated with spelling attainment'*, a relationship supported by others including Bearne [1998], who relates the connection between handwriting and spelling to kinaesthetic memory.

We have published on the use of handwriting recognition for text input by children [Read et al. 2002a, 2003a]. This earlier work focused on the general usability of the technology and its usefulness to support the writing process. How children deal with and recover from errors, how the technology compares to other text input methods and the mental models that children have of recognition technology have all been reported [Read et al. 2001, 2002c, 2003b].

3 The Empirical Study

The empirical study reported in this paper was designed to determine the relative usability of handwriting recognition for extended writing, compared with the two more traditional methods of pencil and paper, and keyboarding. It was hypothesized that children would prefer to use the pen and tablet and that it would result in more writing being done than at the keyboard. An earlier study reported by Read et al. [2001] compared mouse, speech and keyboard input with handwriting and concluded that children found the handwriting recognition interface satisfying, and that it compared favourably with the keyboard in terms of efficiency. This earlier study used very short samples of writing and it was not possible to make any judgements about quality.

3.1 Design of the Experiment

Earlier work by the authors had established that a short training session with the handwriting recognition interface produced much better recognition rates. Training for the pencil and paper was considered unnecessary, but it was felt to be important to check familiarity with the keyboard and so a simple task was prepared which established whether the children could find and use the space bar, the full stop and capitalization. For those who had problems, guidance was given.

3.1.1 Design of the Handwriting Recognition Training Interface

This interface presented text in a single line at the bottom of the screen for the children to copy. An alternative to presenting the text visually would have been to present the text in audio, via headphones or loudspeaker. This was considered to be a bad idea as the children using the technology would be unlikely to be able to spell the words fluently and this would cause errors, and increase the children's anxiety.

It was decided to use three phrases in the training, on the assumption that the first would be badly recognized, the second would be significantly better and a third would act as an insurance against spurious results for the first and second. From the third phrase a 'recognition rate' would be derived that could be used in the analysis of the results. Using three phrases also allowed the identification of repeated poorly formed letters. There were two possible approaches to the design of the text to be copied. One was to use the same phrase three times; the other was to provide similar but different phrases. In earlier work, the latter approach was taken as it reduced the effect of familiarity and boredom, and allowed for a meaningful activity; however, for this experiment it was decided to use one repeated phrase as it was considered that this would help the child see what was happening and help construct a more useful mental model. As the child was only writing three phrases (as opposed to ten in the earlier study) boredom was seen to be less of a problem. Additionally, there was a meaningful activity following this training exercise; this had not been a feature of the earlier work.

The training text to be copied was **'a big dog climbed down the tree'**. It comprised 25 characters and 6 spaces. The writing fitted on one line on the computer screen in a large font.

There were a number of ways in which the recognized text could be presented to the children. Errors could have been highlighted by the use of wiggly lines under the text as is common in many word processing applications. It was also possible to extract confidence scores for each recognized character, and these could have been displayed or interpreted to give the child some clues about difficult recognitions. These two methods were not used as it was felt that they may cause too much anxiety for the children and they did not necessarily reflect the real world task.

3.1.2   Design of the Writing Task

The recognition software had a dictionary that could be turned on or off. The dictionary is used during the recognition process to allow for word matching — this can result in better recognition rates, although its usefulness with children, who may use non-standard spellings, is less obvious. We decided that, as the dictionary was likely to be present in most applications, having it turned on was the most appropriate model for this work.

Children were given a writing task in line with normal English primary school activities. Each task had a stimulus and an activity. The children were given 12 minutes to write, and they were warned when they had 2 minutes remaining in case they wanted to edit their work. Spell checking of the final text was not enabled in either the recognition-based application or on the keyboard; this meant that if a word was spelt incorrectly but was accurately recognized, the child would not see an error. Children writing by pencil and paper were also not given spelling support.

It is common for children to make errors when they write. These are sometimes discovered during the writing activity, and sometimes noticed later. In all three writing methods, children were given the opportunity to correct errors.

3.1.3   Subjects

Eighteen children aged between 7 and 8 were recruited from an English Primary (age 5–11) School in Lancashire. The class teacher selected the children, choosing a mixed sample of abilities and gender, but each child came to the test as a volunteer

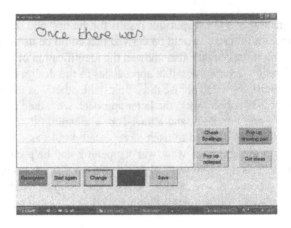

Figure 1: The Writing Interface.

and was given the opportunity to leave the research activity both before and during the work. All the children had English as their first language and none had used handwriting recognition-based technology, or the pen and tablet before. There were seven boys and eleven girls; two of the children were left-handed.

3.1.4   Apparatus

Three story stimuli were prepared with assistance from the class teacher. These were identified as S1, S2 and S3. Each child taking part in the experiment was identified by a code (C1–C18) and the input modalities were identified as P, K, and T (for pencil and paper, keyboard and tablet).

For the handwriting application, an experimental interface (Figure 1) was constructed using Visual Basic 6 and the Calligrapher recognition engine. This was presented to the children on a standard laptop that had a Wacom graphics tablet attached to it.

The children used the pen that was supplied with the tablet to construct their writing. Prior to beginning the experiment, children had the equipment explained to them. They then carried out the training activity as described above.

The keyboard interface comprised a regular word processing package with a standard QWERTY keyboard. The font size was preset to 14 and the spell checking and grammar checking was disabled. Prior to doing the experiment children were asked to type a short phrase to ensure that they could use capitals, the space control and punctuation.

The pencil and paper interface comprised a pencil, a piece of lined paper and an eraser. No training was given!

3.1.5   Procedure

The design was within-subjects single factor with three conditions: writing using paper, writing at the keyboard, and writing with the tablet. A 3×3 Latin Square was used to determine the order in which children did the three activities, and within this

Figure 2: Smileyometer used to record children's opinions.

a further 3×3 square was used to determine which of the three writing stimuli each child used.

Children attended the study in groups of three, with each child being directed to one of the three input methods on entering the room. This meant that each cluster of three children had the same experience with regard to the story stimulus and the environmental conditions. The room that was used was a storeroom with a large table in the centre of it and the children sat on three sides with the two researchers seated between them. On entering the room, each child was asked to indicate on a smileyometer (Figure 2) [Read et al. 2002b] how good they thought the activity to which they had been directed was going to be. The rationale for this was that this gave a measure of expectation that could indicate whether or not the child was subsequently let down by the activity, or pleasantly surprised.

Following any training, the three children were presented with one of the writing stimuli, and then given ten minutes to write their story. After ten minutes, they were told to stop and given the opportunity to edit their work if they wanted to. They were then asked to rate the input modality for user satisfaction using a new smileyometer to give a rating for 'actual' experience.

For each activity, measurements were taken of:

- Quality of the writing (Teacher assessed).

- Quantity of the writing (Word count).

After the children had done all three input modes, they were asked to assess the relative user experience with the three modalities. Two other tools that have been developed by the authors, a fun sorter and an again-again table [Read et al. 2002b] were used for this. The fun sorter required the children to rank the three writing methods in order of preference, and the again-again table invited them to indicate whether or not they would like to use each method again. This was presented to the children on a single sheet, and was given out a week after the study.

3.2 Results of the Study

The class teacher measured the quality of the writing; the results can be seen in Table 1. All the stories were collected, and made anonymous in such a way that the teacher did not know what method had been used for the writing, nor which child had done the work. Initially, each piece of text was awarded a grade of 1, 2c, 2b, 2a or 3c (as used in the National Literacy Strategy [DfEE 1988]) and these were then converted to numbers between 1 and 5 where 5 represented a piece of work

	Mean	Standard Deviation
Tablet	3.0	1.0
Keyboard	2.9	1.1
Paper	3.7	1.2

Table 1: Quality of writing.

	Mean	Standard Deviation
Tablet	58.8	25.5
Keyboard	44.0	24.7
Paper	72.6	38.1

Table 2: Quantity of writing.

at Level 3c. Nationally children of the age under investigation were expected to be working at a Level 2b, i.e. a score of 3.

The quantity of writing (Table 2) was measured using a word count. This was generated automatically using the tool in Microsoft Word.

The results from the two smileyometers were converted into numbers between 1 and 5 where 1 represented the choice 'awful' and 5 represented the choice 'brilliant'. These were averaged across the children and the resulting scores, for both the expected fun and the actual fun, are shown in Table 3.

A week after the event, each child completed the short pictorial questionnaire that comprised the fun sorter and the again-again table. The results from these are summarized in Table 4.

4   Discussion of the Results

4.1   Quality of the Writing

The best writing was from the pencil and paper. The stimulus for this writing was a parable about an ant and a grasshopper in which the ant stored food for the winter, while the grasshopper played his cello all summer and subsequently went hungry in the winter. The children were asked to write a story about what happened the next year.

4.2   Quantity of the Writing

The children wrote more using the tablet than they did on the keyboard (N = 17, t = 4.7, P = 0.0001). When writing at the keyboard, children spent a lot of time looking for the right key to press. It was interesting to note that children using the keyboard asked for spellings whilst those using pencil and paper and the tablet did not. Given that these were the same children, it can be hypothesized that the keyboard creates more anxiety or more uncertainty about spellings. The tablet and

	Expected	Actual
Tablet	4.2	4.3
Keyboard	4.6	4.7
Paper	4.1	4.3

Table 3: Children's preferences.

Hardest to use	Tablet
Easiest to use	Paper
Most fun to use	Keyboard
Least fun to use	Paper

Table 4: Results from survey after all three events.

the pencil and paper both support word-based construction as opposed to letter-based construction.

4.3   Child Preferences

The children marginally preferred the keyboard to the other methods, however, the results were not significantly different. We observed that, when the children were completing the smileyometers, some commented about the quality of their own work (their story) and so it was difficult to be sure about what the child was evaluating, whether it was his or her own work or his or her experience with the interface.

We had expected that the children would prefer the pen and tablet to the keyboard, as it was new to them. It later transpired that only one child had used a word processor for writing before, for all the other children, this too was a novel experience although they were all able to use the keyboard, albeit it slowly.

Children commented after the three activities that one thing that they did not like about the tablet interface was that it didn't allow them to write their entire story on one screen. When the children wrote on paper and on the keyboard, all their work was visible in the same place, whereas with the handwriting interface, their work appeared both to the right of the writing surface (as ASCII text — and with errors) as well as on the writing surface. It is clear that the children found the tablet hard to use; given that they had only a short time to practise, this was not a surprise.

5   Discussion of the Key Findings

In this section we examine some of the key findings with respect to the fit between the technology, the user, and the task. We introduce some data about recognition rates, and explore the errors that occurred at the tablet interface, and investigate the potential of the three technologies for writing.

5.1   Recognition Rates and Experimental Design

While the children were composing on the tablet, one of the researchers copied their writing (including spelling errors) onto a notepad in order to create a corpus

	Mean	Standard Deviation
Training phrase 1	50.4	25.0
Training phrase 2	34.8	23.2
Training phrase 3	41.2	20.4
Composed text	27.8	15.7

Table 5: Error rates.

of presented text. There may have been some errors in this text as the researcher had to make some assumptions (for example she had to sometimes guess what character the child was forming), and also may have inadvertently missed a word or misspelled a word. This presented text was then compared with the transcribed text (stored by the software) to derive a character error rate for the text that the child had composed [MacKenzie & Soukoreff 2002a]. The three phrases of the copied text that had been used for training were similarly analysed. The results are shown in Table 5.

This table (Table 5) demonstrates that error rates fall significantly between the first and second training text. What is interesting from Table 5 is that the error rates for the composed text were considerably lower than the error rates for the (copied) training phrases. We suggest that there are two main reasons for this effect; these are discussed in the next two subsections.

5.1.1   The Occurrence of Spaces

When the children are copying text, many spaces are introduced into the generated text due to the time taken by the children to complete words. This is caused by a feature built into the recognizer that inserts spaces between words when there is a 'pen-up' of a specified duration. For adult usage, this is an essential and useful feature, but for children who may be copying words character by character it is a problem. Thus, if a child writes 'climbed' too slowly, it can be recognized as seven one-letter words rather than as one seven-letter word. This, and the resulting effect on error rates, is demonstrated below:

> Presented text   `climbed`
> Generated text   `c l i m b e d`
>
> MSD = 6 (represents 6 inserted spaces)
> CER = 46.15% (from 6/13 which is the number of errors divided by the number of characters in the transcribed text))

It is therefore likely that copied text will result in higher error rates than composed text.

5.1.2   Focus of Attention

The term *focus of attention* (FOA) was introduced by MacKenzie & Soukoreff [2002b] to describe the attention demands of a text input task. For an expert typist, copying text from a piece of paper is a single FOA task, as the typist needs to look only at the text to be copied and not at the screen or the keyboard. If children are

	Example	Solution
Spelling error	Child misspells words.	Phonic spellcheckers and phonic dictionary support.
Construction error	Child doesn't form the letter or word correctly; 'a' may look like 'd' or 'd' may be constructed in the wrong order.	Training for the child Some flexibility in the recognition algorithms.
Execution errors	The child doesn't touch the tablet with the pen when he writes.	Child to look at the screen.
	The child cannot correctly position the pen on the writing space.	Child to look at the screen.
	The child continues writing once the pen has turned into a pointer (this happens when the pen moves away from the writing area onto a menu area, it is discussed by Read et al. [n.d.].).	Haptic feedback Child to look at the screen.
	The child writes too slowly for the recognition software — introducing spaces.	Training Cursive writing Changing the recognizer 'pen-up' time lag.
	The child may be writing outside the writing capture area.	Haptic feedback Child to look at the screen.
Software error	The software misrecognizes the word or character.	Better algorithms.

Table 6: Errors at the interface and some solutions.

composing on paper with a pencil, they similarly have only one FOA. When children are composing at a keyboard or using the writing tablet they have two FOA — the stylus or the keyboard, and the computer screen. When children are copying text, an extra FOA is created in each case. This overburdens the feedback channels and therefore makes the task more difficult and more error prone.

5.2 Improving the Usability of the HR Interface

Observations made during this and previous experimental work have identified a range of usability problems with the handwriting recognition interface. We have previously classified four types of errors that arise when the child is composing writing at the interface [Read et al. 2001]. These are presented in Table 6 together with some new suggestions for solutions to the problems.

In addition to these errors there are some usability issues that relate to the fit between children writing and the use of the interface. These 'task conformance' issues concern behaviours that will be expected from the children, which are not well supported by the handwriting recognition interface. We have identified four such behaviours and we discuss them below.

5.2.1 Rubbing out / Scribbling out

When children write, they commonly revisit the last word they have written and scribble it out (or rub it out) before substituting another word. Scribbling out

she   she

Figure 3: The effect when children go back and correct their writing.

has a disastrous effect on recognition, so rubbing out needs to be encouraged and supported! This requires an eraser (often the other end of the stylus) with a different set of behaviours attached to it than those attached to the pen.

5.2.2 Starting at the Top of the Page

Children start to write in the extreme top left hand corner of the page and seem to want to completely fill a line before moving down. The effect of this is that sometimes the pen stroke goes off the writing space. If menus are placed at the top of the screen, they are likely to be opened during the writing activity. It is prudent to put all the controls at the bottom of the screen when children are writing. As writing so close to the edge is not a trait that children should carry into adult life, it is acceptable to encourage them to start writing a little way down the page and to write within right and left margins. This can be implemented by putting a greyed border around the writing area, thus encouraging the children to keep away from the edges.

5.2.3 Fixing Bad Writing

Children are encouraged to produce 'good' handwriting in school. As the children's writing is normally assessed as an end product, it is quite usual for children to go back to their writing and 'correct' it so that it looks better when visually examined. An example of this is given in Figure 3 where the child saw '**she**' after it was written and, realizing that the ascender on the '**h**' was a little short, went back and added more ascender. The recognition software finds this difficult to deal with, particularly where there is a time lag involved. It is likely that the correction in Figure 3 will be recognized as **snel**.

The recognition software could cope with this behaviour but it needs complex algorithms that can be made spatially aware. A delayed stroke solution is commonly applied when a late dot over an i or a late stroke through a t is encountered in handwriting. This could be extended to short ascenders and descenders, to poor hoops and to open joins, all of which children commonly correct on detection.

5.2.4 Adding Missing Things

This is a similar problem; the children go back and insert words, or insert letters into words. This cannot be easily coped with by recognition algorithms. The only way that this can be effectively managed is by identifying these corrections as 'mark up', at which point the recognition can behave in a different way. For this to happen, there needs to be a different pen that has different functions. This could be a physical device or could be a virtual instance of the same pen. With this enabled, the writer could add words and phrases between existing words and phrases with the additions being 'placed' in the correct place rather than occurring at the end of the writing (as determined by time sequence).

5.3 Writing Quality and Digital Ink

As can be seen from Table 2 above, the children did not write huge stories. Some children were unable to fully develop their plots in the time allocated. Only a few read over their work when it was done. We had expected that children might edit their work, but they didn't. Research indicates that editing and revision is uncommon at this age [Latham 2002]. What was apparent was that children were able to write quite fluently at both the tablet and the paper.

Writing is typically broken into three overlapping phases, these being [Hayes & Flower 1986]:

- Planning and collecting.

- Initial drafting leading to more final writing.

- Revising and editing.

In all phases of this process, the use of tablet technology and digital ink is supportive for children writing. In the first phase, pencil and paper have traditionally been used for note taking, and for storing and recording creative ideas and thoughts. A word processor allows for no annotation and, as we have identified in this study, children become over concerned with spellings. Notes for subsequent writing, sketches, and diagrams can be made almost as easily with the pen technology as with paper.

The second phase does seem to favour the keyboard input, as it will result in reasonably reliable ASCII text. However, children need to break their words into characters, and it is possible that this has a negative effect on the writing that is produced. In addition it is slow to use for children who have not been taught keyboarding, and there is therefore an extra focus of attention. With a tablet PC, like pencil and paper, the child needs only to focus on one thing.

The third phase of this process, revising and editing, is greatly facilitated by the use of computer aided text processing. Traditionally, this has been enabled by word processing software manipulating ASCII text, but it may be more beneficial for children to preserve their handwritten work and manipulate this as digital ink. In Table 6 above, the majority of the execution errors can be eliminated if a tablet PC is used instead of a separate graphics tablet. This is a result of there being a reduced focus of attention when the pen and the screen are joined. The errors that are caused by the child having to focus on two locations at once are eliminated.

6 Conclusion

The results reported in this paper have implications for the design and evaluation of handwriting recognition based technologies and digital ink technologies.

The first finding is that once children get over the usability problems of the tablet technology, they can write fluently using a stylus. This bodes well for tablet PCs and for digital pens, as they not only reduce the foci of attention to one, (for better error reduction and better ease of use) but they may also reduce the number of execution errors caused by the pointer behaviour, and the separation of the pen and screen. We are currently conducting a user trial with digital pens and tablet PCs in the writing classroom to investigate these claims.

The second finding is that the digital ink technology supports cursive text construction, which has been shown to improve the spelling of children (as does the pencil and paper). Where the digital text has an advantage over pencil and paper is in its ability to be either recognized and thereafter treated and manipulated as ASCII text, or to be manipulated in its own right as digital ink.

An observation that is of interest to the writing community is that text that is constructed at the computer interface can be logged over time, resulting in rich data for research and development. It is now possible to track the multiple changes that a child (or an adult) may make to a piece of writing.

We have identified some of the problems with using copied text for the recording of recognition rates and error rates. It is likely, where children are involved, that error rates with copied text will always be higher than for composed text, due to the additional focus of attention, and the difficulties that children have in remembering the exact composition of the words to be copied.

Future work will investigate the usefulness of digital ink for writing and the usability of the tablet PC and the digital pen for child users.

References

Bearne, E. [1998], *Making Progress in English*, Routledge.

Card, S. K., English, W. K. & Burr, B. J. [1978], Evaluation of Mouse, Rate-controlled Isometric Joystick, Step-keys and Text Keys for Text Selection on a CRT, *Ergonomics* **21**(8), 601–13.

DfEE [1988], The National Literacy Strategy as a Framework for Teaching.

Frankish, C. [1999], Pen-based Computing, *in* J. M. Noyes & M. J. Cook (eds.), *Interface Technology: The Leading Edge*, Research Studies Press, pp.59–72.

Frankish, C., Hull, R. & Morgan, P. [1995], Recognition Accuracy and User Acceptance of Pen Interfaces, *in* I. Katz, R. Mack, L. Marks, M. B. Rosson & J. Nielsen (eds.), *Proceedings of the SIGCHI Conference on Human Factors in Computing Systems (CHI'95)*, ACM Press, pp.503–10.

Goldberg, D. & Goodisman, A. [1991], STYLUS User Interfaces for Manipulating Text, *in* J. R. Rhyne (ed.), *Proceedings of the 4th Annual ACM Symposium on User Interface Software and Technology, UIST'91*, ACM Press, pp.127–35.

Hayes, J. R. & Flower, L. S. [1986], Writing Research and the Writer, *Amercan Psychologist* **41**(10), 1106–13.

Hermann, A. [1987], Research into Writing and Computers: Viewing the Gestalt, Paper presented at the Annual Meeting of the Modern Language Association.

Kurth, R. [1987], Using Word Processing to Enhance Revision Strategies During Student Writing Activities, *Educational Technology* **27**(1), 13–9.

Latham, D. [2002], *How Children Learn to Write*, Paul Chapman Publishing.

Lewis, C. & Norman, D. A. [1986], Designing for Error In User Centred Systems, *in* D. A. Norman & S. W. Draper (eds.), *User Centered System Design: New Perspectives on Human–Computer Interaction*, Lawrence Erlbaum Associates, pp.411–32.

MacKenzie, I. S. & Chang, L. [1999], A Performance Comparison of Two Handwriting Recognizers, *Interacting with Computers* 11(3), 283–97.

MacKenzie, I. S. & Soukoreff, R. W. [2002a], A Character-level Error Analysis for Evaluating Text Entry Methods, *in* O. W. Bertelsen, S. Bødker & K. Kuuti (eds.), *Proceedings of NordiCHI 2002*, ACM Press, pp.241–4.

MacKenzie, I. S. & Soukoreff, R. W. [2002b], Text Entry for Mobile Computing: Models and Methods, Theory and Practice, *Human–Computer Interaction* 17(2), 147–98.

Mankoff, J. [2000], Providing Integrated Toolkit-level Support for Ambiguity in Recognition-based Interfaces, *in* M. Tremaine (ed.), *CHI'00 Extended Abstracts of the Conference on Human Factors in Computing Systems*, ACM Press, pp.77–8.

Mankoff, J. & Abowd, G. [1999], Error Correction Techniques for Handwriting, Speech and Other Ambiguous or Error Prone Systems, Technical Report GIT-GVU-99-18, GVU Centre, Georgia Tech.

McHale, K. & Cermak, S. [1992], Fine Motor Activities in Elementary School: Preliminary Findings and Provivional Implications for Children with Fine Motor Problems, *American Journal of Occupational Therapy* 46(10), 898–903.

Newell, A. F., Boothe, L., Arnott, J. & Beattie, W. [1992], Increasing Literacy Levels by the Use of Linguistic Prediction, *Child Language Teaching and Therapy* 8(2), 138–87.

Norman, D. A. [1981], Categorization of Action Slips, *Psychological Review* 88(1), 1–15.

Noyes, J. [2001], Talking and Writing — How Natural in Human–Machine Interaction?, *International Journal of Human–Computer Studies* 55(4), 503–19.

Papert, S. [1980], *Mindstorms. Children, Computers, and Powerful Ideas*, Basic Books.

Peters, M. L. [1985], *Spelling: Caught or Taught: A New Look*, Routledge and Kegan Paul.

Plamondon, R. & Srihari, S. N. [2000], On-line and Off-line Handwriting Recognition: A Comprehensive Survey, *IEEE Transactions on Pattern Analysis and Machine Intelligence* 22(1), 63–84.

Read, J. C., MacFarlane, S. J. & Casey, C. [2001], Measuring the Usability of Text Input Methods for Children, *in* A. Blandford, J. Vanderdonckt & P. Gray (eds.), *People and Computers XV: Interaction without Frontiers (Joint Proceedings of HCI2001 and IHM2001)*, Springer-Verlag, pp.559–72.

Read, J. C., MacFarlane, S. J. & Casey, C. [2002a], Designing a Handwriting Recognition Based Writing Environment for Children, *in Proceedings of the 8th International EARLI SIG Writing Conference*, EARLI SIG, p.9.

Read, J. C., MacFarlane, S. J. & Casey, C. [2002b], Endurability, Engagement and Expectations: Measuring Children's Fun, *in* M. Bekker, P. Markopoulos & M. Kersten-Tsikalkina (eds.), *Interaction Design and Children*, Shaker Publishing, pp.189–98.

Read, J. C., MacFarlane, S. J. & Casey, C. [2002c], Oops! Silly me! Errors in a Handwriting Recognition-based Text entry Interface for Children, *in* O. W. Bertelsen, S. Bødker & K. Kuuti (eds.), *Proceedings of NordiCHI 2002*, ACM Press, pp.35–40.

Read, J. C., MacFarlane, S. J. & Casey, C. [2003a], Good Enough for What? Acceptance of Handwriting Recognition Errors by Child Users, *in* S. J. MacFarlane, A. Nicol, J. C. Read & L. Snape (eds.), *Proceedings of Conference on Interaction Design and Children (IDC 2003)*, ACM Press, p.155.

Read, J. C., MacFarlane, S. J. & Casey, C. [2003b], What's Going On? Discovering what Children understand about Handwriting Recognition Interfaces, *in* S. J. MacFarlane, A. Nicol, J. C. Read & L. Snape (eds.), *Proceedings of Conference on Interaction Design and Children (IDC 2003)*, ACM Press, pp.135–40.

Read, J. C., MacFarlane, S. J. & Casey, C. [n.d.], Pens Behaving Badly — Usability of Pens and Graphics Tablets for Text Entry with Children, Available on the CD-ROM issued at the UIST 2002 conference, published by ACM Press.

Sassoon, R. [1990], *Handwriting: A New Perspective*, Stanley Thornes.

Sturm, J. [1988], Using Computer Software Tools to Facilitate Narrative Skills, *The Clinical Connection* **11**(4), 6–9.

Swanson, H. L. & Berninger, V. W. [1996], Individual Differences in Children's Working Memory and Writing Skill, *Journal of Experimental Child Psychology* **63**(2), 358–85.

Tappert, C. C., Suen, C. Y. & Wakahara, T. [1990], The State of the Art in On-Line Handwriting Recognition, *IEEE Transactions on Pattern Analysis and Machine Intelligence* **12**(8), 787–808.

BMX Bandits: The Design of an Educational Computer Game for Disaffected Youth

Atif Waraich[†] & Gareth Wilson[‡]

[†] *Department of Computing and Mathematics, Manchester Metropolitan University, Manchester M1 5GD, UK*
Email: *a.waraich@mmu.ac.uk*

[‡] *Bizarre Creations, Liverpool, UK*
Email: *gareth.wilson@bizarrecreations.com*

This paper briefly describes the design, development and evaluation of a prototype multimedia Interactive Learning Environment (ILE). This utilized narrative and a game type environment in an attempt to provide an engaging and motivating learning experience for a group of young people attending Salford Youth Service. The main area addressed was how to ensure that the ILE would appeal to children who found traditional approaches to learning difficult. Additionally, an important aim of the project was to engage the learners in the design process as they were identified as having low self-esteem.

A previously developed design framework which focuses on the needs and views of the learners and aims to facilitate both requirements gathering and design issues using a narrative based approach was used. The ILE that has been developed is influenced by the design of computer games as this was a common interest of the focus group who participated in the design. The ILE is briefly described and an initial evaluation of its use presented. The paper concludes by identifying the aspects of the ILE, which appealed to the students and assesses the affect of the motivational aspects.

Keywords: multimedia, learning, narrative, informant, design, games, motivation, interaction.

1 Introduction

The development of educational software that is focused on the learner requires the use of design and development approaches that are user centred. Informant Design (ID) [Scaife et al. 1997] is such a methodology and has been successfully used to develop educational software for children.

An important aim our work with Salford Youth Service was to empower children who had significant social problems by including them in the development of a computer based learning environment that would teach a domain that was relevant to them. The Youth Workers who worked with the children suggested that the process of developing the game could provide an opportunity to encourage the group to participate in a project and thereby improve their social skills and encourage creativity. An early goal of the project therefore, was to ensure that the development process would appeal to the children. Previous work by Waraich [2002] using an adapted version of ID, has shown that the development of games based teaching environments appeals to children, particularly if they are directly involved in the design process. A similar approach was adopted for this study.

2 Narrative and Learning

Educational theorists, such as Piaget [1973], have argued that the interpretation and integration of knowledge occurs within a specific social and cultural context. Bruner [1991] and Berger [1997] have extended these ideas to suggest that stories may be the primary way that we assimilate our knowledge of the world and make sense of it.

Mandler & DeForest [1979] and Trabbasso et al. [1984] have shown that narrative is important in the recall and comprehension of material. From this perspective narrative is viewed as a mechanism to make sense of the material that we are presented with or, more significantly, as a fundamental property of meaning making. When appropriately designed and integrated, it has been shown that narrative can act as a useful structural mechanism to help guide students through a learning environment [Quinn 1996].

It is clear that if we are to design motivationally engaging learning environments narrative can play a very important role, both as a structural device to help with meaning making and to engage the learner.

3 Motivating Learners

Lepper & Cordova [1992] and Lepper et al. [1993] report the results of studies on educational activities with identical instructional content but differing motivational appeal. These studies have shown that gains in learning can occur when the learning activities take place in a motivationally enhanced setting. The embellishments used were the provision of a number of fantasy contexts for simple educational games providing a basic narrative. Students exposed to the motivationally enhanced programs showed significantly increased motivation for learning target domain knowledge, even when the motivational factors where removed. Lepper et al. also distinguish between intrinsic and extrinsic rewards for learning. Intrinsic rewards are based on a high congruence between the material being taught and the motivational techniques used. Lepper notes that extrinsic rewards can have a detrimental effect on learning.

For any learning task to be meaningful to the learner they must have both a sufficient context for the learning and motivation to perform the tasks that will help them to learn. We believe that game based learning environments that incorporate a strong narrative can meet these requirements as the learning tasks, if appropriately designed, can be tightly coupled with the narrative.

We have used an approach that is based on designing a meaningful and engaging narrative for the users of the system so that they will be motivated to continue using the system rather than explicitly trying to determine their motivational state.

4   Computer Games and Education

Adventure games and simulations have often been used in educational systems [Sherwood 1991]. Adventure game based learning environments allow the learner to be presented with a series of tasks and puzzles to solve in a goal oriented environment. This can be a powerful motivational device if appropriately designed and implemented. A fantasy context and narrative can also be introduced including interaction with a variety of characters and elements of surprise and 'cognitive curiosity' can be incorporated into the system [Malone 1981; Sherwood 1991; Quinn 1994].

Amory et al. [1999] have suggested that adventure games may have cross gender appeal when compared to other genres of games and educational games often use an 'adventure game' approach [Prensky 2001].

Quinn [1996] has described the development of an educational adventure game designed to teach low-literacy youth about independent living skills. The system 'Quest for Independence', was designed to run on low specification computers and to use a game format to motivate the intended user group. The game itself consists of a simulation of the tasks the learners would have to complete in the 'real' world if they were to survive by themselves on a day-to-day basis (e.g. getting a job or opening a bank account). It does not attempt to simulate all the possibilities — just those that are considered most important by the games developers.

As the target audience for 'Quest for Independence' had low literacy levels the use of a mainly graphical environment was considered an important design parameter. The appeal of the system was also emphasized as the users had "little tolerance for any material of a low entertainment value". The game provides guidance for learning within the simplified environment, not all the actions available in the real world are available to users of the system — those discarded were the ones that either did not contribute to relevant knowledge acquisition or to game play.

In developing the ILE for use with Salford Youth Service it became apparent from initial conversations with both Youth Workers and the children that we would need to adopt a similar approach. The children were all interested in computer games and quickly decided that they would like a game-based ILE as opposed to a more traditional approach.

4.1 Narrative Computer Games and Education

There are a number of commercially available school level educational adventure games (such as the *Where in the World is Carmen San Diego* series). Such games often use a basic narrative as a device to structure the environment and provide pedagogical goals and tasks for the learners.

We believe the adventure game genre has proved popular because it presents a number of potential advantages for the development of an ILE that uses narrative:

1. It allows the incorporation of the motivating characteristics of computer games.

2. It provides a framework for the development of a suitable diachronic narrative.

3. The narrative can easily incorporate both macro-level and micro-level story-lines if appropriately designed.

4. The computer-based interactivity allows the possibility of context-based practice of key skills and concepts.

5. The narrative itself can act as a navigational and pedagogical scaffold for the learners (if it is appropriately integrated).

We chose an adventure game style format for the BMX Bandits (our ILE) for the reasons stated above; in addition, as previously discussed, consultation with the children in the focus group indicated a strong preference for a game type environment.

5 Developing Educational Computer Games

5.1 The User Centred Design and Cognitive Engineering Approach

Quinn [1994] has suggested a cognitive engineering methodology that incorporates elements of user centred design — specifically for the design of learning environments that incorporate both narrative and game like elements as motivational and pedagogic devices. Quinn asserts that a user-centred design approach that uses cognitive engineering is most appropriate and that the principles used in these methodologies can be applied to the design of educational systems.

Quinn suggests that games can provide a situated context for learning that can enhance motivation but that a meaningful game must be chosen or developed if this is to be effective. In this context games are considered constructivist in nature as they can allow the user to explore the environment and discover the actions/knowledge required for success. He suggests that reflection is not always specifically supplied in games and that some games only allow this when they have concluded.

We agree with Quinn that the target learner group must be involved in the design process of educational games but we argue that the narrative must be the central focus of the design if the system is to have meaning for the users rather than the designers. In addition, though Quinn's model is useful in identifying the importance of an iterative, user centred design based methodology it does not outline specifically what games techniques, in practical terms, may be of use to the developer of educational games.

We suggest an adapted form of the Informant Design framework [Scaife et al. 1997] that incorporates narrative based techniques to help to ensure that the design has meaning for the target learner group (see Section 5.3 below).

5.2   Game Object Model

Amory et al. [1999] have suggested a model that focuses on the interface of an educational game, the Game Object Model (GOM). The elements of the game environment such as graphics, sound and technology are related to the categories of learning/skills that can be addressed such as memory, mathematics, reflexes and so on. The model does not directly address theories of drama or narrative which we consider important for the development of adventure games. Amory & Govinder [2000] claim that an evaluation of the use of this model showed that it was 'useful in the creation of an interactive story' though the users who evaluated the system felt that the 'story line should be more complex'.

5.3   Narrative Centred Informant Design

The development approach used for this work was based on an adaptation of Informant Design [Scaife et al. 1997] known as Narrative Centred Informant Design (NCID) [Waraich 2002]. Conventional approaches to user centred design revolve around the evaluation of prototype designs and careful requirements gathering to ensure that the needs of the user are met. Informant Design is intended to involve a range of experts in the development of software and treats the potential users as partners in the design process. NCID adapts the Informant Design model to use narrative centred techniques. There are four phases to the design process as per Informant design but the first two phases use narrative focused techniques to help to design and develop the macro and micro narratives that will form the basis of the ILE.

The narrative techniques include initial discussions with the target group to determine what sort of narratives appeal to them. A proto-story is then developed from the use of character templates and narrative events derived from Propp's universal story elements. Story-boarding and scenario mapping are used to develop this story further with the informants.

NCID uses a number of informants in the design process, as does Informant Design. In the work with Salford Youth service the roles were adapted as some experts (such as teachers and psychologists) were not available. Their roles were filled by others where possible. As the target learners had some literacy problems some of the techniques outlined in Table 1 were adapted for the project. The adapted version of NCID used is shown in Table 2.

5.3.1   Narrative Structure

The narrative elements that have been used as the basis of NCID are based on Propp's [1968] model of a universal narrative. Propp's identification of a common narrative structure and characters provides a useful basis to identify major plot events and characters with informants [Waraich 2002]. A simplified version of the Proppian model was used directly with the informants.

Design Phase	Main objectives	Methods	Contributors	Outcomes/Techniques
(1) Define domain and problems & identify basic narrative elements	Identify basic nature of narrative Identify basic narrative elements; Narrative awareness	Teacher interviews Theoretical analysis of external representations Talk about nature of narrative	Teachers Children Design team Software designer Narrative facilitator	User requirements document Learning objectives Preliminary documentation produced Questionnaires
(2) Translation of specification & plot/character definition	Identify specific narrative elements & theme, character, setting & plot elements	Storyboarding & sketching, scenario creation	HCI analyst Psychologist Software designer Narrative facilitator	Storyboards; index card based narrative description; Paper based narrative scenarios; Children's stories Story analysis
(3) Design Low-tech materials and test	Create low-tech materials Complete narrative spec. & evaluate	Storyboarding Scenario creation Design through scenarios plot definition; character matrices	Psychologist Software designer Children Narrative facilitator	Storyboards; index card based narrative description; Paper based narrative scenario Character matrix
(4) Design and test high-tech materials	Validate design Validate cognitive & pedagogical aims Evaluate interactivity & narrativity	Prototype (high-tech) Multimedia Pre- and post-tests Cognitive analysis	Psychologist Software designer Children HCI analyst Teachers Narrative facilitator	Prototype systems; non-functional & functional; Pre- & post-tests Questionnaires

Table 1: Narrative Centred Informant Design.

Design Phase	Methods	Contributors	Outcomes/Techniques
(1) Define domain and problems & identify basic narrative elements	Interviews Analysis of existing materials & software Talk about nature of narrative	Youth workers Children Designer Narrative facilitator	User requirements document Learning objectives/goals Preliminary documentation produced Group discussions
(2) Translation of specification & plot/character definition	Storyboarding & sketching, scenario creation	HCI expert Software designer Narrative facilitator Children	Storyboards; index card based narrative description; Paper based narrative scenarios; Children's stories/group work Story analysis
(3) Design Low-tech materials and test	Storyboarding Scenario creation Design through scenarios plot definition; character matrices	Youth Worker Social Worker Software designer Children Narrative facilitator	Storyboards; index card based narrative description; Paper based narrative scenario 9cut outs)
(4) Design and test high-tech materials	Prototype (high-tech) Multimedia Pre- and post-tests Cognitive analysis	Psychologist Software designer Children HCI analyst Youth Worker Social Worker Narrative facilitator	Prototype system (BMX Bandits) functional; Pre- & post-tests Questionnaires Observation Interviews

Table 2: NCID as used with Salford Youth Service.

6 NCID at Salford

Salford Youth Service work with children who have problems with truancy and other related problems. Twelve children were involved in this study 4 girls and 8 boys. The children were aged between 13 and 15 and attended Irlam and Cadishead Youth Club. The children in the group were from a number of schools in the local area and had varying success with the school environment. Several of the children had been identified as having behavioural problems at school and other social issues, which meant that they did not respond well to the 'traditional' classroom environment.

The project was conducted over a four-month period with fortnightly meetings with the focus group.

The application of the NICD as used at Salford is briefly outlined below.

6.1 Phase 1: Definition of the Domain

The target learners were given some influence over the domain to be addressed to encourage their involvement. A group exercise was used to encourage discussion of possible areas and this process produced an agreement to address the set up of a small business. This was a common interest for the group as the Youth Service were undertaking a project to obtain funding for a BMX/skateboard park in Salford which would involve input from the children in the study. Learning goals were derived from this process by the designers, Youth Workers and social worker. The original learning goals included addressing issues involved in running a business on a day to day basis, these were not completed due to time constraints.

6.2 Phase 2: Translation of the Specification

Initial discussions centred on narratives and games that appealed to the focus group. The design of the characters and the basic storyline was facilitated by the use of index cards that the group used to define the actions, appearance, personality, desires and needs of the characters they envisaged would be part of the game. Before the characters were discussed the basic characters defined by Propp were introduced as 'templates' (such as the villain). The group were encouraged to discuss the characteristics of each others characters. Simple scenes were then generated using these characters forming a proto-story. The children appeared to enjoy this activity and were enthusiastic participants. The plot lines were documented as the discussions proceeded.

6.3 Phase 3: Design of Low-tech Materials and Evaluation

Having established a basic storyline and identified a number of possible characters for the narrative, the next phase of the design was establishing a 'look and feel' for the environment. Screenshots of existing games were presented to the group for comment and ideas for the interface of the system were discussed. Again the children generated a number of useful ideas for the designers. For example the majority (10) wanted a 3D style immersive environment and suggested that the player could use a mobile phone in the game to obtain help.

6.4   Phase 4: Design of High-tech Materials

The prototype ILE BMX Bandits that was produced for evaluation is described in detail in Section 7 below. The prototype was developed using Bliztbasic.

7   BMX Bandits

BMX Bandits is the prototype ILE developed for this project and was developed using the Blitz3D (http://www.blitzbasic.com) environment. This uses a C like, compiled language that allows the control and manipulation of 3D objects and worlds. Blizt3D is designed to facilitate the development of 3D computer games. Significant advantages of Blitz3D for game development include support for a number of standard 3D file formats (such as .3ds and .x) and it's provision of a 3D control language that allows the developer to concentrate on the 3D world rather than memory allocation or hardware issues.

The basic architecture of the software is based on the model proposed by Rollings & Morris [2000] which has three components: World Update, Render 3D World, Display 2D Images.

7.1   Characters

Based on the documentation produced from design phases 1 and 2 a number of characters were developed for use in the game. It is important to note that the final selection of characters and the narrative used was determined by the designers and not the focus group. This was to ensure that the narrative was cohesive and that the features of the game were not familiar to the group (for evaluation purposes).

The basic storyline revolves around a hero (the learner) who is sent on a quest by a Youth Worker to set up an appropriate business for a skate park. In carrying out this task the hero must interact with several other characters including a bank manager, an estate agent, and a BMX Biker.

The learner has an inventory which acts as a basic scoring system; by completing tasks within the environment they receive parts necessary to make a 'super' BMX bike.

Interactions with the characters are through a simple point and click interface and are text based. The children suggested the use of emoticons to convey emotions in the text and this feature was implemented (see Figure 1).

7.2   Help System

A help system was implemented which had two main features. Firstly, there was a 'scanner' that provided the learner with basic information on buildings and characters if they passed the mouse over such objects. Additionally there was a mobile phone which displayed text relating to the game (see Figure 2).

8   Evaluation Procedure

The software was evaluated in three main ways. A pre- and post-test was used to determine whether there was any effect on the learning of the domain material with the target group.

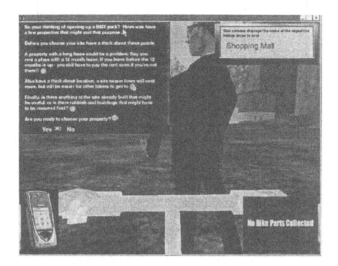

Figure 1: Dialogue with a character showing emoticons.

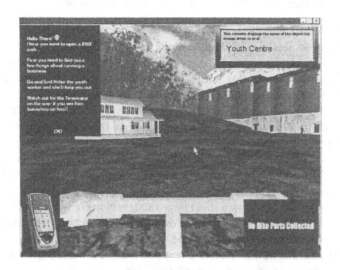

Figure 2: Help system showing textual communication via 'phone'.

Student ID	Pre	Post	Post-Pre	Help Used (Y/N)
1	1	3	2	Y
2	1	3	2	N
3	4	6	2	Y
4	3	5	2	Y
5	3	4	1	N
6	3	1	2	N
7	2	5	3	Y
8	4	6	2	N
9	5	7	2	N
10	5	6	1	N
11	3	4	1	Y
12	8	8	0	N
Mean	3.50	4.83		
STDev	1.93	1.95		

Table 3: Pre- and post-test results (maximum possible score 10).

A major aim of the project was to increase the group's motivation to learn and this was assessed using a combination of observation, questionnaires and post-test interviews. The group's attitude to the ILE was assessed by comparison to traditional approaches to learning such as teacher centred classroom approach, the use of books or multimedia aids (e.g. video). Each student was assigned a numerical ID to provide anonymity and these have been used in reporting the results here.

8.1   Pre- and Post-Test

The pre- and post-test consisted of 10 multiple choice questions (MCQ) relating to the set up of a small business. MCQ style questions were used as, after discussions with the Youth Workers it was felt that more discursive questions would not have been appropriate as some of the children had literacy problems.

Some of the children (ID 1 and 2) had very little prior knowledge of the domain, whereas one (ID 12) had very good knowledge as they were studying Business Studies GCSE.

As the group were involved in both the design and evaluation of the software it is not possible to assign any improvement in learning solely to the use of the ILE.

The pre-test and post-test scores are shown in Table 3.

The post-test results show a small improvement in overall mean mark from 3.50 to 4.83. 10 of the 12 students improved on their pre-test scores, with one student's score remaining the same (ID 12) and one whose score reduced (ID 6).

A post-test interview of student 6 revealed that his pre-test score was largely a result of guesswork as opposed to prior knowledge.

Table 3 shows the post- minus pre-test scores. There appears to be some correlation between the time spent using the ILE and performance. The longer the learner spent on the game the higher the score. This may indicate that the learners who spent longer on the task were carefully reading the material as opposed to quickly reading through it.

There also appeared to be a correlation between material tested in the ILE and learning as previously reported by Lepper & Cordova [1992]. Questions 1, 2, 3, 5 and 7 from the tests were fielded by the Bank Manager character within the environment whereas the other questions were not. The group answered 4 of the 5 questions tested within the game correctly after using the ILE. Of the questions that were not tested in the game accuracy for two increased, one remained the same and two decreased. Again due to the small sample size these results are not statistically significant and further work is required to investigate this effect.

8.2   Observation of the Group

Direct observation of the group using the ILE revealed two main approaches to using the software. The first approach was skewed towards the goals of the game. When asked by the characters in the game whether they wanted help, students adopting this approach would refuse help even if their domain knowledge was poor. They were focused on obtaining the parts for the BMX bike and therefore completing the game in the fastest time. They were observed to be skimming through the text and would often repeatedly answer questions incorrectly in a trial and error approach. There was no direct penalty for adopting this approach in the game and this is an area that could be addressed by monitoring and responding to such strategies.

A second strategy adopted by four learners was more considered. They took significantly longer than the others to complete the ILE and they would often accept help when it was presented within the environment; because of this they were often able to answer questions correctly straight away. They passed the in-game test with 1–2 attempts at the questions. They were also observed to read the text within the ILE in much more detail.

8.3   Post-Test Interviews

One focus of the interviews was to determine why some students appeared to rush through the ILE whilst others were much more methodical in their approach.

It appears that for 4 of the 5 children that adopted this approach the main reason was that they were keen to be involved in other activities in the Youth Centre on that evening of the evaluation and therefore external factors were affecting their strategy. Five of the twelve learners (ID 4, 5, 6,10 and 12) stated that they wanted to finish the ILE as quickly as possible to 'show off' to their friends. Three (ID 4, 8 and 10) said that they found the text in the ILE 'boring' and just used the trial and error approach discussed above to answer the questions.

One of the learners suggested the use of a scoring system to prevent 'guessing'; the learner would receive additional points for answering questions correctly at the first attempt.

All the children felt the software improved their understanding of the domain material and all reported that they enjoyed using it — an important initial goal of this work. When asked if the software had helped to improve their understanding of the target domain knowledge all either 'strongly agreed' or 'agreed' with the statement.

9 Conclusion

The original goals of this work were to produce a game based ILE that would engage the target learners and motivate them to interact with the system and to teach them about the development of a simple business. Additionally, in this case the actual development process itself was considered important as we were working with children who had low self-esteem. The use of NCID was considered useful in this instance both because it focuses on the target learners and because it uses a narrative based approach to requirements gathering which has previously proved successful [Waraich 2002]. The use of low-tech prototyping of the narrative aspects of the ILE was particularly well received by the focus group. NCID and the techniques it encapsulates may provide a useful way of gathering requirements from children on a range of projects where children's views are considered important.

The Youth Workers who worked with the children stated that the children were attentive when participating in the sessions and generally less disruptive than with other activities. In addition, the Youth Workers noted that the children were particularly pleased to see their ideas incorporated into the ILE. They were also willing to consider the needs of other children outside of the group and empathize with them, as they often speculated whether their own preferences would appeal to their peers.

It is not possible to state categorically from this pilot study whether there was a significant improvement in learning of the target domain for this group. As the group were involved in the design of the prototype it is possible that the results have been affected by repeated exposure to some of the principles we were evaluating. However, it is clear that the development process was a valuable exercise for this group of children and that it was an enjoyable experience for them.

Overall, we believe that we have demonstrated that the development approach used to design an ILE can be valuable to children who have social problems and low self-esteem. Game based learning environments must appeal to the target group if they are to be successful; it is essential to use a user centred design approach in these circumstances and in this case we believe that NCID proved to be an effective method of both requirements gathering, developing the design and engaging the children.

References

Amory, A. & Govinder, D. [2000], Interactive Fiction: Model Development and an Example Created with DHTML and Microsoft Agent, *in Proceedings of ED-MEDIA 2000*, AACE.

Amory, A., Naicker, K., Vincent, J. & Adams, C. [1999], The Use of Computer Games as an Educational Tool. Identification of Appropriate Game Types and Game Elements, *British Journal of Educational Technology* 30(4), 311–22.

Berger, A. [1997], *Narratives in Popular Culture, Media and Everyday Life*, Sage Publications.

Bruner, J. [1991], The Narrative Construction of Reality, *Critical Inquiry* 18(1), 1–21.

Lepper, M. & Cordova, D. [1992], A Desire to be Taught: Instructional Consequences of Intrinsic Motivation, *Motivation and Emotion* 16(3), 187–208.

Lepper, M., Woolverton, M. & Mumme, D. [1993], Motivational Techniques of Expert Human Tutors: Lessons for the Design of Computer-based Tutors, *in* S. Lajoie & S. Derry (eds.), *Computers as Cognitive Tools*, Lawrence Erlbaum Associates, pp.75–105.

Malone, T. [1981], Towards a Theory of Intrinsically Motivating Instruction, *Cognitive Science* **5**(4), 333–69.

Mandler, J. & DeForest, M. [1979], Is There More Than One Way To Recall a Story?, *Child Development* **50**, 886–9.

'Piaget, J. [1973], *Memory and Intelligence*, Basic Books.

Prensky, M. [2001], *Digital Game Based Learning*, McGraw-Hill.

Propp, V. [1968], *Morphology of the Folktale*, second edition, University of Texas Press. Translated from the Russian original by Laurence Scott.

Quinn, C. [1994], Designing Educational Computer Games, *in* K. Beattie, C. McNaught & S. Willis (eds.), *Interactive Multimedia in University Education: Designing for Change in Teaching and Learning*, Elsevier, pp.45–57.

Quinn, C. [1996], Designing an Instructional Game: Reflections on Quest for Independence, *Education and Information Technologies* **1**(1), 251–69.

Rollings, A. & Morris, D. [2000], *Game Architecture and Design*, Coriolis.

Scaife, M., Rogers, Y., Aldrich, F. & Davies, M. [1997], Designing For or Designing With? Informant Design for Interactive Learning Environments, *in* S. Pemberton (ed.), *Proceedings of the SIGCHI Conference on Human Factors in Computing Systems (CHI'97)*, ACM Press, pp.343–50.

Sherwood, C. [1991], Adventure Games in Education: A Far Cry from A Says Apple…, *Computers in Education* **17**(4), 305–15.

Trabbasso, T., Secco, T. & van den Broek, P. [1984], Causal Cohesion and Story Coherence, *in* H. Mandl, N. Stein & T. Trabasso (eds.), *Learning and Comprehension of Text*, Lawrence Erlbaum Associates, pp.83–111.

Waraich, A. [2002], Designing Motivating Narratives for Interactive Learning Environments, PhD thesis, Computer Based Learning Unit, University of Leeds.

Tales, Tours, Tools, and Troupes: A Tiered Research Method to Inform Ubiquitous Designs for the Elderly

Jay Lundell & Margaret Morris

Proactive Health, Intel Research, 2111 NE 25th Avenue, MS JF3–377, Hillsboro, OR 97124, USA
Email: *{jay.lundell, margaret.morris}@intel.com*

As the elder population continues to increase throughout the world, there is a tremendous need for technologies that will keep elders healthy and self-sufficient in their homes. Ubiquitous, smart home technologies can fulfill this role, but a thorough understanding of elders' routines, lifestyles, and home environments is required in order to develop effective aids. This paper describes our research approach, which evolved from stories related in household interviews ('tales'), ethnographic observation of elders' routines and environments ('tours'), analysis of artefacts ('tools') and finally interactive performances ('troupes') to convey and elicit feedback about the capabilities of future home technologies for the elderly. This combination of methods revealed a range of user values, behaviours, coping styles, and requirements for ubiquitous technology that would otherwise have been difficult to gather in this domain of ubiquitous, 'invisible' computing.

Keywords: design methods, elders, ubiquitous computing, focus troupe, ethnography.

1 Introduction

It is generally recognized that as people age and become less capable of performing daily activities, they nevertheless want to retain as much independence as possible. They want to pursue their interests, live in their own home, and continue to be active and social in spite of declining physical and cognitive abilities [Gibson et al. 2003]. Meanwhile, governments and health care officials are beginning to recognize that current medical models of elderly care are insufficient to deal with the coming global wave of elderly people. In nearly every country in the world, the percentage of people over the age of 65 will increase dramatically over the next 50 years [MMWR 2003]. The model of care that has frail elders being sent to live in nursing homes will cause the collapse of health care due to the sheer number of people it will need to support in this manner.

This situation implies a mutually beneficial solution — if we can keep elders self-sufficient and living in their homes, we can save the prohibitive costs to the health industry, and provide elders with a more desirable quality of life. But how is this done? How can we ensure that elders remain able to navigate their home, cook meals, shop for groceries, and maintain their health? How can we provide much of the care and assistance elders would get in a nursing home, while still keeping them independent and in control of their lives?

Several research projects are underway to address these issues by developing ubiquitous computing approaches to the home. At the Broadband Institute Residential Laboratory [Kidd et al. 1999], for example, researchers are installing a wide range of sensing equipment into a house that will be used as a 'living laboratory' for designing aids to support elders and other ubiquitous home applications. MIT's house_n project [Intille 2002] built by the MIT Department of Architecture, is used by the Media lab and other departments to explore a variety of technologies for elders as well as other applications. The Center for Future Health at the University of Rochester [Marsh 2002] has a smart medical home research laboratory that is focused more narrowly on the area of health research, and features an intelligent medical adviser and technologies to help detect changes in gait that indicate potential health problems. The Gloucester Smart House[1] is more specifically targeted to support elders with relatively simple 'low tech' solutions, such as a bath and basin monitor to prevent overflows, and a locator for finding lost items such as keys and glasses.

These are just a few of the efforts in ubiquitous computing that use the laboratory 'home' as the dedicated research site in which prototype technologies are implemented and later evaluated by bringing in people from the community. This 'living laboratory' approach can be effective as a method for testing and evaluating ubicomp technology, but it is costly — it requires the ongoing maintenance of a living environment and the construction of embedded prototypes.

Our group has taken an approach that is complementary to the 'living laboratory' approach. Rather than build out the technology and test in a dedicated laboratory, we have focused on conducting more extensive field research to uncover hidden needs and values, generating many different concepts, and testing these concepts using interaction scenarios. We plan to bypass the living laboratory framework and deploy technology into actual homes from the concepts that are validated in the interaction scenarios. This paper describes the methods we have used to gather requirements from elders, turn these requirements into high level concepts and test these concepts before building expensive ubiquitous computing prototypes.

---

[1] See http://www.bath.ac.uk/bime/projects.htm for details.

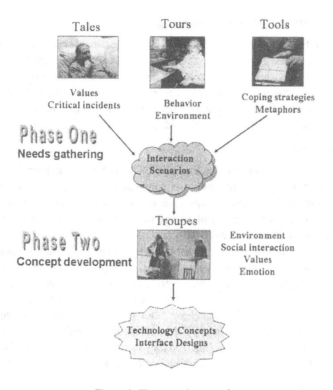

Figure 1: The research approach.

2 Research Approach

The research reported here occurred in two phases. In the *needs gathering* phase, we conducted interviews that elicited elders' stories (tales), 'day in the life' tours of the house, and key artefacts (tools) that they use in their day-to-day activities. These data types revealed elders' values, critical incidents in their lives, key aspects of their behaviour and environment, and coping strategies.

In the *concept development* phase, we conducted focus troupes to elicit feedback from our target audience. The focus troupe method uses dramatically staged scenarios to convey concepts to an audience that highlights the environmental, social, and emotional aspects of the concepts as well as the technical capabilities. Figure 1 illustrates this two-stage approach. We believe that this approach has produced insights into the development of solutions that might not have been obtained otherwise. By closely examining the lives of elders, their environment, their social networks, and daily routines, we develop insights into problems and opportunities in keeping elders healthy and active. By using the focus troupe method of obtaining concept feedback, we obtain actionable feedback from elders before investing expensive engineering resources in system development.

3 Phase One — Needs Gathering

In the needs gathering phase, we adopted a layered qualitative approach, using expert interviews and focus groups first, and then recruiting individuals from the focus groups for interviews and ethnographic observation. The focus groups provide the ability to identify the most important issues for elders and to narrow our focus for ethnographic study. This narrowing of focus has been recommended by others for naturalistic observations [Hirsch et al. 2000].

3.1 Participants

We recruited participants in five regions of the US — New York, Florida, California, Oregon, and Washington. In total, we conducted 44 household interviews, and 7 focus groups. Of the focus groups, one was with healthy elders, two were with elders with mild cognitive impairment and their spouses, two were with dementia patients and spouses, and two were with professional caregivers.

Of the household interviews, eight households involved healthy ageing elders, six suffered from mild cognitive impairment, twenty-five were in various stages of dementia (ranging from mild to severe), and four were family caregivers of deceased dementia patients. Elders and their spouses and/or other family members participated in the household interviews. Our participants (not including children caregivers) ranged in age from 56 to 97. Most were recruited through affiliations with University ageing research programs, and they represented a diverse socio-economic background, from rural poverty level housing to upscale urban care settings.

3.2 Procedures

Focus groups of eight to ten participants were conducted to uncover basic themes. We discussed how life has changed as they have aged, strategies for staying healthy, challenges with everyday household objects, daily activities, hobbies and interests, and strategies for organizing, reminding, and staying connected with friends and relatives.

From the focus groups, we invited participants to volunteer for home interviews. Interviews lasted about two hours and were videotaped. In these interviews, we followed up on issues that were revealed in the focus groups. We asked details about the participants' social support system, and discussed in more detail how their life has changed in retirement. For the cognitively impaired, we probed on the history of the impairment, how it was discovered and how they now cope with their disability. Finally, we toured their house, asking them to lead us through a typical 'day in the life'. We took copious notes and hundreds of photographs of artefacts in the home environment.

4 Phase One Results

The interviews produced data from 44 households. The data consisted of three broad categories. First, we analysed the tales that elders related to us. These stories reveal critical incidents in their lives and the values that are important to them. Second, we analysed the videotaped home tours that elders took us on. These tours reveal the daily routines and opportunities for enhancing and preserving the elders' lifestyle and habits. Third, we analysed the tools and artefacts that we captured in photographs around the house. These tools reveal many of the coping strategies and provide clues to the types of technologies that are acceptable to elders. Each of these provided different perspectives of their lives that contributed to our technology concept ideas. This section provides only a broad overview of our phase one results in order to illustrate the method. More detail is provided in another publication.

4.1 Tales

Elders told many stories describing critical incidents in their lives. For example, Gayle B. described when she first realized her husband Allen had dementia: she discovered that he had spent most of their retirement savings on uncharacteristically frivolous investments. These types of critical incidents in the lives of elders reveal major breakdowns in life processes that technology might be helpful in solving. Perhaps in Gayle B's case, intelligent technology to monitor investment behaviour might have been able to signal her or her adult children that Allen was behaving erratically, long before he lost so much of his money.

Tales revealed challenges in maintaining lifestyle in the face of functional decline. Mrs H told of the time she went hiking and found herself unable to get back to her car as darkness ensued. One of her favourite pastimes, hiking, now has become a fearful activity. Other elders related stories about giving up their hobbies. Clark showed us his extensive woodworking area while his wife revealed that she fears for his safety with all his dangerous equipment. Can technology help elders pursue their pastimes while keeping them safe?

Elders' stories also reflected their values. Randall and Naomi A. told us of their decision to sell their home and move into an adult care facility because they wanted to avoid the eventuality that their children would need to make living arrangements for them. In this case, they placed greater importance on their need to control their future than to remain in their home of thirty years. Although the values we extracted from this research did not always directly impact our technological solutions, they often helped to provide context and constraints on our ideas. For example, the values of independence and control often reminded us of the need to design solutions that allow elders maximum flexibility and initiative, and to design for a 'continuum of assistance' that provides support only when necessary.

4.2 Tours

In the 'day in the life' tours, elders enacted daily routines that revealed activities and behaviours that might be aided with ubiquitous technology. For example, Molly, a daughter of Chester, who lives nearby, explained why she has to come over every day to start the daily crossword puzzle for him. He often has difficulty getting started on the puzzle, but if she starts it, he will be more likely to finish it himself. We saw many examples of elders who routinely play games and puzzles, often more for the purpose of keeping their mind sharp and active than for their entertainment value.

Tours also gave us insights into the home environment and how elders utilize space in their household. We observed many instances of 'reminding walls' — areas used to display photos and memorabilia. These are more than simply places to hang photos — they are dedicated areas for reminding elders of their legacies and key

Figure 2: Household tours reveal behaviours. Doing crossword puzzles keeps elders mentally active. Photos and mementos are used much more frequently than computers that are sequestered in back rooms.

periods of their lives. These areas are in prominent locations of the house so they can be easily seen by visitors. They serve to maintain perspective, to reveal their values, and to preserve their identity. We also observed areas of the house that are seldom or infrequently used. For the elders that had a computer, the computer was always located in one of these spaces.

Tours also gave us insight into everyday behaviour. For example, nearly everyone struggled to remember to take their medications, and these attempts often failed. We observed that while some elders organize their medications in a single location, others distribute their medications at key locations throughout the house. For example, Ben keeps his morning medications in the bathroom, and his evening medications in the kitchen so he remembers to take them before dinner. In these households, even a 'smart' pillbox would fail to meet the needs of elders who prefer to take their medications in different locations of the house.

4.3 Tools

We took approximately 1700 photographs of household artefacts, from remote controls to microwaves to refrigerator magnets. These photos revealed the tools that elders use to support everyday coping strategies. They also revealed ways in which technology fails. For example, remote controls were often heavily taped, with the tape serving to provide more informative and readable instructions and to cover up unneeded and confusing buttons.

Virtually every household had at least one calendar, and most had many. There were monthly calendars on kitchen walls, and weekly calendars on dry-erase boards on the refrigerator. There were daily planners and pre-printed calendars of social events. Elders frequently transferred appointments from one calendar to another, and often had to synchronize multiple calendars into the daily schedule. Calendars were typically maintained by more than one member, and were collaborative in nature. Calendars served a variety of functions — as daily schedulers, as reminders of the past, as planning aids for the upcoming weeks or months, and even as a means of assessing goals and strategies. For example, one elder told us that he often records in his calendar what he had planned to do and what he had actually accomplished. Thus, he uses his calendar to gauge how well he has matched his actions to his goals over the course of a few months.

Figure 3: Calendars and reminders were in every household and showed elders' coping strategies in managing their lives.

There were many examples of notes and other reminding tools distributed in key locations. These attempt to serve as contextually appropriate reminders. However, we observed some problems with them. For example, Nancy proudly showed us the timer she wears around her neck to remind her when the laundry is done or the baking is done. Because she can wear it around the house, she will always hear the alarm. As we watched, she set the timer for 30 minutes. One half hour later, as we were taking a tour of her house, the alarm around her neck went off. "What's that?" she said, and we had to remind her that it was her alarm. In this case, the reminder failed to provide enough context and information for her to recognize it. This and other examples drove home the importance of contextual relevance in technologies.

Tools also served as metaphors to inform solutions. For example, the newspaper in the driveway served to notify neighbours that the resident elder had not yet gotten up. This use of a signal that indicates an elder's daily status led us to think about other ways that an ambient message might indicate an elders' status to loved ones living far away.

5 Phase Two — Interaction Scenarios

As we examined the tales, tours, and tools of these interviews, it became obvious that elders' requirements go beyond the ability to keep track of their medications, to perform daily activities, or even to remain safe. Elders were struggling to maintain their social ties, to keep involved in their cherished hobbies, and to preserve the unique identity that they had taken a lifetime to build. These values have driven the research in ways that other approaches would not have driven it.

From these perspectives, we developed conceptually based solutions that address the needs of these elders, and that were also grounded in technology that is feasible in the near future. We developed descriptions and concept photos of our ideas, and set out to obtain feedback from elders via focus groups and interviews. In spite of instructions to the contrary, many elders reacted to these descriptions by critiquing detailed (non central) aspects of the concepts (e.g. the colour of the device) vs. the capability that we were trying to assess. Other elders clearly misunderstood the descriptions of the concepts, and provided feedback that was irrelevant.

We decided that showing pictures and text descriptions of our concepts would not work well — the audience was not familiar enough with technology to understand which aspects were relevant to provide feedback and which were not. Additionally, the abstract, ubiquitous nature of many of our concepts was not conducive to a simple text description and a picture. We decided that the concepts needed a method of description that included the social, emotional, and environmental context in which it would be used. We decided to use focus troupes for this purpose.

A focus troupe (aka informance) is a method of depicting a technology concept via dramatic scenarios [Burns et al. 1994; Salvador & Howells 1998]. In this method, actors demonstrate the concept by dramatizing its use in a staged context. The audience consists of target users, and a facilitator leads a discussion after each scenario about the concept and how it might be used (or not used) by the audience. Like a focus group, this method is qualitative — data is collected on people's reactions and comments.

The value of a focus troupe is that the emphasis is on the context of use and the social interactions among the actors, as opposed to the technology or device. In fact, we conducted the dramatizations with no technology props at all. For example, when an actor was interacting with a display, she simply mimed the act of touching a screen and revealed through her comments and actions what was being displayed.

5.1 Method

We recruited three types of participants: healthy ageing, mild cognitive impairment, and leading segment boomers. The healthy ageing group consisted of elders 65 and over who had no diagnosed dementia or cognitive impairment, and were in generally healthy condition. The mild cognitive impairment group consisted of patients (and their spouses) who have been diagnosed with mild cognitive impairment. Finally, the leading segment boomers group consisted of people between 46 and 57 who have had some experience in caring for an elder family member. This group was included for two reasons. First, as caregivers, we wanted to obtain reactions to the concepts that facilitated remote care giving and relieving the caregivers' burden. Second, as the generation that will soon enter retirement age, we wanted to obtain their advance opinions regarding the solutions presented.

We worked with an outside agency that enlists actors for purposes of management training. We have also worked with this agency on previous informance group studies. We jointly developed a script that depicted our concepts within a typical 'at home' setting that we had observed. There were four dramatic scenarios presented.

In all there were seven sessions — three healthy elder sessions, and two each of MCI and boomers, for a total of 35 healthy elders, 16 MCI, and 28 boomers. Each session lasted about 2.5 hours. In each session, the moderator introduced the topic area, described the informance group process, and had each participant do a short introduction. Then the actors were introduced, and they acted the first scenario. Participants wrote down their initial impressions about the concepts that were dramatized on a notebook, and the moderator then engaged them in discussion.

These interaction scenarios were dramatic presentations that showed advanced ambient intelligence and ubiquitous computing applications. Even though none of these applications were developed, we were able, through these scenarios, to show rich interaction in the environmental and social context of an elders home. This proved particularly valuable for the types of applications that are ubiquitous and that attempt to facilitate social interaction and provide better quality of life rather than accomplish specific tasks.

Elders and boomers alike were able to easily grasp the capabilities as well as the potential problems of our scenarios. It was clear from the responses that participants could easily imagine variations in the applications that would better suit them. For example, several people felt that a system to help them rehearse names would not be nearly as helpful as a highly portable system that would provide name-face recognition 'in the moment'.

5.2 Example Interaction Scenario — The Pervasive Calendar

In all, we presented 13 concepts in the focus troupes. For purposes of brevity, we describe one example, and show how the concept was evaluated.

From the phase one study, we observed the challenges elders had in managing their lives with the calendars, post-it notes, and other tools. Elders talked about the difficulty in keeping calendars synchronized, the problems of remembering to write appointments down on calendars, and the problems of accessing calendars when away from the home. We developed the notion of the pervasive calendar — a calendar that is easily accessed, always synchronized, and easily modified. The calendar would interface with written paper and could be voice activated as well. Elders would access the calendar through multiple displays throughout the house.

The following dialogue shows how some of these aspects were conveyed through the characters of Sam and Jean, a retired couple:

Sam: What are we doing tomorrow?

Jean: It's on the calendar. Remember, you can look at it on the photo frame if you want.

Sam: Oh, yeah, right. (*picks up the photo frame prop*) (*To photoframe*) Calendar. Tomorrow. (*Showing speech recognition*) (*Reads it*) Golf. That's good. And shopping? (*To Jean*) Did you put that on there? (*To photo frame*) Erase shopping.

The scenario went on to show how Jean could update the calendar by writing on a paper calendar hung on the refrigerator.

Reactions to this concept were strongly positive. Many people's first reaction was "I want this now!" Some talked about the value of having a shared calendar for family and friends outside the home. To them, the calendar was a valuable means of staying in touch. For example, one participant described how he used to put sticky notes around his father's house that reminded the father of family activities that were planned — "he lived vicariously through us — through a shared calendar, he could be experiencing our life". As the discussion of the shared calendar progressed, some people realized the need to keep certain data private.

Elders liked the idea of a central calendar that automatically synced up to various peripheral calendars and date books. Said one participant, "I don't like to have to write things in three different places". They also greatly preferred speech recognition to other forms of input and output.

Another aspect that came up with the calendar scenario was the 'always on' aspect of ubiquitous computing. Several people mentioned the pain of having to start up a computer, and how they avoided electronic calendars because of that. The idea of always having immediate access to information was very appealing for baby boomers, and was a requirement for elders — they won't tolerate having to go to their isolated computer room to use these applications.

As a result of this type of feedback, we have modified our calendar concept to include more features for sharing, and have begun to implement components that will enable the pervasive calendar. More generally, the focus troupes have provided the information to allow us to guide the development of the most effective technology. We are currently developing the infrastructure that will be deployed into elders' homes this year to test and further refine our concepts.

6 Results and Implications for Ubiquitous Technology

From the results of our home visits and the focus troupe, we drew several general implications for ubiquitous technology to support elders in the home. Although the reaction to the specific concepts was very positive overall, elders expressed some general themes and areas of concern that apply globally to ubiquitous computing technology.

6.1 Flexibility

Participants made it clear that the technology must be flexible in accommodating an individual's lifestyle or functional needs. For example, people often commented that an interface modality would not fit all people. In one scenario, the actors demonstrated that a blinking light would signal the user about a situation, people quickly responded with comments such as "if the elder had poor eyesight, a light would not work". The technology needed to be adaptable for it to be acceptable as a solution in people's homes.

6.2 Device Intrusiveness

Participants also were concerned about the possible intrusion of technology that might make life more difficult instead of easier. Related to this issue is *control* — people want to be able to control the technology, not have the technology control them. One respondent stated, "I don't want beepers going off all the time — I have enough intrusion as it is". Technologies need to show value that clearly outweighs any actual or perceived inconvenience. A related concern was that the technology would foster premature or unnecessary reliance on devices for assisting in everyday living. This is a balancing act — technologies need to provide assistance only when needed, and allow the elder to act independently otherwise.

6.3 Privacy and Reciprocity

Elders raised issues of privacy and who would have access to data collected by ubiquitous sensors. Most participants want control over what information is shared and many felt that they only wanted to share information that was vital to their health or safety. Some expressed reservations about sharing even with a spouse or close relative. Any home monitoring or personal data collection technology needs to satisfy users that the information is secure and under their control. Furthermore, a reciprocal relationship would be preferred in which elder and caregiver share data with each other about their activities. If technology is used to monitor elders, elders in turn should be able to obtain availability information about the caregiver.

6.4 Robustness

Participants were quick to identify failure modes of the technology. For example, one participant noted that wearing the 'smart' tennis shoes for an activity other than exercise might incorrectly notify an exercise partner that their exercise buddy was ready for a walk. The technology needs to be tailored appropriately for the elder's situation and environment. People — especially elders — will abandon the use of a technology if there are even a few situations where it fails to work properly.

6.5 Natural User Interfaces

It was clear that elders want user interfaces that demand little or no learning, and interact in a way that is familiar to them. For example, in one interview, a caregiver showed us her mothers' fifteen-year-old microwave, which had been repaired numerous times at a cost much higher than a brand new microwave because she could not learn to use the newer appliances. Natural language understanding was very well received by elders because of its natural and effortless interaction style.

7 Conclusion

The individual methods described — tales, tours, tools, and troupes — have been variously illustrated in other papers. For example, Hirsch et al. [2000] have described using ethnography to study elders' needs, and Sato & Salvador [1999] have described the use of focus troupes. What is unique is the way these methods have been put together, and the application of these methods to the domain of ubiquitous computing.

These methods have allowed us to address some very challenging issues in the design of ubiquitous technologies for the home. We wanted to gather requirements from a population of users who had no familiarity with the capabilities of ubiquitous technologies, and little technical experience. Our focus was intentionally wide, as we wanted to understand the broad life challenges faced by this population. Thus, methods that focused on the critical stories, 'day in the life' tours, and a detailed understanding of the way everyday objects were used to solve problems proved very valuable and insightful.

Our phase one research led us to conclude that most solutions should be completely embedded into the existing home environment, and as such, should be 'invisible'. Thus, it was challenging to gather feedback on concepts that were not yet developed, and could not be instantiated as a particular concrete device. The focus troupe was a useful technique to present our concepts in a way that users could understand and relate to. By presenting these concepts in a social and environmental context, we were able to elicit deep values and emotions that might not have been obvious. As one participant commented about the value of the dramatizations:

"I think that if you had just presented pictures, I think of how much would be lost compared to the drama ... after seeing it acted out, you could feel how it would feel to use this technology".

This two-stage process can be extended to other projects. We believe that it is most useful for projects with the following attributes:

- *When social and environmental interaction is critical to the application.* In many standard business office or ecommerce applications that involve a single user and a well-defined goal, standard usability methods can be effective [Nielsen 1993]. However, it is difficult to identify social and environmental nuances of a technology without *in situ* observation, and testing applications in a usability lab will not reveal how the environmental or social context will interact with the use of the technology. With the focus troupe, we were able to evoke insightful discussions about the context of use that we were not able to obtain in interviews or focus groups.

- *When emotions are likely to play a key part of the product domain.* The role of emotion is just beginning to gain recognition in the design of products [Norman 2002], and is likely to play a greater role in the future. Ethnographic methods can elicit the emotions that are key in a particular domain, and the focus troupe can evoke those emotions and spur discussion about how designs can accommodate these relevant feelings in users.

- *When personal and cultural values are likely to be an important design consideration.* The ethnographic style of the home interviews allowed us to uncover values that were relevant to the domain of elder care, and the focus troupe method allowed us to position these values in the context of using the technology.

- *When the domain of interest might generate many concepts that need to be tested.* In this research, we generated and tested thirteen concepts. It would have been very expensive to develop working prototypes and embed them into a home environment or even to test them in a laboratory setting. With the focus troupe method, we were able to obtain useful and reliable feedback for many concepts without prototype development.

In addition, the process of designing the interaction scenarios and developing the script served to clarify our thoughts and helped to solidify our common understanding of our users' needs. As Burns et al. [1994] have pointed out, the process of doing this alone has great value in designing interactive products.

Acknowledgements

We would like to thank Eric Dishman, Brad Needham, Paul Pilat, Karen Howells, and Judy Straalsand for their work on this project, and the anonymous reviewers of this manuscript.

References

Burns, C., Dishman, E., Verplank, W. & Lassiter, B. [1994], Actors, Hairdos and Videotape: Informance Design, *in* B. Adelson, S. Dumais & J. Olson (eds.), *Proceedings of the SIGCHI Conference on Human Factors in Computing Systems: Celebrating Interdependence (CHI'94)*, ACM Press, pp.119–20.

Gibson, M., Freiman, M., Gregory, S., Kassner, E., Kochera, A., Mullen, F., Pandya, S., Redfoot, D., Straight, A. & Wright, B. [2003], Beyond 50: A Report to the Nation on Independent Living and Disability, http://research.aarp.org/il/beyond_50_il.html.

Hirsch, T., Forlizzi, J., Hyder, E., Goetz, J., Strobeck, J. & Kurtz, C. [2000], The ELDer Project: Social, Emotional and Environmental Factors in the Design of Eldercare Technologies, *in* J. Thomas (ed.), *Proceedings of the ACM Conference on Universal Usability (CUU 2000)*, ACM Press, pp.72–9.

Intille, S. S. [2002], Designing a Home of the Future, *IEEE Pervasive Computing* **1**(2), 76–82.

Kidd, C. D., Orr, R. J., Abowd, G. D., Atkeson, C. G., Essa, I. A., MacIntyre, B., Mynatt, E., Starner, T. E. & Newstetter, W. [1999], The Aware Home: A Living Laboratory for Ubiquitous Computing Research, *in* N. A. Streitz, J. Siegel, V. Hartkopf & S. Konomi (eds.), *Cooperative Buildings: Integrating Information, Organizations, and Architecture. Second International Workshop, CoBuild'99*, Vol. 1670 of *Lecture Notes in Computer Science*, Springer-Verlag, pp.191–8.

Marsh, J. [2002], House Calls, *Rochester Review* **64**(3), 22–6.

MMWR [2003], Public Health and Aging: Trends in Aging — United States and Worldwide, *Morbidity and Mortality Weekly Report* **52**(06), 101–6. Also avaialble at http://www.cdc.gov/mmwr/preview/mmwrhtml/mm5206a2.htm.

Nielsen, J. [1993], *Usability Engineering*, Academic Press.

Norman, D. [2002], Emotion and Design: Attractive Things Work Better, *Interactions* **9**(4), 36–42.

Salvador, T. & Howells, K. [1998], Focus Troupe: Using Drama to Create Common Context for New Product Concept End User Evaluations, *in* C.-M. Karat & A. Lund (eds.), *CHI'98 Conference Summary of the Conference on Human Factors in Computing Systems*, ACM Press, pp.251–2.

Sato, S. & Salvador, T. [1999], Playacting and Focus Troupes: Theatre Techniques for Creating Quick, Intense, Immersive and Engaging Focus Group Sessions, *Interactions* **6**(5), 35–41.

Designs for Lives

The Re-design of a PDA-based System for Supporting People with Parkinson's Disease

Bengt Göransson

Uppsala University IT/HCI and Enea Redina AB, Smedsgränd 9, SE-753 20, Uppsala, Sweden

Email: *Bengt.Goransson@enea.se*

This paper describes the re-design of the user interface and the interaction for the PDA-based (Personal Digital Assistant) system *mediPal*. The aim with the system is to help people with Parkinson's disease to a better life by supporting them in their day-to-day struggle with their chronic illness. In the paper we discuss the re-design — the process and the resulting user interface. The focus is on the evaluation of an earlier version of the system and how that led up to an improved user interface through user-centred systems design (UCSD). The paper also discusses how a practitioner can accomplish UCSD in the context of product development and consultant work.

Keywords: Parkinson's disease, personal digital assistant, design for special needs, usability, practitioner, user-centred systems design, quality in life.

1 Introduction

In this paper we will describe and discuss a design case where we re-designed a potentially highly useful system, to make it easier and more intuitive, i.e. usable, to use. The PDA-based system, called mediPal, was at the time still under development, but had been tried out and tested by approximately 6–8 users. The author was hired as a consultant and usability designer to improve the usability of the new release, which was intended to become the first commercially available version. My reflections on how a usability designer consultant can promote a user-centred attitude and process in a constrained product development setting will also be summarized. The conditions for my work were to finalize a product that was considered 'almost ready' by the client. This had impact on my 'space' for designing and focusing on usability, and called for a cost-effective use of user-centred techniques.

1.1 The Reflective Practitioner

To *reflect-in-action* and *reflect-on-action*, and be a reflective practitioner as Donald
Schön [1983, 1987] suggests are important and effective methods for practitioners
to analyse and extract conclusions from their practice and then communicate them
to others. In doing consultant work as a practitioner in a project, you are expected to
contribute and to make a difference in the project, but relevant research results can
nevertheless be obtained, as long as the reader bears in mind the particular context
and work situation. This paper is aiming to communicate how this particular re-
design project was conducted, the resulting artefacts and the reflections made.

As the system aims at helping people with chronic diseases such as Parkinson's,
and given that the design of such an interactive system undoubtedly will
be influenced by that, I think it is necessary to include a background to the
characteristics of Parkinson's disease.

2 Background to Parkinson's Disease

Parkinson's disease (Parkinson for short) is a chronic neurological condition.
Parkinson is a slowly progressive disease that affects a small area of cells in the
mid brain known as the *substantia nigra*. Gradual degeneration of these cells causes
a reduction in a vital chemical known as 'dopamine'. This decrease in dopamine can
produce one or more of the classic signs of Parkinson:

- resting tremor on one side of the body;

- generalized slowness of movement (bradykinesia);

- stiffness of limbs (rigidity); and

- gait or balance problems (postural dysfunction).

In Sweden between 10,000–20,000 people have some kind of Parkinson
related disease (in US there are approximately 1.5 million with Parkinson
(http://www.parkinson.org/)). Although 15% of the patients are diagnosed before
the age of 50, Parkinson is generally considered a disease which strikes older adults.

Parkinson often begins with an episodic tremor of the hand on one side of the
body. Tremors may be distressing because of their visibility to others, but fortunately,
this symptom rarely leads to serious disability.

Resting tremors may be accompanied over time with slowness and stiffness on
the affected side. As symptoms progress, patients may notice impairment on the
other side of the body, almost always less severe than the primary side. Due to fine
motor deficits, finger and hand movements requiring skilled coordination, such as
brushing teeth, shaving, and buttoning clothes may become slow and difficult. Some
patients notice a slight foot drag on the affected side, or a feeling of walking with
great effort ('as through quicksand') at times. Steps become shorter, or freezing may
occur when initiating movement. The voice can decrease in volume and take on a
raspy quality. While there is yet no cure for this condition, progressive treatments
allow many patients to maintain a high level of function throughout their lifetimes.

Many Parkinson symptoms can be controlled with currently available medications. Levodopa (also called L-dopa), the active anti-Parkinson substance in drugs such as Madopark, is the single most beneficial substance to relieve symptoms of Parkinson. L-dopa is a short-acting substance that enters the brain and is converted into dopamine, the neurotransmitter that is low in Parkinson. L-dopa is combined with another substance called carbidopa, which enhances L-dopa's action in the brain and minimizes side effects such as nausea.

Low-dosage of a drug containing L-dopa is commonly started when the patient experiences enough inconvenience or incapacity from Parkinson symptoms to interfere with his or her ability to carry out normal activities. Maximal results are obtained the first few years on this medication, although most patients continue to benefit for many years. With long-term use, some patients notice a shorter duration of effect from each dose (known as the 'wearing off' phenomenon), and some can develop an 'on-off' effect in which symptoms may come and go at unpredictable intervals.

3   Objectives for the Medical Friend — mediPal

Medication for a patient suffering from a chronic disease such as Parkinson is highly individual and also situation based with many influencing factors. Knowledge about these factors as well as the relationship between cause and effect is only partially available due to the complexity of the human system. This makes it virtually impossible to construct successful medication schemes based on causal knowledge. The *mediPal* concept is therefore based on real observations by the patients themselves and the usage of an inductive learning method to detect suitable medication schemes. These schemes are stored and a pattern recognition technique is used to retrieve medication advice based on the current situation.

The purpose of the adaptive learning method used in mediPal is to gradually and automatically discover successful medication schemes for an individual and to store and use these schemes as future medication advice.

The man who invented mediPal suffered from Parkinson himself. He discovered how important it was to monitor how his mobility changed in relation to the specific medications he was taking. This in turn led to the idea to constantly reporting and gathering information about his illness to a 'medical friend'. The result is the mediPal product, which the Swedish company Meditelligence initially developed.

The essence of the mediPal product is its ability to remind the patient about medication, and then collect data or information from the patient. The major reason for physicians to encourage their patients to use systems like mediPal is the systems' reporting accuracy — a PDA has a better ability to 'memorize' than a person does. The reports do not only give physicians a better basis for treating their patients, but also better data for research purposes.

4   The Re-design of mediPal

The development of the mediPal system had been going on for some years, mostly focusing on the adaptive learning algorithm and the internal system architecture, when our re-design of the user interface started. The mediPal had a user interface, which was designed by the developers of the system, and partly by the inventor of the mediPal concept. The earlier design of the user interface was based on expertise knowledge about Parkinson and its effects, but little usability or design knowledge. At this time the company understood that the user interface of the system needed some improvements before becoming a commercial product, i.e. a more usable and 'nicer' looking user interface. They also realized the importance of the usability aspect for such a product, but did not fully appreciate the impact that our work would have on the system.

Below is a short background on how the mediPal system is supposed to work, and some rationales for our design decisions. A typical scenario on how the system works would be:

- The patient gets a PDA with the mediPal system (pre-installed) in which the physician has entered a scheme for medication, and a set of feedback questions regarding vital symptoms and conditions.

- If relevant, the physician can add questions such as: "have you been drinking coffee?", "have you been sleeping well?", etc.

- The patient gets an alarm or reminder when it is time to take some medication, and answers some follow-up questions.

- Whenever a crucial condition changes, such as tremor, the patient is invited to register that: *Spontaneous registration.*

- During the next visit to the physician, he or she will use the stored information to make any necessary changes in the patient's medication scheme.

- The physician can, based on the information provided via mediPal, see patterns and guide the patient in his or her day-to-day life.

The initial goal of the system was for it to automatically adjust the patient's medication scheme, in real time. However, everyone involved in the project realized that this would take a long time to accomplish and that it also involved major legal, medical and ethical concerns. Today, only the treating physician is allowed to modify a drug prescription and medication scheme. Instead, the results and the predictions from the system were still to be treated as added information for the physician to act on.

The PDA itself can be used for other purposes than mediPal, e.g. taking notes, browsing the Internet, e-mailing, etc. The mediPal system is a local system with its own database and no on-line communication. Data from the mediPal system is uploaded to the doctor's computer[1] for review through a standard synchronization program. Uploading can be done during visits to the hospital only.

For the data to be of any real value, the user must use mediPal for several consecutive weeks, providing enough input to the adaptive learning algorithm for it

---

[1] A special program was also developed for the purpose of reviewing the data and customizing the mediPal system with attributes for an individual user (patient). This program is not a part of this design case and paper.

- A PDA running Microsoft Windows for Pocket PC environments.

- The screen is 240×320 pixels, and in colour.

- Pen input, no traditional keyboard.

- Touch sensitive screen.

- Runs on battery.

Figure 1: The PDA that was used for mediPal and some of the major technical concerns.

to make valid conclusions and finding patterns in the variation of the user's condition with the intake and effects of the medication. Thus, the system is to be used daily and must be at hand at all times.

Designing for a PDA (see Figure 1) compared to designing for, e.g. a desktop computer, is quite different and challenging. Some of the more notable differences are:

- The limited space on the screen and its physical size.

- The way you interact: the stylus pen and the handwriting.

- A touch screen.

- Availability. The PDA is always carried around and instantly available when needed.

Designing for people with Parkinson was challenging in itself, and gave us a couple of surprises, but the main challenge was designing for the PDA rather than for the special needs of the users. We introduced some new concepts for layout and interaction, based on careful interaction design.

Our position on, and our solutions to these challenges are described later on, as the design and the process is detailed.

4.1 The Re-design Process

A 'lightweight' and tailored design process was used, based on the usability design process proposed by Göransson [2001]. This process included:

- Reviewing of all feedback from different stakeholders, including early test users.

- User profiling.

- Analysis of all windows and dialogues.

- Usability evaluations and user interviews.

- *Report — analysis report.* (milestone)

- New design phase — paper and pencil, sketches in a drawing program.

- Usability evaluations with users.

- Continued design — prototype on the PDA.

- *Report — design report.* (milestone)

The development team contained a nurse, specialized in Parkinson; a usability designer; a product manager; a technical project manager and three developers. In addition, a technical writer and some administrative staff were also involved, but not part of the project team.

Taking part as a usability consultant in a product development project, and joining late in the process, affects what you can do and accomplish. Nevertheless, my aim was to introduce usability and user-centred methods and techniques in the project. We used the key principles for UCSD defined by Gulliksen et al. [2003] as a starting point. They include principles such as: active user involvement, iterative design, prototyping, dedicated design activities, evaluations and usability championing. The team used a mixed development process approach with influences mainly from Rational Unified Process [Kruchten 1998]. I introduced user-centred activities where and when suitable, and did not try to 'force' UCSD on the development team.

My reflections on what we did and did not accomplish, in regard to UCSD, are discussed in the concluding section of this paper.

4.1.1   Review of the Earlier Version

The first thing that we did was to print all the current windows and dialogues in the mediPal system, and put them on the walls of the project room. We did also go through all available documents with comments, etc. on the system and extracted the most vital pieces of information, for the usability, and compiled them in a list. This was information that had been collected by the nurse in the project, for the most part during communication with the early 'test' users. (The 6–8 patients that had been trying out the earlier version of mediPal for some months.)

Then we conducted several sessions going through different usage scenarios on these 'paper windows'. We annotated them with potential, and sometimes already known, usability problems and also with suggestions for improvements. By doing this we built a 'picture' of the current status of the system and it also gave all members of the development team a common ground to relate to. It was clear that by doing this, the developers got an insight into how the users actually had to, or were forced to, use the system. By building the 'big' picture, we could e.g. discuss things such as navigation structures and interaction design, instead of just details in one single window.

In order to place the focus on the users and their background and current situation, we developed a user profile of a typical Parkinson patient.

We used our own version of *personas* [Cooper 1999] with the following objectives and characteristics:

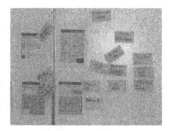

(a) Screen dumps on the walls   (b) Example detail.
   of the project room.

Figure 2: Review of windows and dialogues in the earlier version. Screen dumps were put up on the walls and annotated with yellow stickers for possible usability problems and green stickers for suggested improvements.

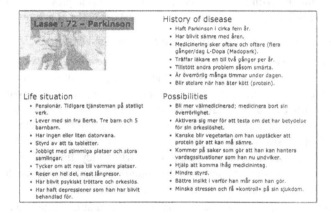

Figure 3: A persona-like description of the main and targeted user group.

- *Goal for the persona*: to focus the team on the users and the usage of the system.

- Based on accurate data about persons suffering from Parkinson, mostly already known 'facts' collected by the nurse in the team.

- A fictitious character (patient), but with real attributes.

- Placed on a wall in our project room, for everyone to see and be influenced by. It was placed next to the screen dumps, relating it closely to the system.

We used the persona solely for analysis and design issues. When it came to evaluations, we evaluated with real users. This is somewhat different from the

Figure 4: Evaluating the earlier version of mediPal with a patient.

original purpose that Cooper suggests where the personas are also used for evaluation purposes. Evaluating with real users is one of the key principles behind UCSD and can not be replaced with or simulated by virtual walk-troughs of personas.

4.1.2   Studies of Users, Actually Using the Earlier Version

In parallel to this, we conducted user interviews and evaluations with three users (patients) at a University hospital. Before the usability evaluation of the system we interviewed the users to find out how they used the system in their day-to-day life. They were told to describe in what context they used it, how they used it, what they liked and did not like about it, etc. The actual evaluation of the system was carried out as a think-aloud session. The users were asked to carry out some of their more frequent activities with the PDA and think aloud while they did this. We took notes as well as still photos during the sessions. No video was used, mostly due to the legal and integrity aspects on using a recording video at a hospital.

Two additional users were also briefly interviewed at our office, and asked to give their opinion on the system.

The analysis of the results was then done at our office. I, as the usability designer, and the nurse discussed and compiled the findings in a workshop together with the other team members. We used our notes and the photos as input in this activity.

4.1.3   Problems in Earlier Version

After the user evaluations and review of the dialogues and windows we delivered an analysis report, stating usability problems and suggesting improvements. Listed below are some of the most prominent findings:

- *Users did not feel in control.* They 'got lost'. The window structure and interaction were not clear and intuitive to the users.

- *Some long interaction sequences* and even illogical sequences, e.g. when attending to an alarm.

Figure 5: Main window.

Figure 6: Window for entering data.

- *The aesthetic design was defective*, e.g. background images, colour scheme, sizes of buttons. This lead to, among other things, unnecessary cognitive problems.

- *Users did not have a good enough overview of events.* Users could not foresee the next couple of events and plan in accordance with them.

Figures 5 & 6 show example windows from the earlier version[2].

The usability problems did also have an immediate impact on the quality and the accuracy of the system. Since the adaptive learning algorithm is totally dependent on valid and correct information from the users, the usability problems that were found did not only irritate and stress the users, but did also lead to 'bad quality' in the entered information. This was not because of users not being able to tell their current condition, but depending on a less usable user interface, making users hesitate and be confused about what information to enter where, etc.

Based on theses findings we suggested a set of usability goals or 'user aims'. They were not measurable usability requirements, but served as the team's guidance for the future development of the user interface and interaction design:

- Guidance to a better life, i.e. to feel better.

- Easy to learn. Short learning period (minutes).

---

[2]The earlier version of mediPal was only available in Swedish so all screen dumps are therefore only available in Swedish.

- Consistent and correct data, i.e. intuitive and error prohibiting data input mechanism. Gives the physician better data for decision-making, e.g. about changes in the medication.

- Support and help to remember: diary, reminders, etc. Reduce the user's cognitive work load.

The first goal of 'feeling better' is not really what you expect as a usability goal, but it has the character of being unavoidable when working with users suffering from a chronic disease. We were guided in our design by this goal in the sense that we were actively and constantly searching for possible design solutions that would give the users visual feedback about trends in their condition, and recommendations about e.g. food habits. The rest of the goals were more concrete and straight forward to interpret and put into design solutions.

The earlier version of mediPal was based on the assumption that users would use their fingers to interact with the PDA. This, in combination with the tremors that are part of, had led to a window design with rather large active touch areas. The real estate of the screen was therefore not efficiently used. Our user evaluations and investigations did lead us in another direction. All the users we studied, as well as other users we communicated with, used the stylus pen to interact with the PDA. And further, when they used the stylus pen the tremor seemed to be less disturbing. This finding made it possible for us to reduce the size of the touch areas and to come up with a design that took advantage of the screen's real estate much more efficiently.

4.2   Designing the Next Version

After delivering the analysis report we went ahead with the re-design of the user interface and the interaction. We based our design process on some high level design criteria and decisions deduced from the findings during the evaluation and from the usability goals:

- A virtual 'timeline': The user (patient) should have the possibility to view forthcoming as well as previous events and activities — overview and detail. This would presumable lead to a kind of calendar function and a diary.

- User in control: The user must feel in, and have total control, i.e. always be sure what to do, and immediately see what can be done. There must be no situation where the user hesitates about the next action.

- Graphics and layout: Significant improvements in screen layout and graphics were necessary. This included: an obvious and consistent conceptual design with clear navigation paths; efficient usage of the screen space (real estate); a pre-defined colour scheme; eligible fonts and font sizes, etc.

The limitations of the PDA led to the below design decisions, among others:

- No handwriting as input. This meant that there were no such things as free text input fields, just optioned input and button commands. The reasons for this were many; the most significant was the time it takes to enter free text that is correct with the stylus pen.

Figure 7: Design sessions. Starting on paper; using pencil, sticky notes, etc.

- *Minimize erroneous and unintentional input* by having interaction actions be activated in two steps. Two-step interaction prevents users hitting for example a command button and executing some functionality, by mistake. This might happen, for instance, if the PDA gets 'squeezed' when in a pocket or purse.

We started the re-design using a number of different low level prototyping tools; paper, pencils, whiteboard, sticky notes, etc. The design was guided by the persona and the design decisions described above.

We did most of the design in informal design sessions. Most often the usability designer and the nurse met alone, but occasionally we had sessions with the developers and the whole development team. We also met with the users a few times, to discuss design issues. We went through a loop of conceptual design, interaction design and detailed design, and also interchanged the different design phases [see for example Crampton Smith & Tabor 1996]. Details in the design are explained in the next section where the final design is showed.

The evaluation of the new design took place at the same hospital in Lund, Sweden. We evaluated with three users, two of them were the same as in the first evaluation. We used a paper prototype together with the PDA. We took the paper sketches and designed them in a drawing program. Then we printed the windows on carton paper, and cut them to fit the display of the PDA.

During the evaluation sessions one person sat next to the user and asked questions as well as took notes. The user was asked to carry out scenarios of their more frequent activities and think aloud while they did this. They interacted with the system by using the stylus pen and point on the 'paper window' on top of the PDA. They explained what they did, why and what they expected to happen. A third person then swapped the paper windows according to the user's action. After the session we interviewed the user about their experience with the prototype.

The resulting material was analysed in the same manner as in the first evaluation. The results were unambiguous and did, in comparison with the prior

Figure 8: Evaluating a paper prototype placed on top of the PDA screen.

evaluation, give much better result, i.e. it seemed like the new version was more usable than the earlier one. All users managed to carry out their most frequent activities or tasks easily and reasonably quickly. They also expressed their positive opinion about the new look and feel of the system.

The main reasons for using a low-fidelity prototype were that no investment in programming was necessary and that the designers spent less effort on the design, making it easier to discard it and replace it with another. The main drawbacks were that it was only a simulation of the real user interface, only the designed actions could be simulated, we could not measure the exact timing of events or system feedback and that the feel of the interface was not the real thing. But, given the time constraints and the resources available, it was much wiser to spend time and money on a paper prototype instead of having programmers code a functional prototype.

4.3   Final Design

Even though it seemed that the new user interface was an improvement compared to the earlier one, the results from the evaluation led to some re-design. The most notable was re-arranging some of the areas on the Start or *Main window*. We wanted some fields to be more prominent and to be more visibly attractive, so we moved them to the top of the window. We also changed some of the visual appearances and introduced a set of icons. But in general, the design was acceptable, so we focused on finalizing all windows. In parallel the developers worked on a running prototype.

4.3.1   Conceptual Design

The overall design of the user interface focuses on effectively supporting the users in their day-to-day life. Based on the design implications identified in the earlier activities, we decided on using the *workspace metaphor* [Henderson & Card 1986; Borälv & Göransson 1997] for the conceptual design. In our implementation of this metaphor we strived to design an effective user interaction with logical and minimized navigation. In the workspace metaphor, the application window is divided into distinct areas, each containing a workspace with all the information and functionality needed by the user to perform a certain work task or activity. The workspace and navigation between workspaces are in focus. Within the workspace, information and functions are grouped into *panels*. Due to the physical screen limitations of a hand held device, certain deviations from the principles of simultaneous viewing and a minimum of navigation were necessary.

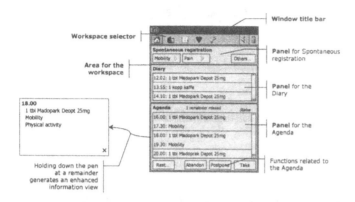

Figure 9: The final design of the Main window. Components in the conceptual design have bold text.

Figure 9 shows the Main window which is visible most of the time. Acting on, for example, alarms, will generate a new window, but after attending to the alarm, the Main window will appear again. It contains the most important user features: the *Agenda*, the *Diary* and the *Spontaneous registration* facility.

The rationale underpinning the conceptual design was in short: *a stable and intuitive framework where the user can be and feel in total control*. The workspace is not to be confused with so called tab controls. Tab controls can be used within the workspaces to group information that belongs together. There is always one workspace active. That means, for example, that the user navigates between the workspaces on an imaginary horizontal level, and uses functions within a workspace on a vertical level. All (with some exceptions) functions are modal: the user has to go back (or up) before selecting a new function. Functions are usually encapsulated in function windows that occupy the whole screen and are application modal (see Figure 10).

In the Remainder window we typically had to adapt to the limited screen space and design for sequential instead of parallel viewing. If there are more than five actions, or questions for the user, a 'dynamic panel' is visible with sets of five actions per window to go through.

Among the graphical components we developed were a collection of so called *editors* (see Figure 11). Each editor supports a certain category of information to be entered by the user.

After finalizing all windows we delivered the Design report. The report was then 'approved' and the construction phase (programming) started. Even though some construction had been going on during the design phase, mostly prototyping, the bulk of programming took place after the design phase. When this construction phase started I left the team and the nurse was supposed to see to that the design was consistently and coherently implemented.

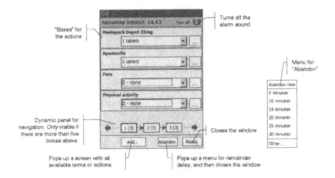

Turns off the alarm sound

"Boxes" for the actions

Menu for: "Abandon"

Dynamic panel for navigation. *Only visible if there are more than five boxes above*

Closes the window

Pops up a screen with all available terms or actions

Pops up a menu for remainder delay, and then closes the window

Figure 10: Example of a function window: Remainder, attending to an alarm.

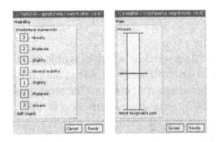

Figure 11: Example of editors for entering information in: Mobility (left-side) and Pain (right-side).

5   Discussion on Results and Reflections

We re-designed the user interface and the interaction for the mediPal system to better fit the needs of the users. And we did this by using a user-centred approach. The managers at the product company were surprised that the re-design had such a great impact on the system. What they expected to be a minor 'face-lift', turned out to be a major make-over. We did not just change the look of the system. We eventually changed the whole interaction (dialogue), and also altered quite a lot of the functionality. The usability focus and the UCSD approach had a much greater influence on the re-design than they could foresee.

5.1   What Can Be Learned?

I, the usability designer, spent approximately 190 hours in the project. A very modest effort, but well in line with what we, as consultants, typically put into projects. We started in mid October 2001 and the analysis and design phase ended in early March 2002. It was a great advantage to work with people who know the domain and the user characteristics thoroughly. In this case the relation between the nurse and me (the usability designer) turned out to be fruitful. We complemented each other in knowledge and experience, and worked efficiently together.

The tailoring of the UCSD process was necessary. We could not have pushed harder for a change in the company's development practices. We realized that it had to be a step-by-step process, changing the work practices for the team members as well as for the managers. Reflecting on how we worked actively with the users and the UCSD process, I must admit that I have mixed feelings about what we succeeded with in comparison to what we wanted to do:

- The design phase, with dedicated activities for going through conceptual design, interaction design, and lastly detailed design, was considered a good approach, in general.

- The team managed to focus on usability, e.g. via the usage of a persona, but we did not succeed in having active user participation.

- We spent too little time with users. We wanted to do more evaluations, as well as studies of users in their homes and bring users into design sessions etc. The main reason why we did not do this was that we could not convince management to give us the resources needed for these kinds of studies. Another major concern related to this was the limited access to users. That might have been solved if we had succeeded in getting more resources.

- Having the usability designer leaving the project right at the start of the construction phase was a logical decision in the managers' eyes, but resulted in a lack of user and usability focus during this phase. This was reported numerous times by team members in later communications. The usability championing aspects can never be overrated.

- The adaptation of the workspace metaphor to the small format of the PDA was a challenge, but turned out quite well. We did have to make some compromises such as having sequential windows for some tasks.

- The evaluation of the prototype with paper windows used on top of the PDA was seen as an elegant and effective way of carrying out the usability evaluation.

Working with users that have a chronic disease such as Parkinson does inevitably have an effect on what you are doing. You get emotionally involved, but exactly how this affects your job is very hard to tell. I like to think about it as the practitioner being humbled by the experience, trying to do his/her very best, and even adding a little bit extra without including it on the invoice.

5.2   How Did the mediPal System Succeed as a Product?

There were three studies with approximately 80 users planned for when I left the project. The results from these studies are unfortunately not published and therefore inaccessible. The commercial introduction of the product has for various reasons been postponed, and mediPal has now been sold to another company and is hopefully ready for release this year. So, it is hard to say if mediPal will really help people with Parkinson in the future or not; it is unclear at the moment.

References

Borälv, E. & Göransson, B. [1997], A Teleradiology System Design Case, *in* I. McClelland, G. Olson, G. C. van der Veer, A. Henderson & S. Coles (eds.), *Proceedings of the Symposium on Designing Interactive Systems: Processes, Practices, Methods and Techniques (DIS'97)*, ACM Press, pp.27–30.

Cooper, A. [1999], *The Inmates are Running the Asylum: Why High-tech Products Drive us Crazy and How to Restore the Sanity,*, Sams Technical Publishing. ISBN-0-672-31649-8.

Crampton Smith, G. & Tabor, P. [1996], The Role of the Artist-Designer, *in* T. Winograd (ed.), *Bringing Design to Software*, Addison–Wesley, pp.37–61.

Göransson, B. [2001], Usability Design: A Framework for Designing Usable Interactive Systems in Practice, Licentiate Thesis in Human-Computer Interaction, Uppsala University. http://www.it.uu.se/research/reports/lic/2001-006/.

Gulliksen, J., Göransson, B., Boivie, I., Blomkvist, S., Persson, J. & Cajander, Å. [2003], Key Principles for User-centred Systems Design, *Behaviour & Information Technology* 22(6), 397–409. In special section "Designing IT for Healthy Work".

Henderson, A. & Card, S. [1986], Rooms: The Use of Multiple Virtual Workspaces to Reduce Space Contention in a Window-based Graphical User Interface, *ACM Transactions on Graphics* 5(3), 211–43.

Kruchten, P. [1998], *The Rational Unified Process – An Introduction*, Object Technology Series, Addison–Wesley Longmans.

Schön, D. [1987], *Educating the Reflective Practitioner: Toward a New Design for Teaching and Learning in the Professions*, Jossey-Bass.

Schön, D. A. [1983], *The Reflective Practitioner: How Professionals think in Action*, Basic Books.

Designing for Social Inclusion: Computer Mediation of Trust Relations Between Citizens and Public Service Providers

Michael Grimsley[†], Anthony Meehan[‡] & Anna Tan[*]

[†] *Centre for Regional Economic & Social Research, Sheffield Hallam University, Pond Street, Sheffield S1 1WB, UK*
Email: *m.f.grimsley@shu.ac.uk*

[‡] *Department of Computing, The Open University, Walton Hall, Milton Keynes MK7 6AA, UK*
Email: *a.s.meehan@open.ac.uk*
URL: *http://mcs.open.ac.uk/am4469*

[*] *London Borough of Camden, Town Hall Extension, Argyle Street, London WC1H 8NG, UK*
Email: *anna.tan@casweb.org.uk*

Trust has a direct impact on the extent to which citizens engage with public and community services. This paper advances a framework which seeks to support HCI designers and managers in promoting ICT-mediated citizen engagement with public services through a strategy of trust promotion. The framework is based upon an analysis of evidence from large-scale community surveys which demonstrate a significant relationship between levels of user trust and users' experience of public services and reveals experiential factors that promote users' trust.

Keywords: trust, e-government, public services, social inclusion, social exclusion.

1   Introduction

"Those who are left outside the development of information and communication technology are often the same people ... who most need the welfare state's services in any case. This is why special attention should also be paid to the needs of these people when developing a human information society." [Pekonen & Pulkkinen 2002]

Some people avoid contact with public and community services they do not trust unless it is absolutely essential [Duffy et al. 2003]. Trust promotion can have a direct impact on how well services such as schools, hospitals, justice (both criminal and civil), police, housing, environment, can meet individual and wider community needs. In the UK, the government is promoting on-line delivery of public services through its e-Government initiative. At the same time, the government is concerned to address the problem of social exclusion, associated with economic and other forms of social disadvantage. In this context, it seems timely to examine ways in which information and communication technologies (ICT) can be designed to promote trust-based relations between citizens and public service institutions; otherwise there is a risk that the increased reliance on electronically mediated interaction with public services may reinforce social exclusion. The work described in this paper is part of a research programme which aims to identify principles, and develop frameworks, that designers and managers of ICT systems can use to facilitate community engagement with public services through the medium of trust.

There is a growing body of work examining trust in human-computer interaction in the context of e-commerce; Egger [2002] provides a useful review. The dominant focus of this research seems to be the experience of the computer interface in respect of graphical design, ease of navigation, brand recognition and reinforcement (e.g. use of colours, logos), etc. Some of this research extends to include transaction feedback i.e. a customer's experience of the outcome of an electronically mediated transaction (e.g. did the goods arrive on time, in good condition, etc.) [Minocha et al. 2004]. This aspect of experience is often seen as adjacent to HCI, but, in our view, is integral to the design of systems that mediate human-human or human-institution relations.

For a number of reasons, the e-commerce model of transaction experience is not best suited to understanding user interaction with public services. Many important services are delivered over prolonged time scales and satisfaction can depend more upon how a service *is* (not was) provided, rather than the specific outcome (e.g. consider the attitudes of chronically ill patients towards hospital staff). Further, in promoting first-time engagement with public services it is important to identify the experience of service delivery that is sought or anticipated by the user and find ways of conveying, via design of the user interface, that this experience is available.

In seeking to use ICT to promote engagement with community services, the first step in our strategy is to identify experiential factors that promote trust between citizens and the providers of public services (human-institution interaction). Thence we shall seek ways to incorporate these factors into the users' experience of a computer-mediated interaction with a public service. Accordingly, this paper examines results from large scale public surveys which describe, from a users perspective, trust-promoting experiences of public services and then proceeds to develop a framework which supports incorporation of these experiential determinants of trust into the design of computer-mediated interactions with service providers.

The remainder of the paper is organized as follows. In Section 2 we very briefly describe our view of the role of trust in community strategy; for a fuller account, see Grimsley et al. [2003]. Section 3 describes the evidence relating trust to peoples' experience of public services and identifies the experiential basis of this relationship. Section 4 describes framework for incorporating the experiential dimensions of trust relations into the computer-based mediation of users' interactions with public services. Section 5 makes some concluding remarks and describes future work.

2 Trust in Communities

We consider, briefly, the role of trust in communities. We then examine the forms of trust that arise within communities and outline the relation of ICT to the community relations that give rise to trust.

2.1 The Role of Trust

We view trust as an expression of Social Capital [Bourdieu 1986]. Within any community, individuals relate to a wide range of institutions: families, cultural, community and political associations, institutions providing public services, democratic and legislative fora. Relations with (and between) these institutions operate on the basis of some level of mutual trust. Trust makes possible the achievement of community objectives that would not be attainable in its absence [Coleman 1990; Fukuyama 1995]. Community trust relations are an expression (possibly the principal expression) of a community's capacity to achieve a better quality of life than would otherwise be available if its members acted merely as individuals [Lin 2001; Warren 2001].

2.2 Forms of Trust

Braithwaite & Levi [1998] distinguish between two form of community trust. *Horizontal trust* arises in relations with family, friends, neighbours, work colleagues. *Vertical trust* arises in relations with community institutions. Grimsley et al. [2003] have also demonstrated that horizontal and vertical trust are correlated (in a statistically significant sense) and have articulated a Community Trust Cycle which provides a framework for locating the generation and propagation of trust arising from relations within a community (Figure 1). Levels of vertical trust are promoted both by a sense of being able to influence policies and provision of public services and by experience of the service's actual provision and practice. Statistically, vertical trust is correlated with experience of public service provision but horizontal trust is not. This suggests (but no stronger) that horizontal relations mediate the community's experience of individuals' vertical trust relations.

2.3 ICT and Trust Relations

ICT has a number of distinctive roles in mediating the trust relations in this cycle and the development of the Internet and associated technologies (including

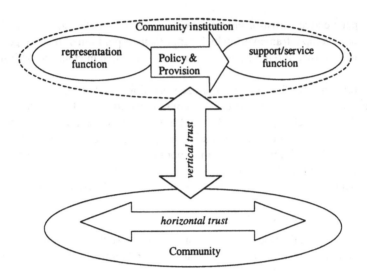

Figure 1: Community Trust Cycle.

---

interface technologies) has significantly extended the potential scope of this role. Most commonly perhaps, intranets facilitate internal social relations of institutions and organizations; see, for example, Nandhakumar & Montealegre [2003]. E-Commerce has led to significant changes in the extent to which ICT mediates peoples' experiences of community institutions in the commercial sphere and trust is seen as an important factor in its continued development [Egger 2002]. Recently, there has been a significant growth in technology to support the availability of government and public services, so-called e-government; where the metaphor of e-commerce seems to have been transplanted, appropriately or otherwise, into systems of public governance and service provision. ICT to support contributions to the formation of policy and to the election of officials/representatives is at an earlier stage of development. ICT can contribute to the connectivity of community, e.g. at the level of family, friends, neighbourhoods, community organizations. It can disseminate information about the role of community institutions and can mediate peoples' interaction with, and participation in, those institutions; though its impact in terms of trust and social capital appears to be relatively complex and uneven [Wellman et al. 2001].

Our strategy for promoting community participation is to first identify the elements of positive trust relations that exist between members of a community and its participative institutions and thence seek ways to mediate access to these same trust relations using ICT, and, indeed, extending this opportunity to those who are otherwise socially excluded. This is one part of a vision for electronically mediated access to community agencies and public services.

3 Trust and the Experience of Public Services

In this section we describe two large-scale surveys that provided data for our enquiry, the means used to analyse the data, and the results of the analysis.

3.1 Surveys

Two sample surveys were conducted in economically deprived UK communities. Over the last decade or more, the communities have experienced significant, deleterious, economic and social change, mainly as a result of the loss of employment. Social exclusion is a policy concern in these areas.

One survey was commissioned to evaluate UK government and European Union regeneration strategies. It was designed and supervized by a local consortium of agencies. Interviews were undertaken by 50 trained members of the local communities surveyed. It elicited responses from 4220 individuals in homes within nine distinct communities with one adult selected per randomly sampled household [Green et al. 2001]. Another survey was commissioned to examine issues related to housing and health, and forms the first part (wave 1) of a longitudinal research programme. This postal survey covered eight similar, but not the same, communities. More than one person per household was sampled and social housing households were over represented by design. Responses were obtained from 1341 individuals [Green et al. 2000].

Both surveys featured a combination of direct and indirect questions and responses to questions were expressed on five-point ordinal, or Likert, scales. The surveys measured user satisfaction with a variety of public services, and levels of community trust.

3.2 Data Analysis

Many of the issues upon which respondents were questioned are believed non-independent. Accordingly, in analysing the responses, we have used oblique principal component analysis (OPCA) when attempting to identify the underlying components of trust.

3.2.1 Community Services and Trust

For both surveys, the relation between satisfaction with community services and the level of community trust was explored. The first survey elicited responses on satisfaction with, and trust placed in, health services, police, local environment management and transport services; the second survey for health facilities, transport and schools. For all surveys, and for all services considered, there was a strong positive correlation between satisfactory experience of the service and the level of trust expressed. Having established a relationship between experience of services and expressed trust, the first survey was used to identify the dominant experiential factors that seemed to underpin expressed levels of trust in services.

3.2.2 Experiential Factors Determining Trust Levels

The first survey allows an analysis of three experiential factors that were conjectured to influence levels of community trust arising from individuals' relations with public services and other community institutions [Grimsley et al. 2003]. These are complex factors for which any single label risks misrepresenting their meaning. We have labelled the factors as follows:

- Information: the extent to which individuals felt well informed.

- Control: the extent to which individuals felt they enjoyed a sense of personal control in their lives.

- Influence: the extent to which individuals felt they could exert influence.

Control has many interpretations in the literature [Skinner 1996] and it is best to try to clarify its use here. In the context of HCI and social capital it is perhaps most readily related to *affordances* [Gibson 1977] and perceived affordances [Norman 1999; McGrenere & Ho 2000]. We suggest that if the set of anticipated affordances is greater than the set of *perceived affordances*, a sense of reduced control is induced. In this context, a sense of personal control also captures the scope for alternative courses of action (sequences of affordances), towards the same end, as individuals juggle the demands of work, home, care of children, the elderly and the sick and other community responsibilities.

The concept of influence, too, has a number of interpretations in the literature. However, in the context of civil society, we adopt Rodin's interpretation of influence as access to, and/or participation in, democratic processes; "the expectation of having the power to participate in making decisions in order to obtain desirable consequences" [Rodin 1996]. This interpretation appears to be shared by Warren [2001] when examining political empowerment and 'voice' in the context of social capital. Skinner [1996] summarizes some deleterious effects that absence of the ability to exert control, and influence the world one experiences, has on mental and physical well being.

For each the three experiential factors investigated, there is a strong, positive, relationship between the level of the factor and the level of trust expressed (Figure 2). (Space does not permit a fuller exploration of the relation of these experiential factors to trust but we do wish to point out there are important distinctions to be made on the basis of community, gender, ethnicity and education/training.)

4 Mediation of Users' Experiences to Promote Trust

We have seen above that trust is determined (partially) by three experiential variates. The identification of these variates, and their role in promoting trust, suggests that they should each be addressed in planning, designing and managing ICT systems which will mediate relations between community members and community institutions such as public services. The framework we are developing aims to support that objective.

The element of the framework explored below is an Experience Management Matrix, which supports each party in the trust relation in determining its participative strategy.

4.1 Experience Management Matrix

The Experience Management Matrix is based upon the inter-relation of the three experiential factors we have identified as contributing to trust. The intuition behind

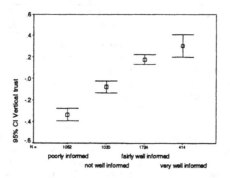

(a) Sense of being well informed.

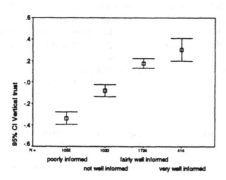

(b) Sense of personal control.

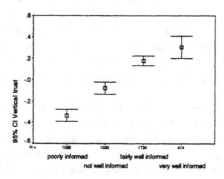

(c) Sense of influence.

Figure 2: Experiential factors underpinning trust in public services. (Vertical scale is the 95% confidence intervals for levels of vertical trust expressed over all services.)

Trust Strategy	Target Experience in User		
	Sense of being Well-informed	Sense of Personal Control	Sense of being able to Influence
Information Strategy Questions	How should information be structured and organized to promote well-informedness?	What information is needed and how can it be organized to promote a sense of personal control?	What information is needed to facilitate the formation of informed views and how to convey them appropriately and effectively?
Distribution of Control Questions	With whom should the initiative lie in the elicitation and provision of information?	How might responsibility for the subtasks that together achieve the objectives of the relationship be distributed between the parties?	With whom should the initiative lie in the elicitation of views on current and future policy?
Deployment of Influence Questions	What balanced and (preferably) independent evidence is available to legitimate current policy and practice?	How might perceptions of needs be changed so that any diminution of the space of alternative courses of action/opportunity is not experienced as a diminution of a sense of control?	What negotiation strategies will be perceived as trustworthy?

Table 1: Experience Management Matrix — nine dynamics arise from the 'product' of three experiential factors promoting trust in a two-party relationship.

---

the instrument is that the experiential factors we have identified apply to both parties in a trust relationship. Thus, for each party, there is scope for shaping the overall trust relationship by managing the communication of information, the distribution of control, and the deployment of influence, in respect of the other party. This gives rise to nine separate dynamics in the trust relation, each of which features a range or scale of behaviours that will shape the experience of the other party.

If we consider ourselves in the role of a designer and/or manager of ICT systems which mediate the users' interaction with our (public) service, we need to formulate three strategies; an Information Strategy, a Control Strategy, and an Influence Strategy (leftmost column of the matrix). Each of these has a desired experiential outcome in the user (top rows of the matrix). (Of course, there is a complementary user perspective in relation to the provider.)

The matrix is illustrated in Table 1. In each cell of the matrix, we identify the central design question to be addressed in devising the trust-mediation strategy. To illustrate the use of the matrix, we provide some examples of how these dynamics may be elaborated.

Control (of Information) Strategy	Induced Sense of Well-informedness
Basic-reactive: Information provision is entirely request driven.	*Dependent*: user must take the initiative in researching the information needed to act.
Minimal-standard: basic or routine information on levels of service availability is published.	*Non-standard dependent*: if the user needs any variation in the basic provision they must take the initiative in acting to meet their need.
Explanatory: explanations are published in relation to 'routine' service standards.	*Informed-dependent*: the user knows and can take a view on the reasonableness of the service standards they experience.
Responsive: information is provided about how the service can be adapted to (individual) users' needs.	*Facilitated*: the user can negotiate provision for their specific circumstances.
Enabling: information is provided which allows the users to achieve goals by reference to alternative courses of action or even 'competing' service providers.	*Emancipated*: the user is able to pursue alternative courses of action which achieve their desired goal.

Table 2: Relation of chosen control of information strategy to user experience of a sense of being well-informed.

4.1.1 Example 1 (Row 1, Column 1)

First, consider the problem of determining an information strategy that will engender a sense of being well informed in the second party. Complex organizations need complex structures to organize the information they need to convey to widely differing parties. Key issues include determining an appropriate volume of information to be provided, the quality and depth of the information (e.g. accuracy/clarity/accessibility), and the scope of the information (e.g. does it cover the most common/basic requirements of users, does it extend to special/unusual requirements, does it refer to alternative, possibly competing, sources of support/service). There will, inevitably, be a variety of constraints in relation to this task, for example, in relation to UK e-Government strategy, there are standards designed to enforce interoperability (e.g. determining search categories, multilingual capability, and more — see http://www.govtalk.gov.uk).

4.1.2 Example 2 (Row 2, Column 1)

Second, consider how control can be deployed to induce a sense of being well informed in the other party. In relation to control of provision of information there are two poles to a strategy: the first represents a purely reactive strategy (information is provided only when asked for), the alternate pole is wholly proactive information provision. The experience of these different strategies will range, respectively, from a sense of dependence and low levels of a sense of personal control through to a sense of emancipation (Table 2). (It is possible to construct comparable figures to illustrate the examples that follow but we have avoided this for reasons of space.)

4.1.3 Example 3 (Row 2, Column 2)

Third, consider how control can be distributed between service provider and user. Here, there is a considerable body of literature that is of relevance. Sources include the CSCW, Adjustable Autonomy and Mixed-initiative Interaction communities. Bradshaw et al. [in press] are currently seeking to identify and describe some conceptual dimensions that are, in some sense, common to these research communities, with a view to understanding and formalizing policy-governed, dynamic task distribution between autonomous entities, be they ICT systems, or human individuals or institutions. The policy framework that is anticipated appears to have two elements. The first builds a model those tasks that can be achieved unilaterally and those that require collaboration. The second, more ambitious, element will seek to drive the distribution of tasks over this first model on the basis of dynamic, integrated planning and scheduling, and the psychological needs of humans. One such need is (mutual) trust. This project offers the prospect of sophisticated and complex control strategies.

4.1.4   Example 4 (Row 3, Column 1)

Fourth, consider how the deployment of influence may promote a sense of being well-informed. The strategic options in this case range from absence or denial of access to information which has been used to inform policy in respect of service provision and practice, through to the provision of a clear rationale, for current policy. The positive effect of this latter strategy is enhanced if the evidence is seen to be independent. The experience of these alternatives ranges from a sense of informational exclusion in which it is only possible to speculate as to the rationale behind a policy through to informational inclusion in which it is possible to construct both an appreciation of the service rationale and to formulate proposals for alternative provision and practice on the basis of shared evidence.

4.1.5   Example 5 (Row 3 Column 3)

Finally, consider how the deployment of influence may promote a sense of being able to influence. The relevant literature in this situation comes mainly from negotiation theory. The strategic alternatives range from denial of influence, through a coordinative style, to an integrative approach. The corresponding experiences range from exclusion (seeming antagonism), through to an experience of having the issues one advances being at least acknowledged, to an experience of mutual trading of priorities/constraints (subject to the relative priorities of the respective parties) [Pruitt 1981]. There is an appreciable body of literature on computer-based (agent) negotiation to inform designers of ICT systems in which negotiation with users is to be facilitated [for example Zlotkin & Rosenschein 1996a,b; Faratin et al. 1997; Kraus et al. 1998]. Grimsley & Meehan [2002; 2003] have begun work on automating integrative negotiation styles in the context of e-commerce.

5   Conclusion and Future Work

This paper has addressed the problem of promoting user engagement with public services as part of a social inclusion strategy based upon trust promotion. It describes the analysis of two large-scale surveys among users of public services that demonstrate a link between users' experiences of services and trust in those services. Further, it has identified three experiential factors that appear to promote expressions of trust in public services: how well informed users feel, the extent to which they experience of sense of control in their lives, and the extent to which they feel able to exert influence.

The paper then proceeded to explore a framework to aid designers and managers of ICT systems that will mediate user interaction with public services. The framework features an Experience Management Matrix which supports the development of interaction strategies based upon managing the experiential factors promoting a sense of trust in users.

Future work will focus upon evaluating the medium and long-term effectiveness of the framework as part of a new e-Government initiative, CASweb, (to be launched in 2004) which provides a portal for selected public services in a pilot project covering five London Boroughs.

References

Bourdieu, P. [1986], The Forms of Capital, *in* J. G. Richardson (ed.), *Handbook of Theory and Research for the Sociology of Education*, Greenwood Press, pp.241–58.

Bradshaw, J. M., Jung, H., Kulkarni, S. & Taysom, W. [in press], Dimensions of Adjustable Autonomy and Mixed-initiative Interaction, *in* M. Klusch, G. Weiss & M. Rovatsos (eds.), *Computational Autonomy*, Springer-Verlag.

Braithwaite, V. & Levi, M. (eds.) [1998], *Trust and Governance*, Russell Sage Foundation.

Coleman, J. S. [1990], *The Foundations of Social Theory*, Harvard University Press.

Duffy, B., Browning, P. & Skinner, G. [2003], Exploring Trust in Public Institutions: A report for the Audit Commission, Technical Report, MORI. http://www.mori.com/sri/pdf/final.pdf.

Egger, F. N. [2002], Consumer Trust in E-Commerce: From Psychology to Interaction Design, *in* J. E. J. Prins, P. M. A. Ribbers, H. C. A. van Tilborg, A. F. L. Veth & J. G. L. van der Wees (eds.), *Trust in Electronic Commerce: The Role of Trust from a Legal, an Organizational and a Technical Point of View*, Kluwer, pp.11–43.

Faratin, P., Sierra, C. & Jennings, N. R. [1997], Negotiation Decision Functions for Autonomous Agents, *International Journal of Robotics and Autonomous Systems* **24**(3–4), 159–82.

Fukuyama, F. [1995], *The Social Virtues and the Creation of Prosperity*, Free Press.

Gibson, J. J. [1977], The Theory of Affordances, *in* R. Shaw & J. Bransford (eds.), *Perceiving, Acting and Knowing: Towards an Ecological Psychology*, Lawrence Erlbaum Associates distributed by John Wiley & Sons, pp.67–82.

Green, G., Grimsley, M. & Stafford, B. [2001], Capital Accounting for Neighbourhood Sustainability, Technical Report, Centre for Regional Economic and Social Research, Sheffield Hallam University.

Green, G., Grimsley, M., Suokas, A., Prescott, M., Jowitt, T. & Linacre, R. [2000], Social Capital, Health and Economy in South Yorkshire Coalfield Communities, Technical Report, Centre for Regional Economic and Social Research, Sheffield Hallam University.

Grimsley, M. & Meehan, A. [2002], Measuring Behaviour-based Trust Between Negotiating Agents, *in* M. Klusch, S. Ossowski & O. Shehory (eds.), *Cooperative Intelligent Agents VI: Proceedings of the 6th International Workshop on Cooperative Information Agents, CIA 2002*, Vol. 2446 of *Lecture Notes in Artifical Intelligence*, Springer-Verlag, pp.112–22.

Grimsley, M. & Meehan, A. [2003], Dynamic Inference of Perceptual Categories in Negotiating Agents, *in* J. Liu & N. Zhong (eds.), *Proceeding of the IEEE-WIC International Conference on Intelligent Agent Technology (IAT-2003)*, IEEE Publications, pp.89–95.

Grimsley, M., Meehan, A., Green, G. & Stafford, B. [2003], Social Capital and Community Trust and e-Government Services, *in* P. Nixon & S. Terzis (eds.), *Proceedings of the 1st International Conference on Trust Management*, Vol. 2692 of *Lecture Notes in Computer Science*, Springer-Verlag, pp.165–78.

Kraus, S., Sycara, K. & Evenchick, A. [1998], Reaching Agreement through Argumentation: A Logical Model and Implementation, *Artificial Intelligence* **104**(1-2), 1–69.

Lin, N. [2001], *Social Capital: A Theory of Social Structure and Action*, Cambridge University Press.

McGrenere, J. & Ho, W. [2000], Affordances: Clarifying and Evolving a Concept, *in Proceedings of Graphics Interface 2000*, Peters. Avaialble at http://www.graphicsinterface.org/proceedings/200/177/.

Minocha, S., Dawson, L., Roberts, D. & Petre, M. [2004], E-SEQUAL: A Customer-centred Approach to Providing Value in E-commerce Environments, Technical Report 2004/12, Department of Computing, The Open University.

Nandhakumar, J. & Montealegre, R. [2003], Social and Organizational Aspects of Internet-based Information Systems, *Information Systems Journal* **13**(2), 109–112. Special Issue on Internet as an Agent of Social and Organisational Change.

Norman, D. A. [1999], Affordance, Convention and Design, *Interactions* **6**(3), 38–42. http://www.jnd.org/dn.mss/affordances-interactions.html.

Pekonen, O. & Pulkkinen, L. [2002], Social Capital and the Development of Information and Communication Technology: Report for The Committee for the Future of the Parliament of Finland, Technical Report, University of Jyväskylä.

Pruitt, D. G. [1981], *Negotiation Behaviour*, Academic Press.

Rodin, J. [1996], Control by Any Other Name: Definitions Concepts and Processes, *in* J. Rodin, C. Schooler & K. W. Schaie (eds.), *Selfdirectedness: Cause and Effects Throughout the Life Course*, Lawrence Erlbaum Associates, pp.131–48.

Skinner, E. A. [1996], A Guide to Constructs of Control, *Journal of Personality and Social Psychology* **71**(3), 549–70.

Warren, M. E. [2001], Social Capital and Corruption, *in* D. Castiglione (ed.), *Social Capital: Interdisciplinary Perspectives. Proceedings of the EURESCO Conference on Social Capital*, School of Historical, Political and Sociological Studies, University of Exeter. Available at http://www.ex.ac.uk/shipss/politics/research/socialcapital/papers/warren.pdf.

Wellman, B., Haasse, A. Q., Witte, J. & Hampton, K. [2001], Does the Internet Increase, Decrease, or Supplement Social Capital? Social Networks, Participation, and Community Commitment, *American Behavioral Scientist* **45**(3), 436–445. Special issue on The Internet in Everyday Life.

Zlotkin, G. & Rosenschein, J. S. [1996a], Mechanism Design for Automated Negotiation and its Application to Task Oriented Domains, *Artificial Intelligence* **86**(2), 195–244.

Zlotkin, G. & Rosenschein, J. S. [1996b], Mechanisms for Automated Negotiation in State Oriented Domains, *Journal of the Artificial Intelligence Research* **5**, 163–238.

Decentralized Remote Diagnostics: A Study of Diagnostics in the Marine Industry

Jonas Kuschel & Fredrik Ljungberg

Application Development Group, Department of Applied IT, IT University of Göteborg, Box 8718, 40275 Göteborg, Sweden

Tel: *+46 31 772 4895*

Email: *{jonas.kuschel, ljungberg}@ituniv.se*

We present the results of a study of diagnostics work in the marine industry, with the purpose of exploring design implications for remote diagnostics. We divide diagnostics work in three analytical categories, called 'defining the problem', 'investigating cause and solving the problem', and 'involving central experts'. The three main characteristics of these categories are; the importance of being co-located with each other and the boat, the collaborative practice, and the reliance of local knowledge. Against this background, we suggest a decentralized approach to remote diagnostics, which focuses on the local service technician. The decentralized approach suggested contrasts our research from the prevailing centralized model of remote diagnostics, in which the local technician plays a minor role.

Keywords: remote diagnostics, empirical study, collaboration, local knowledge, CSCW, design implications.

1   Introduction

In the marine industry, as in the vehicle industry in general, companies are showing an increased interest in remote diagnostics. This concept denotes the process of accessing, diagnosing and programming the control and support systems of modern vehicles remotely. In the past, diagnostics work was restricted to the workshop, but technological evolution increasingly makes this possible remotely. Vehicles become more and more computerized, and consequently, problems and solutions are nowadays often concerned with digital technology.

In Computer Supported Cooperative Work (CSCW), authors often claim the importance of going beyond the common sense understanding of practice when developing new applications to evolve that practice [see for example Hughes et al. 1997]. From that starting point, we may argue that the design of applications for remote diagnostics should be informed by empirical studies of how diagnostics actually takes place today. Based on this assumption, we have conducted fieldwork investigating diagnostics in the marine industry. The objective was to discern design implications for how diagnostics, as currently undertaken, can be evolved, or 'cultivated' [Dahlbom & Mathiassen 1993], into remote diagnostics. The results complement, we argue, the existing body of knowledge in the area, which mainly consists of technical implementations and visionary speculations, with empirically grounded implications for design. Our main thesis is that diagnostics should be evolved into 'decentralized' remote diagnostics, which, in contrast to the vision of completely centralized diagnostics often promoted in industry (e.g. GM OnStar), takes three main aspects of the current diagnostics practice into account: the local knowledge of the technician, the collaborative work practice, as well as involved actors being co-located to each other and the boat.

The paper is structured as follows. In Section 2, we introduce the area of remote diagnostics, in Section 3 we describe the research site and method used in the study, Section 4 presents the results of the study, which are discussed in Section 5, and finally, concluded in Section 6.

2   Remote Diagnostics

Before reporting the fieldwork and its results, we wish to introduce the concept of remote diagnostics in some more detail.

2.1   The Modern Vehicle

A modern vehicle, such as a boat, is to large extent controlled by computers, often called Electronic Control Units (ECUs), which are interconnected via a serial bus. Each ECU controls different parts of the vehicle. The electronic injectors, for example, optimize the amount of fuel to be injected into each cylinder. The ECUs execute software and can thus be programmed to behave in different ways. Experts from DaimlerChrysler estimate that 80 percent of all future automotive innovations will be driven by electronics and 90 percent thereof by software [Grimm 2003], indicating the growing importance of software components.

Data values beyond a predefined scope automatically trigger so called Diagnostic Trouble Codes (DTCs) that are stored in the ECUs. Consequently, mechanics of today have to rely on advanced computer programs to perform a service. With such computer applications, mechanics can read out DTCs, display status parameters, update the ECUs with software patches, etc.

2.2   What is Remote Diagnostics?

There are no generally agreed upon definitions of neither 'remote diagnostics'[1] nor the closely related concept of 'telematics'. However, in general 'telematics' denotes the wide set of vehicle related services enabled by wireless communications, while 'remote diagnostics' concerns the subset of services concerned with diagnosing and

---

[1] 'Remote diagnostics' and 'remote vehicle diagnostics' are often used interchangeably.

solving vehicle problems remotely. For example, a route guidance service for drivers would be an example of 'telematics', while a system that sends DTCs from vehicles to a central service centre would be an example of 'remote diagnostics'.

In the automotive industry, there is a set of common assumptions about how remote diagnostics will be applied in the future. These assumptions may be worth mentioning as a background to the fieldwork. First, remote diagnostics is often believed to bring the possibility to reduce, or even remove the need for local service technicians — "if less experts could solve vehicle problems remotely, then why do we need all these local technicians?" Second, the person who accesses the vehicle data is assumed to be an expert technician of some kind, who typically would be situated at a central service centre. Third, the expert technician is believed to have significant knowledge of the vehicle electronics, and inasmuch as he has access to the vehicle he is expected to be able to solve most ECU related problems. Fourth, it is often assumed that the customer simply does not want to know about remote diagnostics, i.e. remote diagnostics should be transparent. One or several of these assumptions you will find in most research on remote diagnostics.

2.3   *Research on Remote Diagnostics*

Originally, remote diagnostics was concerned with diagnosing a problem with a vehicle from a remote geographical location, typically a central service centre. Increasingly, however, remote diagnostics has been used to denote the entire process of defining and solving problems with a vehicle remotely. Consider, for example, the definition by market analysts Frost & Sullivan. They define remote diagnostics as:

> "The ability to access the vehicle's performance parameters and trouble codes in case of malfunction using a wireless network, and provide necessary support services." [Frost & Sullivan 2002, p.3]

During the late 1990's, the forecasts for usage of remote diagnostics were optimistic. In 1998, Jameel et al. [1998] predicted that new vehicles within five years probably would incorporate basic telematics services, such as sending status data reports via the Internet. Even though this has not happened, the vehicle industry still considers remote diagnostics to be a very important area. Customers also believe in the prospect of remote diagnostics, a recent survey by Gartner G2 [2002] concludes. In the study, 28% of the subjects reported their next car is likely, or very likely to have a remote diagnostics service, which is a 133% growth compared to the year before (ibid.). This may seem remarkable given the current economic downturn and general IT pessimism. However, there are already some examples of commercial services such as GM's OnStar.

Despite the commercial interest in remote diagnostics, the research in the area is still rather limited. It is mainly very technologically oriented, with a main interest in connectivity and security [see for example Duri et al. 2002; Bisdikan et al. 2002]. One strand of research in the field reports reference architectures and implementations of infrastructure. Campos et al. [2002], for example, report a novel reference-architecture for remote diagnostics applications, based on Java 2 Enterprise Edition (J2EE) and Open Service Gateway Initiative (OSGi). The reference-architecture builds upon the idea of context-awareness as a means of predicting future action. The assumption is that we can apply AI (e.g. agents, data mining) on data collected about the vehicle, to predict future purposeful action. However, the planning model that systems like this rely upon has documented to be problematic in the case of interactive systems [see for example Suchman 1987].

There is also a body of research concerned with 'diagnostics' as such, e.g. how experts solve diagnostics problems [see for example Rasmussen 1993; Besnard & Bastien-Toniazzo 1999]. This is, of course, important input to our project. At the same time, it is not straightforward how to transform those findings into the design of remote diagnostics systems.

Before going through the results of our study, let us introduce the research site and method.

3   Research Site and Method

Ethnographic workplace studies are today commonplace in CSCW and HCI [see for example Hughes et al. 1994; Bellotti & Bly 1996], and the use of social science approaches to inform computer science has become widely acknowledged in the literature [see for example Dourish 2001; Luff et al. 2000; Hughes et al. 1995]. The objective of our research is to apply a social science approach as a means to understand diagnostics work, and based on such an understanding be able to sketch design implications to evolve that practice towards remote diagnostics. In the terms of Dahlbom & Mathiassen [1993], we want to 'cultivate' diagnostics into remote diagnostics. We want, simply put, to understand what parts of diagnostics to preserve, what to evolve, and what to remove. Our aim is to, inspired by the idea of cultivation, change diagnostics, but not to more than necessary.

We conducted our research at Volvo Penta (VP), a leading manufacturer of engines for leisure boats, work boats and power generating industrial equipments such as generators or fork lifters. VP has one of the industry's largest dealer networks, which is supported by a central support organization. The support organization starts with a regional support team that covers several countries, e.g. Scandinavia and Western Europe, followed by the Global Support Department (GSD) that supports all regional departments, and finally the Quality Action Centre (QAC) specialized in solution-finding for recurring problems reported from the field. Our study investigated the Scandinavian regional support team, GSD and QAC, which are located at VP's headquarter in Göteborg, Sweden.

We collected our empirical material by conducting a 'quick and dirty' ethnographic field study. Hughes et al. describe such an approach as follows:

> "What the quick and dirty fieldwork provides is the important broad understanding that is capable of sensitising developers to issues which have a bearing on the acceptability and usability of an envisaged system rather than on specifics of development." [Hughes et al. 1994, p.434]

We wanted to understand the main characteristics of diagnostics work and by doing so be able to discuss overall implications, or principles for how to evolve that work practice with new applications. Against this background, we found quick and dirty ethnography a useful starting point for our project.

Figure 1: Local service technician, customer and researcher at the site.

Our study consists of two parts, first, a study of local service technicians and second, a complementary study of central experts at VP. The first part took place at four different local service centres in Sweden and involved eight service technicians. With the exception of one informant, all technicians were highly skilled and worked single-handed. All technicians worked with modern boats, i.e. boats equipped with ECUs, which was a requirement in the selection of study objects. A challenge for ethnographic fieldwork is to become accepted by the study objects in the field as smoothly as possible so as to minimize the disruption to their work patterns. This was especially important in our case as seasonal changes limited the time for the study. We gained quick access through actively participating at the scene. We tried to help the technicians thus becoming 'observers as participants' [Junker, 1960 described in Hammersley & Atkinson 1995]. It was suggested to us that, in 80%, of the cases customers were present when servicing was undertaken, so customers were included in our study. The second part of our study focused on studying seven experts at the customer support centre (regional support, GSD, QAC). The whole study was conducted during a period of two months and involved informal interviewing and shadowing of experts at work.

4   Results

In the study, we identified three analytical categories of diagnostics work carried out by the local technician: defining the problem, investigating the causes and solving the problem, and involving central experts. We also found it useful to make distinctions between symptoms, effects and causes. Let us start this part of the paper with an excerpt that illustrates these concepts:

Local service technician Niklas tells about a case where three service technicians, independently from each other, at three different occasions replaced an injection component because a DTC indicated it to be malfunctioning. The customer experienced that the boat was not operating with the usual effect, i.e. not driving fast enough. Niklas got confused and made a profound analysis, finding that filth in the fuel tank was the underlying cause of error, blocking the injection component.

Symptom is a customer-experienced deviation from expectations, e.g. the customer identifying a decrease in speed. Effect is a measurable deviation from the standard value, usually distinguished by DTCs that are stored by the system (DTC pointed to the effect, i.e. the injection component). Cause, we define as the underlying cause for measurable deviation (filth in the fuel tank).

In the following sections, we detail our results from the empirical study using the three analytical categories mentioned above.

4.1 Defining the Problem

A repair process starts with either a problem incident or a scheduled maintenance. If the customer experiences a problem, the technician typically defines the problem by asking questions concerning the symptoms. The customer, who usually is present, then describes his or her experiences of the problem, and the technician tries to 'index' the problem by asking follow-up questions. The following excerpt from the field notes is a typical example:

Local service technician Niklas meets with a customer to solve a problem. He has already received a short problem description from the customer by telephone and therefore he has had the chance to do some preparations. The customer recognized the oil level falling beneath minimum. Due to experience from similar cases, Niklas assumes that metal chips from the production may be blocking the oil valves in the engine. To get his suspicion confirmed he asks the customer for more details, such as how and when the problem occurs. The customer remembers to have recognized the problem when watching the oil level display, being confident that the display would be malfunction. The problem reoccurred, according to the customer, when entering, for instance, a marina. Niklas wonders whether the customer usually abruptly slows down in these cases, which is confirmed by the customer thus confirming Niklas' hypothesis.

During this 'interview' with the customer, the technician confirms and falsifies hypothesis about the problem by discussing different possible causes. Sometimes discussions defining problems are long, sometimes they are short, depending on many different things. For example, if the workshop visit is a follow up of a visit last week, then the technician may know much about the boat and just needs a short status update. In cases where the technician does not know much about the boat or is uncertain about the problem cause, the discussion may last for some time. Gradually, the technician starts to form an opinion about the problem, but this may require some discussion. His *local knowledge* is a determining factor in order to define problems. Local knowledge includes both knowledge about boats in general and perhaps most importantly knowledge about the customer and the boat in particular. Also, where he cannot quickly identify a solution, the technician knows who among the colleagues or central experts to ask for help.

There is a mutual interest to involve the customer in the diagnostic process. The customer usually wants to participate to learn more about the problem and its solution. The technician wants to involve the customer because he knows how the problem has appeared, which is important in the process of defining the problem.

However, it is not obvious that all technical problems identified should be defined as 'problems'. Consider the following notes from the study:

> "All fault codes are relevant since they indicate that something is wrong in the system. Whether they are relevant in each case depends on what the customer complains about. [...] If the customer complains about the engine power and there is an indication at the audio system it is not relevant, but if he complains about the sound quality it is indeed very relevant." [Volvo expert, personal communication]

As this quote points out, diagnostic data has to be put in relation to the customer experience. If the customer does not experience the technical problem, then it may not constitute a problem. Technicians told us that the primary goal in every repair process is to satisfy the customer by solving those problems he experiences. This implies that the technician's job is to identify the problem *as experienced by the customer*, as opposed to technical problems in general. The primary objective is to satisfy the customer, not to resolve technical problems as such.

4.2 Investigating the Cause and Solving the Problem

During the study it became obvious that not all problems could be defined at once and even though the technician thinks he knows the problem cause, he often wants to try to 'reproduce' the problem. Thus, he needs to know the circumstances of its occurrence. The customer, for example, could tell the technician that the problem occurs when operating the engine between a certain span of revolutions per minute or when accelerating abruptly with a cold engine. The technician then uses this knowledge when trying out the machinery.

When reproducing the problem situation, the technician could very well find out that the initial hypothesis of the problem was incorrect. Consider the following example:

> *The customer is complaining about vibrations at 3000 revolutions per minute, which Niklas promptly relates to a defective propeller trim. This is a frequent problem caused by a malfunctioning pump. During test-driving, however, Niklas recognizes that the propeller trim is not adjusted properly, which is a totally different cause of error than assumed ('same symptom, different cause').*

The excerpt above is just one example of the multitude of possible causes of a particular problem. The technician wants to try things out. You can never be too sure.

In trying to reproduce the problem, the technician in many cases needs to use computerized diagnostic tools to, e.g. read out DTCs and real-time parameters. In doing so, the technician can monitor how, for example, the acceleration of the crankshaft may go up and down depending on speed, which indicates whether cylinders and injectors are properly adjusted to each other. Similarly, the technician can switch ECUs on or off to see what happens.

Throughout the study, we recognized a general scepticism towards computerized diagnostic data among service technicians. It is regarded unreliable, complex and overrated. This is different from most (commercial) remote diagnostics solutions that tend to believe that diagnostic data is sufficient in order to diagnose a vehicle. Even when DTCs seem to point to malfunctioning components it is important to question the results. DTCs have to be scrutinized. Diagnostic data may indicate the effect instead of the cause and possible problem causes may be located at totally different places:

> "When performing a diagnosis you are not finished before you have located the fault and know which component or part you need to change or repair. Since a fault code can point to one or several components it often requires a continued fault-localization after the fault codes have been read." [Expert technician at VP, personal communication]

This quote shows that diagnostic data might be misinterpreted because the data represents the effect, not the cause of an error. It highlights two more interesting facts as well; on the one hand, a perceived requirement to make a continuous fault trace and on the other hand, the observation that a successful diagnosis often involves mechanical problems as well. Robert, an expert technician at VP working with quality issues, told us that problems with the electronics or software seldom occur. Facing mechanical problems, e.g. incorrect components, wear to materials etc., means that the mechanic needs to put hands on in the diagnostic process.

Daniel reads out DTCs using a diagnostic tool, indicating a serious problem concerning a multi steering unit. In order to be sure that the component is actually defective, he detaches it and reads the DTCs. No DTCs appear, so he can be sure that the component is defective. The next day he replaces the component, solving the problem.

Mechanical intervention is in this case necessary in order to delimit the error to a single replaceable component and to verify sensor diagnostic data. Loose contacts are mentioned as a frequent problem which can be excluded if the sensor data is verified by, e.g. detaching components. This shows that despite the increasing amount of sensors, diagnostics work still requires mechanical intervention. Thus the technician needs to be *co-located* with the boat.

In order to investigate and solve a problem, the technician needs, beside diagnostic data, knowledge about, for example, known problems with different boats and engines. You cannot just rely on the data as such. A particular engine problem can for instance be regarded as resolved even though DTCs are still displayed. One reason for this to happen would be that the engine in question virtually *always* displays DTCs, although there are seemingly no problems.

A service technician reports on DTCs causing irritation because no solution could be found. After contacting VP he got to know that it was caused by an internal software error. Keeping this in mind it seems rather difficult for him not to become sceptical.

Furthermore diagnostic data sometimes requires complementary information. Injector tests, for example, can be conducted using the diagnostic tool, but analysing the result requires listening to the engine's sound in order to trace a problem. In these cases, the technician again has to be co-located with the engine. Not all problems can be solved during the service session. Some problems require test driving, as well as involvement of the customer in the investigation.

Niklas installs a potentiometer in a boat instructing a customer to observe its values during long term operation. The customer drives the boat for about an hour in order to see if any abnormal values occur.

Involving the customer in the investigation process gives him a feeling of having control and being sure that the faults are attended to. Being part of the problem solution process requires confidence in the local technician. Throughout our observations we noticed a personal and friendly relationship between customers and service technicians.

4.3 Involving Central Experts

Experts at VP customer support are another important part of the diagnostic process. The support organization consists of various experts who in turn can access several knowledge resources and take advantage of similar problems previously resolved at other sites. In problematic cases, it is possible to get help from product development teams with exceptional knowledge regarding technical issues.

When the local service technicians cannot solve problems they contact VP customer support, either by telephone or email. Experts may give answers immediately, or they can work out a solution that is returned by email or telephone some days later. To solve the problem, the central experts sometimes need to go to the local workshop.

The following two examples are problem descriptions posted to VP by email. They illustrate how experts and local service technicians collaborate today:

"We have undertaken extensive testing of the middle engine [...]. The owner noticed a problem [...] with the middle engine RPMs fluctuating and as yet we have been unable to resolve the problem. We have swapped turbo between engines, carried out compression and computer tests and more and more. I have been adamant that we check every avenue of service and maintenance of the entire boat, including having the fuel cleaned. [...] the local Volvo specialist is convinced that it is the configuration of the middle engine, lowering the water due to the V that is causing the RPM fluctuations."

"I was also at site to troubleshoot one unit of engine KAD191kW @3800rpm, the engine unable to start due to ECU problem with following fault code. [Listing two fault codes] [...] I also tried to reprogram the ECU, unfortunately after reprogramming the fault code still exist." [Listing datasets and engine serial number]

The first excerpt shows typical failures in the problem description. In this case, it is the customer who contacts VP. He gives a very vague description of the problem. He neither mentions the engine type nor gives a useful fault description. In the email, he mentions several tests but does not detail any results. In order to solve the problem, the expert needs more detailed information, requiring him to contact the customer.

The second excerpt shows a more detailed fault description. This case is reported by a local service technician, which might explain the detailed description.

However, the hypothesis is rejected by the experts. In both cases, the email is the only information available to the expert. He must, therefore, either try to get complementary information, or (which is more common) try to map the information to prior problem cases, in order to find a solution. To get more information, the expert could also carry out tests in a test bed.

The knowledge the experts apply in these processes was not formalized in a knowledge base. We observed an ongoing collaboration between experts, discussing and analysing problems.

The experts we have studied and interviewed emphasize carefully that the customer's problem description, despite its varied quality, is an essential part in order to get an understanding of the problem. Local service technicians are not always aware of that. They neglect the definition and investigation process, which results in insufficient problem descriptions.

Kjell complains about too many insufficient problem descriptions. Most cases are described from a subjective point of view, narrowing the problem and resulting in an inadequate picture.

Insufficient case descriptions are considered to be a problem at VP's customer support. In most cases, the expert has to request more information. New engine series with extended electronic components makes it even more difficult to give a detailed problem description. It is impossible for a local service technician to give a summary of sensor diagnostic information in an email or a phone call.

While technicians get more sophisticated diagnostic tools, experts still have to rely on their conventional tools, such as email, telephone and visiting the site. The central experts spend approximately 100–150 days travelling on a yearly basis, which implies the importance of 'being there' to define and resolve problems. The challenge is to offer detailed information to the remote expert.

5   Discussion

The focus of most research on remote diagnostics is highly technical and does not start from an understanding of how diagnostics takes place today. Inspired by the idea of 'cultivation', our objective is to explore how to evolve current diagnostics practice towards remote diagnostics.

Based on the fieldwork presented above, we can discern three characteristics of diagnostics practice; co-location, collaboration and local knowledge. These characteristics are, we argue, important to acknowledge in the design of remote diagnostics applications.

5.1   Co-location, Collaboration and Local Knowledge

With the exception of the central expert and situations where customers were requested to try out the boat themselves and report back to the workshop, the diagnostics work we observed was *co-located* — as opposed to remote. The work takes place in the workshop, where the technician, the boat, and often the customer, are present. This implies, first, that remote diagnostics will have to evolve from 'co-located diagnostics', and second, that remote diagnostics is more likely to enhance 'co-located diagnostics' than replace it.

Another observation is the importance of *collaboration* between the actors involved. Diagnostic work can be described as a collaborative process between customers, local service technicians and central experts. The customers are involved to share their experiences of the vehicle, to discuss the conditions under which problems occur, or even to try out the boat again and report back. The central experts become involved in assisting when the local technicians have problems in defining or solving problems, sharing their experiences from having dealt with similar problems in other workshops. The actors are, in the words of Schmidt & Bannon [1992], 'mutually dependent', and as a consequence, they need to join together in collaboration. The mutual dependency, as explained by Schmidt and Bannon, origins from the fact that none of the actors can solve the problem on their own, which clearly was documented in the study. You may also argue that this is just an example of the collaborative nature of work, which has been documented in many studies. Consider, for example, the collaborative practice documented in the well cited study of line control rooms in the London underground [Heath & Luff 1992], or how people cooperate to assure a 'smooth flow of work' on the shop floor, as documented by Bowers et al. [1995]. In fact, the rich collaboration between co-located people has been used to explain why remote collaboration using IT is so hard to achieve. Contemplate, for example, the well-known attempts of using 'media spaces' [see for example Bly et al. 1993] or video communication for informal, spontaneous communication [Fish et al. 1993].

In the automotive industry, remote diagnostics is often thought of as a way of making the local technicians redundant. The idea is that remote diagnostics will enable a smaller number of central experts to do the work now being performed by the local technicians. Based on our study we do not think this is likely to happen, at least not in the near future, simply because the local service technician seems to play such an important role in the diagnostics work. One reason for this is that, where problems involve mechanical faults the remote repair is currently impractical and a local technician will still be needed to do the repair. A second reason is the local knowledge of the service technician, which the central expert never would have the possibility to get.[2] For example, central experts would never get knowledge about things like:

- which customer actually has knowledge about boats (an important background information when interpreting the customer's problem description);

- which customer you can request to try out the boat and report back;

- what previous problems there have been with a particular boat; and

- what kind of driving style the customer has, e.g. aggressive or calm.

Such knowledge is obviously important in order to work effectively with diagnostics. Similar observations, in other domains, have been reported by Bowers et al. [1996], Fagrell et al. [1999] and Randall et al. [1995].

---

[2]There is no generally accepted definition of local knowledge in the literature. However, a typical description of the concept can be found in Bowers et al. [1996, p.382]: "To know who knows what, who is busy, who is worth asking about 'x'."

To some extent, our empirical findings echo those presented by Orr [1996], who studied the diagnostic work practice among photocopier service technicians. However, our approach and focus differ from Orr's. To us, the fieldwork is a means to an end. We simply wanted to get some grounded insights in diagnostics work as a basis for our application development. For Orr, the study as such was the main purpose. He wanted to understand, in detail, the work practice of the service technicians. Our focus is on application development. Orr's focus is on social science. At the same time, Orr's study is clearly relevant input to our project.

5.2   *Implications for Design*

Based on the results of our study, in particular the importance of the local service technician in diagnostics work, we argue in favour of a decentralized approach that acknowledges the importance of collaboration, co-location and local knowledge. The typical, centralized view on remote diagnostics focuses on the central experts and assumes they, by using remote diagnostics, can do much of the work now being performed by the local technicians.

The decentralized approach starts from the three main actors in today's diagnostics work: the technician, the customer and the central expert. Starting out from the local technicians, the three major ways we want to enhance this model are: first, remote access to diagnostics data (of the boats), second, remote collaboration with customers, and third, remote collaboration with central experts. Let us now discuss these three ways of enhancing the current diagnostics practice.

5.2.1   *Remote Access to Diagnostics Data*

The local technician would clearly benefit from getting remote access to information from customer boats. Such access would include both reading out DTCs and getting alerts when certain DTCs occur. This would, for example, be useful as a way of following up boats with problems, or to get the possibility to contact customers when certain problems have occurred. These possibilities would render the diagnostics process more efficient and improve customer satisfaction.

The difference between giving the local technician and the central expert access to remote diagnostics services is important. The local technicians, embodying local knowledge, could interpret the DTCs in relation to the context, e.g. what kinds of problems the particular customer actually experiences as problems. A DTC does not equal a problem, simply because what constitutes a problem is defined by the customers-if the customer does not experience the problem as such, then it is not a problem. Furthermore, since solving a problem could change the behaviour of the boat (e.g. increased fuel consumption as a consequence of improved cold start), fixing a DTC could mean the customer becomes dissatisfied. The local technician is more likely than the central expert to be able to handle these kinds of complex issues.

5.2.2   *Remote Collaboration with Customers*

Since the customer plays an important role in diagnostics work, the possibilities for collaboration with the customer remotely would be beneficial. Let us give some examples: First, a DTC has been set, but the technician is not sure whether or not the customer experiences a problem. Therefore, the technician needs to contact the customer to find out. Second, certain parameters indicate a DTC is about to be set in a boat, and the service technician knows the customer is going away on a long trip shortly, which makes it sensible to contact the customer to discuss the issue. Third, a problem with a boat could not be solved. The technician is notified that a DTC has just been set, and he can now contact the customer to discuss the local setting, which may influence the problem.

A system to handle this would not need to be very sophisticated. A mobile phone may be enough, as long as it is possible to track the communication to make it searchable at a later stage. Together with a remote diagnostics tool, such a communication system would make it possible for technicians and customers to collaboratively conduct parts of the diagnostics work remotely. For example, the technician could ask the customer to do things he cannot do remotely, e.g. turn off the power.

5.2.3   Remote Collaboration with the Central Expert

In some cases central experts have knowledge that local technicians do not have, e.g. general problems with a new engine, which implies the importance of remote collaboration between the local technicians and the central experts. It could be improved by, for example, giving the central expert access to diagnostics data about a particular boat. Currently, the technician will need to summarize a problem in an email or in a voice conversation with the expert, which is regarded as difficult. According to Kraut et al. [1996] less experienced technicians improve by collaborating with remote experts, but the choice of communication technology does not seem to have any impact. By publishing the diagnostics data to the expert, and being able to discuss the topic orally, the collaborative situation is likely to be more efficient than today at VP. Today, the central expert quite frequently needs to travel to meet the technician and get access to the boat, which is something all parties want to reduce; the central expert wants to be accessible to assist technicians, and the local technician wants to solve the problem.

6   Conclusion

In order to explore design implications for remote diagnostics applications in the marine industry, we have conducted an empirical study in cooperation with Volvo Penta in Göteborg, Sweden. The study revealed details regarding how the actors involved collaborate to define problems, investigate causes and solve problems. Three main aspects of these activities are: the importance of being co-located with each other and the boat, the importance of collaboration, and the reliance on local knowledge. Based on these results, we suggest a decentralized approach to remote diagnostics focusing on the local technician. In particular, we suggest a model where the local technician has, first, remote diagnostics access to the boats of their customers, second, the possibility of collaborating remotely with customers, and third, improved possibilities of collaborating with central experts.

These suggestions conform to typical CSCW issues and may thus seem rather straightforward and not very innovative. Against that, we would like to present two arguments. Firstly, the purpose of our project was to discern how diagnostics practice, as conducted today, could be improved by using remote diagnostics, as opposed to, for example, what remote diagnostics may be like in ten years from now. With a focus on current practice and an application domain that most people would recognize, the implications are likely to be incremental, as opposed to radical. Secondly, most actors in the vehicle industry suggest centralized models of remote diagnostics that do not acknowledge the importance of co-location, collaboration and local knowledge, appearing to ignore these aspects of diagnostics work. In this sense, our results could be considered somewhat radical. We argue, however, that exactly these empirically grounded insights, and the suggested decentralized approach, constitute the main contribution of this research.

One interesting insight of the study is that technicians define their job as identifying problems *experienced by the customer*, as supposed to technical problems as such. Simply put, a technical problem is a problem only to the extent the customer experiences it as a problem. In this sense, the job of the technician is similar to that of a salesman; to identify what problems the customer experiences, and based on that offer solutions. It should be noted, however, that the technician would always tell the customer about technical problems that could cause damage. At the same time, the distinction between an 'experienced problem' and a 'technical problem' is interesting, since it challenges the common understanding of what diagnostics work is all about. As a consequence, a remote diagnostics system should, in a sense, diagnose the problems experienced by the customer, as supposed to the technical problems of the vehicle. The customer experienced and the technical problems would probably overlap in many cases, but to assume that they would overlap completely in all cases would be wrong.

Acknowledgements

We would like to thank our collaborators at Volvo Penta, our colleagues at the IT University of Göteborg, Ian Newman, the anonymous reviewers and Guy Lefleur.

References

Bellotti, V. & Bly, S. [1996], Walking Away from the Desktop Computer: Distributed Collaboration and Mobility in a Product Design Team, *in* G. Olson, J. Olson & M. S. Ackerman (eds.), *Proceedings of 1996: ACM Conference on Computer Supported Cooperative Work (CSCW'96)*, ACM Press, pp.209–18.

Besnard, D. & Bastien-Toniazzo, M. [1999], Expert Error in Trouble-shooting: An Exploratory Study in Electronics, *International Journal of Human–Computer Studies* 50(5), 391–405.

Bisdikan, C., Boamah, I., Castro, P., Misra, A., Rubas, J., Villoutreix, N., Yeh, D., Rasin, V. & Huang, H. [2002], Intelligent Pervasive Middleware for Context-Based and Localized Telematics Services, *in* M. Viveros, H. Lei & O. Wolfson (eds.), *Proceedings of the 2nd International Workshop on Mobile Commerce*, ACM Press, pp.15–24.

Bly, S., Harrison, S. R. & Irwin, S. [1993], Media Spaces: Bringing People Together in a Video, Audio and Computing Environment, *Communications of the ACM* 36(1), 28–47.

Bowers, J., Button, G. & Sharrock, W. [1995], Workflow from Within and Without: Tehcnology and Cooperative Work on the Print Industry Shopfloor, *in* H. Marmolin,

Y. Sundblad & K. Schmidt (eds.), *Proceedings of ECSCW'95, the 4th European Conference on Computer-supported Cooperative Work*, Kluwer, pp.51–66.

Bowers, J., O'Brien, J. & Pycock, J. [1996], Practically Accomplishing Immersion: Cooperation In and For Virtual Environments, *in* G. Olson, J. Olson & M. S. Ackerman (eds.), *Proceedings of 1996: ACM Conference on Computer Supported Cooperative Work (CSCW'96)*, ACM Press, pp.380–9.

Campos, F. T., Mills, W. N. & Graves, M. L. [2002], A Reference Architecture for Remote Diagnostics and Prognostics Applications, *in* P. Griffin & D. Gratz (eds.), *Proceedings of IEEE Conference Autotestcon*, IEEE Publications, pp.842–53.

Dahlbom, B. & Mathiassen, L. [1993], *Computers in·Context: The Philosophy and Practice of Systems Design*, Blackwell.

Dourish, P. [2001], *Where the Action Is: The Foundations of Embodied Interaction*, MIT Press.

Duri, S., Gruteser, M., Liu, X., Moskowitz, P., Perez, R., Singh, M. & Tang, J.-M. [2002], Framework for Security and Privacy in Automotive Telematics, *in* M. Viveros, H. Lei & O. Wolfson (eds.), *Proceedings of the 2nd International Workshop on Mobile Commerce*, ACM Press, pp.25–32.

Fagrell, H., Kristoffersen, S. & Ljungberg, F. [1999], Exploring Support for Knowledge Management in Mobile Work, *in* S. Bødker, M. Kyng & K. Schmidt (eds.), *Proceedings of ECSCW'99, the 6th European Conference on Computer-supported Cooperative Work*, Kluwer, pp.259–75.

Fish, R., Kraut, R., Root, R. & Rice, R. [1993], Video as a Technology for Informal Communication, *Communications of the ACM* **36**(1), 48–61.

Frost & Sullivan [2002], The European Remote Vehicle Diagnostics Market, PowerPoint presentation at http://www.transportation.frost.com/prod/servlet/cpo/2658558.pps.

Gartner G2 [2002], Telematics Industry Outlook: Think Outside the Vehicle, Technical Report RPT-0902-0163, Gartner G2.

Grimm, K. [2003], Software Technology in an Automotive Company: Major Challenges, *in* L. Clarke, L. Dillon & W. Tichy (eds.), *Proceedings of the the 25th International Conference on Software Engineering (ICSE'03)*, IEEE Computer Society Press, pp.498–503.

Hammersley, M. & Atkinson, P. [1995], *Ethnography: Principles in Practice*, second edition, Routledge.

Heath, C. & Luff, P. [1992], Collaboration and Control: Crisis Management and Multimedia Technology in London Underground Control Rooms, *Computer Supported Cooperative Work* **1**(1–2), 69–94.

Hughes, J. A., O'Brien, J., Rodden, T., Rouncefield, M. & Blythin, S. [1997], Designing with Ethnography: A Presentation Framework for Design, *in* I. McClelland, G. Olson, G. C. van der Veer, A. Henderson & S. Coles (eds.), *Proceedings of the Symposium on Designing Interactive Systems: Processes, Practices, Methods and Techniques (DIS'97)*, ACM Press, pp.147–58.

Hughes, J., King, V., Rodden, T. & Anderson, H. [1994], Moving Out of the Control Room: Ethnography in Systems Design, *in* J. B. Smith, F. D. Smith & T. W. Malone (eds.), *Proceedings of 1994 ACM Conference on Computer Supported Cooperative Work (CSCW'94)*, ACM Press, pp.429–39.

Hughes, J., King, V., Rodden, T. & Anderson, H. [1995], The Role of Ethnography in Interactive Systems Design, *Interactions* **11**(2), 57–65.

Jameel, A., Stuempfle, M., Jiang, D. & Fuchs, A. [1998], Web on Wheels: Toward Internet-enabled Cars, *IEEE Computer* **31**(1), 69–76.

Kraut, R. E., Miller, M. D. & Siegel, J. [1996], Collaboration in Performance of Physical Tasks: Effects on Outcomes and Communication, *in* G. Olson, J. Olson & M. S. Ackerman (eds.), *Proceedings of 1996: ACM Conference on Computer Supported Cooperative Work (CSCW'96)*, ACM Press, pp.57–66.

Luff, P., Hindmarsh, J. & Heath, C. (eds.) [2000], *Workplace Studies: Recovering Work Practice and Informing Systems Design*, Cambridge University Press.

Orr, J. E. [1996], *Talking About Machines: An Ethnography of a Modern Job*, Cornell University Press.

Randall, D., Rouncefield, M. & Hughes, J. A. [1995], Chalk and Cheese: BPR and Ethnomethodologically Informed Ethnography in CSCW, *in* H. Marmolin, Y. Sundblad & K. Schmidt (eds.), *Proceedings of ECSCW'95, the 4th European Conference on Computer-supported Cooperative Work*, Kluwer, pp.325–40.

Rasmussen, J. [1993], Diagnostic Reasoning in Action, *IEEE Transactions on Systems, Man and Cybernetics* **23**(4), 981–92.

Schmidt, K. & Bannon, L. [1992], Taking CSCW Seriously: Supporting Articulation Work, *Computer Supported Cooperative Work* **1**(1–2), 7–40.

Suchman, L. A. [1987], *Plans and Situated Actions — The Problem of Human–Machine Communication*, Cambridge University Press.

Searching, Searching, Searching

A First Empirical Study of Direct Combination in a Ubiquitous Environment

Simon Holland

Department of Computing, The Open University, Milton Keynes MK7 6AA, UK

Tel: *+44 1908 653148*

Email: *s.holland@open.ac.uk*

In dynamic ubiquitous environments, end users may need to create services by causing *two or more* devices or resources to interoperate together in ad-hoc circumstances. In general, users can find this kind of process hard to manage. At the same time, existing UI architectures are not well suited to supporting such activities. It is proposed that a good basis for addressing these and related problems in a principled, scaleable way is the principle of Direct Combination (DC). The principle is summarized, and analytical arguments are presented that predict that DC can reduce the amount of search required by the user. Other things being equal, such a reduction in search would be expected to offer interactions which are faster, less frustrating, and impose less mental load on the user. We present a proof-of-concept implementation, and a small-scale evaluation of a DC interface. Within the limitations of a preliminary evaluation, consistent support is offered across several measures for the analytical predictions.

Keywords: ubiquitous computing, handheld devices, mobile computing, input technologies, interaction technologies, interaction theory, interaction design, interaction principles, interaction frameworks.

1 Introduction and Problem

In ubiquitous environments, networked devices on the person and in artefacts, vehicles and surroundings, will be cheap, plentiful and richly distributed. In such environments, there will be numerous opportunities for end users to access, or to dynamically create, services of interest by causing *two or more devices or resources to interoperate together*, often under ad-hoc circumstances [Banavar et al. 2000;

Edwards & Grinter 2001; Newman et al. 2002]. A very simple, non-problematic example is that a user with a PDA in an unfamiliar place might wish to show another user a document on a nearby screen. In general, users find impromptu inter-operation of two or more resources hard to manage [Edwards & Grinter 2001; Kristoffersen & Ljungberg 2000]. Existing programming architectures tend make this kind of task inconvenient [Banavar et al. 2000; Winograd 2001] since the necessary functionality is generally controlled via device-centric application programs [Banavar et al. 2000]. These cannot easily organize the huge number of possible interactions, making it difficult for end users to cope [Banavar et al. 2000; Kristoffersen & Ljungberg 2000]. Whenever three or more distinct resources are involved, the problems for users multiply combinatorially. Consequently, such tasks often involve the user in non-trivial searches of the user interface. The problems are particularly acute when the search is performed on the move via mobile devices with small, resource-poor user interfaces. Typically users are forced to spend time and attention distracted from their main task, searching a sequence of screens and menus [Holland et al. 2002]. The problem of supporting inter-operation in changing circumstances, especially in ubiquitous systems, is called the problem of *spontaneous interaction*. There are few, if any, interaction techniques well suited to spontaneous interaction. Approaches are needed that allow the user to specify what they want as simply and directly as possible, while at the same time taking full advantage of machine-mediated knowledge.

2 Proposed Solution

We propose that a good principled basis for addressing this and related problems is the principle of *Direct Combination* [Holland & Oppenheim 1999; Holland et al. 2002]. We will argue that Direct Combination allows the user interface to be made highly economical, and the amount of search required by the user to be reduced. The principle of Direct Combination, with its associated interaction techniques and architecture is perhaps best introduced by means of an example. For reasons of memorability we will use an imaginary interaction scenario borrowed from Holland et al. [2002] featuring a magic wand. Binsted [2000] has argued that imagined magic is a valuable tool when designing or analysing innovative interaction technologies. More realistic scenarios will be presented below. *Harry raised his wand towards the menacingly advancing Gator[1] and tried to remember the spell for turning it into something harmless. It was no good; he just couldn't remember the right spell* ... Problems of this sort with magic wands are common in fiction and folklore. For example, the story of the Sorcerer's Apprentice deals with an inexperienced wizard who has memorized enough commands to start a process, but does not know, or cannot recall, the commands needed to control or stop it. *Harry suddenly remembered that this was a Direct Combination Wand. He wouldn't need to recall the spell. Quickly looking around, Harry noticed a small stone on the floor. Pointing the wand at the Gator, Harry selected it, and then made a second select gesture at the stone. A glowing list next to the wand presented the two available actions applicable to this particular pair of things: propel the stone at the Gator and turn the Gator into*

---

[1]An imaginary monster, normally docile, but occasionally dangerous.

stone. *Gratefully Harry activated the second command and the Gator froze into grey immobility.* The key principle of Direct Combination (DC), as illustrated by the above scenario, is that if the user is allowed to indicate in advance *two or more interaction objects* involved in an intended action, then, given a supporting architecture, the system can use this information to constrain significantly the search space of possible commands. This allows the system to present to the user a space of focused relevant options to choose from, instead of the unrestricted space of commands. Some terminology is worth introducing at this point: interactions involving a pair of objects are known as pairwise interactions. This pattern with two interaction objects is particularly useful, but *zero or more* objects are the general DC case. Cases that involve selecting a single object are known as *unary* interactions, and cases with three or more objects are known as *n-fold* interactions. Direct Combination encompasses all of these as special cases within a single uniform framework. Note that any potential difficulties, in some situations, with physical pointing for accurate selection of items, are no barrier to DC; the principle works just as well if objects are identified in any other way, e.g. by speech or by selection from a resource discovery menu.

3 The Direct Combination Principle

In practical terms, viewed from the point of view of the user, the principle of Direct Combination [Holland & Oppenheim 1999; Holland et al. 2002] can be stated as follows:

- The user interface must always *permit* the user to select *zero, one, two, three or more* objects (before the user is obliged to choose any action).

- The interface must immediately display the actions that apply to *that particular collection* of objects.

Note that under this principle the user is *not* obliged to specify one or more nouns before verbs — it is just that this is always *possible*. The principle of subsumption [Holland & Oppenheim 1999; Holland et al. 2002] requires that DC should always include conventional interaction patterns as special cases — as illustrated below. To be scaleable and maintainable, appropriate supporting software architecture and analysis methods are required; both of which requirements now have well-founded solutions. These aspects are briefly touched on below, but are outside the scope of this paper. Although DC is at root a very simple idea, it has far reaching consequences.

4 The Domain

The domain of the evaluation is a simulated ubiquitous environment, accessible via a user interface (Figure 1) running on a laptop controlling a model of the environment. In a fully realized environment, and in earlier work [Holland et al. 2002], users may select physical objects in the environment by pointing at them physically with a remote ID reader built into a PDA or wand: remote or virtual objects are selected by selecting items on-screen on the PDA/wand. For the evaluation, all selection is done by choosing from menus on a simulated PDA running on the laptop. A wide range

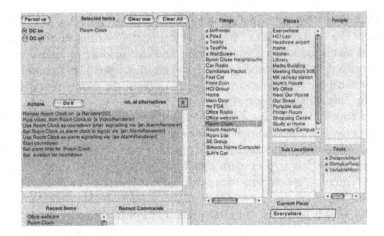

Figure 1: The interface used for the evaluation. For purposes of comparison, Direct Combination (DC) can be switched off. This does not change the appearance of the interface, but restricts its behaviour. DC behaviour always supports not only DC interactions but also conventional interactions (see Section 3). The panes places, people and sub-locations are unused in this study. For reasons of space, the figure has been cropped at the bottom, but this removes no functional detail.

of objects are available in the simulated environment, including wall screens, radios, PDAs, doors, houses, clocks, printers, room lights, cameras, central heating, cars, and text files. Each type of simulated object supports appropriate behaviours and states. Simulated outcomes in the environment are detailed in dialogue boxes. Given our interest in interactions that may involve arranging for two or more objects to work together (some possibly remote), the objects in the simulation are drawn from a range of locations including a residence, a place of work, and outdoors (Figure 1). Note that DC does not apply merely to physical devices — it applies equally well to arbitrary combinations of physical objects, virtual objects, remote objects, and subparts of objects.

5   A Prototype Direct Combination User Interface

The user interface has been implemented to work in two modes, Direct Combination mode, and a reference mode that excludes DC (called for brevity 'non-DC mode'). In the reference mode the interface behaves conventionally, just like most typical user interfaces. Loosely speaking, non-DC mode is as follows: the user may select a single object; this elicits a list of relevant actions; the user may then choose an action from a list, and execute it; this may achieve the task, or it may cause a dialogue box to be opened, so that additional arguments can be provided. Of course, many conventional user interfaces have additional behaviours, such as allowing a collection of objects to be selected, thus permitting the same command to be issued to all objects in the collection; or cut and paste; and also drag and drop. However, all of these behaviours have analogues in DC [Holland & Oppenheim 1999; Holland et al. 2002], hence for simplicity and clarity of comparison these behaviours were not included in the evaluation for either condition. In Direct Combination mode, the user interface appears and behaves essentially identically to the reference mode, but has a single systematic *additional* behaviour to make it conform to the DC principle: namely, the user may at any time select 0, 1, 2, 3 or more objects of interest. The system then shows a list of actions relevant to that particular combination of object types. As in the non-DC case, the user may select any action and execute it: a dialogue box may request additional arguments. This sole behavioural difference is supported by differences in the software architecture 'under the hood', but these differences are invisible to the user.

6 Analytical Arguments about the Predicted Benefits of Direct Combination

It is useful to consider some analytical arguments about the expected benefits of Direct Combination. Given a complete enumeration of the options offered to a user by a given user interface(s) in a given environment and circumstances, an abstract tree representation of the space of user commands available can be constructed. In practice, many factors will affect the user's search space, but, given appropriate assumptions about the user, task, and situation, this can be used as the basis of a *formal model* of the user's search space. Such models can be used to estimate the extent to which Direct Combination can reduce the user's search space compared with conventional restricted command patterns, under various assumptions. Here, we will informally outline three general cases in which DC is expected to reduce the search space, and note two other benefits newly identified from this study:

- Whenever a single object implements a large number of commands, if DC is not available, the user is liable to have a large search space of commands. If the user already knows one or more objects involved in the interaction, DC can be used to shrink the search space simply, rapidly and appropriately.

- In a conventional interface, whenever choosing from actions involving two or more objects, the user must typically select at least one object in a dialogue box. This dialogue box both restricts the user's freedom [Holland & Oppenheim 1999], and introduces new visual elements, making new non-task related demands on the user. Such a step is typically eliminated in the DC case.

- Whenever three or more principal objects are involved in a desired interaction, the combined search space of actions for all three objects considered individually is liable to be large. DC turns the tables to make this combinatorial explosion work in the user's favour. The objects selected reduce the search space to relevant commands only. This is DC's hallmark: a *combinatorial implosion* of the search space, dramatically reducing cognitive load for the user.

- Sometimes, a task that can be achieved using three or more objects happens not to be implemented as a single integrated command by any one of the objects.

Consequently a sequence of actions may need to be composed by the user. This can be difficult for users to manage using conventional application-centric approaches. DC interfaces provide a straightforward way for users to access such behaviour in a single step, by simply selecting the relevant objects (see Task 3 below).

- In situations where objects may be capable of interacting in diverse ways with a wide range of other object types, including some that may not have existed when the object was designed, user interfaces would become cluttered and time consuming to search if they dealt explicitly with all possible interactions — and would need continual upgrading to cope with new kinds of interactions. Third party integrative tools are one important way around this problem. The essential idea is that if needed functionality for some class of spontaneous interactions is not available in the user interfaces of any of the relevant devices, a third party tool may be able to afford those interactions.

However, this puts an additional load on non-DC users to know what general-purpose tools are available, what they are called, what they can do, and when they are applicable. By contrast, the role model servers used for DC interactions allow users to benefit from such tools without needing any knowledge of their existence (Tasks 5 and 6), simply by selecting the relevant objects. Automatic use of third party integrative tools can easily be incorporated into DC role model descriptions.

7   The Evaluation

This was the first empirical evaluation of Direct Combination applied to ubiquitous computing, and was deliberately kept small scale, since it was unknown what might happen with users who had never used this new interaction technique before.

7.1   Assumptions About Subjects

The evaluation required that all subjects should:

1. Be familiar with the use of *conventional user interfaces*.

2. Be familiar with minimal assumptions about an imagined *simulated world of ubiquitous computing*, as envisaged by Weiser [1991], namely that more or less every object is networked; that a PDA or wand can be used to identify and control such objects, locally and remotely.

3. Have exposure to the fundamental *idea or principle of DC* user interfaces, e.g. as expressed in a few sentences.

4. Have heard one or *two short* stories or scenarios to make the idea memorable.

7.2   Subjects

After two pilot runs with solo users, eight subjects (four pairs of two, to promote think-aloud) were used in the evaluation. The eight subjects were chosen from a pool of about one hundred potential subjects. Within this pool, subjects were recruited opportunistically. They had a variety of kinds of computing experience and level of education. In order to ensure that all subjects met assumptions 2–4, they were given three sheets to read, as noted in the protocol. All of the subjects except two were male. Three were computer scientists without particular knowledge of HCI. Another was an HCI researcher. Two were secretarial staff with good office computing skills. Two users were non-technically educated schoolchildren (one aged 12 and one aged 17). Both had experience of computer games and word processing, but no particular computing expertise. Two of the computer scientists had heard oral descriptions of Direct Combination at an abstract level. None of the subjects had ever seen or used a Direct Combination interface.

7.3 Tasks

The tasks were drawn from a wide range of actions possible in the simulated environment:

1. Pipe sound from the Office Radio to myPDA.

2. Display time from the Room Clock onto aWallscreen.

3. Pipe sound from myPDA onto the Car Radio.

4. Get Teddy to vocalize a TextFile over the Car Radio.

5. Arrange it so that if the Front Door opens, the Room Light flickers.

6. Arrange it so that when SJH's Car gets closer than 15 miles to Home, the Room Heating is turned on.

For details of how to complete the tasks using DC vs. non-DC, see Section 7.7.

7.4 Data Collection

Users were observed (with sound recorded, and the screen video-recorded) while carrying out a series of tasks and thinking aloud in pairs. Times taken to complete the tasks were recorded, and whether the task was completed or not. After each task, each subject was asked to grade the task according to mental demand, effort, frustration, and three other dimensions, using the NASA TLX human workload index [Hart & Staveland 1988]. After completing the evaluation, users filled in a short questionnaire (see Figure 2). The video log was analysed to catalogue all user actions and significant comments.

7.5 Training

In order to ensure all subject met assumptions 2–4, subjects were given three sheets to read before the start of each evaluation, each requiring about a minute to read. The first sheet explained that the evaluation takes place in an imagined ubiquitous environment, where every object of interest in the environment is wireless networked and remotely accessible. The second sheet explained that there were two versions of the user interface, and that with one version, only a single object could be selected at a time, whereas with the other version several objects could be selected at once: it was explained that with this version of the interface, when more than one object was involved in a task, selecting more than one object was generally advisable. The third

Direct Combination applied to user interfaces tends to:	Disagree Strongly	Disagree	Disagree Weakly	Neutral	Agree Weakly	Agree	Agree Strongly
reduce the degree of search required to carry out tasks		1	2		1	4	
reduce the amount of time required to carry out tasks		1			1	4	2
reduce the amount of attention required to carry out tasks			2		1	4	
reduce the amount of work required to carry out tasks			2			4	1
reduce the amount of frustration in carrying out tasks			1	2	2	2	2
lessen the need for memorisation in carrying out tasks			1	2		4	1
lessen the demands of interface navigation			1	1	1	4	1
reduce the amount of stress involved in carrying out tasks			1	1	1	4	1

Figure 2: Subjective questionnaire response, showing number of subjects giving each answer. Modal (most popular) answers are highlighted.

---

sheet included the Harry Potter scenario and one other scenario, to make the idea memorable. Before starting to perform tasks on either version of the interface, users were read a short scripted screen tour, describing the function of the different panes of the interface, accompanied by the evaluator pointing at the panes in question. No demonstration of the operation of either version was given. The scripted oral screen-tour told users:

- what pane to use to select simulated objects;

- what pane to use to see the objects selected; and

- what pane to use to select relevant commands.

Part of the screen tour varied depending on the version of the interface about to be used (DC vs. Reference), as follows.

7.5.1 Screen Tour for Reference Condition

Users were told that only a single object could be selected from the selection pane at a time. They were also told that in cases where none of the objects individually appeared to be able to carry out the tasks, it might be necessary to use a general-purpose tool. Users were shown the labelled pane where general-purpose tools can be selected. Finally users were told that it may be necessary to use an object they created in an earlier step in order to carry out some tasks, and are told where such objects can be selected (in the pane labelled 'recent items'). Users were told that they could ignore all other panes and controls.

7.5.2 Screen Tour for DC Condition

Users were told that more than one object could be selected at once, and that actions relevant to that particular collection of objects would then be displayed. They were also told how to clear selected objects using the clear buttons. Users were told that they could ignore all other panes and controls. (The panes *places*, *people* and *sub locations* are unused in this study.)

7.6 Protocol

Each pair was asked to carry out the same set of six tasks twice: using first one, then the other version of the interface. To allow for learning and interference effects, half

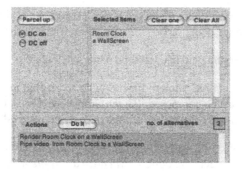

Figure 3: Using Direct Combination. The Room Clock and Wall Screen are both selected (Task 2). Only actions tailored to that particular set of objects are then displayed. To save space, this figure shows just the relevantly different part of the full interface seen in Figure 1.

of the groups used the DC version first and half used the reference interface first. The protocol followed the methodology of Lewis & Reiman [1993]. Users were asked to think out loud to say what they were trying to do next, what they were looking for, what they were uncertain about, etc. After the introductory scripted protocol, the experimenter said as little as possible, except to encourage thinking aloud — any departures from this were recorded. Each task was presented on a new sheet of paper. Tasks were phrased exactly as listed in Section 7.3. After each task was completed, or the subjects gave up, each user was asked to grade each task according to mental demand, effort, frustration, and three dimensions, using the NASA Task Load Index (TLX) [Hart & Staveland 1988]. After both conditions had been completed, subjects were asked to fill in a brief questionnaire (Figure 2).

7.7 Contrasting DC vs. Conventional Interaction

The next section contrasts how tasks can be completed using DC vs. non-DC. To make use of the available figures, we start with Task 2.

Task 2. In DC mode the user may select the *Room Clock* and the *Wall Screen* before having to specify any action (Figure 3). The system then shows a relatively brief list of actions relevant to that particular combination of objects types. The user selects the action *'Pipe video from RoomClock to WallScreen'*. On pressing *'Do it'*, a dialogue box is displayed indicating that video is being piped from the Room Clock to the Wall Screen. Note that, following the principle of subsumption, it is also possible to use the DC interface to complete the task using exactly the same steps as with the conventional interface, itemized next.

In non-DC mode the user selects the *RoomClock*, and then selects the action *'Pipe video from RoomClock to [a Video Renderer]'* (see Figure 1). On pressing *'Do it'*, the user is presented with a dialogue box allowing selection of a Video Renderer — in this case the *WallScreen*. On pressing

'*Do it*' in the dialogue box, a new dialogue box is displayed indicating that video is being piped from the Room Clock to the Wall Screen.

Tasks 1 and 3 are isomorphic in command pattern to Task 2.

Task 4 No single object has enough functionality to be able to complete this task. Two actions must be composed. (Given simple provisos, DC can compose this on the fly, even with objects *types* not explicitly considered before.)

> **In DC mode** the user selects the *teddy*, the *text file* and the *car radio*. The user then selects the option: '*Vocalize a text file using a teddy via a car radio*'.

> **In Non-DC mode** the user selects the *teddy*, then chooses the action '*Vocalize [a vocalizable] using a teddy*'. On selecting and executing this action, a dialogue box is opened allowing the *text file* to be chosen as argument. A dialogue box is then displayed showing that *the teddy is vocalizing the text file*. (Recall that no single object supports the UI functionality to complete the task in a single step.)

> The user now selects the *teddy* again, and chooses the action '*Pipe sound from Teddy to [a Sound Outputer]*'. A dialogue box is opened allowing the *car radio* to be chosen. A dialogue box is then displayed showing that *the teddy is outputting sound via the car radio*. This completes the task.

Task 5 Again, no single object has enough functionality to allow the task to be performed using a single command. But in this case, there is not even a composition of interactions associated with any objects that could complete the task. A general-purpose tool (here the stimulus response tool) must be found and used, as detailed below. (Once more, DC can compose the complete interaction on the fly, even if the particular object types and tools have never been considered together before, and even if the tools are unknown to the participating objects.)

> **In DC mode** the user selects the *front door* and the *Room light*. From the few choices, the user selects the option: '*Program stimulus response from Front door to room light*'. A dialogue box is opened to allow a stimulus to be chosen from those offered by the door (e.g. *open, close, lock, unlock*), and another dialogue box to allow a response to be chosen from the room light (e.g. *on, off, flicker*).

> **In Non-DC mode** given that the neither object has the functionality or UI to complete the task, and given that neither object knows about the existence of the third party tool (which may have been designed after both objects were created), the user must select the *stimulus response tool* (see Section 7.5 *Screen tour for DC condition*; and Figure 1, the *Tools* pane). Selecting this tool opens a single dialogue box, which allows all necessary arguments to be selected (the stimulus and the response). The

user selects the *Front door* as the stimulus source and the *Room Light* as the stimulus responder. A new dialogue box is opened to allow the correct stimulus to be chosen for the door, and another dialogue box to allow the correct response to be chosen for the room light. This task may seem a little hard, but was deliberately chosen as an example of the class of problem noted under Item 5 in Section 6. Such situations are common in spontaneous interactions. It is much more easily handled using DC, but it is one of the advantages of DC that it collapses the search space for this kind of problem so decisively.

Task 6 This task requires not just one, but two general-purpose tools whose functionality must be composed. This is similar to Task 6 but more complex. This task was chosen as an example of a class of spontaneous interaction where both Situations 4 and 5 described in Section 6 are composed.

> **In DC mode** the user simply selects the *car*, the *house* and the *central heating*, and then uses dialogue boxes as directed to program the details of the condition and response.

> **In non-DC mode** the solution is similar to that of Task 5, but both a Distance Monitor and a Stimulus response tool are required (see Section 7.5, screen tour for DC condition, and Figure 1, the *Tools* pane).

8 Results

The evaluation was preliminary and small scale. However, the combination of measures used (four NASA TLX measures, task completion times, whether tasks could be completed or not, and the questionnaire) allowed some triangulation of results. Figure 4 shows the *Mental Load* of the subjects as measured on a 20-point scale by the NASA TLX [Hart & Staveland 1988], averaged over all eight subjects, in the DC condition compared with the non-DC condition, for the six tasks. As Figure 4 shows, the *Mental Load* for the non-DC condition was measured to be bigger for all of the six tasks. Figures 5 & 6 show the same information for *Effort* and *Frustration* as measured by the NASA TLX. Both *Effort* and *Frustration* were measured to be greater in the reference condition than in the DC condition for all of the six tasks. This is also true of the NASA TLX results for Physical Load and Temporal Load (not shown). Figure 7 shows the actual time taken to complete each task (or until the participants abandoned the task). The time taken, averaged over all subjects, was longer for the non-DC condition than the DC condition for each of the six tasks. Given the think aloud nature of the evaluation, time taken must be treated with caution, but, within the limits of a preliminary study, it gives a useful indication. All of the subjects completed all tasks in the DC condition, but in the non-DC condition, two subjects gave up on one task, and two subjects gave up on two tasks. In the questionnaire (Figure 2), seven of the eight subjects rated the DC condition favourably, or at worse, neutrally on all of the questions asked.

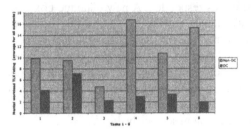

Figure 4: Mental Load for DC vs. non-DC, on a 20-point scale, as measured by the NASA TLX (averaged over all subjects) for Tasks 1–6. DC scores are shown in the darker shade.

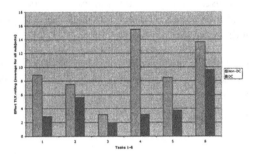

Figure 5: Effort for DC vs. Non-DC, on a 20-point scale, as measured by the NASA TLX. Average ratings over all subjects for Tasks 1–6. DC scores are shown in darker shade.

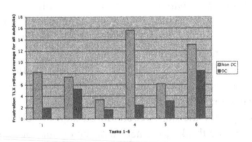

Figure 6: Frustration for DC vs. non-DC as measured on a 20-point scale by NASA TLX (average ratings for all subjects) for Tasks 1–6. DC scores are shown in the darker shade.

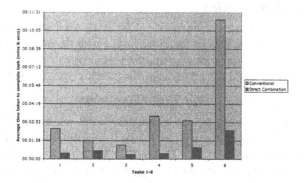

Figure 7: Time in minutes and seconds to complete tasks for DC vs. non-DC. Averages for all subjects shown for Tasks 1–6. (Max time about 11 minutes). DC in darker shade.

8.1 Effect of Order of Presentation

As already noted, half of the subjects encountered the DC condition first, and half encountered the non-DC condition first. Irrespective of the order of presentation, averaged over all tasks, all subjects rated the DC tasks on the NASA TLX scale as having a lighter workload than the non-DC tasks for: mental load, effort, frustration, physical load and temporal load. Similarly, averaged over all tasks, all subjects performed the tasks faster on the DC than on the reference interface. However, the order of presentation did affect the *degree* of out-performance of DC over non-DC differently for different measures and different tasks.

9 Interpretation

9.1 Principal Findings

This is the first empirical evaluation of a DC interface applied to ubiquitous computing, so we were unsure what user behaviour might be found. Consequently the use of a small-scale evaluation was chosen. One problem is that eight subjects are not enough for reliable statistical evidence. Also, think-aloud activity, though useful here (see Section 10.3 confounds precise timing data. Consequently, we must forgo any *precise* claims about timing. However, the timing data *overwhelmingly* favoured DC (Figure 7), even though no user had ever used it before — which might be expected to handicap DC. Given that all of the several data sources yielded similar stories, we claim that, within the limits of a preliminary evaluation, the study gives useful information. On the basis of the results from the various NASA TLX dimensions, the timing data, the completion data, the order of presentation analysis, and the questionnaire, there is consistent evidence, within the limitations of an initial study, that Direct Combination has the capacity to offer interactions which are faster, less effort, less frustrating, and impose less mental load on the user. There was support for all of the analytical predictions (Section 6).

9.2 Order of Presentation

The above findings held true irrespective of order of presentation, although the *degree* of difference of the various measures varied with the order of presentation. However, the degree and direction of variation was inconsistent across the various different measures, so that it is hard to draw firm conclusions about this variation.

9.3 Direct Combination and Task Complexity

Unlike in non-DC, on average the more complex Task 4 was completed in the DC condition in similar times to the simpler Tasks 1–3. Even Tasks 5 and 6 did not take much longer than Task 1 in the DC case, even though both conditions involved the same dialogue boxes for setting up trigger distances and stimulus responses. DC comfortably outperforms non-DC even for the three simple Tasks 1–3, although performance with non-DC does appear to improve over the course of these tasks.

9.4 Learning to Use Direct Combination

Given that all subjects had hundreds of hours of experience with conventional user interfaces, which work more or less exactly like the reference interface, and no experience at all of a DC interface, it was not clear in advance that users would find DC easy to use or quick to learn, especially since users had only about two or three minutes of introduction to DC. However the results demonstrate, as did direct observation, that learning to use a DC interface was almost instant.

10 Alternative Interpretations and Limitations

10.1 Minor Inconsistencies: Questionnaire Results

In the questionnaire, one subject (the HCI researcher) had evaluated DC negatively on several measures (Figure 2), even though, in the NASA TLX, he consistently rated the DC condition better for each task. The key to this apparent self-contradiction was identified when we asked this subject what his responses would have been to the questionnaire with *negated* versions the questions, i.e. asking about the effect of "the *exclusion* of Direct Combination from user interfaces". Surprisingly, the *negated* versions of the questions elicited exactly the same responses, *except* for the question about memorization. The subject agreed that the tasks had been easier, quicker, and less stressful, etc. using DC: his negative responses were not about DC *per se*, but reflected his scepticism about any general statements about interaction techniques. Despite systematic scepticism about general claims for *any* interaction style, this subject actively supported the view that Direct Combination tends to lessen the need for memorization (Figure 2).

10.2 Minor Anomalies: Workload in First Tasks

On all of the workload measures, Task 2 in the DC condition shows a higher load than Tasks 1 and 3, despite the fact that Tasks 1–3 are identical in command structure. There was an accidental ambiguity in the written phrasing of Task 2, which caused all subjects *in both conditions* to be unclear which of two similar actions best fitted this task. The additional time taken in Task 2 compared with Task 1 is accounted for in the video log by time exploring which of the two actions better satisfied the task.

This was observed in both conditions, but in the non-DC condition, the effects seem masked by other factors, possibly learning effects.

10.3   Usability Issues

An earlier heuristic review had removed as many usability problems as possible in both conditions. Because the DC interactions are relatively simple and undemanding on the user interface, most of this earlier improvement effort had focused on the non-DC version of the interface. For example: care was taken with non-DC to avoid a sequence of dialogue boxes where a single combined dialogue box could be used; a 'show matches only' feature was added; and the number of general purpose tools was reduced to only those needed for the tasks, plus a single distractor. Despite this, the think-aloud element of the present study picked up numerous small usability features that could be improved for both conditions equally: for example, the work flow could have been better organized left to right, and some of the 'success' dialogue boxes were insufficiently detailed. Three of these issues may have affected the non-DC side more than the DC side: actions were not categorized; the 'show matches only' feature for selecting arguments in dialogue boxes was not set as the default mode; and the general purpose tools could have been more clearly named. However, study of the video log together with a simple analytical argument (below) suggests that these issues made little material difference. Firstly, the video log suggests that setting 'show matches only' as default could have had only a small impact on overall timings. Similarly, although some of the users expressed confusion about the names of the general-purpose tools, there was no such confusion on the part of other users, and yet there was no material difference in the outcomes. Finally, the first argument in the analytical predictions section shows that simple categorization of actions is soon outrun by a combinatorial explosion of possible object interactions — so that action categorization can help non-DC interactions only to a limited degree.

11   Other Issues

In previous studies, the question was raised whether DC would transfer workload from the user to the domain analyst and maintainer [Holland & Oppenheim 1999; Holland et al. 2002]. There were also at that time technical difficulties with n-fold combination. Although outside the scope this paper, it is worth noting that two innovations, the use of a role-based architecture, and the use of computationally explicit role models, as used in the current implementation give well-founded solutions for both concerns. The architecture appears scaleable, flexible and potentially well suited to distributed use. Various issues have been identified that must be addressed for the general applicability of *any* user interaction techniques in ubiquitous domains (not just DC) [Edwards & Grinter 2001; Bellotti et al. 2002]. These issues include security, resource discovery, feedback, monitoring of tasks in progress, and cancelling. We have implemented crude prototype facilities for monitoring of tasks in progress and cancelling, but for simplicity these facilities were hidden for the purposes of evaluation. Note that this is a completely new architecture compared with Holland & Oppenheim [1999] and (with sound n-fold combination) a leap beyond Holland et al. [2002]. As regards scalability, DC places no burdens on distributed objects beyond those typical for Ubiquitous Computing. i.e. simply to identify their class or identity, and to respond to commands. Similarly, only a very simple client is required on the user devices; all of the heavy lifting can be done by DC servers. Also, because of the use of reflective descriptions, server requests require only modest bandwidth (not complete descriptions of objects).

12 Related Work

The Direct Combination principle may be viewed as generalizing and extending diverse existing user interaction approaches in a parsimonious, elegant way. Use of pointing devices to transfer information between computers or other devices is well established. For example, Pick-and-Drop [Kohtake et al. 1999; Rekimoto 1997] is an extension of Drag & Drop used to copy data between multiple devices via passive pens with IDs. Direct Combination may be viewed in turn as an extension of Pick and Drop, but one that offers far greater flexibility and expressiveness. Similarly, the InfoStick [Kohtake et al. 1999] is an interaction device for inter-appliance computing. It may be used to pick up and store information items between devices. The InfoStick effectively offers a limited special case of Direct Combination where the only available operations are *get* and *put*. Previous work on ad-hoc configuration includes the Proem project, which aimed to provide infrastructure for building special-purpose ad-hoc collaboration applications [Kortuem 2002]. The Aura software architecture [Sousa & Garlan 2002] also addresses dynamically changing resources, but it centres on technical challenges, whereas our concern is on the level of user interaction. The tangible computing system DataTiles [Rekimoto et al. 2001] uses tagged transparent tiles placed on a flat display. Interactions between any two tiles are effected by physical adjacency, or by a pen gesture. The kind of interaction is determined by the tile types, although a pen gesture may be used for limited modifications. However, the affordances are very limited — physical adjacency determines a single interaction type. DataTiles could be given greater flexibility and power, without loss of elegance, by applying the Direct Combination principle. Alternatively, DC may be viewed as a novel way of exploiting a *relational* approach [Ullmer & Ishii 2000] to Tangible User Interface design, *systematically* allowing the selection of multiple objects to determine dynamically bindings between objects and computational operations. Other systems with related goals, but different approaches include Recombinant Computing [Edwards et al. 2002], and the iRoom tuple-space approach [Borchers et al. 2002]. DC relates strongly to Direct Manipulation (DM): parts of DC may be viewed as generalizations or specializations of DM, though the relationship is complex.

13 Conclusion

Direct Combination is a new user interaction principle. Fragmentary, isolated examples of DC can be identified in some existing systems, but as a *systematic principle* and supporting framework, Direct Combination is fundamental and novel. This paper has presented the first systematic, albeit preliminary, empirical investigation of a Direct Combination user interface in the ubiquitous domain. The investigation is small scale and the results must be treated cautiously, but across all data sources there was consistent preliminary evidence that a DC user interface, compared with a conventional user interface offers interactions which are faster, less effort, less frustrating, and impose less mental load on the user. Within its limits, the study also demonstrated that DC is usable for users from a variety of backgrounds, and is rapid for them to learn. Building the test environment led to the identification of three new benefits of DC for users, beyond reduction of search space, not previously explicitly noted. These concern automatic composition of actions, the automatic deployment of integrative tools not associated with specific objects, and the automatic *composition* of the operation of such tools (see Items 4 and 5 in Section 6). One surprising lesson arising from this study was that, once the architecture was in place there was considerably more work needed to implement the programming required for the *conventional* interactions than for the DC interactions. This was because, to eliminate any factors that might unfairly disadvantage the conventional interactions, tuning was carried out *solely in the non-DC case* to ensure that all dialogue boxes would be as clear as possible. For the DC case, no such dialogue boxes, or tuning, were needed, so that work disappeared not only for the user but also for the designer/developer. No comparable tweaking was done for any of the DC interactions — they were all done using the standard elements of the role-based DC architecture. Within the limits of a preliminary evaluation, this study tends to substantiate the theoretical arguments for the benefits of DC. No evidence emerged of undue penalties that have to be paid elsewhere. More generally, the evaluation suggests that the principle is very widely applicable to user interfaces. The principle is particularly useful when it is necessary for an end-user to arrange for two or more devices or resources to interoperate together in ad-hoc circumstances.

Acknowledgements

Thanks to Paul Mulholland for generous and vital advice, Bashar Nuseibeh for urgency, Marian Petre for insightful tips, SJH for vital help, Henrik Gedenryd for the UC connection, David Morse for support, and to the anonymous referees for much appreciated comments and criticisms.

References

Banavar, G., Beck, J., Gluzberg, E., Munson, J., Sussman, J. B. & Zukowski, D. [2000], Challenges: An Application Model for Pervasive Computing, *in* R. Pickholtz, S. K. Das, R. Caceres & J. J. Garcia-Luna-Aceves (eds.), *Proceedings of the 6th Annual ACM/IEEE International Conference on Mobile Computing and Networking (MobiCom'00)*, ACM Press, pp.266–74.

Bellotti, V., Back, M. W., Edwards, K., Grinter, R. E., Henderson, A. & Lopes, C. [2002], Ubiquity: Making Sense of Sensing Systems, *in* D. Wixon (ed.), *Proceedings of SIGCHI Conference on Human Factors in Computing Systems: Changing our World, Changing Ourselves (CHI'02)*, *CHI Letters* 4(1), ACM Press, pp.415–22.

Binsted, K. [2000], Sufficiently Advanced Technology: Using Magic to Control the World, *in* M. Tremaine (ed.), *CHI'00 Extended Abstracts of the Conference on Human Factors in Computing Systems*, ACM Press, pp.205–6.

Borchers, J., Ringel, M., Tyler, J. & Fox, A. [2002], Stanford Interactive Workspaces: A Framework for Physical and Graphical User Interface Prototyping, *IEEE Wireless Communications* **9**(6), 64–9.

Edwards, K., Newman, M. W., Sedivy, J., Smith, T. & Izadi, S. [2002], Challenge: Recombinant Computing and the Speakeasy Approach, *in* I. F. Akyildiz, J. Y. B. Lin, R. Jain, V. Bharghavan & A. T. Campbell (eds.), *Proceedings of the 8th Annual ACM/IEEE International Conference on Mobile Computing and Networking (MobiCom'02)*, ACM Press, pp.279–86.

Edwards, W. K. & Grinter, R. E. [2001], At Home with Ubiquitous Computing: Seven Challenges, *in* G. D. Abowd, B. Brumitt & S. Shafer (eds.), *Ubicomp 2001: Ubiquitous Computing (Proceedings of the Third International Conference on Ubiquitous Computing)*, Vol. 2201 of *Lecture Notes in Computer Science*, Springer-Verlag, pp.256–72.

Hart, S. & Staveland, L. [1988], Development of NASA-TLX (Task Load Index): Results of Empirical and Theoretical Research, *in* P. Hancock & N. Meshkati (eds.), *Human Mental Workload*, North-Holland, pp.139–83.

Holland, S. & Oppenheim, D. [1999], Direct Combination, *in* M. G. Williams & M. W. Altom (eds.), *Proceedings of the SIGCHI Conference on Human Factors in Computing Systems: The CHI is the Limit (CHI'99)*, ACM Press, pp.262–9.

Holland, S., Morse, D. R. & Gedenryd, H. [2002], Direct Combination: a New User Interaction Principle for Mobile and Ubiquitous HCI, *in* F. Paterno (ed.), *Human Computer Interaction with Mobile Devices: Proceedings of the 4th International Symposium on Mobile Human–Computer Interaction (Mobile HCI 2002)*, Vol. 2411 of *Lecture Notes in Computer Science*, Springer-Verlag, pp.108–22.

Kohtake, N., Rekimoto, J. & Anzai, Y. [1999], InfoStick: An Interaction Device for Inter-appliance Computing, *in* H.-W. Gellersen (ed.), *Handheld and Ubiquitous Computing: Proceeding of the First International Symposium on Handheld and Ubiquitous Computing (HUC 1999)*, Vol. 1707 of *Lecture Notes in Computer Science*, Springer-Verlag, pp.246–58.

Kortuem, G. [2002], Proem: A Middleware Platform for Mobile Peer-to-Peer Computing, *MC²R Mobile Computing and Communications Review* **6**(4), 62–4.

Kristoffersen, S. & Ljungberg, F. [2000], Representing Modalities in Mobile Computing: A Model of IT-use in Mobile Settings, White Paper, Norwegian Computing Center. Available at http://www.nr.no/documents/imedia/publications/work_in_the_future/mopas_kristoffersen.pdf.

Lewis, C. & Reiman, J. [1993], *Task Centered User Interface Design: A Practical Introduction*, University of Colorado, Boulder, Colorado, USA.

Newman, M. W., Sedivy, J. Z., Edwards, W. K., Smith, T., Marcelo, K., Neuwirth, C. M., Hong, J. I. & Izadi, S. [2002], Designing for Serendipity: Supporting End-user Configuration of Ubiquitous Computing Environments, *in* B. Verplank, A. Sutcliffe, W. Mackay, J. Amowitz & W. Gaver (eds.), *Proceedings of the Symposium on Designing Interactive Systems: Processes, Practices, Methods and Techniques (DIS'02)*, ACM Press, pp.147–56.

Rekimoto, J. [1997], Pick-And-Drop: A Direct Manipulation Technique for Multiple Computer Environments, *in* G. Robertson & C. Schmandt (eds.), *Proceedings of the 10th Annual ACM Symposium on User Interface Software and Technology, UIST'97*, ACM Press, pp.31–9.

Rekimoto, J., B., U. & Oba, H. [2001], DataTiles: A Modular Platform for Mixed Physical and Graphical Interactions, *in* J. A. Jacko & A. Sears (eds.), *Proceedings of SIGCHI Conference on Human Factors in Computing Systems (CHI'01), CHI Letters* **3**(1), ACM Press, pp.269–76.

Sousa, J. P. & Garlan, D. [2002], Aura: An Architectural Framework for User Mobility in Ubiquitous Computing Environments, *in* J. Bosch, W. M. Gentleman, C. Hofmeister & J. Kuusela (eds.), *Proceedings of WICSA 2002*, Kluwer, pp.29–43.

Ullmer, B. & Ishii, H. [2000], Emerging Frameworks for Tangible User Interfaces, *IBM System Journal* **39**(3 & 4), 915–31.

Weiser, M. [1991], The Computer for the 21st Century, *Scientific American* **265**(3), 94–104.

Winograd, T. [2001], Interaction Spaces for 21st Century Computing, *in* J. M. Carroll (ed.), *Human–Computer Interaction in the New Millenium*, Addison–Wesley.

The Geometry of Web Search

John D McCarthy, M Angela Sasse & Jens Riegelsberger

Department of Computer Science, University College London, Gower Street, London WC1E 6BT, UK

Tel: *+44 20 7679 3644*

Email: *{j.mccarthy,a.sasse,j.riegelsberger}@cs.ucl.ac.uk*

This paper introduces the concept of a *search geometry* to describe the eye behaviour of users searching with different tasks across multiple sites. To validate the concept, we present results from an eye tracking study of four common tasks on three different Web portals. The findings show a consistent search geometry that describes eye behaviour across the different sites and tasks. The geometry illustrates that a small set of page regions account for a large proportion of eye movements. The results are briefly discussed in relation to theories of information foraging and information scent.

Keywords: Web design, information architecture, visual scanning, search geometry, eye movements, eye tracking, information scent, information foraging.

1 Introduction

A problem facing users in a wide variety of interfaces is selecting the right option to achieve their goal. This problem is especially acute on Web interfaces where users are presented with a large number of simultaneous choices.

Faced with many options, users must search the interface to find the appropriate link to take them closer to their goal. We review the factors that can influence search (Section 2) and distinguish between the identity and location of page elements (Section 3). Drawing on this distinction, we introduce the concept of a *search geometry* to classify search behaviour that is consistent across different websites and search tasks (Section 4). We validate the concept in an eye tracking study (Section 5), with 4 different tasks across 3 websites, and examine how performance is affected when task targets lie outside the *search geometry*. Finally (Section 6), we conclude with a brief discussion of the utility of the concept for practitioners and researchers and discuss the relationship to theories of information foraging and information scent.

2 Factors Influencing Search

The search of Web interfaces is governed by both the design of the page and the expectations of the user. Careful manipulation of design factors such as layering, separation, colours and contrast can draw the eye to important pieces of information and reduce competition between display elements [Tufte 1990]. Similarly, motion or animation is an effective cue to draw the eye to certain locations [Hillstrom & Yantis 1994]. Alongside the myriad of design factors, users will also have expectations about *where* things should be found in an interface. Such expectations are learnt through experience across multiple websites. A recent study by McCarthy et al. [2003] illustrates how expectation of a navigation menu on the left of screen could draw eye movements to this location — even though the menu was actually located on the right.

This result confirms finding from the psychological literature, which show that unless a unique physical feature — such as colour, contrast or motion — identifies a target, search proceeds by fixating the screen elements one by one [Treisman & Gelade 1980]. To reduce the number of things that must be looked at, people rely on expectations about where they might find what they are looking for. And instead of searching every possible location they devote their energy to looking in just a few.

It is important to distinguish this account of search from the concept of information scent [Pirolli 1997]. Scent is perceived when the proximal cues provided by page elements such as such as WWW links, graphics, icons or menu items are evaluated relative to the current goals. This gives an indication of the value, cost, and location of the distal content on the linked page. Thus, information scent is a basis for clicking on a link, but it cannot be perceived unless an element is actually looked at. It therefore cannot guide the visual search process itself.

3 What vs. Where

Evidence from search studies in psychology, psychophysics and neuroscience suggests that there are two main 'streams of processing' in the human visual system. These have been referred to as the '*what*' system and '*where*' system [Milner & Goodale 1995; Wolfe 1996]. The '*what*' stream of processing goes towards the temporal cortex, and is primarily concerned with object recognition. The '*where*' stream goes towards the parietal cortex, and is mainly concerned with object location. The '*what*' stream operates on fixated objects and integrates across fixations but there is no evidence that we can identify things without first fixating them [Treisman & Gelade 1980]. Even if people *could* identify things without fixating them, the mental representation of their goal may not match what is actually present on the page [Jacob & Karn 2003]. A simple example is someone looking for 'houses' or 'flats' when the page represents this as 'property' or 'real estate'. Given these considerations it seems likely that search is primarily driven by information about '*where*' the target might be found. Rensink [2000] claims two types of information can be extracted from the '*where*' processing stream. One type of information is a representation capable of directing subsequent eye movements. The other type of information is the abstract meaning or *gist* of the scene.

The *gist* is defined by the spatial arrangement or layout of objects on the page and may give a general indication of *what type of interface* is being looked at without active identification. Gist appears to be extracted without attention [Oliva & Schyns 1997] and may be based on the statistical features of low-level visual structures such as edges, textures and colours. In terms of Web search, *gist* would distinguish the particular type of site facing the user, e.g. Web portal, e-commerce site, search engine, forum, blog site, etc. By comparing the current layout with experience of previously identified layouts the user *can* identify *what* type of site they are viewing very quickly from the *where* stream or layout alone.

4 Search Geometry

To investigate whether search does indeed follow stereotypical spatial patterns or whether it is driven by the identity of screen elements we conducted an exploratory study of search on three complex websites. If search is primarily driven by prior experience then we should expect similar search patterns across very different websites. To compare search across different websites and tasks we draw on the concept of a geometry. The properties studied in a geometry are the properties that are not changed (i.e. are invariant) under transformation. In the case of Web search, we ask the question:

- Is there a set of objects that are consistently looked at (i.e. invariant) across changes in site and task (i.e. transformation)?

Before proceeding however, we needed to develop a classification scheme to identify equivalent objects across different websites. The scheme we adopted parallels the distinction between the *what* and *where* streams of visual processing.

4.1 Where are the Screen Objects?

There are many conventions adopted and advocated by usability experts that constrain the variety of possible layouts [for example NCI 2002; IBM 2003]. Two websites can have the same spatial configuration but quite different functions. This is especially true with the wide use of Web templates in the design process [Nielsen 1998].

To examine people's search patterns in purely spatial terms, we classify webpages into distinct spatial regions. To simplify interpretation, we define positions relative to the page and use the HTML concept of a table element to identify different screen positions. Tables can be located at the top, left, centre, right or bottom of the visible page. The precise position is identified as a row and cell index in the table (Figure 1):

1. Top Table (Row Y Cell X)

2. Left Table (Row Y, Cell X)

3. Centre Table (Row Y, Cell X)

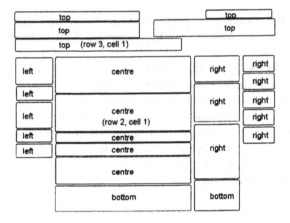

Figure 1: Layout of screen objects.

4. Right Table (Row Y, Cell X)

5. Bottom Table (Row Y, Cell X)

All three sites in the study can be described by this scheme. Our primary goal is to investigate whether a geometry based on '*where*' objects are on the screen actually exists. In other words, do people consistently look at certain locations across changes in site and task?

4.2 What are the Screen Objects?

Another way to identify corresponding objects across different sites is to define objects in terms of *what* they are. But one complication with the notion of '*what*', are the differences in interpretation. What a screen object is — and what it is for depends very much on perspective and the task being performed. Such differences in perspectives are evident in current schemes for classifying screen objects. For example, a recent book by Nielsen & Tahir [2002] deconstructs 50 homepages into five areas:

1. Welcome and Site ID.

2. Navigation.

3. Content of Interest.

4. Filler Image.

5. Advertising and Sponsorship.

6. Self Promotion.

Krug [2000] has a different take on the types of homepage objects, outlining 9 regions of importance (Figure 2):

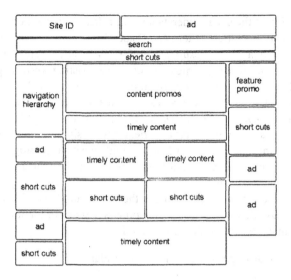

Figure 2: Identities of screen objects.

- Identity/Site ID/Mission.

- Registration.

- Navigation Hierarchy.

- Search.

- Short Cuts.

- Content Promos.

- Feature Promos.

- Timely Content.

- Deals/Ads.

Krug's conception is a more detailed categorization, but there are also semantic differences. For example, what should Registration be classified as in the Nielsen scheme? As Krug's scheme is finer grained, we adopt this to identify corresponding objects across different websites. This will make it more difficult to identify types of object that are consistently looked at across changes in site and task.

4.3 What is Where?

The previous distinctions ignore the fact that there is often a correlation between the location and identity. For example, *Welcome and Site ID* are usually associated with the top left of the page, *Navigation* with the top or left side and *Content* with the middle. Indeed, this is the usual understanding of a design convention — associating meaning with location, colour, pattern and shape.

It seems reasonable to assume therefore that any search geometry has both identity and location properties — reflecting existing knowledge of design conventions. Thus, when searching for information, a user will seek out '*what*' objects are necessary to complete a task but the process of searching will be guided by location expectations of '*where*' these elements might be found. These expectations are based on previous experience with similar interfaces alongside the processing of the current screen layout. With novel technology, expectations are weak as users have little experience — with more established technologies expectations become embedded[1].

These distinctions reflect processing in the '*what*' and '*where*' visual pathways outlined earlier. By identifying a search geometry with both identity and location properties we can address a number of questions:

- Is search primarily governed by location or identity?

- What are the consequences when an interface does not match the search geometry in terms of what is where?

In practical terms it is useful to know where screen objects are best placed to match user expectations about where they should be.

5 Exploratory Study

To investigate the validity of a search geometry to describe search behaviour, two types of transformation are directly manipulated: site transformation (T_S) and task transformation (T_T). Each person was exposed to 12 variations; 3 site transformations, each with 4 task transformations. The 3 sites where homepages of large Internet Service Providers (ISPs) in the UK. These sites varied widely in their use of colour, contrast and layout. We reasoned that to find consistency among such heterogeneous sites would be a strong test of search invariance across sites. To create useful comparisons across these sites, we classified the screen objects of these sites according to layout and identity as outlined above. None of the sites used dynamic interface elements.

To investigate task transformation we examined four visual search tasks based on a recent survey of Internet use [PC Almanac 2000]. This suggests that the most common uses of the Web are:

1. To search for something.

2. To read the latest news.

3. To shop for something (a digital camera).

---

[1] It is worth noting that the establishment of generic expectations does not necessarily mean an interface is more usable. In some cases, such as the QWERTY keyboard, the embedding of what is where may be non-optimal in terms of task performance, user satisfaction and user cost perspectives but still culturally endemic [Shneiderman 1998, p.307].

4. To send an email.

Again, the variety of tasks present a strong test of search geometry because 'a priori' these tasks are not associated with any particular screen position or object.

5.1 Method

5.1.1 Participants

We tested 40 undergraduates. However, to ensure high quality data we excluded from the analysis any participant who was tracked less than 90% of the time — (due to head movements). This strict criterion led to the exclusion of 23 participants from the analysis. The remaining 17 participants had tracking rates of 90% or greater. Of the 17 participants 12 were male and 5 female. The mean age of the participants was 22. All participants were experienced Web users who used the Internet at least 2 hours/day. Participants were paid £5.

5.1.2 Stimuli and Equipment

Eye movements were measured using the EyeGaze system from LC technologies. The system samples eye position at a rate of 50Hz. Raw eye co-ordinates were converted to fixations using an algorithm that assumes a fixation time of 100ms and gaze deviation of 7mm.

5.1.3 Design

The experimental design was a $4 \times 3 \times 4$ mixed design. The between subject variable was *Order*. Within subject variables were *Site* and *Task*. All participants performed all four tasks on each of the three sites. The effects of presentation order were counterbalanced between subjects using presentation orders based on a Latin squares design.

5.1.4 Procedure

Participants were briefed about the nature of the experiment and the measures that were going to be taken. The eye tracker was then calibrated to the participants gaze. They were presented with an alternation of instruction and test screens. Instruction screens provided participants with the current goal — e.g. "Where would you go on this site to.. search for something on the Internet". They were then presented with the homepage on which to complete the task. All participants received a single practice trial.

6 Results

Eye tracking data was first processed to measure the number of glances to a particular object on a page. This rectifies differences in processing time across individuals [McCarthy et al. 2003]. A glance is defined as one or more successive fixations to the same object. Figure 3 shows a scan path with 6 fixations. The first two to Object A followed by three to Object B followed by another to Object A. When reduced to a glance analysis this scan path would be recorded as a total of 3 glances, 2 glances to Object A and 1 to Object B — or A–B–A as a sequence. Thus, multiple glances to an object correspond to a re-sampling or re-visit to that object.

There is a close relationship between the number of glances made and the task completion time. The Pearson's correlation between the natural log of these two

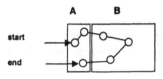

Figure 3: From fixations to glances.

	Top Table Row 3 Cell 1	Top Table Row 2 Cell 1	Centre Table Row 1 Cell 1
I	1.0	0.92	0.83

	Navigation Hierarchy	Search Box	Content Promos
I	1.0	0.92	0.92

Table 1: Invariant spatial and functional regions.

measures $= 0.82$, $p < 0.001$. The average time to complete a task was 6 seconds with an average of 11 glances. The longest search took 50 seconds and the maximum number of glances was 68.

6.1 Search Geometry and Invariance

To investigate whether a consistent set of objects is glanced at across sites and tasks we first extracted the screen objects that received the most glances across all subjects for a particular site-task combination. We defined these as the most frequently glanced objects that cumulatively account for 50% of all glances. For any particular site-task combination 4–5 objects (~20%) accounted for 50% of all glances made. Among these objects we looked to see whether objects with particular functions or spatial positions where consistently looked at. To give an indication of invariance to site and task we calculated an index of invariance, I, to the transformations in site and task. The index is the proportion of times an object received a large proportion of fixations across the 12 site and task variations. If an object consistently receives a large proportion of glances across all 12 conditions the index, $I = 1.0$. If an object is glanced at in only 6 of the 12 conditions the index, $I = 0.5$. Table 1 illustrates the three spatial and function objects with the highest scores on the index of invariance. Clearly, there are spatial and functional areas that receive a large proportion of glances across changes in *Site* and *Task*.

These findings suggest the existence of a search geometry to describe how people search the ISP home pages. Task targets that fall within this geometry should be found more easily than those falling outside the geometry. To investigate this we examined the relationship between search geometry and task performance.

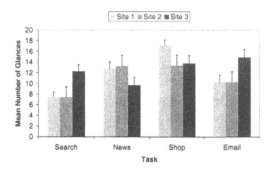

Figure 4: Interaction between Site and Task.

6.2 Search Performance and Task Geometry

We performed an 3×4 repeated measures ANOVA to investigate whether the number of glances to complete a task was sensitive to changes in *Site* or *Task*. Figure 4 illustrates the number of glances across all 12 *Site–Task* combinations. The analysis revealed no overall difference in the number of glances to different *Sites* $F(2,30) = 1.18$, ns; but significant differences between *Tasks*, $F(3,45) = 6.1$, $p < 0.001$ and an interaction between the *Task* and the *Site* it was performed on, $F(6,90) = 5.4$, $p < 0.001$. Averaging across sites, the *Search Box* task took the least number of glances, followed by *News* and *Email*, with *Shopping* being the most difficult task to complete.

The invariance to changes in *Task* and *Site* can be examined visually in Figures 5–9. For any particular site-task combination, the page regions highlighted in grey are the frequently glanced objects accounting for 50% of all glances. The locations of task targets are indicated with a black spot. On 10 out of the 12 conditions examined task targets lie outside the frequently glanced regions — suggesting that they do not attract attention in there own right. To understand the relationship to task performance we examine the glance pattern of sites that perform well and poorly relative to the other sites. On each of the four tasks there is always one site that performs either significantly better of worse than the other two (Figure 3). Site 3 was poor on both the *Search Box* and *Email* task but good on the *News* task relative to the other two sites. Site 1 was especially poor on the *Shopping* task.

6.3 Search Box Task

Site 3 performs poorly on the search task (Figure 5). On this site both targets for the task are outside the frequently glanced regions. The search boxes are therefore in unexpected positions and are not recovered quickly from the search. From this preliminary study it is not entirely clear why the upper right of the screen is not looked at more during the search. One possibility is that the right or upper right of the screen is an unexpected position for the search box. There are however alternative

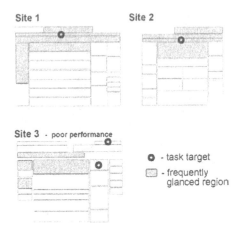

Figure 5: Frequently glanced objects in the SEARCH BOX task.

explanations for the poor performance. The contrast or colouring of the search boxes may have been less salient for this site, and there was also a banner ad, just below the search box, that may have led people to ignore this region of the screen. Without a second study specifically focused on this issue these possibilities cannot be ruled out. Nevertheless, moving the search box to a region with a high index of invariance should improve its visibility. The logic of this is simply to place an object that are used often (search) in a position that is looked at often (Top Table, Rows 2/3).

6.4 News Task

All three sites have a target or targets within the core geometry, but Site 3 clearly outperforms the other two (Figure 6). Therefore this factor cannot be used to explain differences in search performance. Another possibility is that the target may be easier or harder to find within the target object.

Closer examination revealed that all sites have a *News* link on the navigation hierarchy, but site 3 places the *News* link second in the list — to account for the frequent use of this item. In comparison, sites 2 and 3 order their lists alphabetically such that the *News* link is around two thirds of the way down the list. Again this is an example of putting the objects used the most in a position looked at the most but this time it is within an object.

7 Shopping Task

All three sites have task targets within frequently glanced regions — so we cannot use this factor to account for performance differences (Figure 7). Site 1 performed the worst — despite the fact that this was the only site with a second-level navigation hierarchy for different categories of shopping. The top navigation bar of Site 1 had 11 categories for shopping but the only one appropriate to the digital camera shopping task was the first — labelled "A-Z directory". It seemed likely that the poor performance of this site is due to extensive scanning of this region. To test for

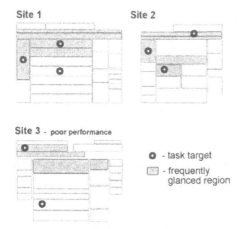

Figure 6: Frequently glanced objects in the NEWS task.

Figure 7: Frequently glanced objects in the SHOPPING task.

this we compared the number of fixations to the top navigation bar on the shopping task across the 3 sites (Figure 8). The results confirmed there were significantly more fixations to this region on Site 1, $\chi^2(17) = 6.95$, $p < 0.05$.

The extensive search of this region on this task can be taken as evidence for the theory of information scent. A second level hierarchy for shopping suggests a potential target with a stronger scent than shopping alone and users invest a significantly longer exploring this region.

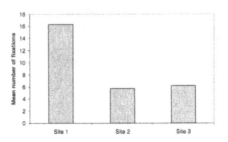

Figure 8: Number of fixations of the top navigation bar.

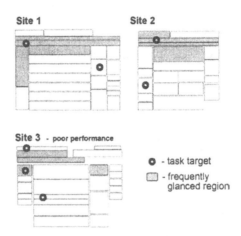

Figure 9: Frequently glanced objects in the EMAIL task.

7.1   Email Task

Site 3 performs poorly on the email task (Figure 9). Two of the three targets
are outside the core geometry. The third is in a position usually associated with
navigation hierarchies, but the region is not actually a menu bar.

For many participants we observed glances to this region but a continuation of
the search as though they didn't really 'see' what was there. This is suggestive of a
mismatch between presentation and representation of *what* the target looks like. It
seems likely that people were looking for a link labelled 'E-mail' but for Site 3 the
links were labelled 'Read Messages' and 'My Inbox'. This subtle difference in what
the target looks like on screen could explain the poor performance.

7.2   Summary

Overall our results reveal that a small set of screen objects receive a large proportion
of all glances. Furthermore, there is great consistency (invariance) in regions glanced
across changes in *Task* and *Site*. This suggests that search patterns are relatively

stereotyped — driven more by expectations from previous experience than by the ambient information on the current page.

We have shown that identifying the core set of objects is a useful tool for interpreting differences in task performance and identifying the scale at which search problems arise. Performance differences on two of the tasks (*Search box & Email*) could be explained in terms of violation of "what is expected where". These results support to the findings of McCarthy et al. [2003] — illustrating how deviations from design conventions can impair search performance. On the other two tasks, (*News & Shop*), difficulty locating the link within an a screen object seems a more likely explanation of search differences.

8 Conclusions

One limitation of the present study is that search was examined with a relatively small number of websites. Although the ISP portals examined have an impact on millions of users, it would still be useful to replicate the finding of a search geometry across a wider range of Web portals. Similarly it would be interesting to study search behaviour across different types of site — such as search engines, e-commerce sites, bulletin boards and weblogs. It seems likely that different classes of site will have different search geometries — called into action from the *gist* or first impressions of the site.

For practitioners, our results show that users devote the majority of their search effort to very few screen objects. With this in mind it becomes important to prioritize the available links, placing the most important within the search geometry. Knowledge of the search geometry for different classes of site could prove an important design tool to improve site usability or to design new sites from scratch. Knowledge of how they change over time could give an indication of design trends reflected in search behaviour.

For researchers, we have presented a novel technique for the analysis of eye movements across multiple individuals, sites and tasks. Difficulties in analysing eye movement data are often cited as one reason why the technique is not more widely used [Jacob & Karn 2003]. The contributions of this paper go some way to simplifying the analysis problem.

In the context of theories of information foraging and information scent, the eye tracking study illustrates that search behaviour is relatively fixed, and limited in terms of what and where people look. There is little evidence of foraging behaviour beyond the boundaries of the search geometry. This however may be a consequence of the tasks examined. Tasks which are performed with a high frequency will have embedded notions of what is where and are more likely to produce predictable scan patterns than a novel task. Future work needs to clarify these issues, identifying the application of the search geometry across a wider range of tasks and exploring the relationship to information scent as a driver for search behaviour.

References

Hillstrom, A. P. & Yantis, S. [1994], Visual Motion and Attentional Capture, *Perception & Psychophysics* 55(4), 399–411.

IBM [2003], Web Design Guidelines, http://www-3.ibm.com/ibm/easy/eou_ext.nsf/Publish/572.

Jacob, R. J. K. & Karn, K. S. [2003], Eye Tracking in Human–Computer Interaction and Usability Research: Ready to Deliver the Promises, *in* J. Hyönä, R. Radach & H. Deubel (eds.), *The Mind's Eye: Cognitive and Applied Aspects of Eye Movement Research*, Elsevier Science, pp.573–605.

Krug, S. [2000], *Don't Make Me Think: A Common Sense Approach to Web Usability*, New Riders Publishing.

McCarthy, J., Sasse, M. A. & Riegelsberger, J. [2003], Could I Have the Menu Please? An Eye Tracking Study of Design Conventions, *in* P. Johnson, H. Johnson & E. O'Neill (eds.), *People and Computers XVII: Designing for Society (Proceedings of HCI'03)*, Springer-Verlag, pp.401–14.

Milner, A. D. & Goodale, M. A. [1995], *The Visual Brain in Action*, Oxford University Press.

NCI [2002], Research Based Web Design and Usability Guidelines, http://usability.gov/guidelines/.

Nielsen, J. [1998], Testing Whether Web Page Templates Are Helpful, Useit.com Alertbox 1998.05.17, available at http://www.useit.com/alertbox/980517.html.

Nielsen, J. & Tahir, M. [2002], *Hompage Usability — 50 Web sites Deconstructed*, New Riders Publishing.

Oliva, A. & Schyns, P. G. [1997], Coarse Blobs or Fine Edges? Evidence that Information Diagnosticity Changes the Perception of Complex Visual Stimuli, *Cognitive Psychology* **34**(1), 72–107.

PC Almanac [2000], What Are You Doing? Online Surfing Habits Remain Similar Across Demographic Boundaries, *PC Almanac* **4**(4), 34–7.

Pirolli, P. [1997], Computational Models of Information Scent-following in A Very Large Browsable Text Collection, *in* S. Pemberton (ed.), *Proceedings of the SIGCHI Conference on Human Factors in Computing Systems (CHI'97)*, ACM Press, pp.3–10.

Rensink, R. A. [2000], Seeing, Sensing, and Scrutinizing, *Vision Research* **40**(10-2), 1468–87.

Shneiderman, B. [1998], *Designing the User Interface: Strategies for Effective Human–Computer Interaction*, third edition, Addison–Wesley.

Treisman, A. & Gelade, G. [1980], A Feature Integration Theory of Attention, *Cognitive Psychology* **12**(1), 97–136.

Tufte, E. R. [1990], *Envisioning Information*, Graphics Press.

Wolfe, J. M. [1996], Visual search, *in* H. Pashler (ed.), *Attention*, Psychology Press, pp.13–73.

Supplemental Navigation Tools for Website Navigation — A Comparison of User Expectations and Current Practice

C J Pilgrim[†], Y K Leung[‡] & G Lindgaard[*]

[†] School of Information Technology, Swinburne University of Technology, Melbourne, Australia

Email: *cpilgrim@swin.edu.au*

[‡] Department of Information and Communications Technology, Institute of Vocational Education, Tsing Yi, Hong Kong

[*] Human-Oriented Technology Laboratory, Carleton University, Ottawa, Ontario K1S 5B6, Canada

One of the challenges confronting website designers is to provide effective navigational support. Supplemental navigation tools such as search, indexes and sitemaps are frequently included on websites. However, due to a lack of guidance for designers a proliferation of designs has evolved leaving users confused about the role and value of each particular tool. This paper reports an empirical investigation into the expectations of users regarding the purpose and design of supplemental navigation tools. Expectations are then compared with a survey of the current utilization of these tools in major commercial websites. The study establishes a relationship between certain types of information goals and the selection of search and sitemap tools.

Keywords: Web navigation, sitemap, index, search.

1   Introduction

It is accepted that the World Wide Web is the most significant information resource ever devised. It is used by millions of people each day for work and entertainment and continues to grow in terms of content and usage. It is however astonishing that the basic methods for locating information on the Web have remained the same for over a decade. When searching for information, users typically use global search tools to find websites relating to their area of interest. These search tools suffer many problems relating to standards, commercial interests, algorithms and interface usability. Alternatively users sometimes navigate through the Web from site to site utilizing information on the pages to trigger decisions to follow links. This 'hit and miss' navigation method makes it difficult to find specific information resulting in users sometimes feeling lost, confused and overwhelmed [Gershon et al. 1995]. Initiatives such as 'Semantic Web' [W3C 2004] offer some future hope, but the distributed nature of the Web means that global navigation may never be improved.

Given the challenging situation of global navigation, it is likely that when users arrive at a particular website they may be cognitively fatigued from the journey through search tools results and irrelevant sites. According to Nielsen [2000], Web users are impatient, require instant gratification and will leave a site if they cannot immediately figure out how to use it. It is therefore important that users can quickly appreciate the nature of the site's content, its organization and the methods by which to find particular information once they arrive at an individual website.

The standard navigation tools provided by Web browsers are inadequate as they do not provide the facilities to visualize the inter-relationships between pages preventing users from answering questions such as "Where am I?", "Where can I go from here?" or "Which pages point to this page?" [Bieber et al. 1997]. A lack of knowledge of the overall structure of the site can result in confusion and cognitive overload as users jump from one location to another [Mukherjea & Foley 1995]. Users are also prone to disorientation whilst navigating through hypertext [Nielsen 1990]. Kappe [in Gershon et al. 1995] refers to the 'Lost in Space' syndrome:

> "where users cannot get an overview, cannot find specific information, stumble over the same information again and again, cannot identify new and outdated information, cannot find out how much information there is on a given topic and how much of it has been seen."

General hypertext research has raised awareness of the problems of disorientation and cognitive load and has developed a variety of supplemental navigational tools that can be deployed into websites. Three common tools are:

- Sitemaps: A site map is essentially a visual representation of the website architecture allowing users to see where they are, what other information is available and how to access other information. It has been suggested that sitemaps assist site navigation decisions [Danielson 2002], reduce disorientation [Shneiderman 1997; Bieber et al. 1997] and provide a sense of the extent of a particular website without giving detail [Tauscher & Greenberg 1996]. Sitemaps may be considered similar to the table of contents of a book providing a list of the major categories of information (i.e. chapters) and their subsections.

- Indexes: Indexes have long been regarded as the "state of the art in print navigation" [Rosenfeld & Morville 1998]. They are defined as an "alphabetical list with references usually at the end of a book" (Oxford Dictionary) hence whilst sitemaps may be considered similar to a table of contents provided at the front of a book, it is assumed that an index of a website would be presented as an alphabetical list of the contents of the site.

- Search: An internal search tool may be provided to allow users to search the current site for a particular search string.

The use of these supplemental navigation tools in websites is extremely common. However, because there are very few design guidelines available for developers, a wide range of designs and levels of functionality for each tool have emerged. Generally, users are presented with a graphical or textual label providing a link to each of the tools, i.e. Search, Sitemap and Index. The decision to select a particular tool is therefore based on an association the user makes between the information on the link label and their prior experience. Such decisions may lead to fulfilling the user's expectations of a suitable tool that meets a current need. Alternatively, the decision to use a particular tool may lead to disappointment if the tool provides inappropriate functionality to assist the immediate information need.

Due to the restricted amount of descriptive information that can be included on a link label, the design of supplemental navigation tools should be sensitive to the needs and expectations of prospective users. Whilst it is difficult in most cases to predict potential user types, design can be improved by an understanding of the general expectations of users regarding the design and functionality of each of these tools, as well as the types of tasks that users perform when they select a particular tool.

The purpose of this study is to investigate user expectations of the design and purpose of the three common supplemental navigation tools for the Web, namely sitemaps, indexes and search tools. This paper reports three studies. The first study investigates the purpose of each tool through an experiment testing the selection of certain navigation tools for specific information goals. The second study investigates expectations that users have of the design and functionality of each tool. The final study reports findings from a survey of the current utilization of supplemental navigation tools in major commercial websites allowing a comparison of expectation with current practice.

Together, these studies afford an appreciation of the relationship between current designs and user expectations, providing the foundation for the development of design guidelines. This benefits not only current designers but also future research into Web navigation.

2   Expectation of Purpose

2.1   *Information Goals*

Users typically activate a link to a particular supplemental navigation tool in response to an immediate information need. The expected purpose of each tool may therefore be investigated by examining the relationship between information goals and tool choice.

It is recognized that information goals of Web users will vary. At times, users know exactly what they want; others have only a rough idea of what they are looking for; at others they only realize they are interested in something when they see it [Lucarella & Zanzi 1993]. Duncan & McAleese [1987] distinguish between users who know what they want and search for a known item, and users who only know that they have a gap in understanding but may not have sufficient knowledge of the subject area to articulate the need formally. Shneiderman [1997] suggests that the complexity of information goals vary between specific fact-finding, where the outcome can be achieved by visiting a single node in the information space, and extended-fact finding where several nodes are visited to accomplish a goal through aggregation or comparison.

Given this variation, previous research [Pilgrim et al. 2002] has proposed a classification of goal types as lying along a continuum based on the level of 'goal specificity' and ranging from tightly defined closed goals to ill-defined open goals. Closed goals have a discrete answer, or a set of answers, once achieved will result in closure of the need. Open goals do not have a finite answer and hence will not have a specific point of closure where the information need is satisfied. This goal-specificity continuum can be used as a basis for a broad classification of user tasks:

- Open tasks have a low level of goal-specificity. Users may not have an immediate information need, so the purpose of the task is to provide an understanding of the organization of the website and/or a sense of how concepts are related. Consistent with Lucarella & Zanzi's [1993] and Duncan & McAleese's [1987] second group, users may serendipitously switch to other strategies as something of interest appears, or as their domain knowledge increases allowing them to express a need more formally.

- Closed tasks are characterized by a very specific information need resulting in a single outcome. This is consistent with Shneiderman's [1997] first category of information goals.

- Investigative tasks are defined as those where the outcome is the result of an aggregation or comparison of information across several pages (Shneiderman's second category of information goals). The distinctive feature of these tasks is that users are required to visit and revisit multiple pages in the site to compile an outcome.

Previous research [Pilgrim et al. 2002] also identified patterns of browsing behaviour for each of the task types. When confronted with an open task, users employed a 'scanning strategy' involving a broad, shallow browse pattern. It is hypothesized that such a strategy would be supported by an interface presenting the site as a hierarchy, allowing an appreciation of the major categories of content with the ability to examine detail if required. A sitemap presentation displaying a categorical hierarchy of the content would support this strategy by presenting a view assisting the user in gaining a general appreciation of the organization and extent of the site and how the content is related.

The previous study also found that a 'selecting strategy' was employed when performing investigative tasks that required the user to visit many different sections of a site to compile an answer. This strategy is characterized by a broad focus on systematic exploratory strategies at deeper levels in the site. It is hypothesized that such a strategy might be supported by an index tool which facilitates selection and comparison of specific areas of interest at deeper levels in the site.

It is also hypothesized that local search tools would support closed tasks due to the high degree of goal specificity allowing an articulation of a specific search string.

2.2 Study 1 — Aim and Design

This study investigated the relationship between tasks and search tools to understand the expectations of the purpose of each navigation tool. The experiment tested the hypotheses that search tools will be chosen for closed tasks, sitemaps for open tasks and indexes for investigative tasks.

Eighteen volunteer participants took part in the experiment. Participants with less than one year total or one hour/week of Web use were excluded. All sessions were conducted in a usability laboratory using the same system procedure.

Participants were presented with a list containing 12 scenarios and three columns labelled 'Search', 'Sitemap' and 'Index'. Scenarios were set in the context of a university website. The list contained four scenarios related to each of the three task types (open, investigative and closed). The order of the task types was randomized for each subject. Participants were asked to select the best navigation tool for each scenario.

2.3 Results and Discussion

Figure 1 shows the number of times each tool was selected for the three task types across all 18 participants.

Clearly, the level of agreement was very high for the search and open task types with the majority of participants choosing a sitemap for open tasks and a search tool for closed tasks. However, there was considerable disagreement with respect to the investigative tasks. A one way ANOVA performed across the three task types revealed a significant difference in the mean number of responses that were correct according to the hypotheses ($F(2,34) = 22.56$, $p < 0.001$). A post-hoc test using paired-sample t-tests indicated that there was a significant difference between the Index and Sitemap tools ($t(17) = 4.48$, $p < 0.017$) and the Index and Search tools ($t(17) = 6.56$, $p < 0.017$). Significance is tested at $p < 0.017$ using a Bonferroni adjustment.

Table 1 shows the mean number of responses corresponding with hypothesized response for each of the three tools. Random selection would yield a mean of 1.33 for

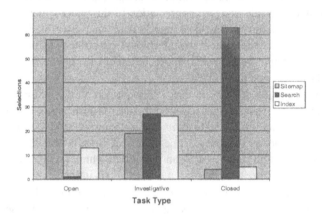

Figure 1: Task Type / Tool Selection.

	Mean	Std.Dev.
Closed task = Search tool	3.56	0.62
Investigative task = Index tool	1.33	1.28
Open task = Sitemap tool	3.22	1.00

Table 1: Means of Expected Responses. N = 18.

each tool. To test the extent to which the observed findings differed from a random selection, a series of single sample t-tests were performed.

The results indicated a significant difference in the mean number of correct responses in the Sitemap/Open task ($t(17) = 7.99$, $p < 0.001$) and Search/Closed task ($t(17) = 15.32$, $p < 0.001$) cases, but not in the Index/Investigative task case. This suggests a relationship between task type and the choice of sitemap and search tools. Choices involving the Index tool were random, and hence no relationship to task has been established.

3 Expectation of Design

3.1 Study 2 — Aim and Design

The aim of this investigation was to establish user expectations regarding the design and operation of sitemaps, indexes and search tools.

Using the same pre-screening criteria as before, eighteen volunteers took part here. The same participation criteria applied as before. All sessions were conducted in a usability laboratory using the same system procedure.

Data were collected using hard copy sketches and video recordings. Participants were provided with three task sheets, each containing written instructions and a blank webpage template. Participants were asked to imagine visiting a university website with a single link called: Search, Sitemap or Index. Participants were requested to sketch the visual appearance and describe the functionality of what they would expect to see if they clicked on the link. Participants completed all three tasks presented in a counterbalanced order. A video camera recorded the sketch and the participant's verbal description of the functionality.

The sketch and associated explanation of each navigation tool were evaluated using the following criteria:

- Categorical, alphabetical, or text field.

- Hierarchical (tree or side), flat or network.

- Interactivity controls.

- Layout (Number of pages and columns).

- Number of levels displayed.

3.2   Results and Discussion

Table 2 shows the results for each of the three supplemental navigation tools. Several types of each tool were established from the criteria of design, structure, interactivity, layout, levels and the sketch. There were two different types of search tools, seven types of sitemap designs and five types of indexes. The N field in Table 2 below indicates the number of responses there were of each particular type.

The results suggest a very strong expectation regarding the design of search tools, with all participants indicating a text field design. There was some consistency in the basic design of sitemaps with n = 17 (94%) of participants indicating that they would expect a categorical organization, most likely structured into a hierarchy. N = 9 (44%) expected a textual hierarchy as shown in Type A and B with a further 27% expecting a more graphical, tree-based hierarchy as shown in Types C and D. Most participants expected that they would be able to view 2 or 3 levels and click through to an area of interest.

There was a reasonable level of consistency in the expected design of indexes with n = 13 (67%) of participants indicating some type of alphabetic representation although the actual organization of the index did vary. Again participants expected that they would be able to click through to an area of interest.

4   Current Practice

4.1   Study 3 — Survey

In order to determine the current utilization of supplemental navigation tools, a survey of 300 major commercial websites was conducted. The survey examined whether each tool (Search, Sitemap and Index) was included. In addition, each of the tools was categorized according to criteria such as design, interactivity, number of initial visible levels, screen dimensions and additional features such as filters or advanced search functions. The survey was limited to major commercial websites. Further surveys would be required to establish current practice in other types of sites such as educational, entertainment and personal sites.

Tool	Type	Structure	Design	N
Search	A	Text Field		10
	B	Text Field & Adv Search		8
Sitemap	A	Categorical Hierarchical Interactive 2 initial levels		8
	B	Categorical Hierarchical 2 levels only		1
	C	Categorical Hierarchical 3 or 4 levels		3
	D	Categorical Hierarchical 2 or 3 levels		2
	E	Categorical 1 level only		2
	F	Categorical Network		1
	G	Alphabetical		1
Index	A	Alphabetical Internal links		8
	B	Alphabetical		3
	C	Alphabetical		2
	D	Categorical Hierarchical Interactive 2 initial levels		3
	E	Categorical 1 level only		2

Table 2: Study 2 Results

4.2 Study 3 — Results and Discussion

The survey results are shown in Table 3. Given the strong advice in recent design guidelines [Nielsen 2000] recommending the inclusion of local search tools, it is noteworthy that only 69% of the sites provided a search tool. All of the sites without a local search tool had either a sitemap or an index tool available for supplemental navigation support. Some 158 (53%) of the sites surveyed provided a sitemap, usually implemented as a link in the basic page template. All sitemaps presented a hierarchical view of the site based on a list of the major categories within the content.

Sitemaps were categorized into four basic designs based on how the levels in the hierarchy were presented and connected. Only six of the maps were of a graphical format with a visual line linking the levels in the hierarchy (C and D in Table 3). More commonly, the sitemaps were presented as a list of textual links using either indenting (A in Table 3 with n = 61; 38%) or columns (B in Table 3 with n = 91; 57%) to visually distinguish the levels in the hierarchy. Almost all of the sitemaps allowed the user to click through to an area of interest with only two sites having additional interactivity such as controls to expand or contract the hierarchy. All sitemaps were presented on a single webpage with n = 114 (72%) requiring some scrolling in order to view the sitemap on a standard resolution.

The survey found that 38% of sites used a single column design as shown in type A. This is consistent with the results of Study 2 which found n = 8 (45%) participants indicated an expectation of this style of sitemap. An inconsistency was that 57% of the sitemaps in the survey had multiple columns as shown in type B, whilst only one participant in the second study indicated that they would expect this design. Also, only six sitemaps in the survey used a graphical design as shown in Types C and D, whereas a relatively high number of participants in the second study (n = 6, 33%) indicated that they would expect a more graphical design.

A total of 22 (7%) sites provided a site index. Of these, only three sites presented the index structured as an alphabetical list of the site contents, with the remaining sites displaying a categorical list resembling many of the sitemaps found on other sites. The most common design (n = 18, 81%) of an index actually presented a tool that resembled a sitemap in the sense that they presented a categorical hierarchy of the content. None of sites surveyed offered both a sitemap and an index.

5 Discussion

5.1 Search Tools

The findings from the studies really confirm the obvious with respect to the current and expected design and purpose of search tools. The results of the first study suggest a strong relationship between search tasks and the selection of a search tool. When confronted with a very specific information need that would result in a single outcome, users are more likely to choose a search tool than other navigational tools. Such a strong mapping is likely to be a result of the consistency of designs of search tools where all search tools take a discrete search string as input. This confirms the initial hypothesis that local search tools support discrete search tasks.

SEARCH TOOLS		
Presence	Search is present	206
Location	Link to search	66
	Integrated into template	140
SITEMAP TOOLS		
Presence	Sitemap is present	158
Categorization	Alphabetical	0
	Categorical	158
Structure	Hierarchical	158
	Network or other	0
Levels	Number of initial levels 1–26, 2–75, 3–52, 4–4, 6–1	
Interactivity	Expand/Contract or other	2
Design: A (n=61) B (n=91) C (n=4) D (n=2)		

INDEX TOOLS		
Presence	Index is present	22
Categorization	Alphabetical	3
	Categorical	19
Interactivity	Expand/Contract or other	0
Design: A (n=2) B (n=1) C (n=1) D (n=18)		

Table 3: Survey Results.

The results of the second study suggest a strong user expectation regarding the design of a search tool with all participants indicating that a search tool would include a text entry field. Many participants also indicated that the tool would also contain advanced search features or filters.

A strong relationship between user expectation and tool design is evidenced in the survey where all sites with a search tool used a text entry field as the major interface component.

5.2   Sitemaps

The findings do result in some immediate design implications for sitemaps. Sitemaps are a popular supplemental navigation tool with just over half of the 300 surveyed sites offering a sitemap tool on their website. The results of the second study suggest some consistency in user expectation with regards to the structure of sitemaps. This experiment established that there is a strong expectation that sitemaps would be presented as a categorical hierarchy of links displayed on a single webpage. In this case, expectation matches current practice with all of the surveyed sites offering a sitemap using a categorical hierarchy design. The expected design of the hierarchy varied, with many participants expecting a textual organization and others expecting a graphical view. Here, expectation conflicts with current practice as most of the surveyed sites used a textual hierarchy. Designers of sitemaps should consider the strong expectation and popular use of hierarchy, especially the need to provide a high level view of the site content.

There is also a strong relationship open tasks and selection of a sitemap tool as indicated in study 1. The results suggest that users who have a low level of goal-specificity and are interested in general information, are more likely to choose a sitemap tool than other navigation tools. Combined with the findings in the second study it is suggested that users who are performing open tasks prefer a supplemental navigation tool that provides them with a high level, hierarchical view of the major categories of the website. These findings inform designers more what not to do than how exactly to design sitemaps. Inappropriate designs would include those that display the complete site structure resulting in a complex view or those that list every key word and heading. Such designs would not assist users in completing open style tasks where overviews are required. Further work is required to determine specific design guidelines for sitemaps which focus on supporting tasks of low goal specificity.

5.3 Indexes

It was hypothesized that users performing investigative tasks are most likely to choose an index tool as this tool would provide rapid access between different sections of the website. The first study shows no preference for any particular tool for investigative tasks. This might be due to the complexity of investigative tasks and the subsequent difficulty of developing a prior strategy. In these cases users might be more likely to perform page-by-page browsing rather than using a supplemental navigation tool.

The results of the second study indicate that most users expect indexes to provide an alphabetical listing of the contents of the site. Many of the subjects in the study said they expected a website index to be similar in structure to an index of a book which is by convention an alphabetic list of keywords and topics. The results only varied in the organization of the alphabetical interface. The remainder of the subjects expected a list of the major categories of the website. This is inconsistent with the results of the survey that found that most sites that provide an index tool do not use an alphabetical organization. The lack of consistency in expectation and the mismatch between expectation and current practice probably contribute to the overall lack of utilization of indexes in commercial websites.

6 Concluding Comments

The strong mapping between closed tasks and search tools and the fact that all of major sites surveyed use a similar design indicates that users will benefit if consistency of design and a clear purpose for a tool can be identified. The study confirms the obvious that users know what a search tool will do for them, when to use it and how to use it.

The study suggests that sitemaps have the potential to be useful tools since there already is a clear purpose for the tool and some consistency in design. The findings inform designers that overview style presentations should be considered. Further research is required to develop more detailed guidelines for the optimal design of sitemaps.

The study does not contribute as much to the design of index tools. There is a lack of consistency with regards to the expectation of the fundamental design of index tools and there is no single task type that such tools support.

References

Bieber, M., Vitali, F., Ashman, H., Balasubramanian, V. & Oinas-Kukkonen, H. [1997], Fourth Generation Hypermedia: Some Missing Links for the World Wide Web, *International Journal of Human–Computer Studies* **47**(1), 31–66. Special Issue on "Web Usability" edited by S. Buckingham Shum & C. McKnight.

Danielson, D. R. [2002], Web Navigation and the Behavioral Effects of Constantly Visible Site Maps, *Interacting with Computers* **14**(5), 601–18.

Duncan, E. B. & McAleese, R. [1987], Intelligent Access to Databases Using a Thesaurus in Graphical Form, *in Proceedings of the 11th International Online Information Meeting (Online Information '87)*, Learned Information, pp.377–87.

Gershon, N. D., Ferren, B., Foley, J., Hardin, J., Kappe, F. & R., W. A. [1995], Visualizing the Internet: Putting the User in the Driver's Seat, *in* R. Cook (ed.), *Proceedings of SIGGRAPH'95 22nd Annual Conference on Computer Graphics and Interactive Techniques, Computer Graphics (Annual Conference Series)* **29**, ACM Press, pp.492–4. Panel session.

Lucarella, D. & Zanzi, A. [1993], Information Retrieval from Hypertext: An Approach Using Plausible Inference, *Information Processing and Management* **29**(3), 299–312.

Mukherjea, S. & Foley, J. D. [1995], Visualising the World Wide Web with the Navigational View Builder, *in* D. Kroemker (ed.), *Proceedings of the Third International World-Wide Web Conference (WWW3)*, Vol. **27**(6) of *Computer Networks and ISDN Systems*, Elsevier Science, pp.1075–87.

Nielsen, J. [1990], The Art of Navigating Through Hypertext, *Communications of the ACM* **33**(3), 296–310.

Nielsen, J. [2000], *Designing Web Usability*, New Riders Publishing.

Pilgrim, C. J., Leung, Y. K. & Lindgaard, G. [2002], An Exploratory Study of WWW Browsing Strategies, *in* G. Dai (ed.), *Proceedings of the 5th Asia–Pacific Conference on Computer–Human Interaction (APCHI 2002)*, Science Press, pp.283–92.

Rosenfeld, L. & Morville, P. [1998], *Information Architecture for the World Wide Web*, O'Reilly and Associates.

Shneiderman, B. [1997], Designing Information-Abundant Websites: Issues and Recommendations, *International Journal of Human–Computer Studies* **47**(1), 5–30.

Tauscher, L. & Greenberg, S. [1996], Design Guidelines for Effective WWW History Mechanisms, *in Proceedings of the Second Conference on Human Factors and the Web: Designing for the Web — Empirical Studies*, Microsoft Corporation. Available at http://www.microsoft.com/usability/webconf.htm.

W3C [2004], Semantic Web, http://www.w3.org/2001/sw/. World Wide Web Consortium.

Papers in Context

Context matters: Evaluating Interaction Techniques with the CIS Model

Caroline Appert, Michel Beaudouin-Lafon & Wendy E Mackay

LRI & INRIA Futurs, Université Paris Sud, 91400 Orsay, France
Email: *{appert,mbl,mackay}@lri.fr*

This article introduces the Complexity of Interaction Sequences model (CIS). CIS describes the structure of interaction techniques and the SimCIS simulator uses these descriptions to predict their performance in the context of an interaction sequence. The model defines the complexity of an interaction technique as a measure of its effectiveness within a given context. We tested CIS to compare three interaction techniques: fixed unimanual palettes, fixed bimanual palettes and toolglasses. The model predicts that the complexity of both palettes depends on interaction sequences, while toolglasses are less context-dependent. CIS also predicts that fixed bimanual palettes outperform the other two techniques. Predictions were tested empirically with a controlled experiment and confirmed the hypotheses. We argue that, in order to be generalizable, experimental comparisons of interaction techniques should include the concept of context sensitivity. CIS is a step in this direction as it helps predict the performance of interaction techniques according to the context of use.

Keywords: interaction technique, interaction sequence, complexity, context, palette, bimanual palette, toolglass, experimentation, performance, theory.

1 Introduction

Research in HCI has produced many novel interaction techniques aimed at improving the usability of graphical applications. Yet very few make it into real products. This may be due to the difficulty of assessing the actual value of a technique before it is integrated into a real interface. Researchers often evaluate new interaction techniques with usability studies. However, the results are often specific to the software and setting, making them hard to generalize. An alternative is a controlled experiment that measures the performance of the technique using a benchmark task. However the choice of the task is crucial: the designers of the technique have an incentive to create test tasks that optimize performance of the technique, as opposed to evaluating its actual performance in context.

How can we capture the context of use to better evaluate an interaction technique? We introduce a new model, Complexity of Interaction Sequences (CIS), that addresses context through the notion of an interaction sequence. This is based on the observation that users organize their interactions according to their cognitive context. For instance, in a copy context, users tend to create objects of the same type in sequence whereas in a problem solving context, they create objects according to their thought process [Mackay 2002]. Even though the two interaction sequences may lead to the same result, a given interaction technique may perform better with one sequence than the other. Therefore, the evaluation of interaction techniques must take into account the various contexts in which they may be used.

The CIS model introduced in this paper was designed to *describe* the structure of interaction techniques, *analyse* them through a set of criteria and to *measure* the complexity of an interaction technique in order to *predict* its effectiveness given a particular interaction sequence. The goal of CIS is to complement other evaluation techniques by helping researchers understand the effect of context on the performance of interaction techniques.

After a review of related work, we present the CIS model and apply it to three techniques: fixed unimanual palettes, fixed bimanual palettes and toolglasses. We use CIS to understand how these techniques are sensitive to context and test these predictions with a controlled experiment. We conclude with directions for future work.

2 Related Work

Few controlled studies have attempted to explicitly take context of use into account. For example, toolglasses [Bier et al. 1993] are semi-transparent movable tool palettes used with two hands. To apply a tool to an object, the user clicks through the tool onto the object. Kabbash et al. [1994] report that toolglasses are faster than other palettes. However, the benchmark task used favours toolglasses because it forces the user to always select a different tool. Selecting a new tool requires a round trip to the palette, while the toolglass is always at hand. Even though the experiment was properly controlled and the results carefully reported, it is not clear that the results can be generalized.

Generalizing the results of such controlled studies requires a better understanding of the influence of context of use on performance. In the Cognitive Dimensions Framework, Green [2000] defines six types of activities such as transcription and incrementation and a set of dimensions such as viscosity and visibility to evaluate information artefacts. He shows that users adapt their behaviour to the type of activity and identifies the most important dimensions for each activity. CIS is influenced by this framework that address the interplay between the task at hand and the properties of the available interaction techniques.

Mackay [2002] compares the efficiency of three interaction techniques (toolglasses, floating palettes and marking menus) used in the CPN2000 interface Beaudouin-Lafon & Lassen [2000] according to two cognitive contexts: copy and problem solving, similar to Green's transcription and incrementation. She observes that the use of a tool varies according to the context as well as users' preference. Users' preference and efficiency are higher with floating palettes in a copy context and with toolglasses or marking menus, i.e. circular contextual menus augmented by a gesture recognition mechanism, in a problem solving context. In other words, which technique is 'best' depends on the context of use.

Unfortunately, such controlled experiments are costly and it would not be practical to test all possible tasks. What is needed is a model that can describe interaction techniques and predict their comparative performance in realistic settings. Formal models of interaction are too numerous to be reviewed exhaustively here. We focus on those that address interaction at a level of abstraction similar to CIS.

Card et al. [1991] introduce a taxonomy of input devices, described as translators from physical properties to logical parameters of an application. Input devices are evaluated by their expressivity and efficiency, as measured by pointing speed and precision, footprint, etc. CIS analyses interaction at a higher level than input devices and elementary tasks by focusing on interaction techniques.

Goals, Operators, Methods and Selection rules (GOMS) [John & Kieras 1996b,a] is a family of descriptive and predictive models based on task analysis. Keystroke-Level Model (KLM) describes a task as a totally ordered sequence of operators while CMN-GOMS, NGOMSL and CPM-GOMS describe a task as a hierarchy of goals with operators as leaves. A goal can be reached by a method, described as a sequence of sub-goals and operators. Selection rules are ad hoc rules to choose a method when a goal can be reached by several methods (for instance, if the goal is 'selecting text' and the text is composed of one word then double click else press mouse button at the beginning of the text and move to the end of the text). KLM and CMN-GOMS predict the time needed to achieve a task by summing the times required by each operator in the sequence (for instance, the operator P, Pointing, requires 1.10s.). NGOMSL and CPM-GOMS are more elaborate models based on cognitive theories. Using Cognitive Complexity Theory [Kieras & Polson 1985], NGOMSL can predict the time required to learn a method; Using the Model Human Processor [Foley et al. 1984], CPM-GOMS predicts how highly skilled users will perform several operators in parallel. Despite tools such as Apex [John et al. 2002] that automate part of building a CPM-GOMS model, constructing a model can be quite hard and long.

Like many of these models, the goal of CIS is to assess performance by predicting execution times. However the approach is different from GOMS: we focus on user interaction rather than tasks and on sensory-motor rather than cognitive aspects of interaction.

3 Describing Interaction Techniques with CIS

The CIS model is based on the description of interaction techniques: rather than describing user tasks (how the system is used), we describe the interface (what the system has to offer). Our hypothesis is that the 'details' of interaction have

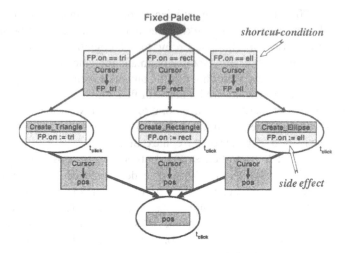

Figure 1: Interaction graph for a Fixed Palette.

---

a significant impact on performance, especially for skilled users who optimize for time, and therefore the sensory-motor aspects of interaction are critical to accurately predict execution times. We are not interested in the cognitive aspects of interaction *per se*, such as how users plan their tasks, but how the results of such planning affect performance. Our notion of interaction sequence captures a 'trace' of the cognitive process and is all we need to model the context of use.

3.1 Defining an Interaction Technique

CIS describes an interface as a set of objects that users can manipulate. Some objects are *work objects*, e.g. geometric shapes, while others are *tool objects*, e.g. menu items and toolbars. The *state of the interface* is defined by the set of work and tool objects and the values of their attributes. A *manipulation* is a creation, modification or deletion of work objects. It is described by a tuple of the form (command, attributes). The *interaction space* is the set of manipulations available to the user in a given interaction state. An *interaction step* is a sequence of *actions* that progressively reduce the interaction space to a single manipulation that it executes, leading to a new state and therefore a new interaction space.

An *interaction technique* is a set of interaction steps. CIS describes it with a directed graph, called the *interaction graph*. Figure 1 shows the interaction graph for traditional fixed palettes in a simple interface that can create rectangles, ellipses and triangles of a predefined size.

The root is labelled with the technique name. A path from the root to a leaf models an interaction step. For example, the leftmost path in the graph (Figure 1) describes the following sequence of actions: move the cursor over the triangle tool — click — move the cursor over a position — click.

We distinguish two types of actions, *acquisitions* and *validations*, described by arcs and nodes in the interaction graph:

- An *acquisition* (arc) identifies a subset of the current interaction space; it is usually achieved by moving an object, typically the cursor, over a tool, a work object or a position. In the interaction graph, the arc is labelled by the object being moved and its target.

- A *validation* (node) confirms the subset identified by an acquisition, which becomes the current interaction space; it is usually achieved by clicking a button or typing a key. In the interaction graph, each node (except for the root) is a validation, labelled by the element(s) of the manipulation it instantiates and the duration of the physical action

The leftmost path in Figure 1 first instantiates the c (command) field of the manipulation with *Create_Triangle* when moving the cursor on the tool that creates rectangles, reducing the interaction space to the set $\{(\text{Create\_Triangle}, p) | p \in \text{position}\}$. It then instantiates the p (position) field when clicking at position *pos*, reducing the interaction space to the single manipulation (Create_Triangle, pos) and executing it.

Nodes can have side effects that describe the change of state of the interface other than the changes of object positions. For example, selecting a tool in a palette activates this tool for future actions. Arcs can have shortcut-conditions: when true, the acquisition and validation actions are skipped. For example, if the triangle tool is already selected, the first step is skipped and a single click on the desired position creates a new triangle.

3.2 Properties of Interaction Techniques

Interaction graphs can describe a large variety of interaction techniques. By comparing these graphs, we have identified the following set of criteria. We have found these criteria both easy to apply and useful to compare the techniques qualitatively:

- *Order* and *Parallelism*: An interaction technique imposes a sequential and/or parallel organization of its constituent actions, visualized by the structure of the interaction graph and the use of the parallel construct. For example, the interaction graphs on Figures 1 & 2 show that a toolglass is highly parallel while a palette is highly sequential.

- *Persistence*: Interaction techniques may have side effects such as setting attributes of tool objects. These side effects may affect how the interaction technique is used the next time, as described by the shortcut-conditions in the interaction graphs. For example, the tool selected when using a traditional palette is persistent, so, for example, creating two rectangles in a row only requires selecting the rectangle tool once. Toolglasses do not have such persistence.

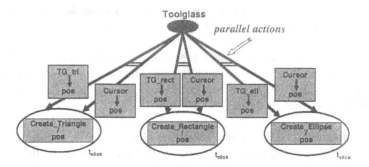

Figure 2: Interaction graph for a Toolglass.

- *Fusion*: Some interaction techniques can modify several work objects by specifying multiple manipulations at once. For example, many drawing tools support the acquisition of several shapes by pressing the SHIFT key and modifying them all at once. Other tools use integrality principles [Jacob et al. 1994] to manipulate multiple attributes of an object at once, such as the style and thickness of lines in a drawing editor.

- *Development*: Some interfaces allow the user to create several copies of a tool with different values for its attributes. For example, in HabilisDraw [St. Amant & Horton 2002], multiple ink wells can be used to colour objects. This is more efficient than using a single colour tool and changing its colour, but uses more screen real estate.

4 Making Predictions with CIS

4.1 Predictive Power: The Complexity Measure

In order to measure the efficiency of an interaction technique, we introduce a *measure of complexity*, inspired by the measure of complexity used in evaluating algorithms. An *interaction sequence* is a sequence of interaction steps that changes the state of the interface. We define a *problem* to be solved as a state to be reached using an interaction sequence. The *size* of the problem is the length of the sequence. The *actions* are the acquisition and validation actions used in an interaction sequence that solves the problem, i.e. which activate manipulations in the sequence. The *complexity* of an interaction technique for the given sequence measures the cost of the actions relative to the size of the problem when using this interaction technique. We use two measures: the number of actions to solve the problem and the execution time of these actions. Figure 3 shows how several interaction sequences can solve equivalent problems, i.e. reach the same state for work objects. As with algorithms, we can explore the best- and worst-case complexities, i.e. the interaction sequences that solve equivalent problems with the lowest and highest values.

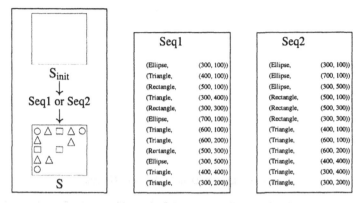

Figure 3: Two sequences transforming S_{init} into S with problem size = 12.

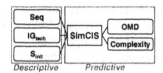

Figure 4: The CIS Model.

We have developed an application, SimCIS, that simulates the use of an interaction technique and predicts its complexity. It takes as input:

- The initial state of the interface, S_{init}.

- The *interaction graph* of a technique, IG_{tech}.

- The *interaction sequence, Seq*.

SimCIS constructs the *sequence graph* that describes the overall interface by merging together the roots of all the interaction graphs and adding *return* arcs from each leaf to the new root. Any path starting and ending at the root of the sequence graph instantiates an interaction sequence (such paths will typically go through the root multiple times). SimCIS computes the path P that activates the manipulations of the sequence *Seq* and evaluates the action and time complexity (Figure 4).

Action complexity is computed as the number of nodes and the number of non-return arcs in the path P. When a shortcut-condition is true, the corresponding arc and end node are not counted. Time complexity is computed by summing the time taken by each non-return arc and node in P. The time taken by an arc is the sum of the time taken to choose that arc at the parent node and the time taken by the pointing action. The former is estimated by Hick's [1952] law which models the choice selection time: $k \log_2(1 + n)$ for n arcs; the latter is estimated by Fitts's [1954] law which models the pointing time: $a + b \log_2(1 + D/W)$ for a target of size W at

 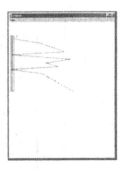

Figure 5: Palette OMD for S_1 (left) and S_2 (right).

distance D. The time taken by a node is the constant time that labels the node. When the shortcut-condition of an arc is true, the times of the arc and its end node are ignored. When two series of actions are parallel, the complexity of the whole is approximated by the maximum of the complexities of each series. We have used the following values, taken from the literature, for the constants in Hick's and Fitts' law: $k = 150$, $a = 0$ms, $b = 100$.

SimCIS also generates a diagram illustrating the different object movements for the sequence, called the Object Movement Diagram (OMD, see Figure 5). These diagrams make it easy to analyse and compare the performance of interaction techniques. The vertical axis represents time (downward) while the horizontal axis approximates the distances between objects. Movable objects and positions of interest are represented by vertical lines and static objects by double vertical lines. When objects are linked together, such as the tools of a palette, they are linked by a double horizontal line. Object movements are depicted by diagonal lines. When two objects move together, such as the cursor and a dragged object, the two lines are linked by a single horizontal bar.

4.2   CIS Predictions and Previous Results

We have used SimCIS to compare techniques on a variety of sequences. Here, we report the results when using a toolglass and a fixed palette on sequences Seq_1 and Seq_2 (from Figure 3). Seq_1 minimizes distances between work objects, while Seq_2 minimizes the number of tool switches.

Figure 6 summarizes the predictions computed by SimCIS: the fixed palette is highly sensitive to context for both time and action complexity. Figure 5 shows the OMD for the sequences Seq_1 and Seq_2 and the fixed palette and illustrates why Seq_1 is more complex than Seq_2 for this interaction technique: S_1 requires many round trips to the palette whereas Seq_2 does not. The toolglass shows no sensitivity to context in action complexity, and very little in time complexity. The fixed palette is more efficient for Seq_2 while the toolglass is more efficient on Seq_1 .

These results are interesting because they confirm some of the experimental results reported in earlier work but challenge others. These sequences operationalize to some extent the problem solving and copy contexts defined by Mackay [2002]: in

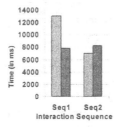 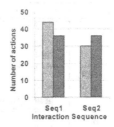

Figure 6: Comparing the complexity measures (light left bar for Pallette and dark right bar for ToolGlass).

problem solving, users tend to create objects according to their thought process and exhibit more locality, i.e. create objects of different types that are close together (as in Seq_1); In a copy context, users can plan further ahead and tend to create objects of the same type together to minimize tool switches (as in Seq_2). Mackay [2002] reports that users prefer palettes in a copy context while they prefer toolglasses in a problem solving context. This matches our predictions if we assume that expert users prefer the most efficient technique. In another study, Kabbash et al. [1994] also compare toolglasses and palettes, but their task forces a tool switch at each step. They conclude that toolglasses are more efficient than fixed palettes. This matches our prediction for sequences with maximal tool switches (such as Seq_1), but does not recognize that a different task (such as Seq_2) would probably have given very different results.

4.3 Hypothesis on Trade-off between Context and Efficiency

In order to achieve a goal, defined as a desired state of the interface, users can choose among multiple interaction techniques and interaction sequences. This choice is informed by the state of the interface, their knowledge of the available interaction techniques, and how many actions they can plan ahead. Some tasks, such as copying, allow users to plan far in advance while others, such as problem solving, are more incremental [Mackay 2002]. We define the *interaction context* as the combination of the current state of the interface and the amount of planning users can do. The former depends on the user's past actions while the latter depends on the task at hand and the next identified goal to be reached. We assume that the choice of interaction sequence is driven by the perceived efficiency of each possible path: once they know what they want to do, users try to do it as fast as possible based on their knowledge of the interface. Highly skilled users are better at planning their future actions because they can anticipate the system's responses therefore they correspond to longer and more efficient interaction sequences in our model, while less skilled users correspond to shorter and less efficient (i.e. more random) sequences.

5 Validating CIS

In order to test the validity of CIS predictions and of our hypothesis, we ran a controlled experiment comparing the three interaction techniques on different

Technique	Interaction	Persistence	Parallelism
Fixed Palette (FP)		Yes	No
Bimanual Palette (BP)		Yes	Yes
Toolglass (TG)		No	Yes

Table 1: The three techniques and their characteristics.

sequences. The techniques are: Fixed Unimanual Palette (FP), Toolglass (TG), and Fixed Bimanual Palette (BP) (Table 1). Bimanual Palettes (BP), implemented in the CPN2000 interface [Beaudouin-Lafon & Lassen 2000], use two hands and two cursors. Each hand controls one cursor: the non-dominant hand is used to select tools in the palette while the dominant hand selects work objects. We chose these techniques because of their physical similarity but different properties (Table 1).

5.1 Task

A set of shapes (green squares, blue triangles and red circles) was displayed. A trial consisted of deleting all the shapes, one after the other, as fast as possible. Each interaction technique contained three tools that matched the three shape types. To delete a shape, the subject had to apply the tool displaying the shape's type onto that shape.

5.2 Experimental Factors

We used a $3 \times 2 \times 2 \times 3$ within-subject design. Factors were:

- Technique: *Fixed Palette (FP), Toolglass (TG) or Bimanual Palette (BP)*.
- Length: *6, 18*.
- Grouping: *Grouped (G) or Distributed (D)*.
- Order: *Radial (R), Spiral (S) or Free (F)*.

We used two interaction sequence lengths to test the effect of the ability to plan the action sequence. Table 2 shows the four different screen layouts associated with Grouping and Order. In all cases, shapes are organized radially along 3 lines of 2 shapes (length = 6) or 6 lines of length 3 (length = 18). When shapes are grouped (G), all the shapes along a line have the same type. When they are distributed (D), all the shapes along a line are different. This factor was used in combination with order (below) to operationalize the context of use.

We imposed the order in which subjects had to delete the shapes for the R (Radial) and S (Spiral) trials, so as to test the validity of the predictions computed

	R (Radial)	S (Spiral)
G (Grouped)	Lo-Near	Hi-Far
D (Distributed)	Hi-Near	Lo-Far

Table 2: The four types of imposed interaction sequences (Length = 18).

by SimCIS. The order was free in F trials, to test the hypothesis that subjects minimize execution time. For imposed-order conditions (R and S), subjects were asked to follow a black line showing the required deletion sequence. In the radial imposed order (R), shapes had to be deleted along each line; in the spiral imposed order (S), shapes had to be deleted along a spiral (Table 2).

The combination of grouping (G, D) and imposed order (R, S) defines four types of interaction sequences, classified as having low or high numbers of tool switches ('Lo' and 'Hi'), and short or long distances between successive objects ('Near' and 'Far') (Table 2). These factors correspond to a typical trade-off when planning a task: is it more efficient to optimize for distance between work objects at the expense of more tool switches, or to optimize for tool switches at the expense of a longer distance between work objects.

5.3 Predictions and Hypothesis

Table 3 shows the time complexity predictions for the imposed order sequences as computed by SimCIS. We extract four predictions from this data that will be tested by analysing empirical data for the imposed order (R and S) conditions:

(P_1) *FP and BP are highly sensitive to the number of tool switches ('Lo' vs. 'Hi') because of the persistence criteria.*

(P_2) *BP is as fast or faster than the other two techniques because it exploits both persistence and parallelism.*

(P_3) *Techniques are sensitive to object distance ('Near' vs. 'Far') because of the effect of Fitts' law on performance.*

(P_4) *A longer sequence length exacerbates the difference between the worst and best cases because of the effect of planning.*

In the free (F) condition, subjects can choose in which order to do the task. The hypothesis underlying CIS is that subjects optimize for time according to the task and interaction techniques at hand. We will test this hypothesis by analysing empirical data for the free (F) condition:

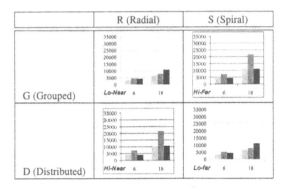

	R (Radial)	S (Spiral)
G (Grouped)		
D (Distributed)		

Table 3: SimCIS prediction for time complexity on imposed order trials.

(H_{Free}) *Subjects optimize for time, i.e. given a technique T, they plan a sequence of interactions that takes advantage of the characteristics of T.*

5.4 Subjects and Apparatus

Twelve adult volunteers, 10 males and 2 females, all right-handed, signed up for 45 minute time slots. Ages ranged from 20 to 56 (mean = 29.41, sd = 9.73).

The training room contained one HP workstation XW4000 running Windows XP Professional, equipped with two WACOM tablets with one puck each for two-handed input. The right tablet was 145×125mm, the left was 456×361mm. The program was written in Java and ICON [Dragicevic & Fekete 2001].

5.5 Procedure

The experiment consisted of 36 conditions grouped in three blocks, one block per technique. Each block consisted of three sub-blocks: a training sub-block to get familiar with the technique, a sub-block with free (F) trials, and a sub-block with imposed order (R and S) trials. The training sub-block was always first. The order of blocks and non-training sub-blocks within a block were counterbalanced across subjects using a 3×2 Latin square. The order of trials in a sub-block was counterbalanced within subjects. Each subject completed a total of 108 non-training trials (36 trials per technique, i.e. 3 repeated measures).

In the training sub-blocks, subjects had to delete shapes appearing one by one in the main window and clicked a button when they felt familiar with the technique. The next shape was always previewed at the top-right corner to allow subjects to plan tool switches (as in the popular Tetris game).

At the end of the experiment, each subject completed a survey. They were asked if they had previous knowledge of each technique, whether they had a preferred technique during the experiment and the cases in which each technique was preferred. They were also shown four free-order trials and asked to rank their preferred technique for completing each of them.

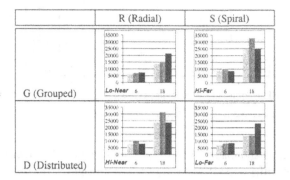

Table 4: Empirical mean time on imposed-order trials.

	TG	BP	FP
length=6	7927	7134	8812
length=18	23142	18903	23100

Table 5: Mean execution time (ms).

6 Results

Data was recorded at the trial level: time between first click and disappearance of the last shape, number of switches, and number of errors. We also recorded time between the disappearance of successive shapes. The Tukey HSD test was used for pairwise comparisons. Data for the Length condition is analysed separately.

6.1 Comparisons between Empirical Data and CIS Predictions

We start by comparing the empirical observations (Table 4) to the SimCIS predictions (Table 3). Although SimCIS underestimates the execution times, it predicts the pattern correctly, i.e. the relationship between interaction sequence and the efficiency of a technique. We next analyse the data from the imposed order conditions to test our predictions.

Technique had a significant effect on execution time (length = 6: $F(2,33) = 8.67$, $p = 0.0009$; length = 18: $F(2,33) = 13.82$, $p < 0.0001$). Only pairs (BP, FP) and (BP, TG) are significantly different, so BP < TG $\approx$ FP. As predicted by CIS, *BP is more efficient than TG and FP* (Table 5) (P_2). Technique had no significant effect on number of errors (length = 6: $F(2,33) = 1.42$, $p = 0.25$; length = 18: $F(2,33) = 0.58$, $p = 0.56$), so differences between techniques cannot be explained by the number of errors. This is important since SimCIS does not take errors into account.

Order interacts significantly with grouping on execution time for both palettes (length = 6: $F(2,132) = 9.63$, $p = 0.0001$; length = 18: $F(2,132) = 105.13$, $p < 0.0001$). As predicted, *both palettes are faster in conditions with low rather than high number of switches* ('Lo', i.e. S×D and R×G vs. 'Hi', i.e. S×G and R×D) (P_1). Also, *BP is less context sensitive than FP* as predicted by SimCIS (Table 3): differences between

Ratio	FP		BP		TG	
	G	D	G	D	G	D
R	2.12	3.08	2.40	3.13	2.98	2.94
S	3.20	1.74	2.91	2.02	2.96	2.75

Table 6: Ratio of mean execution time between length=18 and length=6 trials.

---

minimal mean time and maximal mean time are significantly larger for FP than for BP (length = 6: diff$_{FP}$ = 3348 and diff$_{BP}$ = 2728; length = 18: diff$_{FP}$ = 18465 and diff$_{BP}$ = 10849).

For each technique, *mean execution time is shorter in conditions 'Near' (short distance) than in conditions 'Far' (long distance)* (P$_3$) (Table 4). However differences do not reach significance (length = 6: F(2,66) = 0.15, p = 0.85; length = 18: F(2,66) = 0.22, p = 0.8). This may be due to the layout of the various interaction sequences: in the 'Near' condition, the distances are fairly high when jumping from one branch to the next, while in the 'Far' condition, distances become smaller when spiralling towards the inner circle of targets.

Table 6 shows the ratio between execution times for length = 18 and length = 6 sequences for each condition. We know that both palettes are sensitive to the number of tool switches. The table shows that this sensitivity increases with sequence length (P$_4$):the ratios are smaller in the 'Lo' (S×D, R×G) than in the 'Hi' (S×G, R×D) conditions. We also know that toolglasses are less sensitive to tool switches, and indeed the ratios are all close to 3 for TG.

Kabbash et al. [1994] compared toolglasses to three other palettes, including R-tearoff menus (floating unimanual palettes) and L-tearoff menus (floating bimanual palettes). We were surprised by the poor performance of their equivalent to BP (TG < FP ≈ BP). This difference is not due to their use of floating rather than fixed palettes, since their subjects moved the BP in only 2.9% of trials.

If we consider trials with a low number of tool switches ('Lo' condition), our results show that TG is the worst: BP ≈ FP < TG. This is probably because FP becomes more efficient with fewer tool switches. The connect-the-dots task used by Kabbash et al. [1994] avoided this condition by forcing successive dots to differ in colour. However, we do not explain the difference between our results (BP ≈ TG < FP, predicted by CIS) for trials with a high number of tool switches ('Hi' condition) and their results (TG < FP ≈ BP).

In summary, there is no such thing as the 'best' interaction technique. Showing the advantages of a new technique is legitimate, but it is also important to link it to the context of use by studying multiple scenarios to obtain more generalizable results.

6.2   Subjects Optimize for Execution Time

The combination of imposed order and grouping was designed so that, for each technique, one was close to the optimal time. Subjects approach or even beat this time (Table 7) when they are asked to delete all shapes as fast as possible in the

	Length = 6						Length = 18					
	FP		BP		TG		FP		BP		TG	
	G	D	G	D	G	D	G	D	G	D	G	D
R	6846	10116	5722	7529	7187	7986	14542	31181	13711	23539	21385	23476
S	10194	8093	8450	6834	8312	8403	32570	14105	24560	13802	24632	23075
F	6633	7128	5479	5946	7389	7907	14379	15796	13754	16224	21710	24095

Table 7: Mean execution times (ms) (Optimal execution times on imposed-order trials.

	TG	BP	FP
length=6	3.23	3.12	2.80
length=18	8.40	3.11	2.00

Table 8: Mean number of switches in free order (F) trials.

free (F) condition. We verified that there was no learning effect when the imposed order trials (R/S) were presented before the free ones (F) (length = 6: $F(1,22) = 3.82$, $p = 0.0633$; length = 18: $F(1,22) = 0.28$, $p = 0.6013$). The overhead of having to follow the black line in imposed-order trials may explain why free trials sometimes beat the best imposed-order trials.

Analyses of the effect of technique on number of tool switches is not significant for length = 6 trials ($F(2,33) = 2.67$, $p = 0.0836$) but is on length = 18 trials ($F(2,33) = 64.56$, $p < 0.0001$, pairs (TG,BP) and (TG,FP) are significantly different). Subjects minimize the number of tool switches when they use a palette (FP or BP) but not when they use TG (Table 8). This shows that subjects understood how each technique was sensitive to the context and optimized its use accordingly (H_{Free}).

In the post-hoc survey, only three subjects were able to describe in which trials a technique would be most efficient. One subject always preferred TG, three BP, and five FP, the latter arguing that they were more used to it. The answers to the final question contrast with these preferences yet are consistent with the quantitative data: subjects were asked to rank their preferred techniques to complete a free-order trial drawn on the survey; BP always scored better than the other two techniques, FP was better than TG on trials in condition G (Grouped) and TG was slightly better than FP on the 6-length trial in condition D (Distributed).

Altogether, these results show that users are able to optimize their use of an interaction technique and adapt it to the context at hand. Although they may not always be able to articulate the properties of interaction techniques, they are able to identify the most efficient technique for a given task. This both validates our hypothesis (at least on the techniques we have tested) and opens up new directions for the CIS model and the SimCIS tool.

7 Conclusion and Future Work

We have presented CIS, a model that describes the structure of interaction techniques and predicts the difference between their efficiencies in a given interaction sequence.

We used it to predict differences of efficiency among three interaction techniques: fixed palettes (FP), bimanual palettes (BP), and toolglasses (TG). We conducted a controlled experiment to test these predictions: the efficiency of both palettes (FP and BP) is indeed more context-dependant than TG, and BP outperforms the other two techniques. The experiment also showed that subjects take advantage of this sensitivity to optimize execution time.

CIS is not intended to replace empirical evaluation but rather acts as a tool to help test multiple alternatives and design experiments. It can help explain the sensitivity of interaction techniques to context and identify best- and worse-case scenarios. We argue that, in order to be generalizable, experimental comparisons of interaction techniques should include the concept of context sensitivity.

We intend to develop CIS in several directions. First, we can improve the time complexity predictions by refining the model. For example, the largest differences between Tables 3 & 4 are due to toolglasses because we lack a proper model of double pointing. We plan to extend SimCIS to cover combinations of interaction techniques and automatic identification of best- and worse-cases. This is challenging due to the combinatorial explosion of the number of sequences to explore. Finally, we want to use CIS to help create new interaction techniques. One approach would be to infer possible interaction steps from a set of sequences and use these as a basis for an interaction technique.

References

Beaudouin-Lafon, M. & Lassen, H. M. [2000], The Architecture and Implementation of CPN2000, A Post-WIMP Graphical Application, *in* M. Ackerman & K. Edwards (eds.), *Proceedings of the 13th Annual ACM Symposium on User Interface Software and Technology, UIST'00, CHI Letters* 2(2), ACM Press, pp.181–90.

Bier, E. A., Stone, M. C., Pier, K., Buxton, W. & DeRose, T. D. [1993], Toolglass and Magic Lenses: The See-through Interface, *in* J. Kajiya (ed.), *Proceedings of SIGGRAPH'93 20th Annual Conference on Computer Graphics and Interactive Techniques, Computer Graphics (Annual Conference Series)* 27, ACM Press, pp.73–80.

Card, S. K., Robertson, G. & Mackinlay, J. A. [1991], Morphological Analysis of the Design Space of Input Devices, *ACM Transactions on Office Information Systems* 9(2), 99–122.

Dragicevic, P. & Fekete, J. D. [2001], Input Device Selection and Interaction Configuration with ICON, *in* A. Blandford, J. Vanderdonckt & P. Gray (eds.), *People and Computers XV: Interaction without Frontiers (Joint Proceedings of HCI2001 and IHM2001)*, Springer-Verlag, pp.543–58.

Fitts, P. M. [1954], The Information Capacity of the Human Motor System in Controlling Amplitude of Movement, *British Journal of Educational Psychology* 47(6), 381–91.

Foley, J. D., Wallace, V. L. & Chan, P. [1984], The Human Factors of Computer Graphics Interaction Techniques, *IEEE Computer Graphics and Applications* 4(11), 13–48.

Green, T. R. G. [2000], Instructions and Descriptions: Some Cognitive Aspects of Programming and Similar Activities, *in* V. Di Gesù, S. Levialdi & L. Tarantino (eds.), *Proceedings of the Conference on Advanced Visual Interface (AVI2000)*, ACM Press, pp.21–28.

Hick, W. E. [1952], On the Rate of Gain of Information, *Quarterly Journal of Experimental Psychology* **4**, 11–26.

Jacob, R. J. K., Sibert, L. E., McFarlane, D. C. & Preston Mullen, Jr, M. P. [1994], Integrality and Separability of Input Devices, *ACM Transactions on Computer–Human Interaction* **1**(1), 3–26.

John, B. E. & Kieras, D. E. [1996a], The GOMS Family of User Interface Analysis Techniques: Comparison and Contrast, *ACM Transactions on Computer–Human Interaction* **3**(4), 320–51.

John, B. E. & Kieras, D. E. [1996b], Using GOMS for User Interface Design and Evaluation: Which Technique?, *ACM Transactions on Computer–Human Interaction* **3**(4), 287–319.

John, B., Vera, A., Remington, R. & Freed, M. [2002], Automating CPM-GOMS, *in* D. Wixon (ed.), *Proceedings of SIGCHI Conference on Human Factors in Computing Systems: Changing our World, Changing Ourselves (CHI'02)*, *CHI Letters* **4**(1), ACM Press, pp.147–54.

Kabbash, P., Buxton, W. & Sellen, A. [1994], Two-Handed Input in a Compound Task, *in* B. Adelson, S. Dumais & J. Olson (eds.), *Proceedings of the SIGCHI Conference on Human Factors in Computing Systems: Celebrating Interdependence (CHI'94)*, ACM Press, pp.417–23.

Kieras, D. E. & Polson, P. G. [1985], An Approach to the Formal Analysis of User Complexity, *International Journal of Man–Machine Studies* **22**(4), 365–94.

Mackay, W. E. [2002], Which Interaction Technique Works When? Floating Palettes, Marking Menus and Toolglasses Support Different Task Strategies, *in* S. Levialdi (ed.), *Proceedings of the Conference on Advanced Visual Interface (AVI2002)*, ACM Press, pp.203–9.

St. Amant, R. & Horton, T. E. [2002], Characterizing Tool Use in an Interactive Drawing Environment, *in Proceedings of the International Symposium on Smart Graphics*, ACM Press, pp.86–93.

Enhancing Contextual Analysis to Support the Design of Development Tools

Chris Roast, Andy Dearden & Babak Khazaei

Computing & Communications Research Centre, Sheffield Hallam University, Sheffield S1 1WB, UK

Tel: *+44 114 225 2907*

Fax: *+44 114 225 3161*

Email: *c.r.roast@shu.ac.uk*

URL: *http://www.shu.ac.uk/schools/cms/teaching/crr*

Designing interactive computer systems involves relating informal understandings of practice to the formal language and notations of the computer. For interactive systems that support certain types of 'knowledge work', this relationship is mirrored in the user interface. For example, the users of spreadsheets, aircraft flight management systems, or even domestic heating controllers, can find themselves having to relate their informal understanding of what is required to the notations embodied in such tools. The benefit of effectively utilising these capabilities is considerable, however it requires the use of abstractions and pre-planning, which can impose considerable cognitive burdens on the user.

A key design issue for such innovations is to understand how a new system can be integrated into its environment. These considerations may be critical to the uptake of the system by its intended users. In addition, such technologies commonly promote a qualitative shift in working practices that can challenge the value of traditional contextual analysis assessments.

This paper reports on a study to support the redesign of a novel tool that is intended for use by authors of highly interactive DVDs. The tool provides users with powerful abstractions allowing them to radically extend the interactivity available in the medium of DVD. The investigation shows how contextual studies can be enhanced by combining them with analytic methods to provide an efficient practical framework that is suitable to support successive design assessments.

Keywords: DVD editing, DVD Extra, contextual inquiry, ontological sketch modelling, cognitive dimensions.

1   Introduction

This paper demonstrates how contextual study techniques developed in the field
of interaction design can be combined with analytic techniques to support the
developers of highly innovative technologies in understanding the factors that affect
the uptake of the technology within a work domain. In particular, the paper shows
how ontological sketch modelling and cognitive dimensions analysis can be used
to complement contextual study techniques when designing complex systems that
introduce new abstractions or programming-like activities into a domain.

When a new innovation is introduced, the successful take-up of the innovation
is dependent on the costs and benefits of the innovation as perceived by users' and
customers' within the domain. Different groups of users and customers have very
different perceptions of the balance between the costs and benefits of a technology
depending on its stage of maturity [Rogers 1995]. For the designers of a technology
that seeks to introduce a major innovation in a domain, it is extremely important
to understand these costs and benefits and the perceptions of them by actors in that
domain [Moore & McKenna 1999]. Such costs and benefits may be arise directly
from the usability and usefulness (or otherwise) of the technology, or may arise
indirectly from the compatibility (or otherwise) between current work practices, and
those implied by the innovation.

DVD Extra Studio is a patented technology that enables its users to create highly
interactive DVDs (Digital Versatile Disks). It permits users to formalise an abstract
description of a set of DVD interaction elements that can then be automatically
instantiated. This facility means that DVD Extra Studio can offer a unique benefit
that is impractical to achieve via conventional DVD authoring tools. However, as
with any new technology in its early versions, users and customers for DVD Extra
Studio may perceive considerable extra costs (beyond the purchase price) that could
limit its future success.

This paper describes a study that combines contextual and analytic investigation
methods to uncover factors that may influence decisions about adopting DVD Extra
Studio for potential customers and users. At the time that this study was undertaken
DVD Extra Studio (version 1.2) was under review with a small number of 'early
adopters'. In parallel with the study, and based on earlier informal feedback from
the early adopters, version 1.3 was developed. Following the study, version 1.3 was
also reviewed using the data collected. The combined findings have been used to
guide development of the first full release (which is programmed for Spring 2004).

Experience of the investigation suggests that this particular combination of
inquiry approaches are complementary, and might be useful for other forms of
technical innovation that are based on the introduction of powerful notational
systems. The paper also illustrates how data from such studies can be applied to
support iterative re-assessment of multiple versions of such complex tools.

Section 2 provides the background introduction to the DVD-extra technology.
In Section 3 we discuss the techniques used. Section 4 describes the findings from
the various techniques, and discusses what those findings indicate about the different
methods. Section 5 present our conclusions.

2 Background to the Case Study

DVD Extra is a patented technology that allows its users to create highly interactive DVDs. In general, DVDs can be regarded as high capacity static hypermedia in which users can navigate between nodes, with each node containing text, audio, graphics, animation or video 'assets'. Typical DVDs produced from successful movies may contain a single node for the movie, or a node per chapter within a movie, plus 'extra' nodes that the viewer can access using on-screen menus. It is common for such DVDs to contain between ten and a few hundred nodes. If each node of a DVD is regarded as a state in a state machine, then the level of interactivity available to a viewer of the DVD is restricted by the number of individual nodes and links that the DVD producer has created. DVD Extra Studio allows authors to select and specify a procedure that will 'generate' literally thousands of nodes and links onto a DVD, thus opening the possibility of far richer viewer interaction. Existing examples of such DVDs produced using the technology include implementations of the popular TV quiz game 'Who wants to be a millionaire?' [UPV 2003]. The technology has also been used to develop adventure games including more than 2^{30} discrete states. Thus, developing a DVD using DVD Extra Studio involves a mix of activities, including manually editing parts of the DVD in a way that is similar to existing DVD authoring tools, and defining formal specifications from which other parts of the DVD can be generated.

Whilst DVD Extra Studio is an extremely powerful tool, it is also potentially a very complex tool to use — especially given that many of its intended users are media artists and 'new media' designers rather than programmers. Consequently, the adoption of the tool and its integration with the working practices of its potential customers is uncertain. This uncertainty led to an investigation and evaluation of an early prototype of DVD Extra Studio. The initial study aimed to understand the factors affecting the adoption of the technology and to identify redesign strategies to maximise the uptake of the technology. The study was also used to support a re-evaluation of a revised version of the system.

3 Selecting Methods for the Study

Given the importance of contextual factors discussed above, a decision was made to undertake a study of the working context into which the developers of DVD Extra Studio aim to market their product. The study was conducted in collaboration with three organisations who were 'early adopters' of the technology, and were currently using an early prototype version of DVD Extra Studio to develop interactive DVDs. The investigation was strictly time and resource limited allowing for only 25 person days of investigator effort, including just fours days for studies of the work practices on-site, plus a contribution of time from developers and early adopters to engage in interviews and discussions.

A number of factors limited the range of methods that could be considered to manage the contextual study. The limited time that was available for fieldwork meant that highly detailed ethnographic techniques [Hughes et al. 1995] were not practical. A further problem was that the work to be studied was highly distributed in time and space, a DVD production project may take months to complete and involves activities at many different sites. Dearden & Wright [1997] illustrate how situated techniques, in which an analyst studies work directly in the situation as it is practised, and non-situated techniques, where an analyst seeks to discover more about the work context through discussions and other joint activities with the practitioners, can be combined to study such situations.

Based on these constraints, a decision was made to employ some of the contextual study techniques discussed by Dearden & Wright [1997]. Firstly, contextual inquiry [Holtzblatt & Beyer 1995] sessions would be used to obtain a snapshot of elements of the day-to-day work of the participants. These sessions would provide an opportunity to examine the physical working context and allow the analyst to clarify the role of the various tools being used. However, these studies could only represent a very small sample of the work involved in creating a DVD. Therefore, these situated studies were complemented by rich picture interviews [Dearden & Wright 1997; Monk & Howard 1998] in which the structure of overall production process, the actors within that process and the various influences on it could be explored. Finally, because of the complexity of the tools and the work process that was being studied, the work-study was preceded by a period in which the analyst undertook one day of initial training and practice in the use of DVD Extra Studio. It was hoped that this would assist the analyst in understanding some of the activities that the users were undertaking. Dearden & Wright [1997] describe such pre-study as *cramming*.

Both Dearden & Wright [1997] and Beyer & Holtzblatt [1998] suggest complementing work-studies with model building activities. Beyer & Holzblatt outline 5 major types of model that can be constructed:

- a flow model, which describes the flow of work and work objects around the system;

- a sequence model, which describes the sequence of operations required to undertake some particular task;

- a physical model, which highlights aspects of the physical layout of the space in which the work is conducted, and identifies important artefacts and tools used within the work;

- a cultural model, which highlights different external factors, artefacts and actors that may influence the conduct of work; and finally

- an artefact model, which highlights interesting properties of the artefacts that are employed within the work.

Dearden & Wright use a contextual model that combines aspects of Beyer & Holtzblatt's flow, cultural and physical models, and a model of a particular work process that can be related to Beyer & Holtzblatt's sequence model. In this study, Beyer & Holtzblatt's separate approach was adopted for flow, sequence, physical and cultural models.

However, in studying a complex work system, in which sophisticated computational tools are employed, the question of how the work artefacts are to be modelled is a major problem [Dye 2001]. Beyer & Holtzblatt's example of an artefact model deals with a ring-bound personal calendar. Their discussion suggests a variety of distinctions to consider when analysing an artefact, including: the information content, the parts of the object, the structure of those parts, the annotations that the user may have made to the object, the presentation of the object (colour, shape, layout etc.), the conceptual distinctions reflected in the artefact, the usage of the artefact and possible breakdowns or problems that might arise in using the object. Whilst these distinctions are useful in relation to the study of any artefact, they may be somewhat limited when seeking to understand usability issues for a complex electronic system. In particular, the conceptual distinctions, structure and information content within a system to support computer programming must include aspects of the abstractions and structures within the software, as well as the structure of the programming language. The complexity of understanding how users interact with such artefacts is the basis for an entire field of study, namely the Psychology of Programming. Drawing upon this field, a decision was made to apply two abstract modelling approaches to support the modelling work:

- The first approach was the 'Ontological Sketch Modelling' approach of Blandford et al. [2002]. Ontological Sketch Modelling is a process of enquiring into the concepts and terminology that are used within different domains of work and examining how that terminology maps to the terms and concepts that are available for interaction within a tool. Closer mappings are assumed to contribute to improved learnability and usability. Blandford et al. give the example of users interacting with a drawing package to modify a picture of a whale. In the user's ontology, the tail of the whale may be considered as a single 'entity', but the graphical editor may only recognize objects as curves or text boxes. Ontological sketch modelling was applied informally as a technique to highlight relationships between the entities recognized by DVD Extra Studio and the concepts and distinctions uncovered within the work practices and tools used by the enquiry participants.

- Secondly, the Cognitive Dimensions framework [Green & Petre 1996; Blackwell & Green 2000] was applied to develop a more detailed account of issues that might affect the usability of the design notation provided by DVD Extra Studio. Cognitive Dimensions (CDs) provides a conceptual tool to collect views about the usability of a 'notational system'. This approach considers a range of different 'dimensions' that might impact on the usability of such notations. Table 1 outlines the cognitive dimensions that are examined by the questionnaire. Cognitive Dimensions have previously been used in evaluating software systems, programming languages; prototyping tools and software design notations. For examples, see Roast [1998], Roast et al. [2000], Kutar et al. [2002], Khazaei & Triffitt [2002], Clarke [2001], Dearden et al. [n.d.].

In summary, the enquiry plan combined investigations of the work context using contextual inquiry and a variety of 'non-situated' techniques. These were supported by the development of analytic assessments of DVD Extra Studio using the Cognitive

Dimension	Explanation
Visibility / Juxtaposability	Ease or difficulty of finding various parts of the notation, ability to compare and combine parts, to view different parts of a project at the same time.
Viscosity	Ease or difficulty of making changes to previous work.
Diffuseness	Degree to which the notation is 'terse' or 'long-winded'.
Hard Mental Operations	Requirement for users to perform complex operations 'in the head'.
Error Proneness	Susceptibility of users' to error when using the notation.
Closeness of mapping	Relationship between the notation and the results being described.
Role Expressiveness	Ease of recognising the meaning of notational elements.
Hidden Dependencies	Visibility of dependencies between different parts of a description.
Progressive evaluation	Ease of checking work done so far.
Provisionality	Ability to 'sketch' things out.
Premature commitment	Degree to which the notation imposes a particular order of working.
Consistency	Internal consistency of notational elements.
Secondary notations	Ability to make notes to self, add comments.
Abstraction	Ability to introduce new abstractions, degree to which the notation requires abstractions in order to work.
Novelty	Ability to use the notation in novel or unusual ways.

Table 1: An overview of Cognitive Dimensions

Dimensions framework and sketch of the ontological relations between the tool and existing tools and work practices in the domain.

4 Conduct and Results of the Studies

In this section we examine the conduct and the findings that were uncovered using each of the methods and discuss what these findings indicate about the relationships between these methods.

4.1 *Contextual Studies*

In the contextual strand of the investigation the work context and practice of some early adopters of the DVD Extra Studio technology were visited. Three different organisations were studied. One was a company with a history in interactive gaming software that was using DVD Extra Studio to extend their offerings onto a new medium. The second was a company with a background in film, TV and multimedia authoring, who had used traditional DVD Editing tools in the past, but were using DVD Extra Studio to develop games as an additional part of their product portfolio. The final organisation was a sub-group of Zoo Digital who were using the DVD Extra technology to develop games, thus providing a set of examples that would show the potential of the technology. It was this last group that had produced the 'Who Wants to be a Millionaire' DVD game. All of the organisations studied were small teams with between one and five people directly involved in the creation of the interactive DVDs.

With each of the external organisations, the study consisted of a semi-structured interview conducted with a single member of staff, exploring the existing work structure and practices. This was supplemented by an on-site visit lasting approximately six hours for each site. The in-house group was visited last in order to avoid biasing the investigator when studying the use of DVD Extra Studio by the other organisations.

During the interview sessions study participants were asked to describe the structure of their organisations and the work processes that they used. A rich picture [Monk & Howard 1998] was used to records their observations, and to assist the interviewer in selecting effective supplementary questions. The on-site visits followed the approach of 'contextual inquiry' described by Holtzblatt & Beyer [1995] with the investigator observing the work in progress and acting as an apprentice to learn the way the work was structured and the tools that were utilised. Both the interviews and the contextual inquiry sessions were recorded using a video camera. The recordings were reviewed and significant events were noted together with their approximate times. Full transcripts were not produced because of the limited time available for the whole study.

The contextual study revealed a number of interesting observations about the situation in which the work was conducted. Beyer & Holtzblatt [1998] model the setting of work by describing a 'physical' model of the workplace:

- All of the users of DVD Extra Studio worked with multiple large (at least 20inch) monitors on each of the computers they used. A typical 'workstation' consisted of two large monitors, and two separate computers. One computer, which could drive both monitors, would be used to run the DVD editing package, the second computer would be used for other applications (word processors, email etc.). One of the monitors could then be switched between offering a larger visible workspace for DVD editing, or displaying the other applications. This was particularly useful when the processing capacity of the editing machine was being allocated to 'compiling' the DVD.

- One area of work that was not supported either by DVD Extra Studio nor traditional DVD authoring tools was the initial sketching of interaction designs in this medium. In the games authoring company, one major space for initial exploratory design was the director's sketchpad. This was later supplemented by prototypes developed using Microsoft Power Point. Additionally, some design work was conducted by sticking paper sketches and sticky notes to a wall with navigation indicated using pieces of string.

Whilst these findings were perhaps typical of exercises applying contextual inquiry techniques, and were highly amenable to the modelling techniques described by Holtzblatt & Beyer, there were other observations that challenged the notion of what a 'physical' model might need to include. Three examples are considered below:

- The multimedia authoring company had an established work practice based around the use of Apple Macintosh computers. In their current standard working practice, this company used various tools on the Mac to capture recordings, to edit sequences to achieve the various effects that they wanted, and to compress these sequences in preparation for inclusion in DVDs. Finally, the DVD editing tool that they previously used also ran on a Macintosh. DVD Extra Studio is only available on Windows based PCs. This not only created an extra learning barrier for these users, but also meant that any project using DVD Extra Studio would involve a new file transfer tasks between the two systems.

- In all three work-study sites a number of issues surrounding the management of the digital 'assets', i.e. video, audio, animation and graphics files, were identified. In a traditional DVD production project, only a relatively small number of assets needed to be handled, but a highly interactive DVD could contain literally thousands of different assets, each of which might be undergoing modification at different times during the development project. At all three sites projects using DVD Extra Studio began by making use of 'placeholder' assets whilst the authors explored the interactive behaviours and dialogue structure that they wanted to achieve. When the basic behaviour had been defined, then these 'placeholders' were gradually replaced by the actual media files that were intended for inclusion in the final product. Hence, whenever the project was 'built' or 'compiled', the version created might contain a mixture of the placeholders and the finished items. To manage the complexity of this problem, each organisation had taken a different approach. One site made use of a version control system to support their asset management activities. Another site used a specific file naming convention to refer to different 'areas' of the DVD and different degrees of 'completeness' of the assets. Hence, when the files were sorted in name order, the degree of completeness of the project could be observed. The final site made use of different folders within the file system to maintain distinctions between the different types of assets that were being used.

- In one of the workplaces a company intranet site was used for discussing design concepts for future projects. The structure of this site was similar to a bulletin board, with each project idea being discussed in a single thread. The discussions provided a design history and rationale, in particular the way that technical development issues interacted with the interaction designs that were possible for these possible projects was a common form of debate.

What these examples illustrate is that any attempt to describe the 'physical' model when dealing with a complex computer based activity such as DVD editing needs to consider both tools that are evident in the physical world, and electronic tools and systems that impact upon the way that work is performed. Beyer & Holtzblatt's [1998] include hardware, software and network issues in their list of distinctions to be considered in a 'physical' model. What is novel about the particular situation in which DVD Extra Studio is to be deployed, is that such a large proportion of the work context that needs to be understood is 'virtual' rather than 'physical'.

4.2   Analytical Studies

4.2.1   Ontological Sketch Modelling

Blandford et al. [2002] argue that an important element of ensuring usability is to closely map the entities and operations that a tool recognizes to the concepts that are familiar to its intended users. For DVD Extra Studio, this presents a significant challenge. DVD Extra Studio operates in a way that crosses boundaries between different domains of work. On the one hand, the delivery of highly interactive DVDs that can be used on any DVD player, is constrained by fine details of the standardised specification of the technology; on the other hand, many of its intended users have experience in the (formerly) linear world of Film and TV editing. In combining these domains, the developers of DVD Extra Studio are faced with the communicating a meaningful understanding of the tool across these different domains, each of which already contains its own concepts and language.

The modelling proceeded by identifying key nouns and noun phrases in interviews and contextual studies conducted with 'early adopters' of the technology. In addition, the concepts in DVD Extra Studio were identified by reference to the user interface of the tool and associated training materials. Table 2 shows some of the terminology that exists in the different domains.

Examination of the terminology and ontology shows that, although some terminology differs slightly between DVD Extra Studio and traditional DVD editing tools, many of the essential entities in DVD Extra Studio are quite close. Thus terms such as Stream are common between DVD Extra Studio and traditional tools, whilst the term 'Track' in traditional tools is conceptually similar to 'Component' in DVD Extra Studio (although the term 'Component' covers some additional entities that are not represented as 'Tracks' in traditional tools). Users reported little difficulty in adapting to the slightly different terminology of DVD Extra Studio, although revised terminology could be considered in future re-designs.

One point of interest was that some terms that were common to multiple domains referred to significantly different artefacts in each domain. For example, the concept of a *Storyboard* as implemented by both traditional DVD production tools and by DVD Extra Studio was significantly different in both form and usage from the concept of storyboard as used in the early stages of either film / TV editing or DVD design. Indeed in one of the sites visited, the term storyboard was used to refer to a specific physical artefact used in specifying the structure of the DVD and in monitoring the progress of its development, as well as being used to refer to the software 'storyboard' for the same project, which required a very different structure. However, users did not report any problems in adapting to these differences. They appeared comfortable to simply qualify their use of the term 'storyboard', when necessary, as either a storyboard within the editing package or a storyboard on paper.

Whilst adapting to a slightly different terminology creates some problems for users, more serious problems can occur when key concepts are omitted from the ontology of a tool. In the case of this early version of DVD Extra Studio, problems

Film & TV editing	Traditional DVD production tools	DVD Extra Studio	Underlying DVD spec
Rush	Storyboard	Storyboard	Program-chain
Pan	Track	Component	Cell
Edit suite	Stream	Segment	Sub-picture
Script	Menu	Stream	IFO file
Storyboard	Bit rate	Multi-component	VOB file
	Asset	Button–Set	Video–Title–Set
		Button	
		Asset	
		Exit action	
		Entry action	

Table 2: Terminology and domains relevant to DVD Extra.

were uncovered in relation both to the technical domain of the DVD specification and in relation to the work domain of multimedia production:

- In relation to the underlying technology of DVD, the data encoded on a DVD uses two different file types, one file format (the VOB file) contains the presentational assets, i.e. pictures, graphics and sound, whilst another file type (the IFO file) contains all of the information defining the navigation between these assets. It became apparent during development of highly interactive DVDs that the size of the IFO file that is generated may have an impact on the ability of some DVD players to successfully render the DVD. A minor modification to the tool allowed users to allocate elements of the DVD to different 'video title sets' so that the navigational information was divided between separate IFO files, thus introducing this part of the ontology of DVD production into DVD Extra Studio. However, a more substantial modification will be required to the design to provide users with a suitable visual representation of this concept.

- Another issue that was of concern to DVD authors was the 'bitrate' at which data is written onto the DVD. Because the data on a DVD is compressed, if a very high bit-rate is used when writing the DVD, then the quality of the video reproduction may be compromised. As a result, when producing DVDs using traditional tools, authors may want to monitor the 'bit-rate' at which data is being written to the DVD. The early version of DVD Extra Studio did not monitor this aspect of their existing work domain. This was generally not an issue when creating the automatically generated sections of a DVD which rarely involved the highest quality video footage, however when 'manual' sections of a DVD were being considered, failure to monitor bit-rate could represent a limitation of DVD Extra Studio.

- In relation to existing work practices in DVD and multimedia editing, some traditional DVD Editing tools support a concept of a 'menu'. A file consisting of multiple layers may be imported directly from a graphical editing package, and the behaviour of the buttons can be defined to switch layers on and off. This capability simplifies the work required to create and edit menus, since all of the different states of the menu can be held within a single file, and if any one of those states needs to change its appearance, this change can be made directly in the graphic editing package. In the early version of DVD Extra Studio, this concept is not directly supported. Since a typical interactive DVD may have many different menus, and users of DVD Extra may need to create and alter these menus many times in the process of developing a DVD, this could be a significant usability issue.

These findings appear to support the arguments of Blandford et al. [2002] that the key issue is not the way that items are named, rather that the key concepts in the domain ontology that must be reflected in the design. Subsequent versions of DVD Extra Studio will be designed to better support the key entities recognized in these different domains.

4.2.2 Cognitive Dimensions Questionnaire

The most detailed level of analysis of DVD Extra Studio as an artefact was undertaken using the Cognitive Dimensions framework [Green & Petre 1996]. The analysis was conducted by using the Cognitive Dimensions Questionnaire [Blackwell & Green 2000]. The full questionnaire is available from http://www.cl.cam.ac.uk/users/afb21/CognitiveDimensions/CDquestionnaire.pdf. The questionnaire was first completed by each of the researchers (that is, the three authors of this paper, all of whom have had previous experience with the framework) independently. The results from the three analyses were then consolidated and reviewed to clarify differences in interpretation. Following this, the project managers responsible for the development of DVD-Extra Studio (who had no previous knowledge of cognitive dimensions) were asked to complete the questionnaire, supported by one of the authors to clarify the details of the questionnaire.

The analysis revealed a range of concerns. Some of these concerns were also apparent from the contextual studies, sketch modelling or from earlier feedback from early adopters:

- A previously identified problem was that some of the textual parts of the notation were case-sensitive, and some parts were sensitive to the inclusion of white space. The 'early adopters' had already raised this issue as a usability area requiring attention. Both the investigators and the project managers highlighted this as an issue when discussing the 'error proneness' dimension.

- Another dimension that gave rise to significant discussion was 'visibility and juxtaposability'. When combining different 'streams' for presentation (e.g. video tracks, still overlays, buttons and audio tracks) it was not possible to see all of the tracks that would be presented concurrently to the viewer. This issue was recognised by the project managers but had not been previously picked up by previous interviews with the early-adopters, and was not initially regarded as a major problem when discussed. However, during one part of the contextual study, two specific situations where juxtaposability of parts of the notation would be particularly beneficial were mentioned.

- The lack of support for progressive evaluation, particularly in relation to the management of the assets as early 'placeholders' were replaced by later finished assets, and for secondary notation within the storyboard were also highlighted the cognitive dimensions analysis.

These findings provided triangulation with the contextual study. On the other hand, some issues that arose during the cognitive dimensions analysis could not be related to data from the contextual studies or the ontological sketch modelling, although once identified they were recognised as offering potentially important opportunities for re-design:

- Evaluating the dimension of consistency generated a discussion of the consistency of the role that certain parts of the notation play. For example, a 'component' in DVD-extra may be associated with a problem domain concept (for example a 'question' in a quiz) or may be associated with an implementation issue (for example a randomisation procedure that is run to avoid repetition of questions). This issue is clearly related to the focus of ontological sketch modelling, but had not been highlighted by either the contextual study or the modelling work in this project.

- Similarly, a discussion around the dimension of 'diffuseness' drew attention to a potential mismatch between users' possible understandings of a link between one component and the next, and the particular representation of links, entry and exit actions that relate to the DVD specification and to the representation in DVD Extra Studio. Again, this issue was not highlighted in the contextual studies or the modelling work.

It may be argued that, had a longer period been available for contextual studies and ontological sketch modelling, the investigator might have observed this second problem or a user might have commented on it. However, an alternative hypothesis is that the problem may be difficult for users to recognise and articulate, because it is so fundamentally bound to the design of the notation in DVD Extra Studio. The cognitive dimensions framework provided the investigators with an analytic perspective that prompted the investigators to focus on the issue.

One noticeable feature of the cognitive dimensions analysis was that whilst the general principles of the cognitive dimensions provided useful insights into the properties of DVD Extra Studio as a notation, there was considerable variation of the importance of these insights in relation to different parts of the notation. For example a lack of visibility and juxtaposability indicated a serious problem in relation to one area of the notation, it was a less serious in other areas. The difference being accounted for by differences in the tasks associated with the different parts of the notation.

There were also noticeable differences between the assessments offered by the authors and those offered by the project managers. In general, although the same dimensions were recognised as representing potential problems, the project managers appeared to be more confident that the problems identified could be rectified by minor changes to the tool, the authors often suggested more fundamental changes that might have been more costly to implement. Such differences of opinion might be explained by the different responsibilities in relation to delivering such changes.

Perhaps the most important contribution of the questionnaire was in enabling the dialogue between the researchers and the development project managers to explain the issues raised and to explore re-design options for future versions of the tool.

4.3   Assessing Revisions or Reuse of Studies?

Shortly after the study was completed, a new version of DVD-Extra Studio was released (version 1.3). This new version was not directly influenced by the studies reported because development took place in parallel with the study.

The new version included a number of changes including:

- new software security arrangements;

- facilities to import DVD video created by other applications;

- the ability to assign components to groups which correspond to 'Video Title Sets' on the disk; and

- changes to the editors used to define 'actions' and 'macros'.

The first of these changes was independent of the investigation. The ability to import DVD assets from other applications, and the introduction of component groups address specific needs that had been identified by the contextual study, and by the ontological sketch modelling. The changes to the editors were more directly associated with interaction issues. A key question for the development team was to what extent the revised version improved the ease of integration of the tool into its users' environment. In an evolutionary development process, this question might be answered using observational techniques, e.g. by undertaking a co-operative evaluation. Dye [2001] suggests that such an evaluation, whilst likely to provide useful feedback on details of user interaction, may be limited in its treatment of knowledge intensive parts of the work. On the other hand, the time required for a detailed contextual study of the new version could delay the further development of the tool. A natural compromise was to use data from the previous study to analyse the changes.

In conducting the analysis, the framework offered by the cognitive dimensions enabled the work of the first analysis to be easily employed for comparing the two versions. For example, in assessing the changes to the editors for actions and macros it was possible to refer back to the original cognitive dimensions questionnaires and for each dimension and each individual comment, to ask whether the change addresses that specific comment. The systematic evaluation of this set of data required less than two person-days of effort.

The assessment of the editors showed that the changes had improved the tool in relation to the dimensions of:

- Visibility and Juxtaposability — this was achieved by introducing colour coding, e.g. presenting comment text in green and keywords in blue.

- Error proneness — this was achieved by supporting automatic command completion, so that users were not required to remember the precise spelling of commands and variable names.

- Hard mental operations — this was achieved by enabling users to display the correct syntax of a selected command, thus removing the need to remember the precise order of parameters when making use of built in commands.

However, it was also possible to identify issues relating to these dimensions (and others) that were still outstanding for the next revision of the system.

The colour coding within the editors could also be related to the Ontological Sketch Modelling data, since it introduced various distinctions between key entities in the programmers' world view (comment lines, keywords, functions and macros) into the visual representation of DVD Extra Studio. Likewise, the introduction of 'component groups' can be related to the 'Video Title Sets' from the ontological sketch modelling. Identifying these relationships to examine how well the new design matches users' world views is relatively straightforward because of the structured output from the original modelling activity.

Assessing the impact of the other major change, the ability to import DVD elements produced in other packages, is more difficult. Because this capability was not present in version 1.2, the contextual studies did not examine the different ways in which DVD Extra Studio might be used in conjunction with traditional authoring tools. For this reason, it was difficult to evaluate how the new facilities will interact with the contextual constraints. Such data as was available to support such an evaluation is difficult to identify and select from within the large body of unstructured data from the contextual studies.

These experiences suggest that one particular value of the analytic frameworks applied is the ability to re-use the findings in a systematic way when evaluating multiple iterations in a development process.

5 Summary

Within the study, two of the methods identified unique issues that might not have been possible to identify by the other two. The issue around 'Diffuseness' of navigation rules was uniquely identified by the cognitive dimensions analysis; the issue of easy interoperability with other operating systems arose purely from the contextual analysis. However, a more important observation was the way that the methods complemented each other to permit the investigators to triangulate results and to explore possible redesign options. For example, by deliberately investigating the concept of the menu using the ontological sketch modelling approach, the contextual study was able to uncover specific details and generate design recommendations. On the other hand, the contextual study identified specific areas of the tool where improved juxtaposability would deliver significant user benefits. A major benefit of the analytic methods was in enabling a rapid assessment of the revised version of the system.

6 Conclusions

The importance of understanding work context to support the interactive systems design is widely recognised. Ethnographic techniques have been applied in some domains (for example Hughes et al. [1995]), however, such techniques may require prohibitive amounts of resource, and therefore are unlikely to be adopted (without modification) in general software design [Johnson 1995; Goguen & Linde 1993]. Alternative, techniques such as 'contextual design' [Beyer & Holtzblatt 1998] may offer a cheaper way to conduct studies of work in context, but such techniques may need to be supplemented by 'non-situated' techniques [Dearden & Wright 1997]. However, as Dye [2001] points out, understanding the context of complex 'knowledge work' is extremely difficult. Indeed, the specific area of understanding programming-like activities has given rise to an entire field of research (The Psychology of Programming).

This study shows how, when investigating knowledge work that includes programming-like activities, a contextual analysis can be complemented by two analytic techniques, namely ontological sketch modelling and the cognitive dimensions questionnaire. These analytic techniques can be used to provide important additional details that complement the inevitably incomplete physical and artefact models that can be derived from contextual studies. The findings also suggest that the structuring provided by analytic techniques may be useful to enable systematic re-use of data for future evaluations within an iterative development process.

Acknowledgements

This work was supported by a 'Knowledge Exchange' grant from Sheffield Hallam University, and by EPSRC research grant number GR/R87918 paperCHASTE. We should like to thank all the staff at Zoo Digital, Bruizer Productions and Yeti Studios for taking the time to participate in this investigation.

References

Beyer, H. & Holtzblatt, K. [1998], *Contextual Design: Defining Customer-centered Systems*, Morgan-Kaufmann.

Blackwell, A. F. & Green, T. R. G. [2000], A Cognitive Dimensions Questionnaire Optimised for Users, in A. F. Blackwell & E. Bilotta (eds.), *Proceedings of the 12th Annual Workshop of the Psychology of Programming Interest Group (PPIG-12)*, Corigliano Calabro, pp.24–35. Available at: http://ppig.org/papers/12th-blackwell.pdf.

Blandford, A. E., Wong, B. L. W., Connell, I. W. & Green, T. R. G. [2002], Multiple Viewpoints on Computer Supported Team Work: A Case Study on Ambulance Dispatch, in X. Faulkner, J. Finlay & F. Dètienne (eds.), *People and Computers XVI (Proceedings of HCI'02)*, Springer-Verlag, pp.139–56.

Clarke, S. [2001], Evaluating a New Programming Language, *in* G. Kadoda (ed.), *Proceedings of the Thirteenth Annual Meeting of the Psychology of Programming Interest Group (PPIG-13)*, Bournemouth University, pp.275–89. Available at: http://www.ppig.org/papers/13th-clarke.pdf.

Dearden, A. M. & Wright, P. C. [1997], Experiences using Situated and Non-situated Techniques for Studying Work in Context, *in* S. Howard, J. Hammond & G. K. Lindgaard (eds.), *Human–Computer Interaction — INTERACT '97: Proceedings of the Sixth IFIP Conference on Human–Computer Interaction*, Chapman & Hall, pp.429–36.

Dearden, A. M., Siddiqi, J. & Naghsh, A. [n.d.], Using Cognitive Dimensions to Compare Prototyping Notations, Paper presented at the Fifteenth Annual Meeting of the Psychology of Programming Interest Group (PPIG-15), available at: www.shu.ac.uk/schools/cms/paperchaste/downloads/publications/dsn2003.pdf.

Dye, K. [2001], As Easy to Use as a Banking Machine, *in* A. Blandford, J. Vanderdonckt & P. Gray (eds.), *People and Computers XV: Interaction without Frontiers (Joint Proceedings of HCI2001 and IHM2001)*, Springer-Verlag, pp.3–16.

Goguen, J. & Linde, C. [1993], Techniques for Requirements Elicitation, *in* S. Fickas & A. Finkelstein (eds.), *Proceedings of the IEEE International Symposium on Requirements Engineering (RE'93)*, IEEE Computer Society Press, pp.152–64.

Green, T. R. G. & Petre, M. [1996], Usability Analysis of Visual Programming Environments: A 'Cognitive Dimensions' Framework, *Journal of Visual Languages and Computing* **7**(2), 131–74.

Holtzblatt, K. & Beyer, H. [1995], Apprenticing with the Customer, *Communications of the ACM* **38**(5), 45–52.

Hughes, J., Kristoffersen, S., O'Brien, J. & Rouncefield, M. [1995], The Organisational Politics of Meetings and their Technology — Two Case Studies of Video Supported Communication, *in Proceedings of the First IFIP WG8.6 Working Conference*. Leangkollen, Oslo, Norway, 14th–17th October.

Johnson, C. [1995], The Economics of Interface Development, *in* K. Nordby, P. H. Helmersen, D. J. Gilmore & S. A. Arnessen (eds.), *Human–Computer Interaction — INTERACT '95: Proceedings of the Fifth IFIP Conference on Human–Computer Interaction*, Chapman & Hall, pp.19–25.

Khazaei, B. & Triffitt, E. [2002], Applying Cognitive Dimensions to Evaluate and Improve the Usability of Z Formalism, *in* F. Ferrucii & G. Vitiello (eds.), *Proceedings of the 14th International Conference of ACM on Software Engineering and Knowledge Engineering (SEKE 2002)*, ACM Press, pp.563–77.

Kutar, M., Britton, C. & Barker, T. [2002], A Comparison of Empirical Study and Cognitive Dimensions Analysis in the Evaluation of UML Diagrams, *in* J. Kuljis, L. Baldwin & R. Scoble (eds.), *Proceedings of the Fourteenth Annual Meeting of the Psychology of Programming Interest Group (PPIG-14)*, Brunel University, pp.1–14. Available at: http://www.ppig.org/papers/14th-kutar.pdf.

Monk, A. & Howard, S. [1998], The Rich Picture: A Tool for Reasoning about Work Context, *Interactions* **5**(2), 21–30.

Moore, G. A. & McKenna, R. [1999], *Crossing the Chasm: Marketing and Selling High Tech Products to Mainstream Customers*, Harper Business.

Roast, C. [1998], Modelling Unwarranted Commitment in Information Artifacts, *in* S. Chatty & P. Dewan (eds.), *Engineering for Human–Computer Interaction*, Kluwer Academic, pp.73–90.

Roast, C., Khazaei, B. & Siddiqi, J. [2000], Formal Comparisons of Program Modification, *in* J. Stasko & J. Pfeiffer (eds.), *Proceedings of the 2000 IEEE Symposium on Visual Languages (VL 2000)*, IEEE Computer Society Press, pp.165–71.

Rogers, E. [1995], *Diffusion of Innovations*, fourth edition, Free Press.

UPV [2003], Who Wants to be a Millionaire, Interactive Interactive DVD. Universal Pictures Video.

A Context-aware Locomotion Assistance Device for the Blind

Christophe Jacquet[†‡], Yolaine Bourda[†] & Yacine Bellik[‡]

[†] *Supélec, Plateau de Moulon, 91192 Gif-sur-Yvette Cedex, France*

Tel: *+33 1 69 85 14 90*

Fax: *+33 1 69 85 14 99*

Email: *{christophe.jacquet,yolaine.bourda}@supelec.fr*

[‡] *LIMSI-CNRS, BP 33, 91405 Orsay Cedex, France*

Tel: *+ 33 1 69 85 81 10*

Fax: *+33 1 69 85 80 88*

Email: *yacine.bellik@limsi.fr*

In this paper, we present a study which aims at designing a locomotion assistance device that can deliver semantic information about its surrounding environment at any time. As a first step towards this goal, we introduce an original model suited for the description of building structure, and we present an algorithm that exploits these descriptions. Then, we explain how it is possible to link semantics to structure. Finally, we expose some research directions for user positioning and human-computer interface design.

Keywords: mobility, mobile systems, environment modelling, human interaction, robotics, ambient, pervasive computing.

1   Introduction

Over the past few years, several electronic travel aids for the blind have been developed.   They provide warning signals about approaching obstacles, thus improving users' anticipatory capabilities.

To improve this kind of systems, we develop methods to give them the ability to provide *symbolic information* about pointed objects.

This paper discusses our preliminary results and future directions on this topic. The basic needs for our project are:

- A model and an associated formalism to describe and annotate architectural environments.

- Algorithms to determine what relevant information to provide users with.

- A means to constantly know the 3D positions of the device and of the user.

After giving a short overview of the system, we present a model for the description of buildings and an associated algorithm. Next, we introduce semantic representations, and we show how to link them to building structure descriptions. This represents the work achieved so far. The last part of the paper presents directions for user positioning and human-computer interface design.

2   Towards New Locomotion Assistance Devices

2.1   History of Existing Systems

The basic principle underlying existing locomotion assistance devices for the blind is to measure the distances to obstacles (information capture), and to provide users with warning signals (information presentation).

To measure distances, some devices use infrared sensors (like the Tom Pouce, developed by the LIMSI[1] and the LAC[2]) or ultrasonic sensors (like the Miniguide, see GDP Research [2003]). Both of these techniques detect obstacles within a wide range (roughly 30 degrees), a few meters ahead. To increase precision, other systems like the Teletact 1 [Farcy & Bellik 2002] or the LaserCane N-2000 [Nurion-Raycal 2002] use laser sensors. Their very narrow beams lead to very precise measurements, at a maximum distance of 10 meters, but they fail to detect narrow obstacles upon high incidences. The Teletact 2 combines an infrared and a laser sensor so as to yield good results at short range as well as at long range (see Figure 1).

To provide user feedback, existing systems use either sounds (for instance, the Teletact 1 uses musical notes corresponding to distance intervals) or tactile vibrations (like the Teletact 2).

Our goal is to build upon this kind of existing devices and augment them with contextual information [Salber et al. 1999]. Developed in collaboration with Supélec, the new system will be aware of its current location, and then give relevant symbolic information to the user.

---

[1]Laboratoire d'Informatique pour la Mécanique et les Sciences de l'Ingénieur
[2]Laboratoire Aimé Cotton

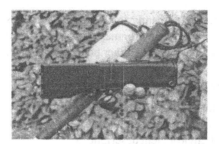

Figure 1: Photo of the *Teletact*.

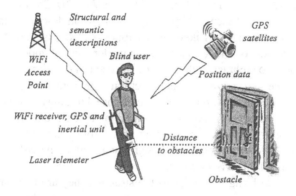

Figure 2: Overview of the future system.

2.2 Overview of the Future System

The system will try to determine its position thanks to a GPS (Global Positioning System) receiver where GPS reception is possible, and otherwise thanks to an inertial unit. The position calculated from these devices will then be matched against structural and semantic information embedded in the environment description retrieved through WiFi connections (see Section 6.1), so as to increase precision and compensate for positioning errors (see Figure 2).

Context-awareness will be enhanced thanks to telemeter data (as in existing devices the new system builds upon) and to light sensors that can provide additional information about light sources (sunlight, artificial light).

When the user's position has been determined, the system will give them context-related semantic information. And when they point at some specific object or location, the system will provide them with information *about* this object or location.

For instance, when a user points at their boss' door, current devices are only able to tell them that "there is an obstacle three meters ahead". The device we are describing here will be able to add that "this obstacle is a door", and that "this door leads to the boss' office".

Such a system can significantly improve blind people's lives, by giving them precise information about their environment. They should therefore gain autonomy, being no longer compelled to rely on other people to find their way.

3 Structure Modelling

To build such a system, we must be able to model users' environments. Up to now, we have worked on building descriptions only. Of course, our model will eventually cover the full range of environment descriptions.

3.1 Existing Description Formats

Currently, formats like VRML (Virtual Reality Modeling Language, see Web 3D Consortium [1997]) or X3D (Extensible 3D, see Web 3D Consortium [2003]) are available to describe 3D scenes. However, they focus on describing the mere visual *appearance* of environments. Likewise, Computer-Aided Design (CAD) tools allow only the description of the *geometrical* characteristics of modelled objects. In contrast, we need to embrace both their *structure* and *semantics*.

Indeed, the *structure* of architectural environments determines how architectural elements are organized to compose buildings. Some elements of this structure may not be visible: we can imagine that a room be divided into two zones, a smoking one and a non smoking one. From a semantic point of view, a frontier exists between the zones. Although this is not a *physical* frontier, we need to model it. We call this a *virtual wall*.

Symbolic data bring semantics to the structure they are associated with. For instance, these data may contain information about the owners of rooms in a building, access restriction schemes, fire instructions, etc.

To put it short, virtual reality models target *sighted people* and try to describe scenes with many accurate visual details in order to be visually as close to reality as possible. Conversely, we target *blind people* and thus we need to model the *organization* of environments.

For these reasons, most existing current 3D description languages do not suit our particular needs.

Geographical databases described by Hadzilacos & Tryfona [1997] represent a useful formalism when dealing with geographic data. But they do not allow the representation of strong structure, so we will not use them for building description.

Thus we define our own model to describe environments, but we aim at being able to perform conversions from existing descriptions (see Section 6.2).

3.2 Modelling Building Structure

3.2.1 A Three-tier Model

At first sight, it seems that building structure is intrinsically hierarchical. A building is composed of several floors, each one containing rooms, that in turn are delimited by walls, and so on. Therefore, the first modelling method that comes to mind is to use a tree structure.

But unfortunately, an only tree cannot account for the structure of a whole building: for instance, in a hierarchical model, a wall located between two different

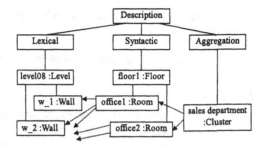

Figure 3: Excerpt of an example description. The *sales department* is composed of two offices, in turn defined by some walls. Intermediate layers of objects have not been represented for the sake of clarity, and have been replaced with dotted vertical lines.

rooms would have to be a descendant of both rooms, which does not fit in a tree model.

To solve this issue, we use three trees, each one inducing a hierarchy over a category of architectural elements. Therefore, there are three such categories of elements, referred to as *tiers*:

- *First tier*: we call *lexical elements* the simple (elementary) architectural elements, such as walls, doors, flights of stairs, and so on.

- *Second tier*: the so-called *syntactic elements* are complex (composed) architectural elements, constituted by putting together several lexical elements. For instance, a room is defined by its walls, a stairway is defined by several flights of stairs and landings.

- *Third tier*: syntactic elements are further aggregated in what we call *aggregation elements*. For instance, several offices can be gathered in a *cluster* called, say, "sales department".

It is possible to draw a parallel between our terminology and the structure of natural-language texts. At a low level, texts are simply made up with words: this is the lexical level. These words are then put together in sentences with respect to a defined syntax. In turn, sentences are aggregated in various units such as paragraphs, bulleted lists and so forth.

3.2.2 Building a Description

A description is composed of three tiers of objects, bound together as shown on Figure 3.

Elements are linked by two kinds of edges:

- *Inclusion links* (solid lines on Figure 3) represent inclusion between elements within a given tier. This gives a hierarchical structure to the tiers, that are represented by trees.

- *Composition links* (dotted lines on Figure 3) enable objects of tier *n* to be composed of elements of tier *n*–1.

For instance, a room is on the one hand *composed* of several walls, and on the other hand *included* in a floor.

3.2.3 Concept Hierarchy

The objects that appear in the description correspond to real architectural elements: a given wall, a given room, etc. These real objects can therefore be considered as instances of general concepts (or classes): a class representing walls, a class representing rooms, etc.

These classes take place in a concept hierarchy. On grounds of genericity, all classes derive from an abstract common ancestor called Element. This class has got three abstract subclasses, corresponding to the three tiers of our model: respectively LexicalElement, SyntacticElement and AggregationElement.

Concrete classes are then derived from one of these abstract classes, depending on what tier they belong to.

3.3 Representation of Descriptions

This model has a strong hierarchical structure, so it is natural to use a representation format that makes this structure explicit. XML (eXtensible Markup Language) allows this type of explicit representation of structure, in addition to being widespread and universal. Therefore, we can use XML to store the three tiers of a description. For instance, the description of Figure 3 would lead to the following XML file:

```
<Description>
  <Lexical>
    ...
      <Level id="level-08" z="16m" height="2.20m">
        <Wall id="w-1" x1="2.3m" y1="4.2m" ... />
        <Wall id="w-2" x1="2.3m" y1="4.2m" ... />
        ...
        <Wall id="w-n" x1="12.3m" y1="13.2m" ... >
          <Door id="d-1" x="2.3m" width="1m" ... />
          <Window id="f-3" x="2.7m" y="0.5m" ... />
        </Wall>
      </Level>
    ...
  </Lexical>

  <Syntactic>
    ...
      <Floor id="floor-1">
        <Room id="office-1">
          <link ref="w-1" />
          <link ref="w-2" />
          ...
        </Room>
        <Room id="office-2" />
          ...
          <link ref="w-n" />
        </Room>
      ...
  </Syntactic>

  <Aggregation>
```

```
      ...
    <Cluster id="sales-department">
      <link ref="office-1" />
      <link ref="office-2" />
    </Cluster>
    ...
  </Aggregation>
</Description>
```

Inclusion links are represented implicitly through XML element imbrication, while composition links are represented explicitly thanks to XML `link` elements.

4   Beyond Structure: Semantics

4.1   Motivation

What are we able to do now? When the user points at an architectural element, the system is able to find it in its cartography. For instance, if the user points at a door, the system *knows* that it is a door, and that there is, say, an office behind.

However, our ultimate goal is to provide the user with *semantic* information. In the above example, the system would not only state that the user is pointing at a door leading to an office: it would also return the office owner's name, the office function, and so on.

To do this, we associate semantic information to the structure description. More generally, such information can be used:

- To add *normative* information to the structure, for example in order to tag restricted areas in a building.

- To identify objects, rooms, and zones.

- To represent connectivity information.

- To add specific information to certain kinds of objects; for instance information about painters could be associated with sculptures in a museum.

4.2   Solutions — Linking Semantics to Structure

Information will be modelled using the Resource Description Framework (RDF) [Manola et al. 2003], an emerging W3C standard quite close to the theory of conceptual graphs [Sowa 1976]. In practice, objects of interest (called *resources*) are associated with each other by properties. Such associations (called *assertions*) are denoted by triples:

```
(subject, property, object)
```

Resources are instances of classes, the class hierarchy being expressed in OWL, the Web Ontology Language [McGuinness & van Harmelen 2003].

Therefore, we end up with two worlds: on the one hand, a world of structure descriptions, and on the other hand, a world of semantic annotations. However, these annotations exist only with respect to the underlying structure of buildings.

This is the reason why semantic descriptions must be linked to the architectural elements of the structure description. This is done thanks to some instances of a class called `Place` in the RDF graph.

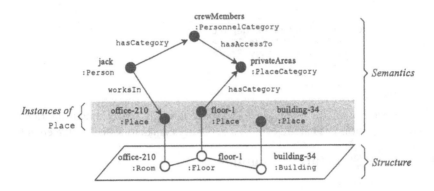

Figure 4: Linking between semantics and structure.

Indeed, instances of `Place` correspond to architectural elements, thus enabling semantic graphs to be *anchored* in the structure description. The actual correspondence is achieved through the use of a common identifier.

On Figure 4, we can see the role played by the instances of class `Place`: such instances belong to the RDF graph, but they correspond one-to-one with the structural elements.

In practice, the structure in Figure 4 looks like this:

```
...
  <Building id="building-34">
    <Floor id="floor-1">
      <Office id="office-210">
        ...
      </Office>
    </Floor>
  </Building>
...
```

The triples of the associated semantic descriptions look like this:

```
(jack, hasCategory, crewMembers)
(crewMembers, hasAccessTo, privateAreas)
(jack, worksIn, office-210)
(floor-1, hasCategory, privateAreas)
...
(jack, rdf:type, Person)
(crewMembers, rdf:type, PersonelCategory)
(privateAreas, rdf:type, PlaceCategory)
(office-210, rdf:type, Place)
(floor-1, rdf:type, Place)
```

The structural elements `office-210` and `floor-1` have counterparts in the semantic description. The latter are instances of the class `Place`, and share the same identifier as their "structural" counterparts, thus linking structure and semantics.

4.3   Current Ontology for Structure Description

Currently, we have defined a basic ontology for structure description. The classes of this ontology take place in three categories:

- *Locations:* in addition to the basic class `Place` already described, we define two classes, `Function` that associates a function to a location, and `PlaceCategory` that allows categories of places to be defined (with respect to an access restriction scheme).

- *People:* likewise, a class `Person` represents human beings, `Role` represents roles played by people within an organization, and `PersonnelCategory` allows to specify categories of people (again with respect to an access restriction scheme). Actually, we do not introduce a new class, but instead we use the existing class `Person` from the FOAF (Friend Of A Friend) ontology [Dumbill 2002].

- *Schedules:* the classes `Schedule` and `Event` are used to associate events to locations.

The ontology also defines a whole set of RDF properties, used to specify relations between class instances. For example, `hasCategory` is used to associate a `PersonnelCategory` to a `Person` or a `PlaceCategory` to a `Place`; `hasAccessTo` states that a `Person` or a `PersonnelCategory` have access to a `Place` or `PlaceCategory`.

4.4 Reasoning

More than just enabling the description of complex relationships, a semantic description allows the definition of reasoning rules.

For instance, in the example of Figure 4 we have the following triples:

```
(jack, hasCategory, crewMembers)
(crewMembers, hasAccessTo, privateAreas)
(floor-1, hasCategory, privateAreas)
```

From that, it seems reasonable to deduce the additional triple:

```
(jack, hasAccessTo, floor-1)
```

Thanks to reasoning rules, it will be possible to implement such *common sense* behaviours, and thus enable the automatic deduction of new triples from the set of existing ones.

5 Determining Relevant Information

5.1 The Problem

From these architectural descriptions, the system will be able to determine:

- The position of the user.

- The object or location pointed at by the user.

However, we still do not know the *level of detail*, i.e. the *granularity* of information needed by the user.

At any moment, we must be able to provide users with relevant — not too detailed, not too general — information. Indeed, too general information is useless, and too detailed information might not be understandable if the user does not know the associated context. To illustrate this, let us look at an example (Figure 5).

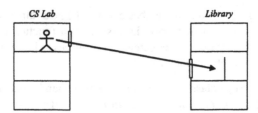

Figure 5: A user points from one building to another one.

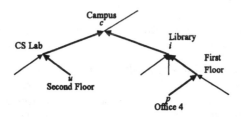

Figure 6: Tree representation of the scene.

5.2   Proposed Algorithm

Suppose that the user is located in u, on the second floor of the Computer Science (CS) Laboratory. He or she points through an open window at p, an office on the first floor of another building, the Library building, located next to the CS building. What information shall we return? Information attached to the room, the floor, the building, the campus...?

To solve this problem, we represent the scene as a tree. This tree is the syntactic sub-tree of our model (Figure 6).

First, let us find the deepest node that is common to both the path leading from u to the root, and the path leading from p to the root. This node is labelled c on Figure 6.

What happens if we return information located on c or above? Such information is too general, because it covers p as well as u. Thus, it will probably be useless for the user, because being in the CS building they already know that they are on the campus.

In consequence, we should return information located below c. However, the returned piece of information must correspond to p, so it must be located on the path leading from p to the root of the tree. That means that eventually we have to focus on the sub-path leading from p to c (c excluded).

We notice that this sub-path is outside of the context of the user. Therefore, if we return too precise information within this sub-path, the user would not understand because he or she would not know the context.

That is why we must return most general information inside the sub-path of interest. It means that we choose to return information located in i.

Note that there is a special case when u and p are on the same branch of the tree. In this case, it is not possible that p be above u, because the user cannot point at an object that *surrounds* them. Therefore, we return information located on the child of u that is on the path leading to p.

In short, the above algorithm enables us to determine a default level of granularity when returning information about the pointed object. However, the user might wish to gain access to another level of granularity. Thus, the final user interface will have to offer some means of climbing up and down the tree.

6 Future Work

6.1 Tracking User Position: Semantic Map Matching

The whole system depends on its ability to track the position of the user. In the open, it should be quite easy thanks to the use of a GPS receiver. GPS positioning has become increasingly accurate over the past, especially since Selective Availability has been turned off (Selective Availability used to allow the US Department of Defense to introduce intentional errors in GPS signals in order to limit accuracy in non-US government user receivers). In consequence, GPS provides a reliable means to position the user *where GPS reception is possible.*

However, there are many place where GPS reception is not possible, for example in buildings and in dense urban areas. For instance Chao et al. [2001] reports very poor conditions in Hong Kong urban areas, regarding GPS and GLONASS (a Russian satellite positioning system similar to GPS). Unfortunately, these are precisely the places where our system would prove the most useful. Therefore we need a means to compute the position of users, even when GPS signal is unavailable.

The basic idea is to embed an inertial unit in the device, and then determine successive positions by means of dead reckoning: at every moment we try to determine our new position by estimating how far we have moved since the last computed position (this is done thanks to gyroscopes, magnetic compasses and accelerometers embedded in an inertial unit). We call this *relative positioning*. Conversely, when GPS reception is possible, we can perform *absolute positioning* because the GPS receiver can compute absolute positions from satellite signals.

In short, our system will use reliable GPS information to find its position *absolutely* when possible, and compute its position incrementally and relatively to the last GPS-acquired position when losing GPS signal.

Unfortunately, dead reckoning has the drawback of being very much error-prone [Fusiello & Caprile 1997]: computed positions are likely to slowly deviate from real positions (cumulative errors). To overcome this shortcoming, the *map-matching* method has been proposed [Bernstein & Kornhauser 1996; Kitazawa et al. 2000]. The basic idea is to restrict the movements of people along well-defined paths on a map. Hence, it is possible to reduce deviation errors by permanently computing the most probable position of the user *along a path* and not in every possible direction.

We do not want to impose such restrictions on the users of our system, but it may be possible to perform some kind of map-matching anyway, because the device has got sensors that give much information about the environment. For instance, from telemeter data we can deduce whether the user is following a wall (and how far the wall is); from light sensors we can know if we are inside a building or outside, etc. These data, coupled with the structural and semantic description of the environment we shall have, are likely to restrict users' probability of presence in some well-defined areas without imposing constraints on their movements.

We call this *semantic map-matching*. Still sketchy at the moment, this method seems to be an interesting research topic and will be further investigated in the future.

6.2 Acquisition of Descriptions

In this whole paper, we have assumed that we had environment descriptions at our disposal. Actually, these descriptions need to be constructed. We have listed three ways of obtaining environment descriptions:

- To write them from scratch, for example by using a graphical editor.

- To perform a conversion from an existing description, either automatically or semi-automatically. As architects are currently defining their own languages for building description [van Rees et al. 2002], it could be useful to be able to reuse their building description data at some point in the future. Similarly, we could use existing Geographical Information Systems to obtain geographical information.

- To scan environments with the device, and label objects on the fly.

The last method seems the most promising — and the most challenging, too. It would allow blind people to use their locomotion assistance devices even in places where there is no available description. We can imagine that they would tag the environment when first visiting a new place accompanied by some sighted person (as blind people usually do). From these data, the system would compute a partial model that could be re-used next time, as in the *map learning* method [Fusiello & Caprile 1997]. Each time the system would return to the same place, it would refine its model based on new information acquired.

It can even be imagined that blind people visiting a new place would be allowed to publish their partial model for others to use it and improve it in turn.

6.3 Presenting Semantic Data

In Section 4 we have defined a way to associate semantic annotations to environment descriptions. However, our semantic graphs have to comply with a given ontology. So far, we have defined a test ontology that covers the fields of basic organizational relations. It is possible to extend this ontology, so as to cover wider fields. Unfortunately, it will never be possible to design an ontology wide enough to cover every situation.

Thus, description designers will have to define their own ontologies, or ontology fragments. As a result, the system will have to be able to deal with new (i.e. unknown) ontologies. In particular, it will have to know how to present users with information conforming to any given ontology. We could impose that every ontology has to be accompanied by a presentation sheet that would explain how to present instance data, within the framework of a multimodal system: for instance, a particular type of relations could be represented by speech synthesis or using a Braille display.

7 Conclusion

Our project builds upon electronic travel aids that have been developed recently. Already useful, these devices are nonetheless capable of only indicating distances to obstacles, and not of giving any higher-level information. To achieve our goal of being able to name objects and give additional information, we have proposed solutions for two critical issues in this paper:

- Defining a formalism to model the structure of visited buildings.

- Designing a model to represent semantic information associated with the structure. When the system has the ability to constantly know its geographical coordinates, it will therefore be able to determine candidate interesting information.

User position tracking, description acquisition and semantic data presentation will be among the topics of our future research work.

References

Bernstein, D. & Kornhauser, A. [1996], An Introduction to Map Matching for Personal Navigation Assistants, Technical Report, Princeton University, New Jersey TIDE Center, New Jersey Institute of Technology.

Chao, J., Chen, Y., Wu Chen, X. D., Li, Z., Wong, N. & Yu, M. [2001], An Experimental Investigation into the Performance of GPS-based Vehicle Positioning in Very Dense Urban Areas, *Journal of Geospatial Engineering* **3**(1), 59–66.

Dumbill, E. [2002], Finding friends with XML and RDF, http://www-106.ibm.com/developerworks/xml/library/x-foaf.html.

Farcy, R. & Bellik, Y. [2002], Locomotion Assistance for the Blind, *in* S. Keates, P. Langdom, P. Clarkson & P. Robinson (eds.), *Universal Access and Assistive Technology*, Springer-Verlag, pp.277–84.

Fusiello, A. & Caprile, B. [1997], Synthesis of Indoor Maps in Presence of Uncertainty, *Robotics and Autonomous Systems* **22**(2), 103–14.

GDP Research [2003], Miniguide Home Page, http://www.gdp-research.com.au/ultra.htm.

Hadzilacos, T. & Tryfona, N. [1997], An Extended Entity-Relationship Model for Geographic Applications, *ACM SIGMOD Record* **26**(3), 24–9.

Kitazawa, K., Konishi, Y. & Shibasaki, R. [2000], A Method of Map Matching For Personal Positioning Systems, *in Proceedings of the21st Asian Conference on Remote Sensing ACRS 2000*, Vol. 2, pp.726–31. Available at http://www.gisdevelopment.net/aars/acrs/2000/ts13/masg0006.shtml.

Manola, F., Miller, E. & McBride, B. [2003], RDF Primer, Technical Report, W3C World Wide Web Consortium.

McGuinness, D. L. & van Harmelen, F. [2003], OWL Web Ontology Language Overview, Technical Report, World Wide Web Consortium (W3C).

Nurion-Raycal [2002], LaserCane Home Page, http://www.nurion.net/lasercane.htm.

Salber, D., Dey, A. K. & Abowd, G. D. [1999], The Context Toolkit: Aiding the Development of Context-enabled Applications, *in* M. G. Williams & M. W. Altom (eds.), *Proceedings of the SIGCHI Conference on Human Factors in Computing Systems: The CHI is the Limit (CHI'99)*, ACM Press, pp.434–41.

Sowa, J. F. [1976], Conceptual Graphs for a Database Interface, *IBM Journal of Research and Development* **20**(4), 336–357.

van Rees, R., Tolman, F. & Beheshti, R. [2002], How BcXML Handles Construction Semantics, *in Proceedings of the CIB W98 Workshop.*

Web 3D Consortium [1997], The Virtual Reality Modeling Language International Standard ISO/IEC 14772-1:1997, Technical Report, Web 3D Consortium. Available at http://www.web3d.org/technicalinfo/specifications/vrml97/.

Web 3D Consortium [2003], Extensible 3D (X3D) International Standard ISO/IEC FCD 19775:200x Final Committee Draft, Technical Report, Web 3D Consortium. Available at http://www.web3d.org/fs_specifications.htm.

Interaction Behaviour (or "Roy Recommends")

Evaluating Usability and Challenge during Initial and Extended Use of Children's Computer Games

Mathilde Bekker[†], Wolmet Barendregt[†], Silvia Crombeen[‡] & Mariëlle Biesheuvel[‡]

[†] *Department of Industrial Design, Eindhoven University of Technology, PO Box 513, 5600 MB Eindhoven, The Netherlands*
Tel: *+31 40 247 5239*
Email: *{m.m.bekker,w.barendregt}@tue.nl*
URL: *http://www.idemployee.id.tue.nl/m.m.bekker/*

[‡] *Communication and Cognition, Tilburg University, PO Box 90153, 5000 LE Tilburg, The Netherlands*

This paper describes a study that examines the amount and kinds of usability and challenge problems, which can be found during initial and extended use of children's computer games. On the one hand the amount of problems might decrease over time, because users become more experienced. On the other hand, new errors may occur during extended use because users start making more errors related to increased carelessness. We discuss the chances of finding problems and relative importance of problems found during formative evaluations of initial and extended use of children's computer games.

Keywords: usability testing, children, initial use, extended use, fun, challenge.

1 Introduction

Research is needed to determine how to assess computer games using cost-effective user testing methods [Pagulayan et al. 2003]. This paper describes research on how user centred evaluation approaches might have to be adapted for children as opposed to adults users and for evaluating games as opposed to applications for work.

There are a number of important considerations when designing and evaluating computer games for children. First of all, for computer games it is important to assess both initial and extended use. For a game to be successful it has to be easy to learn (initial use) and hard to master (extended use). Furthermore, some usability problems may be easily overcome during initial use, because young children often play together with somebody else, like a sister, brother, friend or parent [Feierabend & Klingler 2001]. Thus, the question is how to determine what problems to solve based on whether the problems occurred during initial and, or during longer-term use.

Secondly, because computer games have some different characteristics than productivity applications, evaluation approaches may have to be adapted and extended [Pagulayan et al. 2003]. With productivity applications the focus lies on supporting users to effectively reach their goals, while with games the focus is on ensuring that users experience challenge and engagement while playing a game. As a consequence the evaluation criteria when assessing games should focus on both usability and fun-related issues. Furthermore, games often have goals that are embedded in the game itself, while productivity applications are often used for a goal that is defined externally to the application. This means that evaluation procedures will have to be adapted to determine whether users can reach and understand the embedded goals.

Finally, the suitability of evaluation methods may differ for different user groups. For example, young children may not yet have acquired skills required to participate in product evaluation session, such as the ability to think aloud, or to compare products on multiple aspects [Markopoulos & Bekker 2003]. Assessing usability and fun issues of computer games is often done through a combination of methods. However, user survey methods for gathering data about games are less suitable for use with young children [Pagulayan et al. 2003], because they are less able to reflect on their experiences. Thus, observation-based evaluation methods become relatively more important for assessing usability and fun of products intended for young children.

In this paper we examine cost-effectiveness considerations, such as the chance of finding problems, and the relative importance of problems, when assessing initial and more extended use of computer games in user test sessions.

1.1 Assessing Usability and Challenge

The concepts of usability have been described in the ISO 9241 standard as 'the extent to which a product can be used by specified users to achieve specified goals with effectiveness, efficiency and satisfaction in a specified context of use'. Lavery et al. [1997] provided the following working definition of usability: a usability problem is an aspect of the system and / or a demand on the user which makes it unpleasant, inefficient or impossible for the users to achieve their goals in typical usage situations. Thus, a usability problem description contains four components: a *cause* for the problem, a possible *breakdown* in the interaction, and an *outcome*, which are related to a certain *context* of use [Lavery et al. 1997].

However, in playing a game it might actually be acceptable to be inefficient in reaching a goal if this contributes to having fun. This means that determining whether a breakdown in the interaction is actually an indicator of a problem depends on whether the inefficiency was intentionally designed and contributes to the sense of fun of the user. Thus, a challenge problem is an aspect of the system that is intended to create interesting difficulties for the user in reaching a goal. However, it is perceived by the user to be too difficult, and therefore s/he stops. Other researchers, e.g. Overbeeke et al. [2003], have also argued argue that the emphasis of product design should not be solely on ease of use, but on the whole user experience, which includes for example challenge and enjoyment.

Malone & Lepper uncovered four main elements that contribute to fun in playing games: challenge, control, curiosity and fantasy [Malone & Lepper 1987]. Previous work has shown that breakdowns related to challenge and control can be determined based on observational data, whereas it is less common to uncover breakdowns related to curiosity and fantasy [Kersten-Tsikalkina & Bekker 2001]. For example, children sometimes quit a game halfway through, because they think it is too difficult, or they indicate frustration that they have too little control over skipping an introduction story (control). Children rarely explicitly state that the game does not attract their curiosity or that they do not like the fantasy provided in the game. Often they only make more global statements about the fact that a game is boring without being explicit about the reason why it is boring. Problems with curiosity and fantasy are more likely to be uncovered through other evaluation methods, such as surveys. For example, when children were asked for a first impression of a game as part of a contest for best computer game of the year, they stated that the picture of the dog, which was the game's main character, on the front-cover of the game looked childish. Finally, control is mostly related to having a choice in where to go in a game, and thus is very similar to the aspect of control in the context of usability, such as described in one of the usability heuristics of Nielsen [1994].

Thus, the scope of our study on observation-based evaluation methods is on usability, control and challenge related problems, assuming that other fun-related problems will be uncovered using other types of evaluation methods.

1.2 Initial vs. Extended Use of Games

When a user becomes better trained at using a game it is expected that some of the initial usability and challenge problems may be overcome, thus leading to fewer problems with extended use. However, more experienced user may also run into new usability and fun problems, because they will start using the application in a different manner. Research by Zapf et al. [1992], Frese & Zapf [1991] shows that overall adult users of office applications make less errors after longer term use that during initial use. Some types of errors such as knowledge errors, related to knowledge about computers and tasks and thought errors related to developing correct goals and plans, become less over time. Other types of errors, such as habit errors, related to applying correct actions in a wrong situation increase. Their research gives us an initial idea about how users behaviour may change over time. It does not provide concrete information about how many of the specific problems of initial use still occur after longer-term use, nor does it provide information about how many new problems are uncovered during longer-term use.

This study examines what problems are found during both first and longer time use and what problems can be found uniquely during initial or longer time use. In our study we are interested in determining possible differences in the kinds of problems found during initial use and more experienced use.

1.3   Number of Subjects and the Chance of Finding Problems

In the context of determining how to evaluate products in a cost effective manner research has been conducted to determine how many subjects are needed to find a reasonable amount of all existing usability problems. The overall advise has been that 5 subjects will uncover about 85% of the usability problems of a product for a given user group and a given set of tasks [Landauer & Nielsen 1993; Nielsen 2000]. The number of usability problems found after n subjects can be determined with the following formula:

$$N(1 - (1 - p)^n)$$

where p is the probability of finding the average usability problem with an average subject and N is the total number of problems found in the design [Nielsen 2000]. This is calculated for each test as the mean of the proportion of problems found by each user, assuming that users find an average number of problems and that usability problems have an average chance of being found. For example, when a total of 10 unique problems are found, and users uncover an average of 5 problems this will result in a p of 0.5.

Lewis [1994] discussed the influence of different values for p on the number of subjects required for uncovering various percentages of the existing problems. He presented data with a p-value as low as 0.16, which results in a larger number of subjects to uncover 85% of the problems. Woolrych & Cockton [2001]; Spool & Schroeder [2001]; Barnum et al. [2003] have discussed the importance of taking considerations about the diversity of users, task complexity and applications into account when determining how many users to involve in a user test.

When the average number of problems per hour experienced by a user is lower after longer time use as in the work by Zapf and colleagues, the chance of finding a problem at a higher level of experience with a product will be smaller than the chance of finding a problem with a lower level of experience.

Thus, another aim of our study is to determine to what extent the probability of finding a problem changes from initial to longer-term use, i.e. to determine a value of p for initial and extended use. Furthermore, the results about problem detection rates will be compared with those found by other researchers.

1.4   Relative Importance of Problems

To prioritize redesign effort in a project problems found are often ranked according to their severity. Nielsen [1994] mentions that severity is a combination of three factors: the *frequency* with which a problem occurs, or whether it is a common or a rare problem, the *impact* of the problem or whether it will be easy to overcome, and the *persistence* of a problem, or whether it will happen once or many times. Examining behaviour of both initial and extended use will provide a richer picture of how severity of a problem may change over time.

1.5 Research Questions

Based on the considerations described in the introduction section a study was conducted to address the following research questions:

- To what extent do observations of initial and extended use uncover problems found uniquely during initial or longer time use? By determining what unique problems are found we can determine the added value of testing both initial and extended use.

- What is the chance of finding usability and fun problems during initial and extended use?

- How is the relative importance of a problem, e.g. in terms of problem frequency and persistence, influenced by considering data from initial and, or extended use?

2 Method

A game ('Milo and the magical stones', 'Max en de toverstenen' in Dutch) was selected to be evaluated in two subsequent sessions. It's a game in which three mice, of which one is called Milo, have to collect magical stones by playing a number of sub-games, such as learning to play a tune, catching flies for a toad and solving logical puzzles. Subsequently, they have to take the stones and distribute them amongst a set of mice-holes. Based on a pilot study we determined that children could become reasonably experienced in playing the game in about 60 minutes. This informed the decisions made about the time that children participating in the study needed to play the game. In the first session children could play the game for about 30 minutes. One month later they were asked to play the game again in another session of 30 minutes. Both sessions were videotaped. A facilitator was present at during both sessions to provide help in case the children got stuck. When children requested help, they were first asked to try again. When they were still stuck, they first received a hint to the solution, and only if that did not allow them to solve the problem themselves, were they told the solution. At the end of both sessions they were asked to rate how much they liked playing the game on a 5 point-scale using a smileyometer [Read et al. 2002]. In between the two sessions they played the game by themselves for another 30 minutes, to ensure that they had played the complete game before participating in the second session. A teacher supervised them to ensure that the children really played the game for about 30 minutes. These sessions were not videotaped. To enable the children to play the game in a natural manner no tasks were provided for any of the three sessions [Barendregt et al. 2003].

2.1 Subjects and Setting

In total 28 children (18 boys and 10 girls) in the age group of 6 to 8 years old (average of 7 years, standard deviation 6 months) participated in the experiment. The study took place in a separate room at school. Both sessions were videotaped, combining a view of the child with a view of the screen. The teacher of the school selected which children could participate in the study.

Code category	Description of code
Wrong action	The user performs an action that cannot be expected in the correct sequence of actions.
Execution/motor skill problem	The user has physical problems interacting correctly and timely with the system.
Passive	The user stops playing and does not move the mouse.
Impatience	The user shows impatience by clicking repeatedly on objects that respond slowly or the user expresses impatience verbally.
Wrong goal	The user articulates a goal that cannot be achieved with the product.
Wrong explanation	The user gives an explanation of something that has happened in the game but this explanation is not correct.
Doubt, Surprise, Frustration	The user expresses doubt, surprise or frustration after executing an action.
Puzzled	The user expresses puzzlement how to proceed before an action is executed.
Recognition of error or misunderstanding	The user indicates to recognize a preceding error or misunderstanding.
Perception problem	The user indicates not being able to hear or see something clearly.
Random actions	The user indicates verbally or nonverbally to perform random actions.
Researcher provides help	The user cannot proceed without help and either asks for it or the researcher has to intervene in order to prevent serious problems.
Stop sub game	The user decides to stop playing a sub game without reaching (one of) the goal(s).

Table 1: Description of codes used to describe behaviour indicating problems.

2.2 Data Analysis

The following measures were taken to check whether the children were really significantly more experienced in the second session: the number of screens that were visited, number of requests for help, and the number of sub-games played and correctly finished.

To create a list of problems for the first and the second session the following process was followed. The video data of each session was analysed using a coding scheme for verbal and non-verbal behaviour indicating problems. The scheme consists of codes to score behaviour indicating hindrances or failures to reach task or challenge-related goals. Table 1 provides an overview of the coding scheme.

Some of these codes, as for example Doubt Surprise Frustration, can in principle also indicate (positive) challenge instead of a problem. However, by analysing the game, it was decided where the designers would have planned challenge and where challenge should not be present. Only in cases where challenge should not be present this type of behaviour was considered to indicate a problem.

	Initial use	Extended use	
	Average (std. dev.)	Average (std. dev.)	Paired t-test
Number of screens visited	20.61 (7.87)	22.50 (9.00)	t (27) = -1.40 p = 0.17
Number of sub-games played	5.11 (1.61)	6.46 (1.80)	t (27) = -4.88 p = 0.00
Sub-games correct without help	3.25 (2.41)	6.36 (2.53)	t (27) = -7.20 p = 0.00
Number of requests for help	5.64 (5.30)	3.36 (5.78)	t (27) = 2.73 p = 0.01

Table 2: Overview of results related to the learning process of the participants.

Two analysts used this coding scheme to detect problems. First, they practised the use of all codes by analysing a number of videotapes together. Subsequently, they separately coded a list of 29 breakdowns in user product interaction that was created by four other evaluators. Of the 29 given behaviours, 26 were coded identically, resulting in a kappa of 0.87. Subsequently, they coded the rest of the tapes separately.

After the coding of all videotapes the indicators were clustered into problems. For example, when a user would first make a remark indicating puzzlement with how to proceed ('Puzzled) and subsequently would click a part of the screen which is not clickable ('Wrong Action') these separate indicators referring to the same breakdown would be clustered. The two evaluators discussed how the indicators were clustered into problems.

To determine how the children had experienced playing the game the children were asked for an overall appreciation of the game at the end of the two sessions using a five-point scale smileyometer [Read et al. 2002]. The scale uses 5 different smiley cartoons that indicate emotions ranging from 'awful' to 'brilliant'. The amount of problems was compared with the overall appreciation of the game in Sessions 1 and 2 to determine whether the findings are compatible.

3 Results

3.1 General Results

According to Nielsen [1993] learnability and thus level of experience can be measured using time needed to fulfil a task, and the ability to finish a task successfully. Another related measure is the number of times that users need help.

Table 2 shows that the children in Session 2 were significantly more experienced than when playing the game in Session 1. They played more sub-games, finished more games without help, and made fewer requests for help than in Session 1.

3.2 Usability and Challenge Problems

A total of 57 different problems was found in the combined data from Sessions 1 and 2. More problems were found during inexperienced use than during experienced

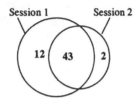

Figure 1: An overview of how many problems were found uniquely in Sessions 1 and 2, and both in Sessions 1 and 2.

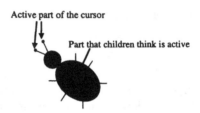

Figure 2: Design of the cursor-shape and the part of the cursor that is active for selecting objects.

use. Twelve problems were only found in Session 1 and two were only found in Session 2, and 43 problems were found in both sessions (see Figure 1).

Most problems that were uniquely found in Session 1 were related to children not (yet) understanding the goal of a sub-game or not being able to determine the next step required to make progress in a sub-game. The two problems uniquely found in Session 2 are: not understanding how to make the main character Milo move in one of the games, and having trouble selecting one of the objects on the screen with the mouse. It seems that these problems are other instances of problems that have already occurred in Session 1 as well, where children also had trouble interacting with objects correctly. All these problems are caused by the fact that it is unclear that only the feelers of the ladybird-shaped cursor are actually active (see Figure 2). So it seems that it is only by chance that these two particular problems are found only in Session 2. These two problems are not the type of omission errors that Frese & Zapf [1991] found in the session with more experienced subjects in their study.

3.3 The Probability of Finding Problems

To determine how the probability of finding problems for initial use and more extended use compares with the probability found by other researchers, the probability of finding problems was determined for both sessions.

We use the number of problems uncovered in the separate sessions, $N = 55$ and $N = 45$, to determine the probability of finding usability problems for Sessions 1 and 2, respectively. The average probability of finding a problem is 0.24 in the first session, and 0.16 in the second session (see Figure 3). Assuming that all subjects find

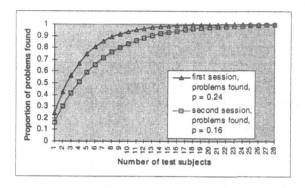

Figure 3: Proportion of problems found with increasing number of subjects, calculated with number of problems found in each session separately.

---

an average number of 13 problems in Session 1 and all problems have an average chance of 0.24 of being found, the total number of unique problems found with 1 subject is 13, with 2 subjects is 23, with 3 subjects is 30, and with 28 subjects is about 55. Users find an average of 7 problems in Session 2. Assuming that all subjects find an average number of 7 problems in Session 2 and all problems have an average chance of 0.16 of being found, the total number of unique problems found with 1 subject is 7, with 2 subjects is 13, with 3 subjects is 22, and with 28 subjects is about 45.

Based on the data of this study Nielsen's formula would indicate that 7 subjects were required to find about 85% of the problems of Session 1 and 11 subjects to find 85% of the problems found in Session 2 (see Figure 3).

3.4 Problem Frequencies in Sessions 1 and 2

By clustering the problems into three different categories of problem frequency an initial description of the relative importance of the problems is created. By determining in which of the three problem categories each problem falls in Sessions 1 and 2 a more detailed view of the relative importance of the problems is generated. Table 3 shows that fewer problems were found in Session 2 than in Session 1.

Overall, the relative distribution over the high, middle and low frequency categories is very similar. However a much larger proportion of the problems is found by only one subject in Session 2.

Determining the relative importance of each of the problems would differ when based on data of Sessions 1 or 2. Table 4 shows that only 17 problems remain in the same frequency category, 36 problems move to a lower frequency category (of which 12 problems occurred only in the first session) and 4 (of which 2 only occurred in the second session) move to a higher, and thus more important category. Thus, prioritizing redesign effort based on the outcome of Session 1 only might mean time is spent on problems which Session 2 would show to be less important.

	First session		Second session	
	Number of problems	% of problems	Number of problems	% of problems
High frequency — problems found by more than 50% of the subjects	6	11	3	7
Medium frequency — 20% to 50% of the subjects	17	31	9	20
Low frequency — 10% to 20% of the subjects	29	53	17	38
Less than 10%	3	6	16	36
Total	55	100	45	100

Table 3: A classification of usability problems according to the percentage of subjects who experienced a problem in Sessions 1 and 2 (in absolute number of problems and in percentages).

	First session				
Second session	High frequency problems — $x \geq 50\%$ of the subjects	Medium frequency problems — $20\% \leq x < 50\%$ of the subjects	Low frequency problems — $10 \leq x < 20\%$ of the subjects	Less than 10% of the subjects	Total
High frequency problems — $x \geq 50\%$	3	0	0	0	3
Medium frequency problems — $20\% \leq x < 50\%$	1	6	2	0	9
Low frequency problems — $10 \leq x < 20\%$	2	8	5	2	17
Less than 10%	0	3	22	3	28
Total in Session 1	6	17	29	5	57

Table 4: An overview of how problems move from one problem frequency category to another from Session 1 to Session 2 (x is % of subjects that experience a problem). The numbers in cells above the diagonal represent an increase in frequency, and those in cells below the diagonal a decrease in frequency.

Second session	First session				Total
	High persistence — $y > 1.5$	Medium persistence — $1.25 < y \leq 1.5$	Low persistence — $1 \leq y < 1.25$	Problems not experienced in first session	
High persistence — $y > 1.5$	1	0	1	1	3
Medium persistence — $1.25 < y \leq 1.5$	1	1	1	0	3
Low persistence — $1 \leq y < 1.25$	1	2	35	1	39
Problems not experienced in second session	0	0	12	0	12
Total in session 1	3	3	49	2	57

Table 5: An overview of how problems move from one problem persistence category to another from Session 1 to Session 2 (y is the total number of times that a problem is uncovered divided by the number of children that experienced the problem).

	First session average (standard deviation)	Second session average (standard deviation)
Opinion after playing the game	4.43 (0.79)	4.79 (0.42)

Table 6: The average and standard deviation of the children's rating of the game on a 5-point smileyometer after Sessions 1 and 2.

We also determined the persistence of a problem in Sessions 1 and 2 by calculating the average of the number of times that children experienced the same problem per session. Table 5 shows that most problems (37 out of 57) have a similar persistence in both sessions. Only 4 problems increase in persistence (of which 2 are problems uniquely found in Session 2), and 16 other problems have a lower persistence in Session 2 as in Session 1 (of which 12 are problems uniquely found in Session 1).

3.5 Subjective Assessment of Subjects

To determine whether children enjoyed playing the game they were asked to rate the game on a five-point scale smileyometer. A significant difference was found in the subject's opinion about the game after the first and second session ($t(27) = -2.79$, $p = 0.01$). They appreciated the game more after the second session (see Table 6). This trend is in agreement with the fact that fewer problems were found in Session 2 than in Session 1.

4   Conclusions

4.1   Problems Specific to Initial and to Extended Use

As expected the study uncovered many problems during initial use that were not experienced any more by subjects in the second session.

We only uncovered two problems in the second session that had not yet been found in the first session. Thus, solely based on the amount of new problems found in the second session, we would not argue for investing effort in evaluating extended use.

4.2   The Probability of finding Usability Problems during Initial and Extended Use

The results on the chance of finding particular usability problems during initial play were different to those reported by [Nielsen 2000]. We found a p-value of 0.16 for the data of Session 2 as compared to the average p value of 0.31 that Nielsen & Landauer [1993] found. Based on the data of the second session we would conclude that *11 subjects* would uncover about 85% of the problems. A p-value of 0.24 was found for the data of Session 1, which means that uncovering 85% of the problems for initial use would require *7 subjects*. Woolrych & Cockton [2001] discuss some of the consequences of the fact that not all problems have a similar chance of being found, and that not all users find the same amount of problems. For drawing these conclusions we are assuming that by selecting a smaller sample of subjects the average number of problems found per subject is the same as in our larger sample, and that the average probability of the problems found will also be the same.

Our findings show that in first instance current rules-of-thumb regarding the number of subjects required to uncover 85% of the problems [Nielsen 2000] may be readily applicable to children user groups and game applications for initial use. However, based on theoretical considerations described in Section 1.1 and the findings of the second session they may not be applicable for longer-term use.

The findings contribute to the discussion of whether it is correct to assume that the chance of finding a problem is on average 0.31 and thus five users are enough in a user test. Moreover, it shows that the chance of finding problems might be related to how experienced users are with using a particular application. More research is needed to determine whether this finding can be replicated and is generalizable to other applications and other user groups.

4.3   Judging Relative Importance of Problems

Having access to data from both initial and extended use does shed a different light on the relative importance of problems. Because the frequency of part of the problem-set decreases, the second session provides extra information for making a priority list of usability problems based on their relative frequencies in both sessions. Only 17 of the total of 57 problems are located in the same frequency category for Session 1 and 2, while 24 problems move to a lower frequency category. The data about more extended use would have a very large influence on how redesign effort should be spent. The persistence of problems in this study seems much more stable, only

4 problems move to a lower persistence category. The extra information of the second session would have a much smaller influence on prioritizing problems. How the frequency and persistence of a problem during initial and longer-term use should be weighed would of course depend on the design goals of a particular project, e.g. whether the emphasis is on optimizing the experience during initial use or extended use.

5 Discussion

The focus of the study described in this paper is on problems uncovered in observational studies. Unfortunately, not all usability and fun problems can be uncovered through observations. For example, fantasy and curiosity related problems are inherently more difficult to observe in a user test. Thus, the findings from initial and extended use from observational data should be complemented with the outcomes of other methods to get a more complete picture. How the combination of the outcomes of the various methods would further influence the decision of how to prioritize problems is outside the scope of this paper.

The study examined problems found during initial and longer-term use. In the present study there was a fairly long gap between the first and the second session in which children played the game. This might have influenced how well children remembered how to play the game. Thus, we might have found even more problems uniquely in Session 1, if the gap would have been smaller. Also, children might have made more omission errors, if they would have still remembered more from the previous session. However, the fact that there was a significant increase in the number of sub-games finished and decrease in requests for help does show that they did become more experienced from Session 1 to Session 2.

Since the study was based on the evaluation of only one computer game, further research is required to determine whether the findings can be replicated and generalized to other games. Also, further research is required to determine whether similar findings occur when observing adult users playing games, or even adults interacting with non-entertainment applications.

Finally, the focus on the quantitative component of the data does not cover insights based on the qualitative nature of the data, such as how the children's playing behaviour changed from Session 1 to Session 2. For example, after children have built up an understanding of the overall aim of the game, they are more inclined to finish playing a sub-game in the second session, because they realize they need the outcome to be able to play another sub-game. In the first session, when they are still unaware of the relationships between the various sub-games they have different motivations for finishing a game or not.

In summary, our study indicates that the chance of finding usability and challenge problems is smaller for extended use than for initial use. The results show that many more than 5 subjects (in this case 11 subjects) are needed to uncover 85% of the problems experienced during extended use. Furthermore, the data on problem frequency and persistence show that problems would be prioritized differently based on the combined findings of Sessions 1 and 2. Doing a more time-consuming study of extended use would provide a better insight into how to prioritize problems. The resources saved by eliminating only those problems which turn out to be serious during longer term use can subsequently be spent on the extra effort required for evaluating extended use with a larger number of users.

Acknowledgements

We would like to thank the teacher of the school from which we recruited the children for her support and the children for participating in the study. We would like to thank our colleagues and Theo Rooden for helpful suggestions about the study set-up and initial drafts of the paper.

References

Barendregt, W., Bekker, M. & Speerstra, M. [2003], Empirical Evaluation of Usability and Fun in Computer Games for Children, *in* M. Rauterberg, M. Menozzi & J. Weeson (eds.), *Human–Computer Interaction — INTERACT '03: Proceedings of the Ninth IFIP Conference on Human–Computer Interaction*, IOS Press, pp.705–8.

Barnum, C., Bevan, N., Cockton, G., Nielsen, G., Spool, J., & Wixon, D. [2003], The 'Magic Number 5': Is It Enough for Web Testing?, *in* G. Cockton & P. Korhonen (eds.), *CHI'03 Extended Abstracts of the Conference on Human Factors in Computing Systems*, ACM Press, pp.698–9.

Feierabend, S. & Klingler, W. [2001], Kinder und Medien 2000: PC/Internet gewinnen an Bedeutung [Children and Media 2000: PC/Internet gain importance], *Media Perspektiven* 7, 345–57.

Frese, M. & Zapf, D. [1991], *Fehler bei der arbeit mit dem computer, Ergebnisse von beobachtungen und befragungen in Burobereich*, Vol. 52 of *Schriften zur arbeitspsychology*, Verlag Hans Huber.

Kersten-Tsikalkina, M. & Bekker, M. [2001], Evaluating Usability and Fun of Children's products, *in* M. G. Helander, H. M. Khalid & M. P. Tham (eds.), *Proceedings of International Conference on Affective Human Factors Design*, Asean Academic Press, pp.450–7.

Landauer, T. K. & Nielsen, J. [1993], A Mathematical Model of the Finding of Usability Problems, *in* S. Ashlund, K. Mullet, A. Henderson, E. Hollnagel & T. White (eds.), *Proceedings of INTERCHI'93*, ACM Press/IOS Press, pp.206–13.

Lavery, D., Cockton, G. & Atkinson, M. P. [1997], Comparison of Evaluation Methods using Structured Usability Problem Reports, *Behaviour & Information Technology* 16(4-5), 246–66.

Lewis, J. R. [1994], Sample Sizes for Usability Studies: Additional Considerations, *Human Factors* 36(2), 368–78.

Malone, T. & Lepper, M. [1987], Making Learning Fun: A Taxonomy of Intrinsic Motivations for Learning, *in* R. Snow & M. Farr (eds.), *Aptitude, Learning and Instruction III. Cognitive and Affective Process Analysis*, Lawrence Erlbaum Associates, pp.223–53.

Markopoulos, P. & Bekker, M. [2003], On the Assessment Usability Testing Methods for Children, *Interacting with Computers* 15(3), 227–43.

Nielsen, J. [1993], *Usability Engineering*, Academic Press.

Nielsen, J. [1994], Heuristic Evaluation, *in* J. Nielsen & R. L. Mack (eds.), *Usability Inspection Methods*, John Wiley & Sons, pp.25–62.

Nielsen, J. [2000], Why You Only Need to Test With 5 Users, Alertbox 2000.03.19, at http://www.useit.com/alertbox/20000319.html, accessed on 2004.05.03.

Nielsen, J. & Landauer, T. K. [1993], A Mathematical Model of the Finding of Usability Problems, *in* S. Ashlund, K. Mullet, A. Henderson, E. Hollnagel & T. White (eds.), *Proceedings of INTERCHI'93*, ACM Press/IOS Press, pp.206–13.

Overbeeke, C. J., Djajadiningrat, T., Hummels, C., Wensveen, S. & Frens, J. [2003], Let's Make Things Engaging, *in* M. A. Blythe, A. F. Monk, C. J. Overbeeke & P. C. Wright (eds.), *Funology: From Usability to Enjoyment*, Kluwer, pp.7–17.

Pagulayan, R. J., Steury, K. R., Fulton, B. & Romero, R. L. [2003], Designing for Fun: User-testing Case Studies, *in* M. A. Blythe, A. F. Monk, C. J. Overbeeke & P. C. Wright (eds.), *Funology: From Usability to Enjoyment*, Kluwer, pp.137–50.

Read, J., MacFarlane, S. & Casey, C. [2002], Endurability, Engagement and Expectations: Measuring Children's Fun, *in* M. M. Bekker, P. Markopoulos & M. Kersten-Tsikalkina (eds.), *Interaction Design and Children*, Shaker Publishing, pp.189–98.

Spool, J. & Schroeder, W. [2001], Testing Websites: Five Users is Nowhere Near Enough, *in* M. M. Tremaine (ed.), *CHI'01 Extended Abstracts of the Conference on Human Factors in Computing Systems*, ACM Press, pp.285–6.

Woolrych, A. & Cockton, G. [2001], Why and When Five Test Users aren't Enough, *in* J. Vanderdonckt, A. Blandford & A. Derycke (eds.), *Proceedings of IHM-HCI'2001, Joint AFIHM-BCS Conference on Human–Computer Interaction: Interaction without Frontiers, Volume 2*, Cépaduès-Éditions, pp.105–8.

Zapf, D., F.C., B., Frese, M. & Prümper, J. [1992], Errors in Working with Office Computers: A first Validation of a Taxonomy for Observed Errors in a Field Setting, *International Journal of Human–Computer Interaction* 4(4), 311–39.

Comparing Interaction in the Real World and CAVE Virtual Environments

Alistair Sutcliffe, Oscar de Bruijn, Brian Gault, Terrence Fernando[†] & Kevin Tan[†]

Centre for HCI Design, Department of Computation, UMIST PO Box 88, Manchester M60 1QD, UK

Tel: *+44 161 200 3315*

Email: *a.g.sutcliffe@co.umist.ac.uk*

[†] *Centre for Virtual Environments, Business House, University Road, University of Salford, Salford, Manchester M5 4WT, UK*

Email: *t.fernando@salford.ac.uk*

An experimental comparison of interaction in the real world and a CAVE virtual environment was carried out, varying interaction with and without virtual hands and comparing two manipulation tasks. The double-handed task was possible in the real world but nearly impossible in the VE, leading to changed behaviour. The single-handed task showed more errors in the VE but few behaviour differences. Users encountered more errors in the CAVE condition without the virtual hand than with it, and few errors in the real world. Visual feedback caused many usability problems in both tasks. The implications for VE usability and virtual prototyping are discussed.

Keywords: CAVE, virtual reality, usability evaluation, manipulation tasks.

1 Introduction

There have been few studies to compare the differences between interaction in virtual environments and comparable real world domains, in spite of the concern over presence in VE research. In mixed reality environments users transfer between real and virtual worlds [Benford et al. 2000]; ethnographic studies on such interaction suggest that users find the transition between real and virtual worlds difficult [Craven et al. 2001]. Virtual prototyping is advocated as an important application for VR, in which the object is to discover usability problems that are attributable to the designed artefact rather than the VE. User behaviour in the VE with virtual prototypes should therefore be as natural as possible. The first motivation for this paper was to discover and qualify the deficit between real world (RW) and VE interaction.

Few usability evaluation studies have been conducted on CAVE environments, and interaction therein normally assumes presence of a virtual hand. However, in contrast to head-mounted displays, CAVEs enable users to see their real hands. If presence and naturalness are to be encouraged for virtual prototyping, then interaction using one's own hands should be an advantage. This formed a second motivation for the study.

Several studies have pointed out usability problems in VEs [Gabbard & Hix 1997; Kaur et al. 1999]. VE applications have interaction styles radically different from standard GUIs, as illustrated in the work of Bowman & Hodges [1997] and Poupyrev & Ichikawa [1999]. These differences concern the ability to manipulate virtual objects interactively, and the VE's immersive capability. However, evaluation methods have not been specifically designed for VEs, posing many problems not encountered in GUI interaction. Some guidelines and generic design issues for VEs can be found in Mills & Noyes [1999], and the more extensive guidelines in Gabbard & Hix [1997]. A preliminary VE evaluation method and usability heuristics were proposed by Sutcliffe & Kaur [2000]; Kalawsky [1999] developed a VE usability questionnaire based on standard GUI principles; to our knowledge no evaluation methods have been proposed for CAVEs. The third motivation was to develop evaluation techniques for VEs.

This paper focuses on investigating the usability problems in fully immersive VE applications and comparing them with user behaviour in the real world; it identifies interaction deficits imposed by the VE technology, and the strategies that users adopt to deal with such problems. In the next section we describe the method and experimental design of the study. We then report and analyse results, and conclude with a discussion of the implications of our findings for the usability and design of VEs.

2 Motivations and Materials

The experimental design had three independent variables: task, user experience and real world vs. virtual world (with and without virtual hand) in a $2\times2\times3$ partially factorial design (task order was fixed), with dependent measures of errors and task completion times. Choice of tasks was motivated by Guiard's [1987] kinematic chain model of haptic interaction, which predicted high cognitive loading for synchronized two-handed interaction, so a double-handed task was selected to create conditions of high performance difficulty, with a second easier single-handed task. The experimental domain was a simple manipulation task of moving chess pieces to reposition them into a target pattern. In the two-handed condition this involved picking up, moving and placing two pieces simultaneously; while in the single-handed condition, subjects were instructed to pick a piece in one hand then pass it to the other hand before placing it in the correct location. The motivation for the hand-to-hand piece-passing was to study the usability problems inherent in visual feedback substituted for haptic interaction in the VE design. Pilot tests demonstrated that subjects had great difficulties in completing the double-handed, synchronous task in the CAVE condition. We changed the original randomized design to study learning effects between the tasks, which were held in the same order: double-handed first, single-handed second. Errors were hypothesized to be higher in the doubled-handed condition for which no learning was possible; in that condition we investigated adaptive strategies. In the single-handed condition, learning was possible where subjects had adopted a similar pattern of behaviour in the previous task. We investigated whether adaptive strategies reduced errors and helped performance in the second task.

The experimental paradigm consisted of two consecutive tests for each subject. All subjects were exposed to the control condition in the real world. The task end state and requirements were the same as the experimental conditions, namely to reorganize randomly placed chess pieces into a desired pattern. Subjects then repeated the task in the experimental condition, performing the double-handed and single-handed tasks in that order. The presence or absence of the virtual hand was randomized following conventional experimental design.

A fully immersive CAVE system [Cruz-Neira et al. 1992] was equipped with shutter glasses to give the users stereoscopic views, and pinch gloves for manipulation. Head-tracking devices mounted on the users' shutter glasses controlled the CAVE viewpoint according to the users' body and head movements.

The application displayed 12 chess pieces: black and white king, queen, bishop, knight, rook, and pawn, and a board with minimal background (see Figure 1). The user tasks were to move the chess pieces from a random layout to the target arrangement shown in the CAVE display. Haptic feedback for piece selection was substituted by colour changes, as follows. When a chess piece was selected by the user operating the pinch glove, it changed colour (from white/black to yellow) in response to the user's action (Figure 1). The piece then moved in tandem with the user's hand until it was released. Once the piece was released it reverted to its original colour.

When a chess piece was placed on the chessboard, the square on which it had been placed changed colour from white/blue to dark red. When the user released the piece, the square reverted to its original colour.

When an already selected chess piece (coloured yellow) was correctly positioned to be gripped for selecting by the other hand, it changed colour from yellow to blue. The user could then release the piece with their first hand and the colour changed back to yellow (= selected) (Figure 2).

Fourteen students from UMIST and Salford Universities took part in the study; they were equally divided between VE expert and VE novice users. Experts had considerable experience in using VEs (mean 1.5 years) and were involved with VR research; novices in contrast had no previous experience with VEs. The average age of the subject group was 29 years, all were right-handed, with good eyesight, and none wore spectacles. Each subject performed the task to arrange the initially scattered twelve chess pieces into the final arrangement.

Figure 1: Selection of a chess piece.

Figure 2: Passing a chess piece from hand to hand.

When they had completed the real world control task, each subject had their inter-ocular distance (IOD) measured to calibrate the VE application to their individual depth perception. Each subject was then introduced to the CAVE, fitted with a pair of stereoscopic shutter glasses and a pair of pinch gloves, and allowed a 10-minute period to familiarize him or herself with the VE chess application. At the end of this period, each subject was asked to complete the two tasks in one of two different conditions: (a) the VE application with the virtual hand represented, or (b) VE without the virtual hand. In both conditions a precise bounding box provided collision detection when the user's hand intersected with the surrounding volume of each chess piece. When the virtual hand was not present the user had to infer the offset between their real hand and its virtual position in the CAVE environment.

The subjects were asked to report verbally any difficulties they experienced while completing the tasks; they were timed and videotaped during their performance. At the end of the study, each subject was questioned during a short debriefing session about the problems encountered during interaction, and their perceptions of the real world and VE application.

The following hypotheses were proposed:

1. Two-handed interaction would take longer and produce more errors than single-handed interaction because it required more conscious motor control.

2. More errors and longer task completion times would be observed in the VE than in the real world because of the limited haptic feedback in the VE.

3. In the VE the presence of the virtual hand would reduce task completion times and errors while the absence of the virtual hand would make task completion more difficult.

4. In the VE expert subjects would perform better (shorter times, fewer errors) than novice users in both conditions.

5. The VE would increase the subjects' cognitive workload, leading to changes in their behaviour and task completion strategies when compared to the real world.

3   Results

3.1   Task Times and Errors

Task times were analysed using a repeated measures ANOVA, with user experience, task type, and task environment as the independent variables. The analysis indicated a significant difference for task ($p < 0.001$) which reflects the quicker mean completion times in the real world environments. In addition, there was a significant interaction between task and environment ($p < 0.01$), and a weaker effect for task and subject experience ($p = 0.05$). Mean task completion times (see Table 1) were much faster in the real world task compared to the CAVE, as might be expected, and the double-handed task times were quicker than the single-handed task, in the virtual environment. However, there was little difference in completion times between the tasks in the real world, which indicates that the virtual environment slowed performance and imposed a different additional load on the subjects for both task. Experts were quicker than novices in the single-handed task but differences were inconsistent in the double-handed task.

3.2   Behaviour and Errors

Videoed subject behaviour was categorized as:

1. task action (indicating subject movement of the chess pieces);

2. errors (indicating mistakes made by the subjects in the movement of the chess pieces); and

3. body moves (movement of the subject's body from place to place particularly in the VE).

Task	RW	VE+hand	VE no-hand
Double-handed:			
Novice	44.14	291.43	531.43
Expert	45.86	308.57	428.57
Total	45.00	295.71	480.00
Single-handed:			
Novice	43.71	488.57	1028.57
Expert	40.29	308.57	745.71
Total	42.00	394.29	887.10

Table 1: Mean task completion time in seconds.

Task	RW	VE+hand	VE no-hand
Double-handed:			
Novice	29.86	35.42	38.00
Expert	24.86	35.57	35.00
Total	27.36	35.50	36.50
Single-handed:			
Novice	60.00	58.43	59.42
Expert	58.29	57.57	58.71
Total	59.14	57.00	59.14

Table 2: Mean frequencies for task actions.

Behaviours were transcribed so sequences could be analysed as well as total frequencies.

ANOVA analysis of the total frequency of task actions (see Table 2) was significant for task ($p < 0.001$) with a weak interaction for task and environment ($p = 0.025$) with the single-handed task taking nearly twice as many bouts, reflecting the additional actions necessary for passing pieces.

Task errors (see Table 3) showed a weak significant main effect for task ($p < 0.05$) with a weak interaction between task and environment ($p = 0.05$). Task errors showed an inconsistent picture: means for the double-handed task were higher in the real world condition; the single-handed errors were higher in the VE conditions. Experts had lower averages than novices.

Usability errors (see Table 4) did not apply in the real world. Frequencies of usability errors were significantly different between the VE environments ($p < 0.05$) and showed an interaction between environment and experience ($p \leq 0.01$). Higher error averages were observed in the no-virtual hand conditions and in the single-handed task, while novices had higher average errors than experts in both VE conditions. This may have been caused by the more complicated manipulation of selecting and releasing pieces when passing them between hands in the VE, and the inexperience of novices in the VE manipulations.

Task	RW	VE+hand	VE no-hand
Double-handed:			
Novice	4.00	1.86	2.54
Expert	2.14	1.14	1.71
Total	3.07	1.50	2.14
Single-handed:			
Novice	2.14	4.57	7.43
Expert	0.71	2.57	4.42
Total	1.43	3.57	5.93

Table 3: Means for task errors.

Task	VE+hand	VE no-hand
Double-handed:		
Novice	2.57	12.57
Expert	1.00	3.14
Total	1.70	7.86
Single-handed:		
Novice	9.43	15.29
Expert	2.14	8.14
Total	5.79	11.71

Table 4: Means for usability errors.

Three usability errors accounted for over 95% of the observed subjects' critical incidents. First, unsuccessful selection of a piece (USP errors, 50% of total) was caused by perceptual difficulty in positioning the virtual hand (or their real hand in the no-virtual hand condition) in the correct position so the bounding box intersected with the chess piece. Once the intersection had been achieved most subjects then pinched the glove to successfully select the piece; however, in 65% of USP errors the subjects failed to complete selection either because they forgot to pinch the glove or because they moved their hand before pinching, which then inhibited selection. The second most frequent problem was the unsuccessful pass piece (UPP), accounting for 39% of the overall usability errors. In these cases the user correctly selected the first piece, then moved the left hand to an appropriate position for hand-to-hand passing, but then released the right hand before selecting with the left. This resulted in an unselected piece floating in front of them. The final usability error, unsuccessful put piece down (UPD, 6%), arose because the user could not select the square on the chess board or, once having done so, did not release the glove pinch in time, consequently disabling the place piece operation. Novices accounted for 74% of the total usability errors, and had higher scores for each type; furthermore, experts had no UPD errors.

The majority of errors were therefore caused by perceptual problems in manoeuvring the virtual hand, causing the collision detection algorithm to be triggered and the appropriate selection highlighted. However, the UPP errors were caused by a complex set of manipulations that had little mapping to the real world task, e.g. gripping the selected piece with both hands before releasing it with the right hand in hand-to-hand passing. A fourth problem, which did not lead to any specific usability problems, was when users experienced difficulty in trying to position their virtual hands to select pieces. We refer to these incidents as the 'cross hands' problem, when users found themselves in a contorted position with their real hands crossed over in a vain attempt to reposition their virtual hands. Their solution was to abandon the movement and start the approach to select a chess piece again.

Sequences of behaviour were analysed by casting transition frequencies for all dyadic combinations of behaviour categories (i.e. frequencies where A followed B, B was followed by C, etc.) in matrices and then constructing behaviour network graphs for each subject. Individual subject behaviour network graphs were inspected for significant commonalities or differences; however, no particular common patterns of behaviour were observed among the subjects for either task of the VE condition. Behavioural frequencies were summed for novice and expert subjects by task and VE condition, and group-level diagrams created. To test for the more significant transitions an expected value was calculated for each cell in the matrix by dividing the total transition frequencies by the number of cells, having eliminated the zero diagonal. The expected value was then used in the Binomial test to calculate the z distribution for sample sizes where $N > 25$.

In the following network diagrams only frequencies above 2% of the overall total are reported. Dashed arrows are non-significant, normal arrows show transitions that were significantly more frequent than the expected value at $0.01 < p < 0.05$, and bold arrows are used for $p < 0.01$.

The subjects showed two patterns for the first double-handed task (see Figure 3): one cycle of picking, moving and placing pieces concurrently, and a separate, more significant cycle of single-handed operation which did not conform to instructions. Only one subject completed the task without error, while three subjects failed to perform any two-handed interaction at all. The expert-only pattern (not illustrated) was similar to Figure 3 with the addition of transitions from Corrections and Hesitations which, although non-significant, may indicate the difficulty of the double-handed task; corrections in the single-handed task were caused by subjects changing their minds on piece selection.

The novice pattern showed an even stronger bias towards single-handed operation, reflecting the difficulty experienced in synchronizing double-handed manipulation even in the real world. Incorrect position errors indicated task knowledge problems with selecting the appropriate square for the piece.

In contrast, the single-handed task was much easier and more natural for all subjects (see Figure 4); furthermore, both experts and novices showed similar patterns. Experts approached a near perfect cycle of picking up a piece, moving it, then passing it from hand to hand before moving it to the required square and placing it (6 black and 6 white pieces required $12 \times 7 = 84$ moves).

The subjects' behaviour pattern in the VE for the double-handed task reverted to single-handed mode, even for experts (see Figure 5), but differed from the real

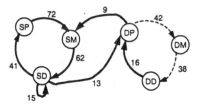

Figure 3: Behaviour network for all subjects: real world double-handed task. Transition frequencies are shown on the arcs (i.e. SD was followed by SP 41 times). SP Single Pick Up; SM Single Movement; SD Single Put Down; DP Double Pick Up; DM Double Movement; DD Double Put Down.

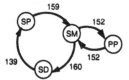

Figure 4: Behaviour network for all subjects: real world single-handed task. PP Pass hand-to-hand.

world pattern with more transitions between piece selects and moves. This suggests that the additional cognitive load of the virtual environment made double-handed synchronization nearly impossible. The expert behaviour patterns also showed some movement and piece selection errors, possibly caused by perceptual difficulties. Novices followed experts in reverting to single-handed performance, but showed more leaning and arm reaching movement, which may reflect their lack of perceptual experience in the CAVE. Perceptual problems may also have been responsible for their high frequency of piece selection errors.

In the single-handed task (see Figure 6), the subjects showed similar behaviour patterns in the CAVE and the real world, with the addition of arm reach body movement to select pieces. Experts experienced few errors in this task condition. Novices, in contrast, showed little body movement apart from arm reaching, so the experts' experience may have made movement more natural for them. Novices also experienced more usability errors, especially in passing pieces which required them to select with both hands before releasing with the first.

In the double-handed task without the virtual hand (see Figure 7), users reverted to a single-handed strategy; furthermore, the cycle of select, move and place was disrupted by piece selection errors. Novices tended to move more, and encountered more errors than experts in trying to pick up and pass pieces. This indicates that experts as well as novices found adjusting to the real-hand cue confusing, until they learned the perceptual offset between the VE depth and their hand. This is indicated by the movement actions preceding the USP errors.

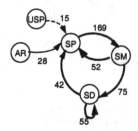

Figure 5: Behaviour network for all subjects: VE, double-handed task with virtual hand. AR Arm Reach; the prefix U indicates an unsuccessful action so USP = unsuccessful select piece error.

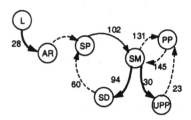

Figure 6: Behaviour network for all subjects: VE, single-handed task with virtual hand. L Body Lean.

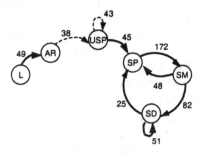

Figure 7: Behaviour network for all subjects: VE, double-handed task, no virtual hand.

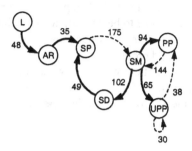

Figure 8: Behaviour network for all subjects: VE, single-handed task, no virtual hand.

The single-handed task patterns without the virtual hand showed many piece-passing errors (see Figure 8). While selection errors were more common in the double-handed task, in the single-handed task placement errors were more frequent. Users in the no-virtual hand condition experienced more repeated pass piece errors (UPP) which may have been caused by the increased difficulty of coordinating both hands as many users commented on the perceptual difficulties of mapping their real hands into the graphical VR world to position and select pieces. The experts' pattern showed less movement compared with the double-handed task and more piece-passing errors. Novices showed frequent place and select piece errors, with several reselect piece actions demonstrating their difficulty in operating without the virtual hand; in addition, they showed more movement than in the double-handed task, indicating more perceptual exploration.

In summary, the behaviour pattern analysis showed that the double-handed task was too difficult for subjects in the virtual environment, and both novices and experts reverted to single-handed operation. The patterns of both experts and novices for both conditions were consistent for each task, while the main novice-expert differences were more usability errors from the novices and more movement by the experts, although this was not a consistent trend.

3.3 Qualitative Data, Subject Comments

Subject comments were grouped into comments about hardware, depth perception and presence, and interaction problems. Five novices complained about interaction, in particular passing pieces where the colour change was confusing; three commented on depth perception, which was worse for more distant pieces; and four subjects commented that they had to concentrate because interaction was difficult. Problems with the shutter glasses led to three subjects' complaints. Only 12.5% of the comments were positive, and all these were about the VE presence.

Four experts complained about the depth perception, although four also commented favourably on the quality of presence, with two subjects sharing both views. Four subjects found the mapping and orientation between the virtual hands and their real hands to be difficult because their real hands 'blocked' the virtual hands and they could not see if the chess pieces were being selected or positioned correctly. This problem was highlighted when passing a chess piece. Most subjects found movement within the CAVE to be natural; however, four subjects experienced a time delay or lag in updating of the VE when moving within it. 50% of the subjects remarked that they experienced problems with depth perception, when the perceived position of a chess piece did not correspond to where they had reached to select it. This was a problem particularly for the novice subjects, whereas expert subjects moved around more in the VE to improve their perception when selecting distant chess pieces.

4 Design Improvements

The VE design could be improved for piece selection (USP error) in several ways. First the 3D perceptual depth could be improved; this was a particular problem in corners of the CAVE where distortion is more severe. Secondly, the bounding box collision-detection mechanism could be improved to map more accurately to the user's virtual hand. Third, the selectable status might be cued more effectively using a handles metaphor to activate users' existing mental models for affordances. Alternatively a 'snap-to' auto-selection function could be triggered when the glove was pinched, or even on collision detection. The extent of automated support for interaction will depend on the demands for naturalness of the VE. Finally, haptic feedback for grip could be provided by vibration-emitting devices in the glove fingers, with movement being calculated from an effective grip by thumb and fingers.

Many of the above improvements could cure the other pass piece (UPP) and place piece (UPD) errors. For UPP errors, adding simulated gravity could have cued rapid learning not to drop a piece before it had been picked by the other hand; furthermore, pressure feedback by finger tip pressure sensors would give better haptic perception of grip by both hands. The cross hands problem might be cured by improving depth perception or by interacting via the user's real hand as in the no-virtual hand condition. However, this condition generally caused more errors than the virtual hand, but a more accurate collision detection with a wider-range bounding zone and a visual cue for a nimbus [Benford et al. 1994] might make this interaction technique more effective. Other improvements which were not explicitly motivated by the observed errors might be to improve the sense of naturalness in the VE by adding gravity, so chess pieces do not float in space when released. This may also improve the users' sense of presence [Slater 1999].

5 Discussion and Conclusions

The first of our research hypotheses (double-handed task longer than single-handed) was not upheld, since the double-handed interaction was quicker and induced fewer task and usability errors than the single hand, apart from in the real world where the opposite results were found. A possible explanation is that usability problems in the VE made the single-handed task longer and more error prone. However, there was considerable variation in subject behaviour in the double-handed task, and in many cases subjects were arguably performing single-handedly.

The second hypothesis (more errors in VE than in RW) was upheld, as more errors and considerably longer times were observed in both VE conditions. This difference was not surprising; however, the quality differences in user behaviour were more interesting. Our experiments demonstrated the difficulty of carrying out complex manipulations in CAVE environments, especially when the task demanded synchronization and double-handed operation. These tasks are known to be difficult in real world conditions, so the degraded performance we observed between the real and virtual world operation of the same task strongly suggests that CAVE environments impose a considerable cognitive burden on users. Furthermore, our subjects changed their task strategies in the face of these difficulties, so CAVE environments might induce a completely artificial pattern of user behaviour. This has important implications for virtual prototyping uses of CAVEs, where the observed problems are more likely to be artefacts of the virtual environment than interaction problems with the designed artefact.

The third hypothesis (virtual hand better than no virtual hand) was upheld, as significant differences were found in both tasks. Interaction without the virtual hand proved to be more error prone than interaction with the virtual hand presence, even though our subjects said they preferred the no-hand condition. Our initial hypothesis was that the no-hand condition would be easier than the virtual hand condition; however, it appears that interaction without the hand gave the users worse perceptual problems. They had to judge the location of a virtual bounding box within the 3D virtual world; unfortunately, the mapping between the depth dimension in the CAVE and the location of the subject's real hand was far from perfect, so our users had to discover perceptual offsets from different viewpoint angles. This led to increased selection errors. However, the virtual hand condition did cause the cross-hand problem, which did not occur when no virtual hand was present. Interaction with no virtual hands in CAVE environments may therefore be advantageous, but only if improved perceptual mapping with the user's real hand and collision detection in the virtual environment can be provided.

The fourth hypothesis (experts better than novices) was partially supported. Experts did show fewer errors than novices, but most differences were non-significant, and task completion times were not consistently quicker. This may be seen as a positive indication that novices can learn to interact in CAVE environments with minimal training, as indeed they did in our study. Alternatively, the persistence of errors shown by experts suggests that perceptual problems do not diminish with training, and these are deeper-seated design defects in the current technology. The behaviour differences between the subject groups indicated that experts got used to CAVE environments and moved around more naturally, whereas novices tended to be rooted to the spot. Experts' use of movement may compensate for perceptual inaccuracies in the CAVE.

The final hypothesis (VE would change behaviour compared with RW) was partially supported. Although we took no direct measure of cognitive workload, it appears that the CAVE environment did induce a radical change in subjects' behaviour, and caused many of them to abandon the cognitively more demanding doubled-handed task. A possible explanation for the additional load is the lack of haptic feedback; poor visual feedback for collision detection imposed an additional cognitive load in maintaining synchronized action. The usability errors we observed were frequent but they could be attributed to a small number of causes. First were perceptual problems in selecting objects. Selection problems caused by difficulty in judging 3D depth in VEs have been reported in other studies [Barfield et al. 1995; Hix et al. 1999; Slater 1999; Sutcliffe & Kaur 2000]. Techniques to make collision detection and bounding boxes more visible to users, e.g. the nimbus concept [Benford et al. 1994] might be one way to improve interaction, although such feedback can be intrusive and impair the user's sense of presence.

Clearly this study has limitations in the generalizability for haptic interaction, and its implications for virtual prototyping. Nevertheless, we argue that the difficulties we found in a relatively simple task do not augur well for more complex manipulations in VEs. While haptic feedback could cure many of the problems we observed, providing a haptic sense for complex manipulations has no easy solution. Simple devices such as the Phantom provide single point (finger) sense of force, but feedback for grip and lift operations necessitate cumbersome and currently unreliable exoskeletons. The implication may be that virtual prototyping needs to consider augmented reality for products where physical interaction will be important. In our future work we will investigate the effects of visual and haptic feedback on more complex manipulations in maintenance tasks, to explore the limitations of what can be achieved in virtual prototyping, and contrast this with augmented reality designs.

References

Barfield, W., Zeltzer, D., Sheridan, T. & Slater, M. [1995], Presence and Performance within Virtual Environments, *in* W. Barfield & T. A. Furness (eds.), *Virtual Environments and Advanced Interface Design*, Oxford University Press, pp.473–513.

Benford, S., Bowers, J. & Fahlen, L. [1994], Managing Mutual Awareness in Collaborative Environments, *Computing* p.39. 12th May.

Benford, S., Greenhalgh, C., Craven, M., Walker, G., Regan, T., Morphett, J. & Wyver, J. [2000], Inhabited Television: Broadcasting Interaction from within Collaborative Virtual Environments, *ACM Transactions on Computer–Human Interaction* 7(4), 510–547.

Bowman, D. A. & Hodges, L. [1997], An Evaluation of Techniques for Grabbing and Manipulating Remote Objects in Immersive Virtual Environments, *in* M. Cohen & D. Zeltzer (eds.), *Proceedings of the 1997 Symposium on Interactive 3D Graphics*, ACM Press, pp.35–8.

Craven, M., Taylor, I., Drozd, A., Purbick, J. & C., G. [2001], Exploiting Interactivity, Influence, Space and Time to Explore Non-linear Drama in Virtual World, *in* J. A. Jacko & A. Sears (eds.), *Proceedings of SIGCHI Conference on Human Factors in Computing Systems (CHI'01)*, CHI Letters 3(1), ACM Press, pp.30–7.

Cruz-Neira, C., Sandin, D. J., De Fanti, T. A., Kenyon, R. V. & Hart, J. C. [1992], The CAVE: Audio Visual Experience Automatic Virtual Environment, *Communications of the ACM* 35(6), 64–72.

Gabbard, J. & Hix, D. [1997], Taxonomy of Usability Characteristics in Virtual Environments, Technical Report 183, Department of Computer Science, Virginia Polytechnic Institute and State University, Virginia, USA. A Report to the Office of Naval Research, Grant no. N00014-96-1-0385.

Guiard, Y. [1987], Asymmetric Division of Labor in Human Skilled Bimanual Action: The Kinematic Chain as a Model, *Journal of Motor Behaviour* **19**(4), 486–517.

Hix, D., Swan, J. E., Gabbard, J. L., McGee, M., Durbin, J. & King, T. [1999], User-centered Design and Evaluation of a Real-time Battlefield Visualization Virtual Environment, *in* L. Rosenblum, P. Astheimer & D. Teichmann (eds.), *Proceedings of IEEE Virtual Reality '99*, IEEE Computer Society Press, pp.96–103.

Kalawsky, R. S. [1999], VRUSE: A Computerised Diagnostic Tool for Usability Evaluation of Virtual/Synthetic Environment Systems, *Applied Ergonomics* **30**(1), 11–25.

Kaur, K., Maiden, N. & Sutcliffe, A. [1999], Interacting with Virtual Environments: An Evaluation of a Model of Interaction, *Interacting with Computers* **11**(4), 403– 26. Special Issue on VR.

Mills, S. & Noyes, J. [1999], Virtual Reality: An Overview of User-related Design Issues, *Interacting with Computers* **11**(4), 375–86.

Poupyrev, I. & Ichikawa, T. [1999], Manipulating Objects in Virtual Worlds: Categorization and Empirical Evaluation of Interaction Techniques, *Journal of Visual Languages and Computing* **10**(1), 19–35.

Slater, M. [1999], Measuring Presence: A Response to the Witmer and Singer Questionnaire, *Presence: Teleoperators and Virtual Environments* **8**(5), 560–72.

Sutcliffe, A. G. & Kaur, K. [2000], Evaluating the Usability of Virtual Reality User Interfaces, *Behaviour & Information Technology* **19**(6), 415–26.

In Search of Salience: A Response-time and Eye-movement Analysis of Bookmark Recognition

Alex Poole, Linden J Ball & Peter Phillips[†]

Psychology Department, [†] Computing Department, Lancaster University, Bailrigg, Lancaster LA1 4YF, UK

Tel: *+44 1524 593470*

Email: *alex@alexpoole.info, l.ball@lancaster.ac.uk*

URL: *http://www.alexpoole.info*

Bookmarks are a valuable webpage re-visitation technique, but it is often difficult to find desired items in extensive bookmark collections. This experiment used response-time measures and eye-movement tracking to investigate how different information structures within bookmarks influence their salience and recognizability. Participants were presented with a series of news websites. The task following presentation of each site was to find the bookmark indexing the previously-seen page as quickly as possible. The Informational Structure of bookmarks was manipulated (top-down vs. bottom-up verbal organizations), together with the Number of Informational Cues present (one, two or three). Only this latter factor affected gross search times: Two cues were optimal, one cue was highly sub-optimal. However, more detailed eye-movement analyses of fixation behaviour on target items revealed interactive effects of both experimental factors, suggesting that the efficacy of bookmark recognition is crucially dependent on having an optimal combination of information quantity and information organization.

Keywords: bookmark recognition, eye-movements, search time, information salience, information re-visitation, World Wide Web.

1 Introduction

1.1 Keeping Found Things Found

Although the World Wide Web serves as the primary information resource for many people, its massively increasing size and complexity has made information overload one of the biggest and most obvious drawbacks of the technological age. In recent years finding resources on the Web has been made easier with modern search engines, together with more refined search functions found within websites themselves. But managing successfully to find a webpage invites a secondary problem: How do you 'keep found things found'? [Jones et al. 2001]. Users have many different methods for maintaining resources that have been accessed on the Web, such as saving whole pages to their hard drives or printing them out. Alternatively, users may send URLs to themselves in an email, write them down on pieces of paper, or add them to the 'bookmarks' list in their Web browser [Cockburn & McKenzie 2000; Jones et al. 2001; Tauscher & Greenberg 1997]. The last method, bookmarking, is the focus of the present research.

1.2 Bookmark Basics and Good Housekeeping

Bookmarks have been in existence since the creation of the first Web browser [Cailliau 1995]. They have since been adopted by most browsers as a standard navigation and re-visitation tool, but tend to be referred to by different names for reasons of marketing. The term bookmark is used in the Netscape Navigator browser whilst the term 'favorites' is used in Internet Explorer. Throughout this paper we employ the term bookmark simply as a convenient shorthand for the generic concept of a stored weblink in a browser menu. The text in a bookmark emanates directly from the title of a webpage as found in the <title> tag in the HTML code used to build the page. However, the text in the <title> tag may not actually appear on the webpage itself, and is also not necessarily the same as the 'title' appearing within the webpage, which has to be defined separately by the author.

Notwithstanding these latter observations, it is generally accepted that there are a few basic things that Web authors should do in order to write acceptable bookmarks, based on the complaints of Web users [Cockburn et al. 2003; Kaasten et al. 2002]. First, they should remember actually to define the <title> tag. If the <title> tag is empty or even missing from the HTML code, then the filename and directory path of the page will be shown, instead of a meaningful title. If authors are using Web publishing software (e.g. Macromedia Dreamweaver), the programme's default text will be displayed if the <title> is left undefined. This can be recognized frequently on the Web by pages marked 'Untitled'. Second, authors should ideally ensure that the <title> tag and the title within the page actually match. Differences between the two have been cited by Web users as a major annoyance during their efforts to locate a bookmark [Kaasten et al. 2002]. Third, authors should ensure that each page on their website has a unique title to aid multiple bookmarking of pages from the same site. Finally, authors should make the title fit within the bookmark character length limit. In Microsoft Windows, the maximum length for a bookmark is 255 characters (including spaces), but, on average, only the first 65 characters will be visible in the favourites menu in Internet Explorer (although all 255 characters should appear in the tool tip).

2 Purpose of the Experiment

2.1 Rationale for Studying Text-Only Bookmarks

Bookmarks are a convenient way to revisit webpages until a bookmark list grows so large that the target item can no longer be found with ease or efficiency. The search task is likely to become even more difficult when returning to a list after a long time, with a fragmented memory of what the bookmark text actually was. To address such problems various research efforts have focused on making bookmarks easier to find and organize [Abrams et al. 1998; Cockburn & Greenberg 1999; Cockburn et al. 2003; Kaasten et al. 2002; Tauscher & Greenberg 1997]. Custom icons can make bookmark references stand out, as can thumbnail images of the websites themselves positioned next to the text bookmarks [Cockburn et al. 2003]. The latter method, however, has yet to be adopted as a standard re-visitation mechanism in contemporary browsers. Furthermore, the advantages of icons and thumbnails may be short lived if their use becomes widespread as their 'pop out' value would be greatly reduced.

Thumbnails also have their own recognizability problems. Text-based pages are hard to recognize at any resolution and pages from websites that are consistently designed are hard to differentiate [Cockburn & Greenberg 1999]. Thumbnails also consume a high proportion of screen real-estate. Each bookmark on the favourites menu in Internet Explorer occupies 20 pixels of vertical space, however, to achieve just a 60% chance of recognizing a particular webpage, a thumbnail 144 pixels high is required [Kaasten et al. 2002]. Accessibility and usability may also be problematic for visual recognition aids. Icons and thumbnails are of little benefit for visually impaired users, but plain text can always be interpreted by voice Web browsers. Similarly, other systems such as file organizers, search engines and databases may not be able to interpret graphical representations. For example, it may be difficult to implement automatic and meaningful bookmark sorting based on graphical properties. In terms of usability, it is not clear if icons and thumbnails will transpose well to PDAs and mobile phones. These devices have extremely limited screen real-estate, and thumbnails, in particular, may have to fill most of the screen to be recognized.

In general, then, whilst studies have shown that visual and graphical aids can make bookmarks stand out, research does not propose how to make webpages easier to recognize when they are represented by standard text-only bookmarks. It is clear that text-based referencing remains a major force on the Web and, as such, warrants continued research and improvement. This study specifically investigates factors that affect the salience and recognizability of text-based bookmarks.

2.2 Types of Bookmark: Top-Down and Bottom-Up Informational Structures

Many Web producers model the <title> tag text on how information is organized on the site. This can help users while they navigate, because their navigation trail is built up in a logical way, thereby providing feedback on where they are and how they got there [Preece et al. 2002]. Two common ways of describing these information structures are 'top-down' and 'bottom-up' [Rosenfeld & Morville 2002]. A top-

| **Top-down structure:** |
| site name $\longrightarrow$ section name $\longrightarrow$ page or article title |
| Example: |
| Nifty News – Middle East – Senior Official Surrenders |
| **Bottom-up structure:** |
| page or article title $\longrightarrow$ section name $\longrightarrow$ site name |
| Example: |
| Senior Official Surrenders – Middle East — Nifty News |

Table 1: Examples of bookmarks relating to a fictitious news website, possessing 'top-down' and 'bottom-up' informational structures.

down structure may list the name of the site, followed by one or more sections, and finally the title of the page. Conversely, a bottom-up structure starts with the title of the page and ends with the name of the site (see Table 1). Both top-down and bottom-up bookmark structures could reasonably identify a page, but which format might be more recognizable to users when they are searching a large bookmark list, with imperfect memory? We set out to address this issue in the present study.

On a priori grounds, bottom-up structures might be expected to be more salient than top-down structures for three key reasons. First, users' actions are driven by goals and tasks [Preece et al. 2002]. Visually searching the bookmark menu is an example of goal-driven behaviour as the user is examining the menu specifically to find a target bookmark with a particular purpose in mind (e.g. to review some information). Bookmark structures that are tailored to the user's task would be predicted to improve usability [Nielsen 1992]. Since a page title describes what the user has read, whilst the site name may be completely unconnected to the page's subject matter, it is likely that the page title may fit the user's task more than the site name, improving relevance and, potentially, recognition. Second, the fuller descriptions afforded by page titles may be more likely to evoke stronger mental imagery, which is known to aid memory and recognition [Clark & Paivio 1987]. Third, bottom-up structures may map optimally on to schema-based knowledge structures, thereby aiding subsequent recognition [Alba & Hasher 1983].

In the light of this previous theoretical analysis, a key prediction was that bottom-up information structures would facilitate bookmark salience (and, thereby, target bookmark recognition) relative to top-down information structures. A second key prediction related to the way in which the number of distinct information cues in the bookmark (i.e. one, two or three cues) might affect bookmark recognition. We predicted that the greater the distinct number of recognition cues displayed, the more the user should be able to infer meaning to facilitate identification of the target bookmark. In other words, the possible interpretations of bookmark information were expected to be constrained or augmented by the context afforded by extra information [cf. Rumelhart & Norman 1985]. Of course, there may well be an optimal amount of information content above which no added value for bookmark recognition would obtain. We were alert to this possibility in our data analysis.

In addition, we sought to examine any potential additive or interactive effects that might derive from the combination of the 'informational structure' and 'number of informational cues' factors that were independently manipulated in our study.

In terms of dependent measures, bookmark recognition was assessed by measuring the overall time taken to find a target bookmark embedded within a menu containing distracter bookmarks. It was assumed that shorter overall search times would be indicative of more effective bookmark recognition. Eye-movement measures were also employed as a means to provide a deeper understanding of information salience within a bookmark-search context. More specifically, the frequency and mean duration of eye fixations on a bookmark component were taken as indices of relative information salience. The use of eye movements in the present study was based on the assumption that they provide a fairly pure, on-line measure of the processing demands associated with items of information, such that more processing (i.e. more fixations and longer fixation times) would reflect decreased salience and interpretational uncertainty, whereas less processing would reflect increased salience and ease of recognition [Cowen et al. 2002; Goldberg & Kotval 1999; Jacob & Karn 2003; Just & Carpenter 1976]. We believed that making use of eye-movement measures in the present study would enable detection of potentially more subtle information-salience effects than might obtain from the rather gross (and inherently noisy) measure of the overall search time taken to find a target bookmark [cf. Zelinsky & Sheinberg 1995]. Thus, we anticipated that the eye-movement findings would serve to clarify and extend effects that might be less extreme in the search-time data.

3 The Experiment

3.1 Participants

Thirty postgraduate students (12 female and 18 male) took part in the experiment (mean age: 32 years; age range: 15 to 65 years). Participants received payment for their contribution to the research. All participants had normal or corrected-to-normal vision and were regular users of the Web, with an average of seven years experience. All but one participant reported that Internet Explorer was their main Web browser. A majority of participants reported that they had never seen the websites used in the study, although six stated that they were familiar with a few of the websites, but did not use them regularly.

3.2 Design and Materials

A 2×3 within-participants design was used (see Table 2). The first factor was the 'Informational Structure' of bookmarks (top-down vs. bottom-up), and the second factor was the 'Number of Informational Cues' (one, two or three). Participants were presented with a series of websites, and the task following presentation of each site was to find the bookmark indexing the previously-seen page as quickly as possible. Twenty-four webpages containing articles on international news and current affairs were collected and saved as static screenshots. These pages had clear site names, article titles and section names, ensuring equal opportunity for encoding and later recognition. The original title-bar text was deleted from each screenshot

Informational Structure	Number of Informational Cues		
	1	2	3
Top-down (i.e. site name first)	Site name	Site name — Article title	Site name — Section name — Article title
Bottom-up (i.e. article title first)	Article title	Article title — Site name	Article title — Section name — Site name

Table 2: Experimental conditions arising from the manipulation of Information Structure (top-down vs. bottom up) and Number of Informational Cues (one, two or three).

to enable systematic manipulation of the bookmark text. For each website, a set of six screenshots (i.e. one for each experimental condition) was created of Internet Explorer with the favourites menu displayed. This enabled webpages to be rotated across all experimental conditions to ensure maximum experimental control. The bookmark associated with a webpage was randomly located in the favourites menu. The presentation order of experimental conditions was counterbalanced across participants to eliminate fatigue and practice effects.

3.3 Apparatus

The website screen shots were presented on a 15″ flat-screen monitor, with a resolution of 1024×768 pixels. Eye movements were recorded with an LC Technologies Eyegaze development system which determines gaze direction by means of the pupil-centre/corneal-reflection method. The tracker consists of a standard desktop computer running WindowsNT/2000, an infrared camera mounted beneath the monitor, and software to process the eye-movement data. An additional, smaller monitor was used to ensure that the eye was in the centre of the camera's field of view. The eye tracker is accurate to within 0.45 degrees of visual angle, which, at 510mm from the screen, covers approximately 3.8mm. This corresponds to 12.8 pixels on the monitor used, which had a dot pitch of 0.297mm. Eye movements were sampled 60 times per second, with tracking errors not exceeding 6.3mm. Although the tracker can tolerate head motion of around 30mm in all directions, participants used a chin-rest to minimize loss of data. Fixations were detected at 100ms or above, an appropriate cut-off point for tracking eye movements in reading tasks [Hyönä et al. 1989; Inhoff & Radach 1998].

3.4 Procedure

Participants completed 24 trials, one for each website and bookmark-menu combination. On arrival participants were shown the tracker and given a brief explanation of how it worked. Adjustments were made to the chin rest and the monitor to accommodate individual variations in seated head position. At all times the same viewing angle between the face and the screen was maintained. Participants were seated at approximately 510mm from the screen. Once the camera's focus and aperture were set the participant was calibrated with the tracker. This procedure lasted 15 seconds and consisted of the participant following a series of 9 dots around the screen. Following calibration, custom software was launched which presented participants with on-screen instructions and which took them through the experiment itself. After reading the instructions participants completed four practice trials while the experimenter sat beside them to answer queries. Care was taken to check that participants understood the study requirements before they proceeded to the main session (e.g. that they had to read each news page for a fixed time and that their ability to recognize a bookmark for that page would then be tested). Each news page appeared for 18 seconds, with each bookmark screen then appearing for up to 30 seconds. Participants pressed the space bar on the keyboard to indicate that they had found the target bookmark. If they could not find the target within 30 seconds, the trial ended and the next trial began.

3.5 Data Processing

Once the eye movements had been measured, logged and error corrected, the data were filtered to enable examination of participants' processing of specific regions of the screen. The main areas of interest were the site name, section name and article title on the website itself and on the associated bookmark screens. Once areas of interest had been defined, parsing software was used to extract the corresponding eye-movement data and format it for statistical analysis.

4 Results

4.1 Overall Search Times

Mean response times per condition were derived for each participant and reflected the time taken between the appearance of a bookmark menu and the participant registering that the target bookmark had been detected. Faster response times were taken to be indicative of superior recognition. To retain as much data as possible, response times were scored even if participants failed to find the target bookmark (such failure was actually extremely rare). If a bookmark was not found, a maximum response time of 30 seconds was scored (again, almost all target items were found within the permitted time frame).

Mean response times are presented in Table 3. Descriptive analyses indicated that these data (and all subsequent data that we report) met assumptions of normality and were suitable for parametric analysis. A two-way repeated measures analysis of variance (ANOVA) revealed that there was no main effect of Informational Structure (top-down vs. bottom-up), $F(1,29) = 0.155$, $p = 0.697$, but there was a main effect of Number of Informational Cues (one, two or three), $F(2,58) = 8.443$, $p = 0.001$. The interaction effect was also unreliable, $F(2,58) = 0.963$, $p = 0.388$. Employing the Bonferroni post-hoc test, significant differences were found between the one-cue and two-cue conditions ($p = 0.001$) and between the one-cue and three-cue conditions ($p = 0.004$). No significant differences were found between the two-cue and three-cue conditions. These results fail to support our stated prediction that the informational structure of bookmarks would impact upon overall search times. The data do, however, indicate that the number of information cues that are present in a bookmark affect search behaviour: Two cues were seen to be optimal, one cue was highly sub-optimal, and a third cue added no value to the two-cue condition

Informational Structure	Number of Informational Cues			
	1	2	3	Mean
Top-down (i.e. site name first)	13.70	9.90	10.58	11.39
	(6.37)	(5.06)	(4.29)	
Bottom-up (i.e. article title first)	12.80	11.10	11.49	11.80
	(6.05)	(4.99)	(5.19)	
Mean	13.25	10.50	11.03	

Table 3: Mean time taken to locate target bookmarks (seconds), with standard deviations in parentheses.

(indeed three cues promoted marginally slower bookmark search than the two-cue condition).

Although the failure to find a predicted effect of informational structure on overall search times runs counter to predictions, we note that there is a clear hint in the pattern of response times for an interaction effect between the Informational Structure and the Number of Informational Cues factors. This is exemplified in the relatively rapid search-time score for the top-down/two-cue bookmark condition (where the site name precedes the article title), when compared against all other conditions. We anticipated that this interaction might manifest itself more clearly in the eye-movement analysis of bookmark salience effects.

4.2 Adjusting Eye-Movement Data for Phrase Length

As the eye-movement data were analysed per area of interest, a raw count of fixations would show misleading results as they do not take into account the differing lengths of the text phrases contained within these areas (i.e. mean phrase lengths of 2.79 words for site names, 6.83 words for article titles, and 1.79 words for the section names). To adjust for these differences, the mean number of fixations per area of interest was divided by the mean number of words in the phrase. In this way, we are able to separate higher fixation frequency due to the simple fact that there were more words to read, and higher fixation frequency because an item was actually harder to recognize. Note that because the mean *duration* of fixations per area of interest is not contingent on the number words in the phrase, this latter measure was not adjusted. Eye movements were analysed for 24 of the 30 participants (the data of six participants was of insufficient quality to warrant inclusion in the analysis).

4.3 Eye Movements During the Encoding Task

We explored the amount of processing effort devoted to different informational cues during participants' initial inspection of the news-oriented webpages. Mean (adjusted) fixation frequencies and mean fixation durations per informational cue are presented in Table 4. A one-way repeated-measures ANOVA was used to assess mean fixation frequencies per informational cue and revealed a main effect of Cue Type, $F(2,46) = 68.962$, $p < 0.001$. Bonferroni post-hoc tests revealed that the element most frequently fixated was the site name, although only the difference between the site and the section name was reliable ($p < 0.001$). The article title was also fixated on more frequently than the section name ($p < 0.001$).

Informational Cue	Mean fixation frequency	Mean fixation duration (ms)
Site name	2.41	241
	(0.88)	(24)
Article title	2.09	225
	(0.63)	(20)
Section name	1.08	227
	(0.39)	(22)

Table 4: Mean (adjusted) fixation frequency and mean fixation duration per informational cue while browsing the websites (standard deviations in parentheses).

A one-way repeated measures ANOVA was also used to analyse mean fixation duration data. A main effect was found according to the type of informational cue being viewed $F(2,46) = 8.948$, $p = 0.001$. Bonferroni post-hoc tests revealed that the mean fixation duration on the site name was longer than on the article title ($p = 0.001$) and longer than on the section name ($p = 0.021$). The mean fixation durations on the article title and the section name were not reliably different.

4.4 Eye Movements During the Bookmark Search Task

4.4.1 Scanning Strategy

In the bookmark-search task, participants consistently scanned down the left-hand side of the bookmark menu, as has been found in similar studies of menu search [Altonen et al. 1998]. Fixations were largely concentrated in the second 8th of the bookmark menu, which corresponds to the first four letters of the first word of each entry (Table 5). Saccadic movements were also concentrated towards the left of the menu (we do not present saccade data for reasons of space). These data suggest that the lead information in a bookmark has a higher psychological 'profile' than other information. For the purpose of our subsequent analyses we focus exclusively on eye movements associated with the lead cue in each bookmark. This restricted focus should enable the eye-movement analyses to augment the search-time findings described previously.

4.4.2 Mean Fixation Frequency

Data relating to the mean fixation frequency (adjusted for phrase length) on the lead cues in bookmarks are presented in Table 6. A higher fixation frequency on lead information was taken to be indicative of greater uncertainty in recognizing the target. A two-way repeated-measures ANOVA revealed a main effect of Informational Structure, $F(1,23) = 73.962$, $p < 0.001$, with bottom-up bookmarks receiving less fixations on lead information than the top-down ones. This finding suggests that having an article title first (as arises in all bottom-up conditions) invokes superior bookmark salience compared with having a site name first (as arises in all top-down conditions). There was also a main effect of the Number of Informational Cues, $F(2,46) = 12.259$, $p < 0.001$, with the two-cue condition being optimal. This latter finding supports the search-time data reported earlier.

Position in Bookmark	Fixation Frequency	Total Fixation Time (ms)	Mean Fixation Duration (ms)
1st	1530	492	322
2nd	13368	4180	313
3rd	5191	1199	231
4th	2906	649	223
5th	1820	404	222
6th	1136	249	219
7th	611	135	221
8th	117	24	202

Table 5: Cumulative fixation frequency, cumulative fixation time, and mean fixation duration in relation to areas (divided into eights) of the bookmark menu.

Informational Structure	Number of Informational Cues			
	1	2	3	Mean
Top-down (i.e. site name first)	1.34	0.87	1.00	1.07
	(0.44)	(0.35)	(0.46)	
Bottom-up (i.e. article title first)	0.75	0.61	0.67	0.67
	(0.22)	(0.19)	(0.27)	
Mean	1.05	0.74	0.84	

Table 6: Mean fixation frequency (adjusted) on the lead cues of the bookmark (standard deviations in parentheses).

Interestingly, there was also a significant interaction between Informational Structure and Number of Informational Cues, $F(2,46) = 4.620$, $p = 0.015$. The number of cues affected fixations differently depending on whether a site name or an article title was the lead cue. Indeed, it appears that top-down structures (which tend overall to be less salient) are much more sensitive to the presence or absence of additional information cues relative to bottom-up structures (whose recognizability seem to be essentially resistant to the presence of additional cues). This interaction effect makes sense in as much as having a site name as the lead information (as arises in top-down conditions) is problematic for bookmark recognition unless the article title appears directly alongside the site name. These fixation-frequency data therefore extend the search-time findings and indicate that users are sensitive to the informational structure of bookmarks. In particular, having bottom-up structures generally improves bookmark salience, with an article-title/site-name structure promoting optimal recognition performance.

4.4.3 Mean Fixation Duration
Data relating to the mean fixation duration on the lead cues in bookmarks are presented in Table 7. In the present study, information which required longer fixations was considered to be less meaningful than information with shorter fixations. A two-way repeated-measures ANOVA revealed a main effect of the

Informational Structure	Number of Informational Cues			
	1	2	3	Mean
Top-down (i.e. site name first)	335 (74)	272 (75)	292 (50)	300
Bottom-up (i.e. article title first)	274 (30)	277 (34)	266 (54)	272
Mean	305	275	279	

Table 7: Mean fixation duration (ms) on the lead cues of the bookmark (standard deviations in parentheses).

Informational Structure, $F(1,23) = 10.437$, $p = 0.004$, as well as a main effect of the Number of Informational Cues, $F(2,46) = 5.742$, $p = 0.006$. There was also a significant interaction between Informational Structure and Number of Informational Cues, $F(2,46) = 5.948$, $p = 0.005$. These findings directly parallel those discussed above in relation to the mean fixation-frequency data.

5 Discussion

5.1 Are There Differences in Bookmark Salience?

In the present study we were interested in the interplay between verbal information structuring and the quantity of informational cues in promoting bookmark salience and recognizability. The study involved taking measures of the overall search time to find target bookmarks, as well as acquiring more detailed eye-movement indices of information salience. In terms of the global search-time measure, faster responses were assumed to indicate superior recognition when participants were searching for a target bookmark within a set of distracter bookmarks. The study revealed no significant difference in the overall time it took to find bookmarks structured in a top-down vs. a bottom-up manner, suggesting that, in a gross sense, both structures may have appeared equally salient. On the other hand, the number of cues on display within a bookmark did emerge as a significant factor affecting search times. Two cues within a bookmark were found to be optimal, whilst one cue was clearly inadequate. Adding a third cue did not bring any significant recognition benefit, and, indeed, the three-cue condition was marginally worse than the two-cue condition. The limited benefits of having a three-cue structure may well be due to the 65 character limit associated with the bookmark menu within Internet Explorer (i.e. the third cue may often only have been partially visible, thereby negating its potential usefulness).

The failure to find a reliable effect of Informational Structure on overall search times challenged our a priori prediction that this factor would be associated with recognition efficacy. We note, however, that the controls implemented in our study during the encoding phase of each trial did not extend to detailed presentational and formatting aspects of the websites that participants were presented with (e.g. in terms of colour schemes, information layout, logo presence or size). Although we had assumed that such factors would add random variance to the bookmark search-time measure, they may instead have had a more systematic impact than expected, thereby weakening the emergence of Informational Structure as a determinant of the global performance metric. On a more positive note, however, closer inspection of the profile of search-time data across conditions does suggest that top-down bookmarks *were* more sensitive to the existence of extra cues than were bottom-up bookmarks. The top-down bookmark with one cue (i.e. displaying the site name alone) was associated with the slowest search time out of all conditions, but this decreased sharply to the fastest search time when a second cue (the article title) was added to the site name. These results indicate that a site name in a bookmark may be relatively less salient than an article title, that is, the site name appears to 'need' extra information to spark the same level of recognition that the article title can attract by itself. The eye-movement data permitted a more detailed exploration of such effects.

The assumption in the present study was that higher fixation frequencies and longer fixation durations in the bookmark-search task would be indicative of uncertainty in recognizing targets [cf Goldberg & Kotval 1999; Jacob & Karn 2003]. Increased uncertainty did indeed seem to arise in the present study in the case of bookmarks with top-down structures, whose lead cues were fixated more frequently and for longer overall than was the case of the lead cues of bottom-up structures. These findings suggest that bottom-up bookmarks have more salience than top-down bookmarks, and can thereby facilitate more rapid bookmark search and recognition. In addition, and as was hinted at by the search-time data, eye-movement measures revealed that top-down bookmarks (i.e. those having the site name first) were far more sensitive to the existence of extra cues than were bottom-up bookmarks (i.e. those with the article title first). Thus, whilst bottom-up bookmarks appeared to be equally salient, regardless of the number of informational cues, top-down bookmarks involving either a single cue or three cues were linked to poor task performance, which was only ameliorated in the two-cue, top-down condition. Indeed, it seems important to emphasize that when viewed in isolation, the site name was considerably less salient than all other conditions, as it was fixated for far longer and with a greater frequency of fixations.

Interestingly, too, when we consider the encoding phase of the test (i.e. when participants read through the news websites) it was observed that site names actually received greater attention than article titles. They were fixated more frequently and for longer on average, serving as further evidence that site names may be more difficult to encode meaningfully. Moreover, despite being subjected to more scrutiny during initial encoding, site names still ended up being less salient for subsequent bookmark recognition than did article titles.

5.2 Factors Promoting the Salience of Article Titles

The improved recognition salience for bottom-up bookmark structures (i.e. those that have article titles as lead cues) raises the issue of what causal factors might promote such effects. One explanation may derive from schema theories of memory organization [Alba & Hasher 1983] which emphasize how existing knowledge can make new information easier to remember. 'Meaning' is essential if we are to remember something effectively [Rumelhart & Norman 1985], and schemas can readily enable the derivation of meaning from information. So, for example, article titles typically 'tell a story' that has intrinsic meaning (e.g. about an election defeat or a terrorist incident). Site names however, at least for news websites, certainly have a lower capacity for rich meaning as they involve abstract names unconnected to the news stories they provide. It is also noteworthy that imaginable and concrete items can be easier to remember as they are represented more richly in memory [Paivio et al. 1968]. Article titles tend to embody more imaginable, concrete words that site names, which can often be rather abstract, so an advantage in recognition value may be further facilitated by this difference.

6 Generality and Future Studies

The study could be criticized on the grounds that any real-life situation might include location memory for menu entries [Hornof & Kieras 1999]. The main counter-argument is that bookmark lists can be left for a long time or re-arranged, and menu positions can be forgotten. Another rebuttal stems from the fact that pages saved on hard drives are often left in archives for a long time and can be re-ordered in many ways, thus disrupting memory for entry location. In these cases the users would have to rely on the text content of the bookmark.

We believe that our findings should generalize most effectively to sites that share a similar information hierarchy to those that were used in the present study, although assessing such generalizability remains an empirical issue. We also acknowledge that our results do not warrant the prescription of a single universal bookmark structure that is applicable to all contexts. Instead, we take the view that optimizing bookmark structures for different kinds of information-retrieval tasks is best assessed through empirical methods of the type that we have advanced here. In addition, there may be more factors affecting the salience of bookmarks than could be revealed in the present research, which tests for short-term recognition. For example, further studies could explore longer cut-off times on the bookmark search task, or introduce longer delays between the viewing of the website and the appearance of the bookmark menu. The effects of familiarity could also be investigated: Are people more likely to recognize pages that come from websites that they use regularly?

Eye-movement data on the websites themselves could be analysed to make recommendations for the bookmark text based on the pattern of eye movements while encoding. For example, the URL was looked at quite often in the present study, which indicates that it may be a significant navigational cue. Similarly, previous research on graphical bookmarks [Cockburn et al. 1999] could be replicated using eye-tracking measures for a more detailed analysis of recognition value. Finally, further studies could be performed to refine the test protocol so that companies can use the technique to find out how to organize information structures in large-scale information-retrieval tasks. Application areas include information architecture, knowledge management, database engineering and Web design. Some specific proposals that can be made in relation to website developers and browser designers, respectively, might be:

- for the former to use additional mark-up in the HTML <title> element to separate and identify the different types of informational cue; and

- for the latter to implement a facility that allowed users to re-order these bookmark cues to show the most salient attribute first (just as can be done with file listings that can be structured by, for example, filename/type/date and the like).

7 Conclusions

The number of informational cues present within a bookmark was seen to affect overall search times to detect that bookmark when embedded in a menu of distracter items. Two informational cues were optimal, one cue was highly sub-optimal, and three cues was marginally worse than the two-cue condition. The informational structure of bookmarks (i.e. whether informational cues were organized in a top-down or bottom-up manner) appeared, perhaps somewhat paradoxically, to have no reliable impact on the basic search times to find a target item. However, more detailed eye-movement analyses of fixation behaviour on target bookmarks revealed interactive effects of both experimental factors (informational structure and number of informational cues), suggesting that the efficacy of bookmark recognition may well be dependent on having an optimal combination of information organization and cue quantity. In particular, the eye-movement data indicated that effective recognition of top-down bookmark structures (e.g. where the site name is the lead information) may be highly context sensitive. In larger-scale information repositories than the one studied here it is possible that the informational-structure factor could be further amplified such that it could have an even more marked effect on search behaviour. Overall, we believe that our findings support the contention that Web developers would do well to exercise caution in designing navigational schemes and data structures to support webpage re-visitation via bookmarks. Even small changes in bookmark salience could have serious consequences for re-visitation efficacy.

References

Abrams, D., Bæcker, R. & Chignell, M. [1998], Information Archiving with Bookmarks: Personal Web Space Construction and Organization, *in* M. E. Atwood, C.-M. Karat, A. Lund, J. Coutaz & J. Karat (eds.), *Proceedings of the SIGCHI Conference on Human Factors in Computing Systems (CHI'98)*, ACM Press, pp.41–8.

Alba, J. W. & Hasher, L. [1983], Is Memory Schematic?, *Psychological Bulletin* 93(2), 203–31.

Altonen, A., Hyrskykari, A. & Räihä, K. [1998], 101 Spots, or How do Users read Menus?, *in* M. E. Atwood, C.-M. Karat, A. Lund, J. Coutaz & J. Karat (eds.), *Proceedings of the SIGCHI Conference on Human Factors in Computing Systems (CHI'98)*, ACM Press, pp.132–9.

Cailliau, R. [1995], A Little History of the World Wide Web, http://www.w3.org/History.html.

Clark, J. M. & Paivio, A. [1987], A Dual Coding Perspective on Encoding Processes, *in* M. A. McDaniel & M. Pressley (eds.), *Imagery and Related Mnemonic Processes: Theories, Individual Differences and Applications*, Springer-Verlag, pp.5–33.

Cockburn, A., Greenberg, S., Jones, S., McKenzie, B. & Moyle, M. [2003], Improving Webpage Revisitation: Analysis, Design and Evaluation, *IT and Society* **1**(3), 159–83.

Cockburn, A., Greenberg, S., McKenzie, B., Smith, M. & Kaasten, S. [1999], WebView: A Graphical Aid for Revisiting Web Pages, in J. Scott (ed.), *Proceedings of OzCHI'99 The Ninth Australian Conference on Computer–Human Interaction*, IEEE Computer Society Press, pp.15–22.

Cockburn, A. & Greenberg, S. [1999], Issues of Page Representation and Organisation in Web Browser's Revisitation Tools, in J. Scott (ed.), *Proceedings of OzCHI'99 The Ninth Australian Conference on Computer–Human Interaction*, IEEE Computer Society Press, pp.7–14.

Cockburn, A. & McKenzie, B. [2000], What Do Web Users Do? An Empirical Analysis of Web Use, *International Journal of Human–Computer Studies* **54**(6), 903–22.

Cowen, L., Ball, L. J. & Delin, J. [2002], An Eye-movement Analysis of Web Page Usability, in X. Faulkner, J. Finlay & F. Dètienne (eds.), *People and Computers XVI (Proceedings of HCI'02)*, Springer-Verlag, pp.317–35.

Goldberg, J. H. & Kotval, X. P. [1999], Computer Interface Evaluation Using Eye Movements: Methods and Constructs, *International Journal of Industrial Ergonomics* **24**(6), 631–45.

Hornof, A. J. & Kieras, D. E. [1999], Cognitive Modelling Demonstrates How People Use Anticipated Location Knowledge of Menu Items, in M. G. Williams & M. W. Altom (eds.), *Proceedings of the SIGCHI Conference on Human Factors in Computing Systems: The CHI is the Limit (CHI'99)*, ACM Press, pp.410–7.

Hyönä, J., Niemi, P. & Underwood, G. [1989], Reading Long Words Embedded in Sentences: Informativeness of Word Halves Affects Eye Movements, *Journal of Experimental Psychology: Human Perception and Performance* **21**(1), 68–71.

Inhoff, A. W. & Radach, R. [1998], Definition and Computation of Oculomotor Measures in the Study of Cognitive Processes, in G. Underwood (ed.), *Eye Guidance in Reading, Driving and Scene Perception*, Elsevier Science, pp.29–53.

Jacob, R. J. K. & Karn, K. S. [2003], Eye Tracking in Human–Computer Interaction and Usability Research: Ready to Deliver the Promises, in J. Hyönä, R. Radach & H. Deubel (eds.), *The Mind's Eye: Cognitive and Applied Aspects of Eye Movement Research*, Elsevier Science, pp.573–605.

Jones, W. P., Bruce, H. & Dumais, S. T. [2001], Keeping Found Things Found on the Web, in H. Paques, L. Liu & D. Grossman (eds.), *Proceedings of ACM's CIKM'01, the Tenth International Conference on Information and Knowledge Management*, ACM Press, pp.119–26.

Just, M. A. & Carpenter, P. A. [1976], Eye Fixations and Cognitive Processes, *Cognitive Psychology* **8**(4), 441–80.

Kaasten, S., Greenberg, S. & Edwards, C. [2002], How People Recognize Previously Seen Web Pages from Titles, URLs and Thumbnails, in X. Faulkner, J. Finlay & F. Dètienne (eds.), *People and Computers XVI (Proceedings of HCI'02)*, Springer-Verlag, pp.247–66.

Nielsen, J. [1992], Finding Usability Problems Through Heuristic Evaluation, *in* P. Bauersfeld, J. Bennett & G. Lynch (eds.), *Proceedings of the SIGCHI Conference on Human Factors in Computing Systems (CHI'92)*, ACM Press, pp.373–80.

Paivio, A., Yuille, J. C. & Madigan, S. [1968], Concreteness, Imagery and Meaningfulness Values for 925 Nouns, *Journal of Experimental Psychology: Monograph Supplement* **76**(1), 1–25.

Preece, J., Rogers, Y. & Sharp, H. (eds.) [2002], *Interaction Design: Beyond Human–Computer Interaction*, John Wiley & Sons.

Rosenfeld, L. & Morville, P. [2002], *Information Architecture for the World Wide Web*, second edition, O'Reilly and Associates.

Rumelhart, D. E. & Norman, D. A. [1985], Representations of Knowledge, *in* A. M. Aitkenhead & J. M. Slack (eds.), *Issues in Cognitive Modelling*, Lawrence Erlbaum Associates, pp.15–62.

Tauscher, L. & Greenberg, S. [1997], Revisitation Patterns in World Wide Web navigation, *in* S. Pemberton (ed.), *Proceedings of the SIGCHI Conference on Human Factors in Computing Systems (CHI'97)*, ACM Press, pp.399–406.

Zelinsky, G. & Sheinberg, D. [1995], Why Some Search Tasks Take Longer Than Others: Using Eye Movements to Redefine Reaction Times, *in* J. M. Findlay, R. Walker & R. W. Kentridge (eds.), *Eye Movement Research: Mechanisms, Processes and Applications*, North-Holland, pp.325–36.

Author Index

Keyword Index